ANIMAL KINGDOM

This edition published by Barnes & Noble, Inc.,
by arrangement with Weldon Owen Pty Ltd.

2001 Barnes & Noble Books

Copyright © 2000 Weldon Owen Pty Ltd

Chief Executive Officer: John Owen
President: Terry Newell
Publisher: Sheena Coupe
Managing Editor: Helen Bateman
Senior Editor: Janet Healey
Senior Designer: Kylie Mulquin
Editorial Coordinator: Tracey Gibson
Production Manager: Helen Creeke
Production Assistant: Kylie Lawson
Business Manager: Emily Jahn
Vice President International Sales: Stuart Laurence

Author and Project Editor: Stephanie Pfennigwerth
Text, pp. 106–149: Sue Grose-Hodge
Designer: Moyna Smeaton
Design, pp. 106–149: Avril Makula

M 10 9 8 7 6 5 4 3 2 1

ISBN 0-7607-2423-7

Color reproduction by Colourscan Co Pte Ltd
Printed by Toppan Printing Co. (H.K.) Ltd
Printed in China

A Weldon Owen Production

ANIMAL KINGDOM

CONSULTING EDITORS

Dr Colin Groves
Reader in Biological Anthropology,
Australian National University, Canberra, Australia

Sally Reader
Department of Ichthyology,
Australian Museum, Sydney, Australia

Joseph M. Forshaw
Research Associate, Department of Ornithology,
Australian Museum, Sydney, Australia

Dr Glenn Shea
Lecturer, Department of Veterinary Anatomy and Pathology,
University of Sydney, Australia

Dr Max Moulds
Collections Manager, Insect and Spider Collections,
Australian Museum, Sydney, Australia

BARNES
&NOBLE
BOOKS
NEW YORK

Contents

HABITATS   8

Tropical Regions   10
Savanna Grasslands   14
Deserts   16
Grasslands, Woodlands, and Forests   20
Alpine Regions   24
Polar Regions   26
World Waters   28

MAMMALS   34

Classifying Mammals   36
Mammals through the Ages   38
Mammal Behavior   42
Endangered Species   46
Monotremes   50
Marsupials   52
Anteaters, Sloths, and Armadillos   56
The Aardvark, Pangolins, and Elephant Shrews   58
Insectivores and Tree Shrews   60
Bats   62

Primates   66

The Bears   72

The Dogs   76

The Cats   78

Carnivorous Relatives   80

Whales, Dolphins, and Porpoises   84

Seals, Walruses, and Sea Cows   88

Elephants   90

Odd-Toed Ungulates   94

Even-Toed Ungulates   98

Rodents   102

Rabbits, Hares, Pikas, and Hyraxes   104

FISHES   106

Classifying Fishes   108

Fishes through the Ages   110

Fish Behavior   114

Endangered Species   118

Jawless Fishes   122

Cartilaginous Fishes   124

Bony Fishes   134

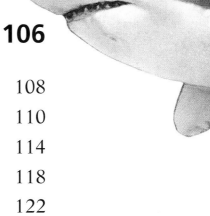

BIRDS 150

Classifying Birds	152
Birds through the Ages	154
Bird Behavior	158
Endangered Species	164
Land Birds	168
Waterbirds	178
Birds of Prey	186
Flightless Birds	192

REPTILES AND AMPHIBIANS 196

Classifying Reptiles and Amphibians	198
Reptiles and Amphibians through the Ages	200
Reptile and Amphibian Behavior	204
Endangered Species	210
Caecilians	212
Salamanders and Newts	214
Frogs and Toads	216
Turtles and Tortoises	222
Lizards	226
Snakes	232
Amphisbaenians	238
Tuataras	240
Crocodiles and Alligators	242

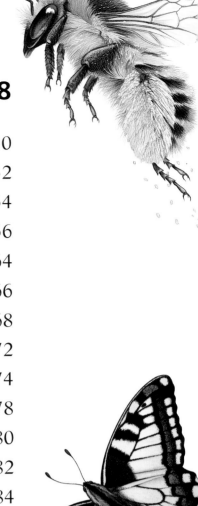

INSECTS AND SPIDERS 248

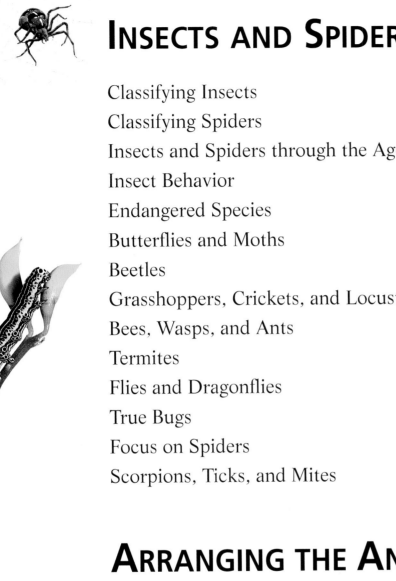

Classifying Insects	250
Classifying Spiders	252
Insects and Spiders through the Ages	254
Insect Behavior	256
Endangered Species	264
Butterflies and Moths	266
Beetles	268
Grasshoppers, Crickets, and Locusts	272
Bees, Wasps, and Ants	274
Termites	278
Flies and Dragonflies	280
True Bugs	282
Focus on Spiders	284
Scorpions, Ticks, and Mites	292

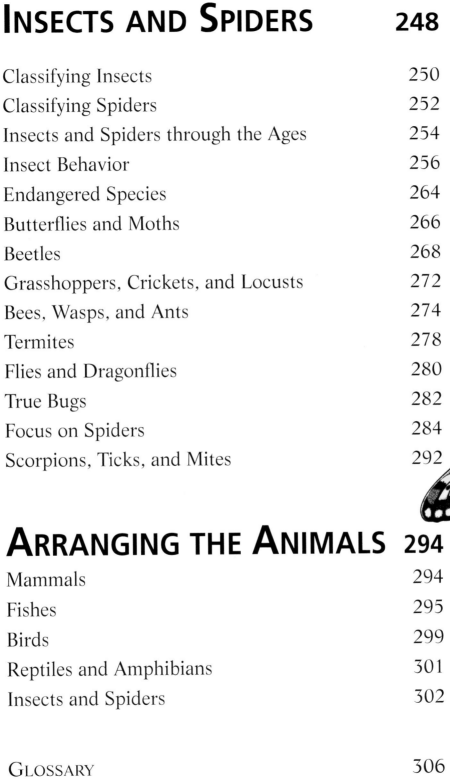

ARRANGING THE ANIMALS 294

Mammals	294
Fishes	295
Birds	299
Reptiles and Amphibians	301
Insects and Spiders	302
GLOSSARY	306
INDEX	312
CREDITS	320

Habitats

Almost every part of our planet is inhabited by an amazing variety of living things. So far, scientists have named about two million species of plants and animals, but there may be between 10 million and 100 million species on Earth!

Desert

Savanna

Tropical forest

The planet's weather system has created a wide range of habitats, from steaming jungles and baking deserts to the stark cold of the poles. Each habitat has its own community of plants and animals. Over time, they have adapted in order to make the most of the food and other resources offered by their habitat—including each other. These changes have given rise to the greatest show on Earth: the animal kingdom.

Conifer forest

Grassland

Oceans

Polar regions

Tropical Regions

THE EARTH'S HABITATS are closely linked to the climate. The Sun strikes the Earth more directly at the Equator than at the poles, so tropical regions are hot and moist. Since the weather determines the kind of plants that grow, these humid conditions create forests that are home to more species than any other habitat.

Steel-blue killifish

Gardens of Eden

Tropical regions have an average monthly temperature of 80°F (27°C). Hot air, laden with moisture, rises into the atmosphere during the day. As the air cools, the water changes from vapor into liquid to form dark clouds that bring heavy rain in the afternoons. In some tropical regions, annual rainfall may reach more than 430 inches (11 m)!

Because there is plenty of warmth and moisture in tropical regions, plants grow quickly. The variety of plants provides a diversity of foods and habitats, from the top of the tree canopy to the rotting debris on the forest floor. Because the days and nights remain the same length all year, the animals that live in these habitats have plenty of time for foraging and breeding. For these reasons, more than half of all living species of animals and plants are to be found in tropical rain forests.

Jungle Gym

Tropical rain forests can be divided roughly into three sections. Ten stories above the ground, the canopy is home to many species—flying frogs, gliding squirrels and snakes, lemurs, sloths, spiders, possums, monkeys, anteaters, bats, hummingbirds, eagles, macaws, toucans, and quetzals—as well as thousands of insect species that remain for the most part unstudied.

The branches of the trees are crowded with epiphytes, or "air plants," such as ferns, orchids, mosses, and lichens. These biological hitchhikers cling to the bark, and a single tree may support more than 100 species of epiphyte. Each miniature jungle is home to numerous creatures that scientists may never have seen before.

Though lacking the bright sunshine of the canopy, the middle forest levels are sheltered from extremes of sun, wind, and rain by the blanket of leaves above. Here, branches and vines wrap, intertwine, and graft together to form a lattice. Palms and tree ferns reach up like giant umbrellas. Monkeys and orangutans forage at this level, and tent and disk-winged bats use the leaves for shelters from predators, rain, and sunlight. Many birds and frogs live only here. The bark of trunks and lower tree branches also shelters a wealth of insects and other small creatures.

The most stable environment is the forest floor. Entirely protected from the elements, this cool, dark, quiet world supports a complex assortment of life forms— elephants, spiders, scorpions, shrews,

Red-bellied piranha

FOREST FISHES
The steel-blue killifish of tropical western Africa lives in small, temporary pools, but the 50 or so species of piranha are found in the river basins and streams of northern South America.

GREEN CATHEDRAL
Elements of different rain forest types are brought together in this South American panorama.

QUEER DEER
The water chevrotain is a kind of deer. It lives in the rain forests of western Africa. About the size of a rabbit, it is an agile climber and often shelters in hollow trees.

LOGGING LAMENT

By the time you have finished reading this paragraph, 2.5 acres (1 hectare) of Brazilian rain forest will have been cut down. In the last ten years the rate of global rain forest destruction has increased by 90 percent. Vast areas are being cleared to supply timber, fuel, and paper, and to make way for towns and farms. We can help to reduce the need for wood by recycling paper. Replanting trees also helps.

gorillas, snakes, civet cats, worms, even crabs. Many plants of the rain forest floor are characterized by their enormous leaves, which help them to make as much food as possible in the dim light. Gingers, ferns, mosses, lilies, bananas, and heliconias also grow here. The heliconias of South America have long stalks of big red or orange canoe-shaped bracts (modified leaves). Water collects in the bracts, and within these tiny pools live a range of aquatic insect larvae.

No Choking Matter

The living things in an ecosystem depend on each other for food and other resources. A simple example is that of heliconia flowers. They are favored by insects and hummingbirds attracted to their sweet nectar. As these animals feed, they pollinate the flowers, thus ensuring the survival of the plant and, in turn, the survival of the animals that feed from it.

These close relationships mean that damage to one part of an ecosystem is likely to affect every other part of it. Humans are as much a part of an ecosystem as any other species. For example, plants make food by absorbing carbon dioxide from the air through pores in their leaves.

The by-product of this process is oxygen, released by the plant for humans and other species to breathe. Widespread damage to tropical forests will therefore have an effect on the amount of oxygen being released into the atmosphere.

Tropical regions also make a huge contribution to the world's climate. The burning of fossil fuels such as coal, gas, and oil has raised the level of carbon dioxide in the atmosphere, but the deforestation of tropical regions has reduced the ability of the planet to absorb this extra gas. So clearing forests not only endangers the life of the animals and plants that live there, but contributes to the most serious threat to our planet: global warming, or the greenhouse effect.

THIRSTY FLIER
The zebra butterfly lives in the subtropical forests of the United States' Everglades. Now irrigation is threatening the supply of fresh water, and the forests may dry up.

GOING HOME
About 3,500 elephants survive in Sri Lanka. But widespread land clearance and development has left little room for them to live, outside of national parks.

FOREST PHARMACY
More than 6,000 plants are used in traditional medicine, and many Western drugs are derived from rain forest plants. The forests may yet contain the cures for diseases such as cancer and AIDS—if they are preserved.

Savanna Grasslands

SAVANNA GRASSLANDS are located in subtropical regions, which lie north and south of the tropical regions. Whereas the weather in most tropical areas remains relatively stable throughout the year, the subtropics have two distinct seasons. These areas do not get as much rain as the tropics, but temperatures can be much higher.

The Wet and the Dry

Parts of India, Brazil, and Australia are located in subtropical regions, but savanna grasslands are found mostly in Africa. During winter, or the dry season, scorching winds blow off the deserts. The ground dries and the vegetation becomes parched. As the Earth moves around the Sun, the dry winds are replaced by hot, humid winds. This marks the beginning of the summer, or rainy season, which may last for several months.

Pursuits That Suit

With rain falling only in summer, savannas have relatively few trees. The hunting style of the cheetah is ideal for open grassland, which not only gives the cat an unobstructed view of its surroundings, but allows it to build up speed in pursuit of prey. A smaller cat, the serval, has adapted to its habitat by becoming the feline equivalent of a giraffe. Rather than adopting the compact, creeping-and-crouching body plan of lions and leopards, the serval has developed stilt-like legs to stalk through the long grass of the savanna. Its uses its huge ears like radar dishes to home in on the rustlings made by rodents as they move unseen through vegetation. When it hears something, it pounces, bouncing high into the air as if on a trampoline.

A Time to Every Purpose

The behavior of the savanna's animal inhabitants is also strongly linked to the weather. During the dry season, elephants and intermingling herds of zebra and gazelle gather around lakes, waterholes, and riverbeds, while some fishes and amphibians wait out the drought in underground chambers. When the rains begin, animal activity changes. Elephants and huge herds of wildebeest begin their annual migration to find fresh growth. Mating also occurs during the rains, so that the births occur when food is most plentiful. But the young animals, and those weakened by their journey, provide rich pickings for carnivores such as crocodiles, which take up positions in the rivers on the migratory paths. Along with catfishes, hyenas, lions, monitor lizards, and vultures, they play their part in the cycle of life and death.

JUMP JET
With their long wings and long tail, harriers fly low and slow over open country. If prey is spotted, they drop down and reach into bushes or grass with their legs.

PAMPERED PROGENY
The langurs of Asia live in extended family groups of 15 to 25 animals. Young langurs are cared for by the group for up to two years.

CHEST CAVITY
African lungfishes live in swamps, floodplain lakes, and shallow pools. At the onset of the dry season, they dig a burrow in the mud. They emerge to feed and breed when the rains fall again.

CHAIN OF EVENTS
The African savanna supports herds of herbivores, which are hunted by lions and other carnivores. Vultures and other scavengers eat the leftovers.

Deserts

DESERT REGIONS cover one-fifth of the Earth's land surface. Although there are many kinds of desert, they are usually defined as dry areas that on average receive less than 4 inches (10 cm) of rain per year. This lack of moisture means desert species have developed special adaptations in order to survive.

Blowing Hot and Cold

Desert regions include the dramatic mesa landscapes of the American southwest; the vast, stony deserts of Australia; and the sand seas of north Africa. Some deserts are found alongside mountain ranges. For example, the Mojave and Great Basin deserts of the United States are dry as a result of the shadowing effects of the Sierra Nevada ranges, which block moist air from the sea. Deserts are also a feature of the western side of some continents in subtropical zones, such as the Atacama Desert of Chile, the Namib Desert of southern Africa, and the western Sahara. Here, the effects of cold water currents, coastal winds, and cold air lower the rate of evaporation from the ocean's surface, reducing available moisture.

On the other hand, some Australian deserts and those in central Asia and the Middle East are dry because they are a long way from moisture sources such as the ocean. Weather systems that do actually reach these areas have usually already deposited their rainfall during their long overland journey.

DESERT GEMS

Oryx, or gemsbok, are large antelopes that live in Africa. Their splayed feet are suited for walking on sand, and their pale coat reflects heat. On cold desert nights they feed and move around to stay warm.

INLAND SEA

The strong winds in deserts often create vast seas of sand dunes. The constantly shifting sand and the lack of water mean that there are few plants in these areas.

While coastal desert climates are characterized by fog, the absence of moisture in the air in most deserts means that clouds are rare and skies are clear for most of the year. The land is heated by the Sun, and daytime temperatures can soar to more than 104°F (40°C). However, the lack of cloud cover means that much of the heat radiates back into the atmosphere at night, when the air temperature plummets to almost freezing.

Not all deserts are hot during the day, however. Cold winds blowing across the Gobi desert of central Asia produce freezing conditions both day and night, but it is still considered a desert because it gets very little rain.

Life and Death Valley

Many people think of deserts as sandy, barren places, but deserts support a great range of life. However, in order to survive such extreme conditions, many species have had to develop adaptations of body shape, function, and behavior. Lizards, for example, have scaly skin that enables them to retain water by reducing evaporation from their body. Lizards also produce solid waste rather than liquid urine, and they can alter the color of their skin to reflect more or less heat.

Desert mammals have also adapted to survive. Many save water and avoid the oppressive heat by sheltering in

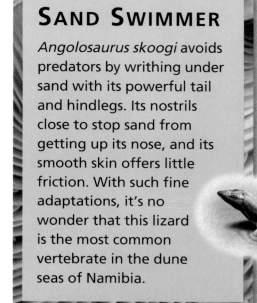

SAND SWIMMER

Angolosaurus skoogi avoids predators by writhing under sand with its powerful tail and hindlegs. Its nostrils close to stop sand from getting up its nose, and its smooth skin offers little friction. With such fine adaptations, it's no wonder that this lizard is the most common vertebrate in the dune seas of Namibia.

THUMBS UP
Ningauis live in the desert heartland of Australia. These thumb-sized marsupials shelter from daytime heat in burrows and undergrowth. They quench their thirst by licking dew from spinifex.

burrows during the day and feeding in the cool of the night. A feature of some desert species, such as the fennec fox and the black-tailed jackrabbit, is their large ears, which they use to lose heat from their body.

The gerbils of Africa and western Asia reflect radiated heat with the white fur on their underbelly. Dense pads of fur insulate the soles of their feet and slow down evaporation. Gerbils also conserve water by concentrating their urine. Kangaroo rats use the high humidity of their burrows to reclaim moisture from their breath, breathing it in through their nasal passages. The roadrunner evaporates water and cools down by vibrating its throat with its bill open.

Water Towers

Many desert plants have also evolved ways to save water. Cacti are good examples. The saguaro cactus stores water in its pleated stems and shallow root system, which can extend up to 70 feet (21 m) in diameter. A single saguaro can store up to 8 tons (7 tonnes) of water, enabling it to feed, house, and provide moisture for many creatures.

In the Mojave desert, aromatic creosote bushes defend their water supply with chemical defenses. Their roots produce a toxin that poisons the ground around them, stopping the growth of any plant that would compete for the limited water. The waxy texture of their leaves also helps to retain precious water. Other plants minimise the evaporation of water during the heat of the day by unfurling their leaves or flowering only at night.

Magic Carpet

In some deserts, rain may not fall for many years. Then, quite suddenly, a storm will break, resulting in a heavy downpour that lasts just a few hours. These rains trigger the germination of thousands of plants. They grow rapidly so that they can complete their life cycle before they run out of water. A few weeks after the rain has fallen, the desert is transformed into a carpet of flowers. During this busy period, animals harvest the seeds, pollen, and nectar before the drought returns.

Rainfall is also the cue for some animals to move into a new stage in their life cycle. For example, winged termites take to the air to find mates and start new colonies. The insects, in turn, provide frogs with enough food to sustain them in their burrows until the rains return.

SNAKE BAKE
Most of the 30 species of rattlesnake live in North America. They are often seen basking on warm rocks.

CACTUS CACHE
In the Sonoran Desert, in the southwestern United States, many animals have a close relationship with saguaro cacti. The cacti, in turn, rely on animals for their survival.

The white-winged dove eats mostly fruit and nectar of saguaro cacti

OUT IN THE RAIN
During hot and dry periods, the crucifix toad of Australia stays buried underground. It emerges after heavy rains to mate, and to eat swarms of winged termites.

The gila woodpecker excavates its nest cavity in a large saguaro

Using the saguaro's huge spines for safety, the cactus wren builds its nest in the branches

The agile Sonoran whipsnake searches the saguaro for nestling birds

The antelope ground squirrel gets water from fruits, seeds, and nectar

The cactus relies almost entirely on the lesser long-nosed bat for pollination

Grasslands, Woodlands, and Forests

THE TEMPERATE ZONES OF THE WORLD experience a mild climate dominated by cool, moist air blowing from the poles toward the tropical zones. Large swings in temperature, the distance from the Equator, and the varying hours of sunlight create a changeable climate and a variety of habitats.

RIVER OF LIFE
Most of the world's people live in temperate regions, where there is an adequate supply of water for much of the year. These regions have four distinct seasons.

Season's Greetings

The temperate zones lie between 35 and 60 degrees latitude, north and south of the Equator. They can be divided into three regions: warm temperate, between 35 and 45 degrees latitude; cool temperate, between 45 and 60 degrees latitude; and cold temperate, experienced by regions in the center of some continents.

Temperate regions have distinct seasons. In spring, plants begin to produce leaves and flowers, and animals begin to breed. This period of growth peaks in summer. As fall, or autumn, approaches, some trees begin to drop their leaves and many animals either migrate or prepare to hibernate. During the winter months, snow may cover the ground for weeks at a time, and the barren landscape may show little sign of activity.

Keep Off the Grass

Warm temperate regions generally receive most of their rainfall in winter and have hot, dry summers.

The lack of water in summer means that the vegetation is dominated by grasses and plants with soft stems; woody-stemmed plants and trees are sparse and shrubby.

The world's temperate grasslands (or prairie) and wood shrublands are found in these zones. They include the Great Plains of North America and the South African Veldt. Here, the plants have adapted to withstand the cutting hoofs and grinding teeth of grazing animals. Since there is little shelter, animals such as toads, voles, ground squirrels, and meerkats live in burrows. The unused chambers of

SHELL-DWELLER
The ornate box turtle of North America prefers dry prairies to moist woodlands. It draws its head and legs into its shell to protect itself and to avoid drying out.

these burrows are also home to snakes and burrowing owls.

The shrublands and grasslands of Australia, by contrast, support native rodents and soft-footed marsupials such as wallabies. Scattered low eucalyptus trees or acacia are home to numerous parrots. Insects are plentiful, and form much of the diet of geckos and other lizards.

But many grassland animals have been wiped out over large areas. In North America, where huge herds of bison once roamed, farmers now graze sheep and cattle, and much of the grassland and shrubland has been plowed to grow crops and grains. In Australia and the pampas of South America, the introduction of cattle and sheep has also degraded sensitive

CATTLE COUNTRY

Hunting, land clearing, and other farming practices have decimated prairie species such as bison and the black-footed ferret. But their loss has been the gain of the cattle egret. Fifty years ago this small heron was unknown in North America, but it is now a common sight in cattle and horse pastures. Such habitats are similar to the bird's native habitat in Africa, where it eats insects disturbed by the grazing of rhino, giraffe, and elephant.

habitats ill-adapted for the pressure of hard hoofs. Nevertheless, these areas remain ideal hunting grounds for birds of prey, which use telegraph poles as vantage points from which to spot their prey and to rest. Freshly plowed fields also provide a variety of birds with plenty of insects, grubs, and worms. Coyotes and other hunting dogs often prey on livestock.

Tree House

Cool temperate areas have cool to cold winters and warm, humid summers. Because rain falls all year round, trees grow well and vegetation is plentiful. These conditions are ideal for a variety of woodland habitats. Each woodland differs from continent to continent. For example, the low woodlands of the Australian east coast support a wealth of frogs, possums, and kangaroos. The tall eucalypt forests harbor parrots, owls, and koalas, while wombats, numbats, and lyrebirds forage on the forest floor.

By contrast, most of the trees in the Northern Hemisphere, such as elm, maple, and beech, are deciduous, which means they shed their leaves in fall. These woodlands are home to species ranging from raccoons to salamanders, black bears to garter snakes. Scorpions, tarantulas, and fire ants prefer Emory oak, the acorns of which provide food for turkeys, quail, and even the gray fox. Some animals migrate in winter, but others survive on food they stored during summer.

Clearing the Air

Cold temperate regions are covered mostly by forests of evergreen trees called conifers. Shaped so that the snow slides off them, conifers are well adapted to survive cold winters. They produce seeds inside cones, and usually have thin, needle-shaped or scaly leaves. These trees support a whole community of wildlife, from the woodpeckers that drill for bark-burrowing insects, to the tassel-eared squirrels that raid the cones for food. Porcupines, cougars, and martens lurk in their cool shadows, and otters, beavers, and loons cruise around nearby secluded lakes.

But these forests are increasingly endangered by air pollution from cars and factories. This pollution can turn rain into a strong acid that kills trees. Fifteen to twenty percent of the coniferous forest of the northeastern United States is dying each decade. Forests in Poland and the Czech Republic have also been destroyed.

Conifers are susceptible to pollution because the needles stay on the tree for up to seven years, allowing toxins to build up on their sensitive surfaces. Exposure to pollution is also worse at higher altitudes, where conifer forests grow. We can help to reduce pollution from cars by walking, cycling, or using public transport. The installation of cleaning stacks at factories will also help to save these forests, and those who live in them.

SPAWN WARNING
Every year salmon return from the sea and swim up cool northern rivers and streams to spawn. Grizzly bears and eagles gather from miles around to take advantage of this fish feast.

FUR, TREES
Cold temperate regions are often covered by conifer forests. Many mammals in this habitat have thick fur, and hibernate during winter. Birds also have thicker plumage, or fly to warmer habitats.

HARE WEAR
Many forest animals tough out the harsh winters. This snowshoe hare exchanges its brown summer coat for a white one to camouflage it from predators in the snow.

LIGHT SUPPER
Wolf packs travel widely to find prey such as deer and elk, but they often fail to catch a meal. A carcass will provide these hungry hunters with a little nourishment.

HEADS IN THE CLOUDS
Mountain peoples make up about a tenth of the global human population. In Nepal, which lies in the Himalayas, the steep slopes have been terraced to provide small, level fields for farming.

ALPINE AMPHIBIAN
The Pacific giant salamander of western North America avoids the cold by living mostly underground. It lays its eggs in alpine streams.

LUNG CAPACITY
Birds like this condor have a respiratory system that extracts twice as much oxygen from the air as other animals. They can fly at high altitudes with no ill effects.

Alpine Regions

THERE ARE MOUNTAINS on every continent, and each mountain has its own weather pattern. In general, however, the higher the land, the less vegetation there is and the colder and windier it becomes. At high altitudes there is also less oxygen, and this "thin air" presents alpine inhabitants with special challenges.

A Restless Planet

From snow-covered alps to the lush highlands of tropical regions, most of the world's mountains are linked in one of two chains. One encircles the Pacific Ocean and can be traced from the Andes in South America, up and around to Alaska, and through Japan to New Zealand and Antarctica. The other chain links the Himalayas with the Alps, ending with North Africa's Atlas Mountains.

Some mountains form slowly, such as when a continental plate collides with or is forced under another, thrusting the Earth's crust into the air. Other peaks have more violent beginnings as volcanoes. On the highest peaks, there is snow and ice all year round, but within a mountain range there may be a variety of climates and habitats: exposed crests, sheltered valleys, cliffs, and glaciers. The side of the mountain facing the wind may receive more snow than the more sheltered side.

Even the position of a rock or tree, creating a barrier to the wind or snow, can have an effect on conditions.

Islands in the Sky

Mountain weather is also variable. Warm temperatures during the day can be followed by bitterly cold nights. With every 1,000-foot rise in altitude, the temperature decreases by about 3°F (5°C per 1 km). Nothing can survive permanently on alpine peaks more than 23,000 feet (7,000 m) high, because the fierce winds and cold would freeze any living cells.

But below this level grow some of the toughest plants—with some of the daintiest flowers—on Earth. Many plants hug the ground to avoid the blasting wind. Some grow in the shelter of rock crevices. Species such as crocuses and lilies grow from bulbs buried below the ground, safe from the worst cold. Others have leaves and stems covered with hairs that trap warm air when the Sun shines. These

hairs also filter ultraviolet radiation, which is stronger at high altitudes.

Animals, too, have adapted to these habitats. Species like the golden toad of Central America are so specialized for a certain combination of rainfall, cloud cover, and altitude that they are found nowhere else. Pumas and wolves have a wider range, following the movements of elk and migrating to lower levels in winter. Most alpine areas also have their own species of goat which, despite being isolated from each other, share similar features, such as hoofs designed to grip rocky slopes.

Some people who travel to alpine regions become ill when their body, starved of oxygen, fails to function properly. But mountain peoples have adapted to living at high altitudes by developing a larger lung volume and a higher concentration of hemoglobin (the molecule that carries oxygen) in their bloodstream. These adaptations enhance their ability to absorb oxygen. Their livestock, such as yaks, llamas, and alpacas, can also breathe easily.

CREATURE COMFORTS
The snow leopard lives in remote terrain in Central Asia. Like all alpine mammals, it has very thick fur. Its tiny ears reduce heat loss, and its long, fluffy tail provides a warm wrap while sleeping.

Polar Regions

THE ARCTIC is an area of frozen ocean surrounded by continents, while Antarctica is a frozen continent surrounded by ocean. Climates near the North and South poles are characterized by extremely low temperatures and permanent snow and ice. In spite of these harsh conditions, many animals live in the polar regions.

The Ends of the Earth

Insulated by ice and warmed by currents, the Arctic Ocean is not as cold as the Antarctic continent. Nevertheless, both the Arctic region and the Antarctic are cold and windy deserts. Antarctica is in fact the coldest, highest, driest, and most windswept continent on Earth. Even during summer, temperatures rarely rise above freezing near the coasts. In winter, Antarctica doubles in size as the sea freezes over and ice encases the continent. Winds rage at speeds of more than 186 mph (300 kmph), and the temperature plummets to an average of –76° F (–60° C)!

The polar regions are cold because the heat of the Sun is weaker at the poles, and the white ice reflects much of the heat from the Sun back into the atmosphere. The poles are also dry because very cold air holds only a small amount of water vapor, and little moisture evaporates from polar seas.

Antarctica and Arctic landmasses such as Greenland are covered with thick ice sheets. Drained by glaciers, these sheets are made mostly from ice and snow that has accumulated over millions of years. Along the coasts, the ice sheets form shelves over the ocean. Giant blocks break off the ice shelves and glaciers and float away as ice floes or icebergs. In 1912, an iceberg from a Greenland glacier sank the *Titanic*.

Midnight Sun

As the Earth tilts on its rotation around the Sun, the poles receive some or no daylight, depending on whether they are tilted toward the Sun

POLES APART

The Arctic is home to several large mammal species, such as caribou, musk oxen, polar bears, walruses, and human beings. Antarctica has no native human inhabitants, nor other land mammals.

FIGHTING THE FREEZE

To stay warm, the polar bear and caribou have extremely dense fur. Penguins have overlapping waterproof feathers, and ptarmigans even have feathered toes. Blubber keeps a seal warm.

Polar bear

Ptarmigans

(daylight) or away from the Sun (no daylight). As a result, the poles receive six months of daylight and six months of darkness. While the North Pole experiences sunshine at midnight, the South Pole has moonlight at midday, and vice versa. The further away from the pole an area lies, the less daylight or darkness it receives.

During the long days of summer, the northern polar region explodes into life. Although there are no trees, the vast tundra grasslands are ablaze with flowering plants. In the warmest areas these bright, ground-hugging blooms attract butterflies, moths, bumblebees, beetles, and many flies. The sea and lake ice melts briefly to provide a home for flocks of migratory ducks, geese, swans, and shorebirds, as well as dragonflies and mosquitoes. Foxes follow polar bears and wolves, feeding on their scraps or competing with snowy owls for their prey of hares, voles, weasels, lemmings, and shrews. Huge herds of caribou roam over the tundra, and fishes such as char and salmon are plentiful in the rivers.

Midday Moon

By contrast, so little of the Antarctic mainland is ice-free that few plants survive. Only in the warmest coastal areas and on ice-ringed mountain peaks do cushions of lichens, liverworts, and mosses grow. Small insects live on these plants, and also in coastal rockpools. Whales, squid, krill, and fishes swim offshore, and seals come ashore to rest and breed. Huge, noisy colonies of seabirds, including petrels, penguins, skuas, and shags, also nest along the coasts and on nearby islands.

As winter approaches, many northern polar animals migrate south to warmer areas. Those that remain, like polar bears, stay active to avoid freezing to death. Only pregnant bears shelter in dens, but even they do not hibernate. In Antarctica, most animals either swim to warmer waters, fly north, or ride out the winter on ice floes. One exception is the emperor penguin, which braves the cold to incubate its single egg on inshore sea ice.

SNOW VULTURES
Petrels are related to albatrosses, but unlike albatrosses they gather food from both land and sea. They are often seen on the Antarctic Peninsula, squabbling over a seal carcass.

ICE BREAKERS
Weddell seals spend their entire life amid the ice surrounding Antarctica. They use their teeth to keep their breathing holes open.

Caribou

Penguin

Fur seal

World Waters

ABOUT 70 PERCENT of our planet's surface is covered by oceans, seas, estuaries, and freshwater rivers and lakes. These habitats are vital not only because they contain a wealth of species, but because they provide humans with food, minerals, energy—and a climate in which we can survive.

Blue Planet

If all the water in the world's oceans was drained away, the landscape of the sea floor would be revealed. With huge mountains and deep valleys, slopes and plains, it is surprisingly similar to the landscape of dry land. But draining the oceans would also kill all life. This is because oceans are the most vital controlling factor in the world's climate. As giant heat reservoirs that capture and release the radiated energy from the Sun, the oceans act as global thermostats, moderating the seasons and the range of temperatures.

Winds and ocean currents also regulate temperature and influence climates by moving warm or cool water along the shorelines. The Gulf Stream, for example, is the current that carries warm water from the Caribbean Sea, up the east coast of the United States, and then to the west coasts of Britain and northern Europe. Without the Gulf Stream, these areas would be much colder and drier.

The oceans are also the Earth's primary source of water—most clouds and the rain or snow they bring are formed as the result of evaporation from the oceans. The oceans also support the algae that provide much of the world's oxygen.

Creatures of the Deep

The world's oceans are teeming with life. Even in the cold, inky darkness of the ocean floor, bristleworms eke out an existence, sifting the mud for particles of food. Sea spiders use their proboscis to suck juices from worms and other invertebrates. The tripodfish smells food in the currents above the mud by propping itself up, like a stilt-walker, on its elongated pelvic fins and tail fin. Glass sponges spread a net of delicate stalks to filter food. Some fishes have adapted to the perpetual gloom by using luminous bacteria to create their own light.

Underwater Oasis

The deep sea is not always ice-cold, however. In some places, volcanic activity allows water to seep under the seabed. As it nears lava-filled chambers, the water is heated to more than 1,100°F (600°C) and returned as hot, gushing fountains. These vents form oases in the deep sea, supporting some of the most extraordinary ecosystems to be found anywhere.

Bacteria living in the hot water and growing on the rocks around the vent openings provide food for giant tubeworms. The worms, which lack a gut, absorb the bacteria directly through their skin. With their red, tentacle-like plumes emerging from their white, tubular body, they look like a giant rose garden clustered around the vent. Enormous 12-inch

TIME AND TIDE

We call our planet Earth, but most of its surface is covered by water. Almost all the water on Earth—97.3 percent—is salt water. Less than three percent is fresh water, and less than one-third is in rivers, lakes, and channels underground. The remainder is frozen in icecaps and glaciers. But the effects of global warming may cause Antarctic ice to become unstable. If some of it melted, the sea level could rise 200 feet (60 m), causing massive flooding and a climate change.

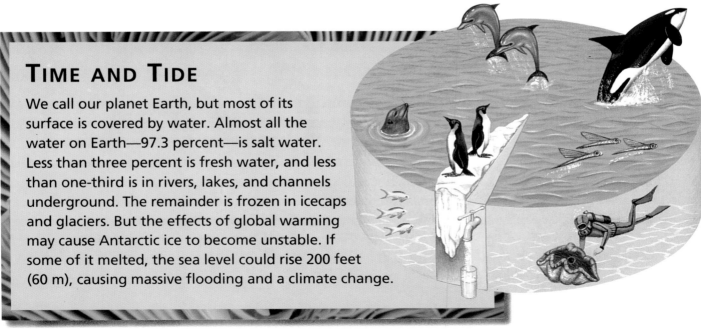

(30-cm) clams and piles of mussels lie among the worm thickets, filtering microorganisms and organic debris from the water. Crabs and shrimps clamber about the clams, and small anemones carpet the floor.

Four Corners

The oceans share many features, and even mix with each other along their boundaries. Nevertheless, the Pacific, Atlantic, Indian, and Southern oceans each has a distinct identity. Differences in water temperatures, salt levels, and geological history have resulted in a wide range of habitats.

For example, each spring the cold waters at the northern and southern boundaries of the Pacific Ocean bloom with tons of plankton. Currents sweep these waters toward the Americas and the Equator, providing food for whale

WATER BIRD
Rays can be thought of as sharks that developed their pectoral fins into "wings" for underwater "flight." This manta ray is common throughout tropical waters.

CROWDED HOUSE
Coral reefs provide food, nests, and shelters for crustaceans, worms, mollusks, clams, and fishes—and the animals that eat them. Snakes such as sea kraits bask and mate on small coral islands.

DRAGONS ADRIFT
Leafy seadragons are related to seahorses. They are found only in southern Australian waters, where, disguised as drifting weed, they suck up crustaceans and swallow them whole.

IN THE SOUP
Sea turtles often rest on coral reefs, in temperate and tropical waters all over the world. This green turtle is endangered because in many countries its eggs and meat are eaten.

sharks, manta rays, and baleen whales, plus millions of smaller fishes—and the predators that eat them.

The Atlantic is like a huge fiord. It is closed in the north and opens at its southern end into the Pacific, Indian, and Southern Oceans. Because of the outflow from the salty Mediterranean Sea, the north Atlantic is the warmest and saltiest of the world's oceans. These waters do not have the diversity of those toward the Equator, such as the North Sea, which is an important area for the fishing industry.

Around the Equator, the warm water becomes deep. Dolphins, sharks, whales, sea turtles, and sunfishes cross these regions on their migration paths. As the Atlantic nears the Southern Ocean, species such as penguins, seals, and whales also abound.

Despite the near-freezing conditions, the waters of the Southern Ocean may produce as much food as those in more temperate climates. The blanket of ice calms the surface, providing a habitat for animals at the base of the food chain, such as zooplankton, and allowing sea-ice algae to develop. The upper surface of the ice supports breeding seals and penguins, which join baleen whales in the water to feast on upwellings of plankton, krill, and squid. Since the plankton grows quickly during the continuous daylight of the summer, there is plenty of food for everyone.

Because the Atlantic is geologically "young" (only about 200 million years old!) the bottom-dwelling animals are not as diverse as those living in the Indo-Pacific. For example, the Caribbean Sea lacks many of the reef-growing corals that make the west Indo-Pacific region the richest marine habitat in the world.

It is estimated that there are between 3,000 and 4,000 species of tropical fishes in the Indian Ocean, often forming colorful "clouds" around corals. Many species are found only in certain areas of the ocean, particularly the Red Sea and the Arabian Gulf. This is because changes in the sea level isolated these regions, providing an opportunity for fishes to evolve in new and different ways.

To Serve and Protect

Coral reefs are to the oceans what tropical rain forests are to the land. Built from the limestone skeletons of soft-bodied coral animals, or polyps, these complex and diverse habitats provide food, nests, and temporary shelters for myriad animals and plants.

Coral reefs occur in the shallow tropical waters of the Pacific and Indian oceans. Humans use reefs for food and shelter, too. They are the home of many food fishes, and also play an important role in protecting low-lying islands and coastal regions from storms.

EEL MEAL
This ribbon moray eel is found mainly in crevices in tropical reefs. It may also burrow into the seabed tail-first, lunging out to seize passing fishes. Unlike this male, the female is bright yellow.

OCEAN GROVE
Mangroves thrive in fresh or salty water. Since they grow in waterlogged mud, their roots develop above ground and reach out to absorb oxygen.

Fish Forests

Some rocky reefs and open coastlines support waving forests of kelp. This form of brown algae may grow more than 165 feet (50 m) long and provide shelter and food for fishes, crabs, sea urchins, sea otters, and seals. Because their dense canopies also reduce the level of light on the sea floor, kelp forests also influence the kinds of plants and animals that will grow beneath them. Humans, too, interact with kelp, using it for fertilizer, food, and other products.

But kelp is not the only "sea tree." Ranging from small shrubs to extensive forests, mangroves are a feature of many estuaries. Birds, spiders, and insects live on their leaves, branches, and trunks, and their roots are home for barnacles and oysters.

The shallow waters of estuaries are nurseries for newly-hatched fishes and crustaceans. Salmon pass through on their way to spawning grounds upstream, while kingfishers and eagles swoop down from above. Estuaries and coastal lagoons also shelter seagrass beds, where turtles and dugongs graze. Fishes, seahorses, and prawns also shelter in these meadows, and some lobsters forage for debris.

The water depth and salt levels of an estuary habitat fluctuate because of the tides, plus irregular surges of fresh water from rivers after rain. But many species have adapted to the changing conditions. For example, fishes swim out into the bay if they prefer higher salinity, or farther up the river for fresh water. Seabirds excrete salt through glands near their nostrils.

Sea Change

Water, sky, and land meet at the seashore, attracting thousands of species. Seashores are especially—

Great egret

Avocets

Crab

and internationally—important areas for wading birds such as plovers, stilts, and curlews. For example, each June and July, more than 30 species of wading birds breed in Alaska, Siberia, Mongolia, and northern China. The birds then migrate to Australian shores for the Southern Hemisphere's spring.

Thousands of birds also find safe havens in wetlands. Although they make up only a tiny percentage of the world's waters, wetlands—rivers and streams, lakes and ponds, marshes, swamps, and bogs—are some of the most beautiful and diverse habitats. Unfortunately, humans have tended to regard wetlands as dumping grounds. But the damage is not confined to

wetlands. The oceans already contain evidence of the changing health of our planet.

Seas and reefs have been robbed of life as a result of overfishing. They are poisoned by oil spills, nuclear waste, industrial dumping, and garbage. Reefs and other habitats are also threatened by the effects of chemical and silt runoff from farmland. Runoff slows coral growth and damages their skeletons. In certain conditions, runoff of fertilizers containing nitrogen and phosphorus also causes an explosion of algal growth. The algae clog the surface of rivers, streams, and oceans, blocking out the sunlight and starving other species of oxygen and food.

Since the oceans make it possible for many living things to survive, any changes to them will have an impact on the life forms that live within them, or rely upon them. Just small changes in ocean temperatures, currents, or even levels can also affect life on the remaining one-third of the Earth's surface, the land. We must stop trashing our oceans, and choking our atmosphere with gases that contribute to global warming. We must act now, for a cleaner future.

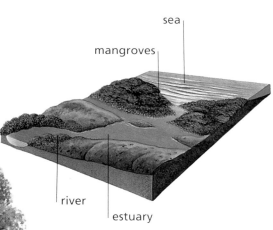

WATER GATE
Estuaries are formed where fresh water from inland rivers merges with the salty sea in protected bays. Salt marshes, mud flats, and tidal creeks can also be found along the edge of estuaries.

sea

mangroves

river

estuary

Ghost shrimp

Bluefish, or tailor

BIRDS OF A FEATHER
Wading birds flock to estuaries and mud flats to feed on crabs and worms under the surface. Humans, too, collect shrimps and oysters.

WETLAND WINGS
Dragonflies can hover and even fly backward to snatch mosquitoes and water boatmen. Dragonflies are, in turn, snapped up by birds, frogs, toads, and hatchling crocodiles and alligators.

FISHING TACKLE
The fishing cat lives near marshes, mangroves, and along rivers and streams in Asia. It scoops up fish with its paws or mouth—or dives headfirst into the water!

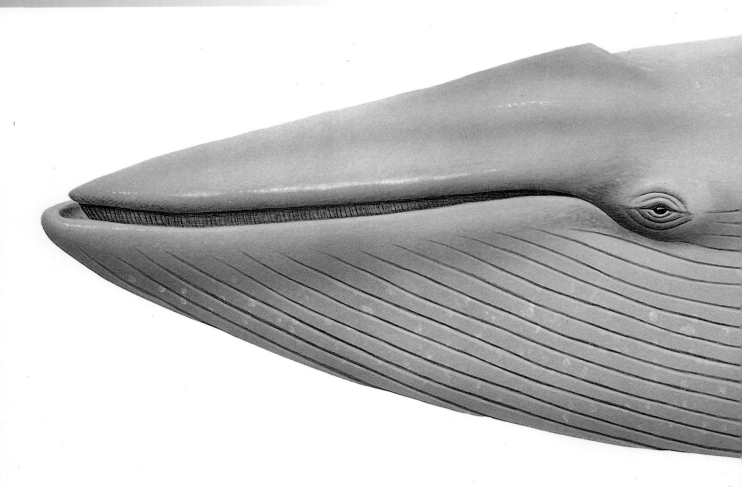

Mammals

Most of the animals we keep as pets, such as dogs, and the animals we use for work, such as horses, are mammals. There are nearly 4,300 species of mammal, and their variety is astounding. From the tiny field mouse to the mighty blue whale; from a mud-wallowing hippopotamus to a flying bat, mammals come in a huge range of different shapes, sizes, and colors.

Mammals live in all sorts of places—some in the sea and some in burrows under the earth; some in trees and others in caves. They have different diets, too—some eat insects, some only meat, others graze on grass and still more, like some whales, use sieves in their mouth to capture plankton. There are mammals swimming, gliding, walking, stalking, swinging, and hopping on almost every part of the planet. There is even a mammal reading this book. That's right—human beings are mammals, too.

Classifying Mammals

MAMMALS ARE CALLED VERTEBRATES—animals with a backbone. They evolved from reptiles that had several bones in their lower jaw. Unlike their cold-blooded ancestors, mammals have a lower jaw of one main bone and are warm-blooded. Mammals are also identified by several other important features.

FANGS A LOT
Mammals, such as this margay, have developed different kinds of teeth: the front teeth are for biting or gnawing at food, the canines are for stabbing, and the molars are for grinding.

In the Beginning

Mammals are divided into three groups: monotremes, marsupials, and placental mammals. All mammal mothers give birth to live young, except for monotremes, which hatch from eggs. Marsupial young are not fully developed when born and are protected in their mother's pouch until they can fend for themselves.

Placental mammals are fed oxygen and nutrients inside their mother's uterus by a blood-rich organ called a placenta. Because of this constant supply of food they are born more developed than monotremes and marsupials, but they are still dependent on their parents. Regardless of their beginnings, all young mammals are fed with milk produced in the mammary glands of their mother.

Sight and Sound

Mammals have a relatively larger brain than other animals. Most also have a well-developed sense of smell and good hearing. Even mammals that don't appear to have any ears, such as moles, have excellent hearing. Whales, dolphins, and some bats that have poor eyesight use sound and hearing to find their food and understand their surroundings.

Mammals that have a weak sense of smell often have keen eyesight. Primates—lemurs, monkeys, apes, and humans—have particularly good binocular vision, which gives a three-dimensional effect and allows them to judge shapes and distances. Nearly all mammals have some color vision, although only some primates can tell red from green.

Coats and Coverings

While some sleek marine mammals have hardly any hair, all land mammals have some fur or hair on their body. This coat can keep them warm by trapping a layer of air against the

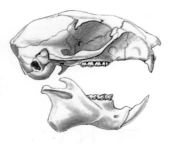

HELPFUL HINGE
In mammals, the lower jaw connects to the skull with a pair of special hinges. These hinges allow the jaw to move without the rest of the skull moving.

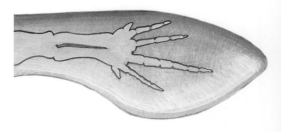

PAWS FOR THOUGHT
The forepaws of a bear and the flippers of a whale have similar bone structures; they are modifications of a basic plan inherited from the same ancestor.

skin, or keep them cool by reflecting sunlight. Some mammals have hairs that are modified into spikes to ward off predators.

Unlike the skin of many other animals, mammals' skin constantly grows, sheds, and renews. A layer of fat under their skin provides insulation, and most mammals have oil glands in their skin, too. For some mammals this oil waterproofs the coat to keep the animal dry while swimming. Some mammals have sweat glands, and others have scent glands that are used to communicate or to protect themselves.

SLEEPING OVER
Food is scarce in winter, so many mammals conserve energy by sleeping for long periods. This allows them to live off fat stored in their body over the summer.

Packs and Loners

Many mammals, such as lions and wolves, live together and work in groups to find food. They have rules of behavior and ways of communicating to make sure that the members of the group survive. But other mammals, such as tigers, live alone, usually only meeting others of their species to breed.

PROUD PARENTS
Lions live in a family group called a pride. Most members of a pride are lionesses and their cubs, which nurse for up to six months.

TRUNK CONNECTION

Elephants are typical mammals in many ways. They have some hair, they feed their young with milk, and they care for their young longer than other vertebrates do. Elephant calves are taught skills and protected by their mother and the other females in their close-knit family for many years. Some calves continue to nurse for up to three years, and female calves remain with their family all their life.

Mammals through the Ages

THREE HUNDRED MILLION YEARS AGO, the Earth was populated by primitive amphibians and reptiles, living in and around tropical swamps. Some of the larger reptiles, called synapsids, had simple teeth with weak jaws and clumsy, sprawling limbs. Fossils tell us that modern mammals evolved from ancestors of these reptiles.

Reptile Relations

We know that synapsids were the first mammal-like creatures because they had a pair of large openings in their skull, behind the eye sockets, similar to the openings found in the skulls of mammals today.

From these reptile beginnings came a group of creatures called therapsids. They developed more powerful jaw-closing muscles and more elaborate teeth, such as canines, or even horny beaks. They also had longer, slender limbs, giving them greater agility and speed. Therapsids probably became warm-blooded and larger-brained.

Therapsids gradually evolved into cynodonts, which looked even more like mammals. Cynodonts had teeth for cutting and crushing meat, with huge jaws and jaw muscles that gave greater biting power. Other bones in the lower jaw became smaller and were used to transmit sound waves—an early development of the middle ear in mammals. One cynodont, called *Cynognathus*, grew to about 3 feet (1 m) in length, but had a head more than 1 foot (30 cm) long.

Early Ancestors

The first mammals appeared during the Triassic Period, about 220 million years ago. They were small, shrewlike animals that were about 5 inches

WALKING WHALES?

Fifty-million-year-old fossils found in India and Pakistan suggest that the land-dwelling relatives of early whales and dolphins may have been dog-sized hoofed animals, known as *Mesonyx*. Studies of the DNA, blood, and muscle structure of modern species have revealed that some of the closest living relatives of whales and dolphins are hippopotamuses!

NEW AND TRUE
Morganucodontids were among the first of the "true" mammals. They were small—the size of a shrew—with sharp teeth to hunt invertebrates, such as insects.

NEARLY BEAR
Ursavus (right) was a small carnivore that appeared about 20 million years ago. It looked rather like a raccoon, and is thought to be the ancestor of most living bear species.

PACK ATTACK
Arsinoitherium defends
her young against a pack of
predators. *Arsinoitherium*
was a herbivore nearly
13 feet (4 m) long. It was a
distant relative of today's
rabbit-sized hyraxes.

(13 cm) long. During the Jurassic and
Cretaceous periods (208–65 million
years ago) new groups of mammals
emerged. Most were carnivores
(meat eaters). But some became
herbivores (plant eaters), such as
the tree-dwelling multituberculates.
Some of these rodent-like animals
were as big as beavers, but they
were not closely related to any modern
mammals. Other mammals developed
teeth and digestive systems to eat both
meat and plant material. Slowly, these
mammals became the ancestors of
monotremes, marsupials, insectivores,
and primates.

Brave New World

Early mammals shared their habitat
with dinosaurs. When the dinosaurs
died out 65 million years ago, the
mammals evolved into thousands of
new species. Their size varied from
tiny rodents to land animals larger
than elephants.

But about 40 million years ago,
a change in the world's climate
caused the extinction of about
one-third of the more primitive
mammal families. Those that
survived this change became
increasingly similar to the
mammals around today. They
spread to every continent and
environment: into jungles, deserts,
and high mountains; across the
grasslands and the tundra; and
even around the polar regions. Some
mammals moved underground, and
others took to treetops, the oceans,
or the sky. The apes also evolved
during this period. Then, about
4 million years ago, the first members
of *Australopithecus* appeared. They
were the forerunners of human beings,
who arose only 2 million years later.

FIRST PERSON?
Australopithecus afarensis
was less than 4 feet (1.2 m)
tall, and lived in Africa
about 3.2 million years
ago. In 1974, an almost
complete fossil skeleton
was discovered in Ethiopia.

Designs for Living

Because mammals have a fairly constant body temperature they can survive in almost any environment, no matter how cold or hot their surroundings may be. To enable them to live in diverse habitats, mammals have developed different body shapes and functions.

Many forest mammals have special toes or thumbs and tails that help them to keep a firm grip on branches. Grassland dwellers that travel great distances for food and rely on speed for survival have long, hoofed legs. Smaller mammals that use burrows for safety and shelter have strong forelegs or large teeth for digging.

Adaptations for survival in the icy Arctic include thick, shaggy coats. Tundra mammals also have broad feet to help them to move across snow in winter and marshy ground in summer. The pale coats of many desert-dwellers reflect harsh sunlight. They also cope with the searing daytime temperatures by sleeping in cool burrows during the day and becoming active at night

(nocturnal). Some desert mammals cope with heat by allowing their body temperature to change throughout the day, while others have body processes that conserve water.

Moving House

Mammals have also evolved as they moved from one environment to another. For example, the ancestors of today's horses lived in forests and were small enough to move among trees and undergrowth. When they began to live on the open plains, however, they grew larger and stronger so they could migrate in search of fresh food, and faster so they could gallop away from the fast-moving predators of the plains.

Whales and dolphins have adapted to their underwater world by doing away with unnecessary hindlimbs. They have fins instead of forelegs, and streamlined bodies. Since there are now whales and dolphins in every ocean of the world—and in some rivers, too—we can understand how body changes such as these allowed mammals to take advantage of different habitats and improve their chances of survival.

PORCU-PAIN
A porcupine's long, sharp quills provide a fearsome defense. They are only loosely attached to the animal, and easily get stuck in the face and paws of any attacker.

SPRINT STAR
A cheetah stride can cover up to 25 feet (7.5 m), and at full speed, the cheetah makes 3½ strides a second. Like other fast runners and jumpers, the cheetah has a long, streaming tail that acts as a counterbalance.

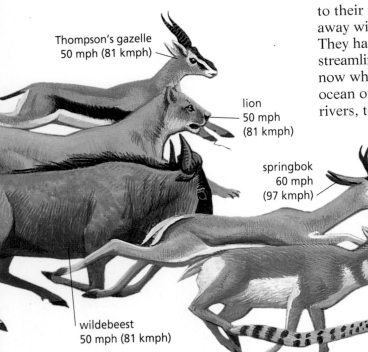

Thompson's gazelle
50 mph (81 kmph)

lion
50 mph
(81 kmph)

springbok
60 mph
(97 kmph)

pronghorn antelope
61 mph (99 kmph)

wildebeest
50 mph (81 kmph)

cheetah
68 mph (110 kmph)

DOG ON STILTS
The maned wolf developed extremely long legs to enable it to see over and travel through the tall grasses of its South American habitat.

SNOW SHOVEL
In Arctic winters the third and fourth claws of the forefeet of the collared lemming (left) become much larger. They help the lemming to dig through snow, ice, and frozen ground for food.

WINTER WONDER
Many mammals in the Arctic adapt to the different seasons by changing color. The Arctic fox (below) has a brown coat in summer, but grows a thick white coat for warmth and camouflage in winter.

SAME, BUT DIFFERENT

Some mammals look similar and behave in similar ways even though they are not related to each other. Although they live in different parts of the world, they have adapted to play similar roles in similar habitats. Scientists call this convergent evolution. For example, the striped possum of Australia, a marsupial, has a long, narrow fourth finger like that of the Madagascan aye-aye, a primate. They both use this finger to hook grubs out of holes in trees. Koalas, also from Australia, look similar to the sloths of Central and South America. Both species are long-legged, almost tailless leaf-eaters that live in trees, and they both conserve energy by moving slowly and resting for up to 20 hours a day.

Striped possum

Aye-aye

Sloth

Koala

Mammal Behavior

SOME MAMMALS, such as bears, snow leopards, and koalas, are solitary animals. They live alone, avoid their neighbors, and only come together to mate. But most mammals are social and live in groups. The way that mammals behave in their group is very important to their chances of survival.

I'M THE BOSS!
By exposing his large canine teeth, an adult male baboon reminds other baboons of his superior power. This warns lower-ranking baboons to stay in line—or else!

Mother Love

Some mammal behavior has to do with day-to-day body maintenance, such as feeding, grooming, and urinating. But a lot of mammal behavior relates to the fact that young mammals must drink their mother's milk to survive.

Some types of mammals, such as whales, elephants, and humans, stay with their mother for years. But most mammals spend only a short time with their mother. For example, rodents are dependent on their mother for less than three weeks. Whatever the length of time they spend together, it is important that the mother cares about her young. As well as feeding and protecting them, many mothers must teach their young skills, especially hunting, to help them to survive as adults.

Play Time

Young mammals of many species, particularly monkeys, dogs, cats, weasels, mongooses, and humans, play games to rehearse for the real-life drama of adult life. Games such as pouncing and play-fighting help youngsters learn how to find food and defend themselves. Playing also teaches them how to form relationships. By learning how to react to the moods and signals sent by others, young mammals come to understand their place in the group.

Safety in Numbers

Living in a group, or a herd or a pack, has many advantages. Mammals that might be preyed on by reptiles, birds, or other mammals can defend each other and their young. Because a predator has many targets from which to choose, most group members have time to escape. Living in a group also means that there are

CLASH OF THE TITANS

SOME male mammals use weapons such as antlers, tusks, and horns in disputes over food, territory, or mates, or to prove their status in a group. The fights are mainly tests of strength and stamina. These male mountain sheep will kick, wrestle, and smash into each other until one ram either stops fighting or flees.

Kicking and growling

Preparing for battle

UNITED WE STAND
Meerkats are very sociable and live together in packs. When a meerkat spots a predator, such as a hawk or eagle, its shrill cry sends the others scampering to the safety of their burrows.

more helpers around to care for the young, and it is easier to find a mate.

To make sure that the members of the group get along—and to ensure the group's survival—many species have a hierarchy in which one member is more important than the rest. Wolves, for example, respect the authority of their leader and rely on him for their survival. The leader decides when the group should rest, and when and what they should hunt.

In some species there may be a few dominant animals in the group, and in others, such as elephants, group leaders are wise old females.

King of the Castle

Dominant animals tell others about their status in a variety of ways. For example, the most powerful males in a troop of baboons are easy to tell because they are bigger than the rest and their

OK CORRAL
When threatened by predators, mammals such as rhinos and whales form a protective circle around their young or wounded companions.

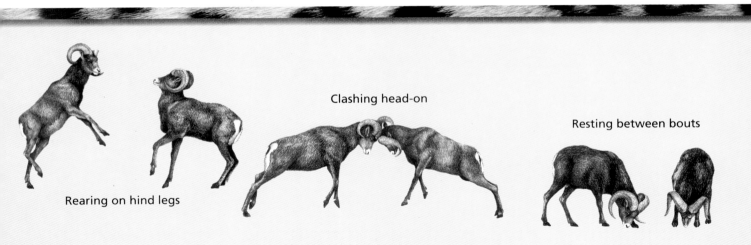

Rearing on hind legs

Clashing head-on

Resting between bouts

manes are thicker. In some other mammal groups, such as blackbucks, the most important buck is black, while all the other males are light brown. In some monkey groups, the most important male has a louder voice than the rest.

However, the most common way that male mammals declare their dominance is to show others what they own and control. Unlike many female mammals, which urinate when their nerves and brain sense that their bladders are full, adult male dogs, male mice, and others use their urine to mark the boundaries of their territory. These stinky "signposts" warn other males to stay away from their land—and the food, females, and other resources found on it.

Animal Attraction

The dominant animal in a group is usually the strongest and fittest. He is responsible for most of the matings in his group. In this way he passes his superior genes on to the next generation.

Some mammals have many sexual partners during their lives. Others— some of the small forest-dwelling antelopes, for example—mate for life. Such mammals spend time getting to know each other before they mate, because they bring up the young together. They court each other using scents and complicated displays of colors, actions, and noises. But other mammals, such as the bandicoot, mate quickly and roughly and never see each other again.

It's Good to Talk

In addition to courtship, social mammals use smells, sounds, facial expressions, or body language to

TAKE THAT!
Many mammals use scent to defend themselves. A skunk ejects a foul-smelling spray into the face of any creature that refuses to leave it in peace.

LUNCH ON THE RUN
A the end of the wet season, wildebeest and zebra (right) travel 2,000 miles (3,000 km) across the plains of eastern Africa in search of water, fresh grass, and leaves. But gerenuks (above) get their food and water from tender leaves and do not migrate.

identify themselves; tell members of the group how they are feeling; locate their companions; warn of danger; and to communicate with other groups over long distances. Dogs, for example, wag their tail when they are happy, and snarl, bare their teeth, and growl when they are feeling aggressive. Male impalas show that they belong to the same group by rubbing scent on each other's faces with their head.

Dinner Parties

Mammals eat almost anything, from plants to other mammals. Vampire bats live on blood, echidnas eat ants, and a pack of wolves will eat a moose or another large animal.

Mammals use many different strategies to find food. Some mammals are scavengers that dine on leftovers. Other mammals are hunters, and members of some carnivorous species band together to catch their prey.

Dolphins, porpoises and seals, lions, and wild dogs work together to save the energy of individual hunters and to make sure that every member of the group eats enough to survive. Together they can catch much larger prey in less time than they could if they were hunting alone. Even humpback whales help each other herd schools of fish. Like the other aspects of group living, cooperative behavior gives social mammals an advantage in the struggle to survive.

STOCKING UP
Squirrels collect nuts and seeds and hide them in hollow trees. They save them to eat during long winters and to have a supply of food ready for the spring.

PUPPY LOVE
In their first year, African hunting dog pups rely on their pack to provide them with food.

Endangered Species

EVER SINCE the first living forms inhabited the Earth, species have gradually died out and been replaced with new types. But now the rate of extinction is speeding up. Experts estimate that we are losing up to 100 species of plants and animals *each day*. If this continues, then almost all mammals will be endangered by 2008.

TIGER TERRITORY
There are only about 6,000 tigers left in the wild. To save the species, we must set aside forested areas large enough to provide food for them—we shall also be saving many other forest plants and animals.

Extinction Is Forever

There are perhaps 10 million forms of life on Earth today. Many more—mostly insects in places like tropical rain forests—have probably not even been discovered yet. What zoologists do know is that there are nearly 4,300 mammal species alive now. That's all.

In the 300 years between 1600 and 1900 about 75 species, mostly birds and mammals, were killed off. Since then the rate has skyrocketed. In 1996, 1,096 mammal species—a quarter of all the known mammals—were listed as endangered or at risk. This means that so many have been killed that there may not be enough healthy adults left to breed and keep the species going. By the year 2015, you will have witnessed the extinction of maybe a million living things. These animals will never be replaced.

Human Error

For thousands of years, humans have been killing other animals. The first North Americans exterminated giant ground sloths and woolly mammoths.

BAD NEWS, BEAR

In Asia, bear body parts are used to treat many health problems. The gallbladder is highly prized because its bile (a fluid that helps digestion) is a powerful medicine used to fight diseases of the liver, heart, and digestive system. So many bears have been killed for their parts that some species are endangered. Because there are so few wild bears left, bear parts are worth a lot of money. For this reason the slaughter continues.

The Maoris in New Zealand destroyed giant eagles and moas completely. European explorers wiped out Steller's sea cows, elephant birds, and other animals on islands around the world. There were between 50 to 60 million bison in America when the Europeans arrived—"buffalo" hunters reduced them to fewer than 800. Sometimes they would take only the tongue, which was a favorite food at the time, and leave the body to rot.

Whenever people move into new habitats, other animals are moved out, by one means or another. This process continues as the growing human population invades the world's last wildernesses. Early humans killed other animals with only simple stone blades. What chance do animals have against today's submachine guns and other killing machines?

No Tree, No Me

It is important to realize that there are many other ways of killing mammals than by simply shooting them. When we dam rivers, drain wetlands, build pipelines, and construct towns and roads, animals lose their habitats—their food, water, shelter, and open areas. Logging forests removes the trees that are the food supply and home of many species. Allowing too many cattle and sheep to graze on land turns it into a dust bowl where nothing can survive. Also, when animals have nowhere else to live and hunt, they may venture too close to where humans have built their homes. For example, much of the cheetah's habitat has been turned into farms and many are shot when they attack farm animals. Others, such as wolves or cougars, have been killed because people think they are dangerous.

BABE IN THE WOOD
The orangutans' forest habitat has been devastated by logging and fires. Mothers are sometimes killed and their young sold as pets.

POLAR PERIL
In 1973, rules were laid down to help control the number of polar bears being killed. But the effects of global warming may eventually destroy the bears' frozen home.

Threats on All Sides

Air and water pollution, acid rain, and soil spoiled by mining or the dumping of chemicals kill an animal's food and poison its home. Oceans fouled by oil spills and toxic and nuclear wastes, and rivers crammed with boats and garbage, can discourage water mammals from breeding and even sicken or kill them.

Sometimes humans bring a foreign species into other animals' habitats for food or recreational hunting. Foreign species also threaten local wildlife. Not only can they kill local animals or give them diseases, but they are more likely to survive and breed to enormous numbers. In the competition for food, water, and shelter, the local animals often lose.

Need or Greed?

Ever since humans first appeared we have been killing wildlife for the resources they give us. For example, the Hawaiian monk seal and several species of baleen whale have almost been wiped out for their fur, meat, baleen, and oil. But some mammals are killed just for fashion. Giant anteaters, for example, are hunted as

trophies. The beautiful fur of species such as giant pandas, snow leopards, and tigers has tempted many hunters. Now these species are endangered.

Other animals are killed because people think they have medicinal or magical properties. There are less than 2,000 maned wolves alive today because their left eye is said to bring good luck. Thousands of bears are slaughtered in Asia every year because their paws are thought to cure rheumatism. Because bear paw is one of Asia's most expensive dishes, some people think eating them is a status symbol. Horns from black rhinos are valued as status symbols when carved into dagger handles. They are prized

CLOSE, BUT NOT QUITE
Europeans had almost wiped out the American bison. At the last moment, land reserves of land were set aside for them. There are now about 30,000 bison living on these reserves.

MONKEY BUSINESS
Habitat destruction has endangered the golden lion tamarin. But other tamarins are threatened because of the pet trade. Thousands were trapped and shipped overseas—a voyage that killed most of them.

DOLPHINS IN DANGER
In the last 35 years, the tuna-fishing industry has killed 6 to 12 million dolphins, especially the pantropical spotted dolphin, Fraser's dolphin, the spinner dolphin (above), and the common dolphin.

A LUCKY ESCAPE
After years of public protest, new rules now exist to protect dolphins. Many tuna nets have special escape hatches, and divers sometimes guide dolphins to safety.

ingredients in some medicines, too, but there is no scientific evidence to prove these medicines actually work. But the people who use the medicines refuse to believe this. Now there are only about 2,700 black rhinos left.

How Can We Help?

One way to stop the slaughter is to stop the reason why the animals are being killed in the first place. For example, African elephants are killed by poachers for their ivory tusks. In 1989, Kenyan wildlife officials confiscated and burned the tusks of about 1,000 elephants to show their support for banning the ivory trade. Ivory prices, and the poaching of elephants, have now declined as a result of the ban, because there is no incentive for poachers to kill them.

Gorillas are killed for food, and their head and hands are also sold as souvenirs. Because of this, and their loss of habitat, only 350–500 mountain gorillas now survive. Perhaps the best way to protect gorillas is by encouraging tourists to visit them. This way the gorillas won't be hurt and the local people will earn the money they badly need from tourism—not from hunting gorillas.

Laws against killing rare species, and zoos that collect them, only go so far. The best way to save mammals in danger is to stop destroying their homes. We must realize that all animals have as much right to exist on Earth as we do. Perhaps as we learn to appreciate and respect mammals more we will be able to think up more ways to conserve their natural habitats. Their survival depends on us. If we don't try to protect them, they are almost certainly doomed.

JUMPING FOR JOY
Due to the efforts of scientists and the public, humpbacks no longer have to fear factory ships and harpoon guns. A ban on commercial whaling became law in 1986.

Monotremes

MONOTREMES ARE MAMMALS that lay eggs instead of giving birth to live young. They are also the only mammals that lack teats, although they do feed their young milk. Monotremes are an ancient group of animals dating back to 130 million years ago. They were on Earth at the same time as the dinosaurs.

Weird and Wonderful

Five species of monotreme are alive today: three species of long-beaked echidna; the short-beaked echidna; and the platypus. All species of echidna are found in New Guinea, and the short-beaked echidna and the platypus are native to Australia. They are found nowhere else in the world.

Monotreme means "one hole." Like birds and reptiles, monotremes have only one body opening, called a cloaca, for reproduction and excretion of wastes. Monotremes lay soft, leathery eggs that are incubated for ten days. The echidna keeps her eggs in a pouch on her belly, and the platypus incubates hers between her body and her curled-up tail. When the young hatch, they are very underdeveloped: A newborn echidna—called a puggle— is less than a half-inch (1.3 cm) long! They feed on milk oozing from patches on their mother's belly.

Prickly Pair

Also called spiny anteaters, echidnas have a finger-like snout, a long tongue, no teeth, and a short tail. At about 12 to 18 inches (30 to 45 cm) long, the short-beaked echidna is almost half the size of the long-beaked species.

DISAPPEARING ACT
In soft soil, echidnas burrow straight down until only their spines poke above the ground. Dingoes are one of the few predators able to dig them out and eat them, spines and all.

KILLER KICK

The male platypus is one of the few mammals that are poisonous. He can paralyze a person's leg or kill a dog by wrapping his legs around the victim and jabbing it with the long spurs on his hindlegs. The male uses his spurs in fights with other males, especially during the breeding season. Male echidnas also have spurs, but they are harmless.

venom gland

venom duct

spur

STICKY BEAK

The short-beaked echidna's tongue is four times longer than its snout. It can lick up thousands of termites, ants, and other small insects during a day's feeding.

The short-beaked echidna uses the thick claws on its short, strong front legs to break into insect mounds and nests. It then captures the occupants with the sticky saliva on its tongue. The long-beaked echidna hunts at night, using its snout to probe for worms. It uses spikes in a groove in its tongue to spear food and draw it into its mouth.

Echidnas' sharp quills, called spines, protect them from predators. On hard ground, a frightened echidna curls into a tight—and prickly—ball, leaving no soft underparts exposed.

Mix and Match

When the first platypus specimen was sent to Britain in 1798, it was thought to be a fake, made by stitching the bill of a duck to the body of an otter!

The platypus is about half the size of a domestic cat. It is shy and meets others only in the winter to breed. It is also amphibious, living in water as well as on land, and feeds mostly at night. It can keep its body temperature steady, even while swimming for long spells in near-freezing water. When not swimming, it spends a lot of its time grooming.

SMOOTH SWIMMER

The platypus stores its prey of water creatures inside its cheek pouches. It grinds its food between the horny plates inside its bill, and then eats while floating on the surface.

WET AND DRY

The platypus lives in burrows dug in riverbanks but spends half of its time underwater in the streams, rivers, and lakes of eastern Australia. Its body has special adaptations to enable it to live in and out of water.

The platypus's eyes and ears are located in a special groove. When it dives, muscles control a fold of skin that tightens to cover this groove. The platypus navigates underwater by using touch and electromagnetic pulses from receptors in the skin of its rubbery bill. The pulses also help it to hunt by detecting the muscle activity of its prey.

The platypus propels itself through the water with its webbed forefeet, using its hindfeet and flattened tail like rudders to control or change direction. On land, it folds back the webs on its forefeet so that it can use its claws to walk and dig.

Marsupials

MARSUPIALS ARE UNUSUAL MAMMALS that appeared at the same time as placental mammals, around 95 million years ago. Like placentals, marsupials give birth to live young. But most marsupials also have a pouch, in which the underdeveloped young nurse and shelter until they are old enough to be independent.

KID KOALA

A young koala spends seven months snug in its mother's pouch, held there by the muscles inside. When it leaves the pouch, the youngster rides on its mother's back as she feeds.

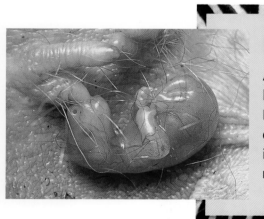

Pouches A-Plenty

There are about 280 species of marsupials. Seventy-five of these are opossums that live in North, Central, and South America. The other species, which vary in size, shape, and way of life, live in Australia, New Guinea, and on nearby islands. They range from 7-foot (2.1-m) tall kangaroos to thumb-sized ningauis. Marsupials live in many habitats, from deserts to rain forests, in trees, in burrows, and on the ground. They hop, glide, run, and swim, and eat plants, pollen and nectar, insects, and meat.

Things That Spring

Sixty or more species of marsupial belong to the macropod family, including kangaroos, tree kangaroos, and wallabies. *Macropod* means "big-foot" and refers to the long back feet and strong hindlegs possessed by most members of this family.

When a macropod needs to move quickly it hops on its hindlegs, using its long, rather stiff tail to help it balance. A hopping kangaroo uses less energy than a running dog or a galloping horse, and the largest macropod, the red kangaroo, can leap 40 feet (12 m) in a single bound. But the design of its hindlegs means that a typical kangaroo cannot walk. The only time a kangaroo can move each hindleg by itself is when the animal is swimming. Only a tree kangaroo can move its hindlegs independently, while walking along branches.

All macropods are herbivores. Some species snatch at plants as they move from place to place, while others stay in one spot and graze like cattle or sheep. If there is not enough food, some kangaroos (like other marsupials) can slow down their baby's growth in

PEA IN A POD

A newborn kangaroo is no bigger than a jellybean. It is tiny, blind, and hairless, and its limbs are only partially formed. But the baby's forefeet have sharp, curved claws, so it can drag itself from its mother's birth canal to her pouch. There it fastens itself to a teat and continues to grow and develop, nourished by its mother's rich milk, for about seven months.

the pouch until there is enough to eat again. Females of some species can also delay the development of a fertilized egg until a young kangaroo—called a joey—leaves the pouch. When the mature joey goes, the mother will give birth to this new joey. Amazingly, she can produce milk suitable for the new joey and a different type of milk for the older joey at the same time!

Koalas and Kin

Macropods belong to a group called diprotodonts. More than half of all Australian marsupials also belong to this diverse group. Diprotodonts have only one pair of well-developed incisors (cutting teeth) in their lower jaw, and the second and third toes of their back feet are fused together to form a two-clawed grooming comb.

The koala is a diprotodont. It spends most of its life in trees and is an agile climber. It gets all of its food

MOBILE HOME
Long after it can move about by itself, a joey returns to its mother's pouch to sleep, travel, and avoid danger. It climbs in head first, then turns so that it can see what is going on outside, or be ready to jump out.

'ROO WITH A VIEW
The Goodfellow's tree kangaroo is the most brightly colored of all the tree kangaroos. It has long, strong forelegs and shortened, broad back feet so it can climb trees and walk along branches.

and water from eucalyptus leaves. Some people think that the koala is a calm, sleepy creature, but it can actually be very aggressive toward other koalas. It can also defend itself against dogs and humans by biting and scratching!

The wombat is closely related to the koala. It looks like a miniature bear, but eats only grass. Timid and nocturnal, it lives in huge burrows, some up to 300 feet (100 m) long. From fossils scientists have learned that Australia was once home to a wombat the size of a hippopotamus.

Possum Posse

Many species of possum live in Australia. The brushtail possum is the most common type. Ringtail possums are so called because of their long,

BOXING MATCH
Male red kangaroos can be 7 feet (2.1 m) tall when sitting down, and even taller when propped up on their tail. In the mating season, the males fight savagely and the winners mate with the females.

DEMON BREED
Some marsupials eat meat. The Tasmanian devil is the marsupial equivalent of a hyena. It does catch some live prey, but it mainly scavenges. Its powerful jaws can crunch up a whole sheep—even the skull!

slender, prehensile (gripping) tail, which they carry tightly coiled when not in use.

Almost all possums live in trees. The smallest are the five species of pygmy-possum, some of which weigh less than a matchbox. Most eat pollen and insects, and use their brush-tipped tongue to lick nectar from flowers.

Mystery Mole

The marsupial mole is the only living member of its family, which dates back at least 50 million years. It is 5 to 7 inches (13 to 18 cm) long and has fine, golden fur that blends in well with its sandy desert home. It uses its flat, spade-like front claws to "swim" through the sand, which collapses behind it. It breathes oxygen from the air trapped between the grains of sand. Since it is blind, it relies on its sense of smell and hearing to catch its prey of burrowing insects and reptiles. But very little else is known of this mole's behavior.

PLAYING POSSUM
When threatened, the woolly opossum (right) of South America pretends to be dead. The yapok, or water opossum (above), is the only amphibious marsupial. It swims with its eyes shut, probing for prey with its sensitive fingers.

Night Scooters

All bandicoots are omnivores (animals that eat both meat and plants). Some are rat-sized, while others are as big as badgers. Bandicoots scamper about at night, using their long snout to sniff out food. They then use their sharp front claws to scratch worms, insects, seeds, and roots from the earth.

A special kind of bandicoot is the bilby, which lives in Australian deserts. Like other bandicoots, the bilby nests in burrows. Its silky fur keeps it warm at night, and its long ears help to keep it cool during the day by radiating body heat. The bilby is endangered because it is hunted by foreign species, such as foxes and feral cats. Much of its habitat has also been taken over by grazing cattle.

Monkey Puzzle

Most cuscuses are found in New Guinea and on nearby islands. They move through the rain forest with their strong, grasping hands, feet, and tail. They have flat faces, and some have bright orange and white-spotted fur. Early European explorers often mistook them for monkeys. Cuscuses eat leaves, flowers, and fruits.

Wild and Woolly

American opossums range in size from one species as small as a mouse to the cat-sized Virginia opossum. Most species, such as the woolly opossum, are omnivores and are able to climb. Those that spend more time on the ground than in trees have shorter tails and eat more meat than tree opossums. They are not afraid of

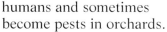

humans and sometimes become pests in orchards.

The seven species of shrew-opossums live in the cool, misty forests in the Andes mountains of South America. They use the two long incisors in their lower jaw to stab their prey of insects and small animals.

Another type of opossum, the colocolo, or monito del monte ("little monkey of the mountain"), lives in the cool rain forests of southern Chile. It eats insect larvae. Unfortunately, some people believe that seeing this rat-size opossum brings bad luck.

ANT-EATER

With its long, sticky tongue, the squirrel-sized numbat is the only marsupial that feeds almost entirely on ants and termites.

FUR FLYING

Some marsupials glide from tree to tree using the furry membrane between their limbs as a parachute. One species, the greater glider, can "fly" more than 300 feet (100 m)!

LOST ... AND FOUND?

The thylacine, or Tasmanian tiger, looked like a wolf with a pouch. It used its huge jaws to catch kangaroos and wallabies. Because it also attacked sheep, the thylacine was hunted. The last known individual died in a zoo in 1936. But there have been many supposed sightings since then. Could some thylacines have escaped the slaughter?

Anteaters, Sloths, and Armadillos

I T IS DIFFICULT TO IMAGINE the similarities between elegant anteaters, armored and speedy armadillos, and shaggy, sluggish sloths. But they all belong to a group of insect-eating mammals called xenarthrans (pronounced "zen-ARTH-rans"), or edentates, which means "toothless." However, only the anteaters have no teeth at all.

TREE HOUSE

The collared anteater, or tamandua, is about half the size of a giant anteater. It climbs trees with the help of its tail and opens ant and termite nests with the huge claws on its forefeet.

Furry Vacuum Cleaners

All xenarthrans are native to Central and South America. The largest species, the giant anteater, grows to about 6 feet (1.8 m) long and weighs up to 55 pounds (25 kg). Its sense of smell is at least 40 times more sensitive than that of humans, and it constantly sniffs the air with its elongated snout. It is active during the day and sleeps at night, using its long, fanlike tail as a blanket.

The anteater's long, wormlike tongue, covered with sticky saliva, slurps up to 35,000 insects per day.

Its strong front legs and long, sharp claws are good for tearing into rock-hard termite mounds. The claws force the anteater to walk on its knuckles—with the two largest claws turned inward—but they also make useful weapons. When threatened, the anteater rears up on its hindfeet and slashes at its would-be attacker. Even powerful cats such as jaguars avoid fighting giant anteaters.

Strange but True

Sloths look like a cross between a bear and a monkey. All three species live in tropical rain forests. They grow about 2 feet (60 cm) in length and have long forelegs and curved, grasping claws. They don't make nests, nor use dens, and they carry their young until the babies are about seven months old. Algae that grows on their fur can actually make them turn green!

SUPER SLOTHS

Giant sloths flourished during the Pleistocene era (2 million to 10,000 years ago.) Some were the size of oxen, while others were as big and as heavy as elephants. The sloths used their huge claws to gather their food of roots, twigs, and leaves. Since sloth fossils have been found in the world's driest place, Chile's Atacama Desert, scientists believe it was once full of lush vegetation.

Sloths are awake for just a few hours a day, during which they move hand over hand, extremely slowly—about 13 feet (4 m) a minute—eating leaves. They move so slowly because their diet contains little energy, but a lot of toxic chemicals. By slowing down their body functions and their movements, sloths reduce their need for food—and also eat fewer toxins.

"Little Armored Things"

The armadillo's name refers to its strong, flexible, bony plates. All 20 species of armadillo have one horny shield over the shoulders, another over the hips, and several around the waist. This armor protects the armadillo from predators and from thorns and cactus spikes.

Most armadillos live in deep tunnels in desert areas with little vegetation. They spend their days

HANGING OUT

Sloths hang upside down to eat, sleep, mate, and even give birth! They are so used to life in the trees that they can no longer walk but drag themselves along with their forearms. This makes them easy prey for predators.

curled up asleep, coming out at night to feed. They have very poor eyesight and rely on their hearing and sense of smell to hunt ants and termites. They also eat worms, fruits, roots, and small vertebrates.

Armadillos are the most widespread of xenarthrans, and also among the most endangered. Cattle grazing has ruined much of their habitat, and their meat is sometimes eaten as a delicacy.

BABY CARRIAGE

The giant anteater lives in woodlands and grasslands. Females give birth standing upright and balancing on their tails. They carry their young on their back for about six months.

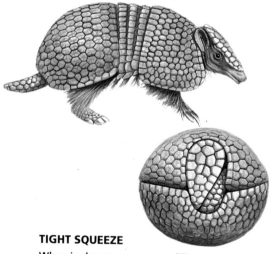

TIGHT SQUEEZE

When in danger, most armadillos either run very fast or quickly dig a burrow with their sharp claws. The three-banded armadillo does not burrow but rolls into a tight ball and uses its thick bony plating like a suit of armor.

The Aardvark, Pangolins, and Elephant Shrews

PANGOLINS AND THE AARDVARK are among the strangest of animals. The aardvark belongs to an order all of its own—Tubulidentata, meaning "tube-toothed." With their horny body scales, pangolins are also one of a kind. They look more like reptiles than mammals. The only feature they have in common with elephant shrews is their diet: insects.

PORKY PREDATOR
The aardvark has an arched back and a long, naked tail. Its skin is lightly covered with bristly hair. Its tough hide protects it from the bites of the ants and termites on which it feeds.

Pigs That Dig

The aardvark is found wherever termites are found: grasslands, savanna, and open woodlands. An aardvark can excavate a termite mound with its shovel-shaped claws in a few minutes, where a human would need to use an ax. It also eats locusts, grasshoppers, and the fruits of a wild South African plant.

When attacked, aardvarks are fierce fighters and will slash and kick with their legs. They can also turn somersaults and balance on their tail to defend themselves with their claws. Aardvarks are nocturnal, sometimes traveling up to 18 miles (30 km) in one night in search of food. By day they sleep in underground burrows.

A LIVING FOSSIL
The aardvark now lives only in Africa. It uses its acute sense of smell to find food. While it is licking up its prey, it closes its nostrils to stop ants from getting into its nose.

Abandoned burrows are important for the survival of smaller mammals, such as hyraxes, which use them as dens or refuges.

The presence of aardvarks in farming areas helps to control crop-eating pests. But aardvarks are still hunted for their meat and hide.

Scale Tale

The seven species of pangolin (scaly anteater) live in Africa and Southeast Asia. Like aardvarks, they are shy, solitary, nocturnal, and have a good sense of smell. Pangolins have short, powerful limbs and sharp claws for digging into ant nests and termite mounds. Some species also use their claws to scoop out underground burrows. Tree-dwelling pangolins spend their days curled up inside tree hollows.

Pangolins have no teeth, so they use their long, sticky tongue to drag food down into their muscular stomach. When they are feeding, a thick membrane shields their eyes and special muscles block off their nostrils to keep ants out. Their scales also protect them from the insects' bites, and from the attacks of predators. For example, when a young pangolin is frightened, it grabs the base of its mother's tail. The

BACK OFF
The pangolin's horny scales cover almost every part of its body. When an enemy threatens, the pangolin lashes out with its tail and slashes with the razor-sharp scales.

CREATURE FEATURE
Elephant shrews are unrelated to either elephants or shrews! They are so named because their flexible snout looks rather like an elephant's trunk.

Traditional people in eastern Africa also use dogs to hunt them for food.

Elephant shrews usually mate for life. Together, each pair defends a fixed territory from other elephant shrews. Within the territory, at least one species builds a system of trails. The male spends much of his time doing housework: clearing debris, such as leaves, from the trails with his paws in order to provide an escape route from danger. Family members also rest, groom, and feed at favorite spots along the trails.

Most species build burrows and nests. They live in a variety of habitats, including open plains, grasslands, and tropical forests. Their survival depends on the conservation of these areas. More than half the known species of elephant shrew are already considered vulnerable or endangered.

mother then wraps the tail around herself, enclosing her baby.

In China, pangolin scales are used in traditional medicines. In Africa, large numbers of them are killed each year for their meat. But the greatest threat to the survival of pangolins is the destruction of their rain forest habitat.

Neat and Tidy

The 15 species of elephant shrew are found only in Africa. Species range from mouse-sized to as big as a half-grown rabbit. They all have large eyes and long, ratlike tails. Some use their sensitive snout to probe leaf litter for worms, beetles, spiders, and grasshoppers. Others prefer to devour ants and termites, clawing and biting to break into the insects' tunnels. Elephant shrews are in turn eaten by owls, snakes, and small carnivores.

STRANGE RELATIONS

Ten thousand years ago mammoths roamed the Earth. Some of their frozen remains have been found in Siberia. Studies of the proteins found in the mammoths' muscles have enabled scientists to trace the mammoth's family tree. They believe that many extinct and living mammals share an ancestor that lived 65 million years ago. Aardvarks are distantly related to elephants!

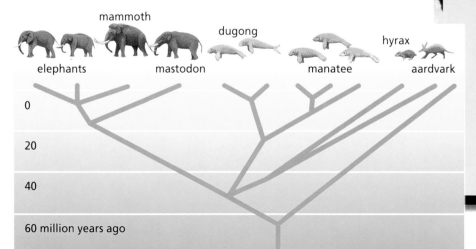

mammoth

dugong

hyrax

elephants   mastodon   manatee   aardvark

0

20

40

60 million years ago

Insectivores and Tree Shrews

ORE THAN HALF OF ALL MAMMALS eat insects as part of their diet. One group of mammals, the insectivores, eats mostly insects, although some also eat meat. Fossils show that the first placental mammals were insectivores. Today their descendants—including moles, shrews, hedgehogs, and desmans—live in almost every part of the world.

NOSE PROBE
The Pyrenean desman is a kind of mole. It swims and hunts its prey underwater, probing beneath rocks for insects and crustaceans with its long, flexible snout.

HIDE AND SEEK
The eyes of the European mole are tiny and useless. It relies on its very sensitive pink nose to smell and feel its underground prey.

SPIKY SPECIES
Hedgehogs are kept safe by their spiny coat. They eat worms, insects, seeds, fruit, and mushrooms. Some species hibernate in winter to save energy.

Bug Breakfasts

With more than 400 species, the order Insectivora is the third largest group of mammals. Insectivores are nocturnal and often solitary. Fast-moving hunters, they have a relatively small brain, but a keen sense of smell, on which they rely far more than their eyesight. They also have up to 44 sharp teeth.

Mighty Bite

Among the largest of the insectivores, solenodons can be found only on the Caribbean islands of Hispaniola and Cuba. As well as insects, solenodons eat meat, including frogs, lizards, and small birds. When they bite their prey they inject it with a small amount of poisonous saliva, which causes paralysis. This poison is very painful, but not fatal, to humans. Two species of shrew also kill their prey in this way.

A female solenodon has one baby at a time. If her burrow is disturbed, she runs to another burrow while the young holds on to her teat. All other members of the Insectivora order carry their babies in their mouth.

Foreign species such as dogs, rats, and mongooses have either killed solenodons or competed for their food. Now solenodons are in great danger of becoming extinct.

Fast and Furious

Shrews live in Europe, Asia, North and Central America, and most of Africa. They have a long, pointed nose, large ears, tiny eyes, and velvety fur. A species weighing $7/100$ ounce (2 g) is one of the world's smallest mammals.

Shrews may be tiny, but they're also very fierce. They are always hunting, darting about and attacking such prey as insects, snails, and centipedes with their sharp teeth. Like many small mammals, shrews cannot store much energy and warmth inside their body. To maintain their energy levels and body temperature, shrews must eat more than their body weight every day. Various species

WINNING STREAK
The streaked tenrec from Madagascar has barbed spines attached to its neck. These spines stick into the skin of an attacker.

hunt in water, on the land—even in moles' burrows! They also defend their kill against other shrews.

Young shrews go on foraging trips from an early age. During these trips, the young of some species line up and grab a tuft of hair on the rear end of the shrew in front. The one behind the mother holds onto her in the same way. This habit is called "caravanning" and helps the young to avoid danger.

Soil Swimmers

Moles are related to shrews. They use their huge, spade-like forefeet and sleek, compact bodies to paddle through soil in pursuit of prey. They are so adapted for burrowing and living underground that they lack external ear flaps. Fur coverings over their ear openings and eyes keep out soil. Also, their stumpy tail is covered in sensitive hairs so they can detect a predator behind them in their tunnels.

Odd One Out

Tree shrews live in the tropical rain forests of eastern and southern India and Southeast Asia. They are highly active, nervous, inquisitive, and generally aggressive animals. Unlike other insectivores, all but one of the 19 species are active by day. They eat fruit and lizards as well as

insects. They also enjoy bathing in water-filled tree hollows.

Tree shrews mate for life and mark their territory, young, and each other with scent. Mothers feed their young only every second day, so the babies suck until they are so full that they cannot move. Enemies of the tree shrew include small carnivorous mammals, snakes, and hawks.

MISSING LINK?
The tree shrew (above) used to be classified as a primate. It's now thought to be a primitive placental mammal—an example of the ancestor from which modern mammals evolved.

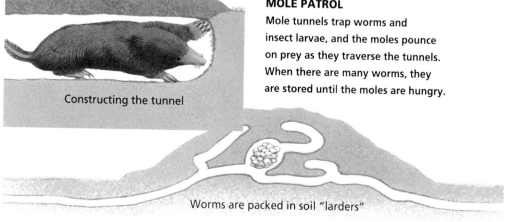

Constructing the tunnel

Worms are packed in soil "larders"

MOLE PATROL
Mole tunnels trap worms and insect larvae, and the moles pounce on prey as they traverse the tunnels. When there are many worms, they are stored until the moles are hungry.

ROUGH AND RATTY
The moonrat (above) is a relative of the hedgehog. Instead of spines it has coarse fur. It lives in wet areas of Southeast Asia, such as mangrove swamps and rubber plantations.

Bats

ABOUT 70 TO 100 MILLION YEARS AGO a group of mammals took to the skies, gliding from tree to tree. These gliders evolved into bats—the only mammals capable of powered flight. Bats can be divided into two groups: the Microchiroptera, or small, mainly insectivorous bats, and the Megachiroptera, or Old World fruit bats.

Wings of Skin

Some 925 species of bat are currently recognized, making bats the second largest order of mammals. Most species are at home in the tropics and subtropics, but bats can be found in almost every part of the world apart from polar regions, cold mountain areas, and some remote islands.

The Greek name for the order is *Chiroptera,* meaning "hand wing." Bats' wings are, in fact, modified hands. Their enormously long fingers support the flight membrane that stretches from their hands and arms down to their hindlegs, and often their tail. The thumb is not usually joined to the membrane, and it has a claw.

Bats' wingspans range from 4 inches (10 cm) to 5 feet (1.5 m). The wings are pulled downward by muscles on the chest and upper arm. They are raised by other muscles on the back. Wing shapes vary—the bats that fly slowly through trees usually have short, wide wings, while bats that fly fast through open spaces have longer, narrower wings.

Air Traffic Control

Bats are active mainly at night when there are fewer flying predators to threaten or compete with them. While no bat is actually "as blind as a bat," Microchiroptera (insectivorous bats) have small eyes that are sometimes hidden in the fur. Because they can't see very well in the dark, they hunt and find their way around using a technique called echolocation.

IN-FLIGHT MEAL

About 70 percent of bats eat insects, spiders, and scorpions. They capture their prey by either grabbing it in their mouth; deflecting it into their mouth with a wing; or by scooping it up in a curled wing membrane.

EARS THAT "SEE"
The long-eared bat has a small flap called a tragus inside the ear, which helps it to sense the location of its prey.

NOSE THAT "SPEAKS"
Like many insectivorous bats, this tent-building bat has a noseleaf—a fleshy structure around its nostrils. The noseleaf is used to focus and direct sound waves through the nostrils.

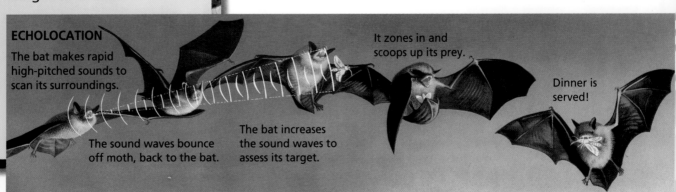

ECHOLOCATION
The bat makes rapid high-pitched sounds to scan its surroundings.

The sound waves bounce off moth, back to the bat.

The bat increases the sound waves to assess its target.

It zones in and scoops up its prey.

Dinner is served!

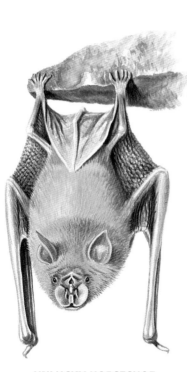

UNLUCKY HORSESHOE
Horseshoe bats get their name from the shape of their noseleaf. They roost in buildings, caves, and hollow trees. The horseshoe bat population in Europe is now in sharp decline.

BATS MOBILE
Free-tailed bats get their name because their tail extends past the flap of skin that joins the hindfeet to the tail. The 90 species are found worldwide. They roost in caves and tree hollows, or beneath tree bark.

SPOT THE BAT
There are 320 species of evening bats. Most live on insects, but a few species catch fish. They roost in all sorts of places, including buildings. Most are drab, but this spotted evening bat is rather handsome!

Echolocation is similar to radar. A bat projects high-pitched squeaks through its mouth or nostrils. (The bat closes its ears so it will not deafen itself.) The sound waves bounce off surrounding objects—the ground, trees, buildings, and also other moving objects in the air, such as other bats and insects. The bat then listens to the type and position of the echoes to interpret its surroundings and the location of its prey. The bat can tell what kind of insect or other prey it is "hearing," and how fast and in what direction that prey is moving. Echolocation is so sensitive and accurate that the bat can track an insect as small as a mosquito.

Dracula Who?

A few species of Microchiroptera eat frogs, lizards, birds, rodents—even other bats! Some species, such as the fishing bat, even specialize in hunting underwater prey. It uses echolocation to "listen" to ripples on the surface of streams. When it senses a fish close to the surface, it rakes its long claws across the water to seize its prey. But of the 925 species of bat, just 3 species feed on blood—vampire bats. They live only in North, Central, and South America. Unlike most other bats, which scurry awkwardly when on the ground, vampire bats are very agile. After spotting their prey from the air, they approach it by walking, hopping, or running using their feet, elbows, wrists, and thumbs. Their razor-sharp front teeth slice open the skin of their prey—a bird or mammal—and their saliva stops the blood from clotting while they lap up their meal. The prey is usually unaware that it is being bitten!

Sweet Tooth

Today there are 160 species of Megachiroptera, including Old World fruit bats, flying foxes, and dog-faced fruit bats. These are medium to large bats—some weigh as much as 3 pounds (1.5 kg). They are found in Australia, Asia, Africa, and many Pacific islands, where their food of fruits, flowers, nectar, and pollen is available all year long.

Most fruit bats can see well enough in the dark to move around and find food. Only one species uses a kind of echolocation, using low-pitched sounds made by clicking its tongue.

Unlike insectivorous bats, whose squeaks are too high for humans to hear, fruit bats make audible calls. The gray-headed flying fox uses up to 20 different calls to communicate. It is especially noisy when squabbling over food, mates, or places to roost.

WORKING TOGETHER
Some flowers open at night and are scented and colored to attract bats. They are even shaped so that bats can land on, or reach into, their flowers. This bat hovers like a hummingbird while it sips nectar.

BAT'S-EYE VIEW
The gray-headed flying fox from Australia (above) eats the flowers of eucalyptus trees. It flies up to 18 miles (30 km) a night to find food, and may migrate 620 miles (1,000 km) to follow the seasonal flowering of its food source.

Many fruit bats are brown or black with a gray or silvery tinge, and often have a brighter-colored back. Other species have speckled ears and wings, or a facial pattern of white spots or stripes—perhaps for camouflage in trees. The tail of most fruit bats is very short or even missing.

Most fruit bats roost in trees or the shadowy areas of caves. They sleep upside down with their wings wrapped around their body. Some roosts can shelter more than a million bats! Fruit bats can also swim, and some live up to 30 years.

Little Cling-Ons

Both male and female bats can store sperm in their reproductive tracts during winter or hibernation. Fertilization usually occurs the following spring. Some bats are also able to slow the development of the

FUNNY FACE
This lesser bare-backed fruit bat has simple ears because it does not use echolocation. Its tube-shaped nostrils help it to sniff out its food.

baby inside the mother's womb. This ensures that the bats are born at those times of the year when food is plentiful.

The smaller species of bat have a gestation period of 40 to 60 days before they are born. The larger species have a gestation period of up to eight months. Usually only one young is born, but some species often have twins, while others can have as many as five babies. They cling with strong claws to their mother and suckle for up to three months from the teats under her arms.

The females of many species group together in nursery colonies to bear and rear their young. Favorite nursery sites are often used year after year. The young of some small species take their first short flights when they are just three weeks old.

Nothing to Fear

Many people fear bats and think that they are evil and dangerous. Perhaps this is because bats are only active at night, when most of us are asleep, or because they have been featured in so many fairy tales and horror movies.

However, bats help the environment in many ways. Insectivorous bats reduce the number of insects, particularly mosquitoes. Fruit bats perform the vital task of pollinating flowers, in much the same way as bees. They also spread seeds as they eat the fruit of cacti and tropical trees.

As living beings, bats have every right to exist. But today many species are endangered due to habitat destruction, the use of insecticides, or hunting by humans. We must make every effort to protect these misunderstood mammals.

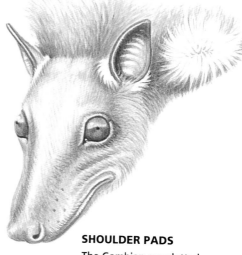

SHOULDER PADS
The Gambian epauletted fruit bat has scent glands surrounded by tufts of hair ("epaulettes") on its shoulders. Old World fruit bats use smell to recognize each other and to find food.

ALL IN THE NOSE
The male hammer-headed bat from Africa has an enormous muzzle and cheek pouches. It makes low, metallic-sounding calls to attract females.

Primates

THE ORDER PRIMATES contains over 230 species of intelligent, mainly tree-dwelling animals. It is divided into two groups. Bush babies, lorises, and lemurs are "lower" primates. Tarsiers, monkeys, apes, and humans are "higher" primates. "Lower" primates share some of the features of their insect-eating ancestors.

Family Ties

Primates share several characteristics. Their hands and feet are modified for grasping, and the tips of their fingers and toes have sensitive pads. Primates have long pregnancies and life spans, and the young remain dependent for months or even years. They also have a large brain, and their forward-facing eyes allow them good binocular vision.

Island of Ghosts

Lemurs are primitive primates. They have ghostlike faces and cry eerily at night. Lemurs once lived all over Africa, Europe, and North America, but became extinct in these regions because they had to compete with monkeys. One family of lemurs is comprised of lorises and bush babies. They are found in Sri Lanka, southern India, Southeast Asia, and Africa. But for the last 40 to 50 million years, all other lemurs have survived only on the island of Madagascar, off the coast of Africa.

HEAD LIGHTS
Tarsiers are fist-sized primates that live in the rain forests of Southeast Asia. They leap from stem to stem as they hunt insects, lizards, and small birds. They also eat fruit and leaves.

Pocket Primates

Mouse lemurs are the smallest of all primates. The pygmy mouse lemur weighs a mere 2 ounces (35 g) and measures only 9 inches (23 cm) long—which includes its tail! Mouse lemurs are nocturnal and live alone in their own territory. They eat mainly insects. The larger dwarf lemurs eat fruit as well as insects. They hibernate throughout the dry season, stirring only when the first rains fall and new food grows.

Spurs and Stripes

Ring-tailed lemurs are about 3 feet (1 m) in length—more than half of which is their stripy tail. These social mammals have unusual adaptations for grooming. The second toe on each foot has a claw that they use to clean their ears. They comb each other's fur with the front teeth in their lower jaw.

Male lemurs have horny spurs on their wrists which are connected to scent glands. They rub their spurs onto trees, leaving a slash in the bark filled with their scent. This scent tells other lemurs who has been there and which troop holds the territory. But female lemurs are dominant and win disputes with males over food or territory.

Stumped Jumper

Four of the six species of indrid are quite small and have long tails. But the largest surviving lemur, the black and white indri, is 3 feet (1 m) long

ON PATROL
A troop of ring-tailed lemurs forages for fruit and insects on the forest floor. Troops can number from 12 to 20 animals.

RUFF RUFF
The long, moist, doglike snout of the red-ruffed lemur is typical of this family of mammals. But it lacks the wrist glands of the ring-tailed lemur, and lives in smaller groups.

and has only a stump of a tail! It has long hindlegs and moves by leaping from tree to tree like a giant furry spring. Indris sleep at night and are active by day, feeding on fruit and leaves. Their loud, wailing cries float through the forest, warning neighbors of territorial boundaries. These lemurs are extremely rare and are now protected in a rainforest reserve in northeastern Madagascar.

Clever Claws

The mysterious aye-aye is nocturnal and solitary. It finds its food of grubs by tapping on tree trunks. It listens for their movements, then gnaws away the bark with its huge incisors. It then uses its extremely long and wiry middle fingers to hook out the grubs and mash them into a paste. These fingers are also used to scoop the flesh from fruit.

The aye-aye has black shaggy fur. Its orange eyes stare out from its white mask. Sadly, the aye-aye's ghoulish looks and bad smell mean it is feared and killed by some local communities.

PAW NO MORE

One of the distinctive characteristics of primates is their special opposable thumb (and sometimes their big toe) that enables them to reach around to touch the tips of the other fingers. This is why primates can grasp small and large objects.

Gorilla hand   Gorilla foot

Gorillas have flattened feet to support their heavy body. Their hands are designed to grasp leaves, bark, and fruit.

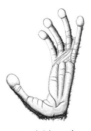
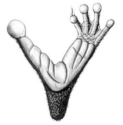

Indri hand   Indri foot

The indri lives most of its life in trees. Its hands and feet give it a strong, wide grip for holding onto tree trunks.

NOWHERE TO HIDE

The sifaka is a kind of indrid. When threatened it runs holding its arms above its head, but it returns to the trees as soon as it can. Like all lemurs, the sifaka is endangered because its home is being cleared for farms. Some species are now confined to tiny areas of land. The forests must be saved, or lemurs will soon have nowhere to run to.

Lemur Losers

About 40 to 50 million years ago, "higher" primates—apes and monkeys—began to take over from the lemurs. Today there are two groups of monkeys: the Old World monkeys, which live in Africa and Asia; and the New World monkeys, which live only in the rain forests of Central and South America.

PICK THE NOSE
New World monkeys of Central and South America (above) have flattened noses with nostrils that face sideways. Old World monkeys of Africa and Asia (below) have prominent noses with narrow nostrils that face forward.

Down to Earth

There are 80 or so species of Old World monkey. Old World monkeys walk on all fours and many spend a lot of time on the ground. They do not have prehensile (gripping) tails.

There are two major groups of Old World monkeys. One group is comprised of monkeys that eat leaves and have stomachs with adaptations for digesting fibrous plant material. These are the colobine monkeys—the golden snub-nosed and proboscis monkeys, langurs, and their relatives.

LIFE AT THE TOP
Cotton-top tamarins are found in Central America. Like many other species, they live in family groups and spend most of their life high up in the canopy of rainforest trees, eating fruit, leaves, and insects.

Who Nose?

Most species of colobine monkey live in Asia, while only seven species live in Africa. Colobine monkeys gallop, rather than walk, along branches. At the end of the branch they launch themselves into space without breaking stride and land in the neighboring tree, grabbing hold with their hooklike, thumbless hands.

SHOW YOUR COLORS

Mandrills live in west African rain forests. The male mandrill (right) has a red and blue nose, red lips, an orange beard, and blue, violet, and red buttocks. Scientists think these colors are used to identify other members of the troop, or to express male dominance—in females and young, the colors are more muted. Geladas, too, use color to communicate. The males of these large, baboon-like monkeys of Ethiopia (in eastern Africa) have a mane of hair and a bright red patch of naked skin on the chest. The red patch is used to attract females and warn other males away.

The largest colobine is the proboscis monkey of Borneo. It eats the leaves and fruit of trees such as mangroves. Young proboscis monkeys have a long nose. Females' noses stop growing at maturity. But in males the nose keeps growing into a huge lobe that droops below the level of the mouth. No one knows what the nose is used for.

Cold Climate Primate

The members of the other group of Old World monkeys have a simple stomach and pouches in their cheeks for storing food. This group includes the baboons and their relatives, which live in herds ranging from ten to hundreds of animals; and macaques. Their diet includes seeds and nuts, birds' eggs, and small vertebrates.

The Japanese macaque is the only primate to live in a cold climate. Also known as the snow monkey, its home is the mountains of Honshu (the main island of Japan), which are covered in snow for more than six months of the year. During winter they survive by eating bark.

A World Apart

There are about 65 species of New World monkey, including marmosets, tamarins, spider monkeys, howlers,

DAY DREAMER
The night monkey is the only nocturnal species. Like titis, night monkeys live in pairs, not troops. But only titis form a close relationship with their mate. They will sit side by side with their tails intertwined.

capuchins, and woolly monkeys. Most New World monkeys are herbivores and spend most of their time in trees. Their thumbs are not as flexible as those of Old World monkeys. Unlike other primates, the larger species have a prehensile tail which they use as a fifth limb to hang on to branches as they travel. Young monkeys also use their tail to keep a firm grip on their mother.

Scientists are puzzled as to how New World monkeys got to America. Their closest living relatives are African monkeys. The earliest remains of American monkeys are 35 million years old—but the continents of South America and Africa broke up long before this.

Siblings, Rivalry

Like other primates, New World monkeys are social mammals. Most live in family groups. The world's smallest living monkey, the 4½-ounce (125-g) pygmy marmoset, is typical: All but one species of marmoset give birth to twins, and the young stay with their parents after they have matured to help rear the next pair of babies, and the next.

Squirrel monkeys of South America are small, greenish monkeys with white faces and black muzzles. The females weigh 18 to 26 ounces (500 to 750 g), half the weight of the males. They live in large troops of 20 to 50 animals. During

TREE DWELLERS
Male howler monkeys (top) defend their territory with howls that can be heard over 3 miles (5 km) away! The woolly spider monkey (above), is the largest and rarest of all New World monkeys. About 300 survive in southeastern Brazil.

the three- to four-month breeding season the males get heavier and become aggressive as they compete for mating opportunities.

Planet of the Apes

Apes are the most highly evolved primates. Like other primates, they have an opposable thumb and a highly developed sense of touch because they have sensitive pads on their fingers and toes. But apes also have flattened fingernails. They move upright more than monkeys, and they have no tail.

The apes also have complex social behavior. The nine or so species of gibbon, which are from South and Southeast Asia, are some of the few primates that mate for life. A pair of gibbons will "mark" their feeding territory each morning by singing a duet of loud hoots and howls.

The smallest of the apes, gibbons are tree-dwellers and swing from branch to branch with their long, narrow hands. They eat fruit, leaves, insects, grubs, and spiders. The adult male of the largest gibbon of all, the siamang, carries and babysits his young until it is at least one year old.

Man of the Woods

Orangutans are found in the wild in only two places in the world—Borneo and the northern part of Sumatra, two large islands in Southeast Asia.

Orangs are covered with clumps of red hair, through which their rough blue-gray skin can be seen. Almost twice the size of females, adult males weigh 175 to 200 pounds (80–91 kg) and can measure 5½ feet (1.7 m) tall. Males also develop fleshy cheek flaps, a mustache, and a beard.

Orangutans live in trees and eat mostly fruit, leaves, and sometimes small animals and eggs. Males wander alone; females are accompanied by a single young, if they have one. Males signal their whereabouts—and their territory—by making a series of deep roars that can be heard from a distance. This roaring attracts

HANDS AS FEET
Wild chimpanzees live mainly on the ground and walk on all fours, supporting their arms on their knuckles.

KING KONG
Each gorilla family is led by a large silverback male. He warns younger males away from his mates and young by standing, roaring, and slapping his chest.

TOOL SCHOOL
Apes use tools for food gathering and then pass on this knowledge to their young. These chimpanzees are using sticks to pick out termites.

females nearby, but warns other males to keep away.

At night, each orang packs twigs and leaves into the top branches of a tree to make a sleeping platform. When lying in its nest, the orang covers itself with other vegetation.

Gentle Giants

Gorillas are peaceful vegetarians that wander through the mountain forests of eastern and central Africa in family troops. The troop may overlap the territory of other troops, but few fights break out.

Adult males stand about 5 feet (1.5 m) tall and weigh 385 pounds (175 kg). After the age of ten they develop silvery gray hair on their back—hence the name, "silverback."

Baby gorillas suckle for up to 18 months and stay with their mother for about 3 years. Young gorillas spend more time in the trees than the heavier adults, and swing from branch to branch.

Like orangs, gorillas are remarkably intelligent and adaptable mammals. Gorillas also build nests each night, often in trees, safe from predators and away from the cold ground.

Close Cousins

Chimpanzees are very social animals. They forage in large communities of 20–100 or more, made up of smaller family groups. The communities are patrolled by adult males, which are larger than the females.

Adult females usually have a baby every four years. Newborn chimps are helpless. They suckle and ride their mother piggyback for several years. When they are older, they eat fruit, leaves, birds' eggs, insects, and some smaller mammals, such as monkeys.

SWINGING SIMIAN
In Malay or Indonesian, *orangutan* means "wild person." The orang's long arms make its legs seem short. Its hook-shaped hands and feet are adapted for grasping.

TALKING HANDS

Scientists have found recently that chimpanzees and gorillas have almost the same ability to learn as we do. They cannot make human sounds, but they can be taught to communicate words, thoughts, and ideas to humans using sign language and special keyboards. They can also work some machinery.

The Bears

CARNIVORA is an order of mammals that has adapted special features for eating meat. The bear family includes the largest of the land carnivores, the polar bear, which can grow more than 11 feet (3.4 m) long and weigh 1,600 pounds (725 kg). Most bears do not eat only meat, but they'll take advantage of a meal when they see it.

Bare Bones

The ancestor to modern bears—a foxlike animal with a long tail—first appeared about 40 million years ago in Europe. Throughout evolution bears have increased in size to become the largest of the land-dwelling carnivores. All bears have a huge head, a thick, strong body, a short tail (except for the red panda), and long, sharp claws.

Fossil bears have been found in southern Africa, but no species survives on that continent. Today, there are only eight species—six of which are endangered. Bears live on the ice of the Arctic; in the temperate forests in Asia, Europe, and North America; high in the Andes mountains of South America; and in tropical forests in Southeast Asia. The South American spectacled bear and the Asian sun and sloth bears are much smaller than their northern relatives.

Munching and Crunching

The uniting feature of the carnivores is their sharp-edged molars, called carnassial teeth, used to tear flesh. But most bears are omnivores: They eat plants, insects, honey, and meat, as they become available. As a result,

HANDY HELPER
Giant pandas feed almost entirely on bamboo, while red pandas eat bamboo, other plants, and insects. Both species have an extra "thumb" so that they can grip slippery shoots.

TOY STORY

In some cultures the bear has come to represent devotion, strength, courage, or spiritual rebirth. Native Americans respect the bear as a wise healer and spirit guide. Other people have a special bond with their teddy bear. Many believe this toy was named after "Ted" Roosevelt, the 26th President of the United States, who refused to shoot a bear while on a hunting trip.

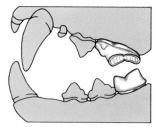

view from inside

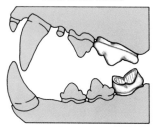

view from outside

STAND AND DELIVER

Bears such as this Asiatic black bear walk on the soles of their feet. They stand upright to look around, or to scare an enemy away.

SCISSOR ACTION

Carnivora have two pairs of sharp-edged molars—carnassial teeth—which slide against each other like scissor blades.

to rake open termite nests. Brown bears dig for roots and pull marmots from burrows with their paws. Skilled brown bears can even snatch jumping salmon in their mouth!

Bears' powerful arms and claws are also designed for climbing. American black bear cubs will shin up a tree to avoid danger and wait there until their mother comes for them. They also climb to reach honey from beehives. Sun bears of Myanmar (Burma), Sumatra, and Borneo climb trees to escape tigers. Like Asiatic black bears, they also make nests of branches in which they sleep during the day.

Smarter than the Average ...

Bears, like other carnivores, are also smarter than their prey. For example, many polar bears know that by easing themselves into water backward, they avoid making a splash that would alert their prey to their presence.

Since bears can live 30 years or more, they gather a great deal of

BIG IS BEAUTIFUL

The brown bear (called the grizzly or Kodiak bear in North America) is one of the largest species. Like the Asiatic and American black bears, it eats berries, roots, fish, rodents, and carrion.

their carnassials are rounded so they can shred and grind the stems and seeds that form most of their diet.

Carnivores have also evolved other modifications, such as acute senses, to find prey before it finds them. Bears' eyesight is like that of humans—black bears are known to have color vision—and their sense of smell and hearing is excellent. Polar bears can smell the breathing holes of their prey, ringed seals, from 3,200 feet (1 km) away!

Paws and Claws

Carnivores must also have speed and skill to catch and kill their prey with little effort. The swiftest bear, the polar bear, can outrun a caribou over a short distance. It can also seize seals in its clawed forefeet, and kill them with a single stomp on the head. But most bears are built for strength, not speed, and their stout legs, short back, and massive paws help them to easily gather food. Sloth bears have large curved claws that they use

PANDA PUZZLE
Scientists are not sure whether
the red panda is actually a type of
bear, or a type of raccoon! Perhaps
it is the surviving member of
an extinct group
of carnivores.

knowledge. A female will pass on some of her learning to her cubs. Most cubs stay with their mother for at least 2½ years, watching her constantly, and learning everything from what to eat and where to find it, to how to find a den for the winter.

The Big Sleep

In the winter, there is no food for the bears that live in colder regions. They store up body fat and retreat into dens dug in hillsides or in snow banks to sleep. This is not true hibernation, however, because the bears' body temperature does not drop.

It is during the winter that females give birth to between one and five blind, helpless, and tiny cubs—a brown bear cub is the size of a guinea pig! The cubs drink their mother's milk until she awakens in the spring.

Black—Not White!

All bears live on land, although the polar bear also lives on ice floes in the Arctic Ocean. These mostly solitary bears are perfectly adapted to the cold. Their thick, water-repellent fur consists of hollow,

clear (not white) hairs that trap heat. Their black skin also helps to absorb heat, and they have a thick layer of insulating fat underneath.

Polar bears often float on ice for 40 to 50 miles (65 to 80 km) to look for prey. They feed almost entirely on seals and fish, although they can kill small whales, such as belugas. They bite or scratch the whale's blowhole so that it cannot breathe, making it easier for the bear to pull the whale onto the ice to eat it.

Chinese Treasure

Giant pandas were unknown outside China until the nineteenth century. Although they sometimes eat birds and small mammals, they spend up to 12 hours a day chewing tough bamboo stalks. Because pandas do not digest the bamboo very well, they have to eat up to 44 pounds (20 kg) of bamboo a day to survive.

Giant pandas have always been rare because they do not breed very often— females generally raise only a single cub.

SHADES OF BLACK
All black bears have a brown muzzle, but their coat can be cinnamon, honey, "blue," white, or even black! Coat color can change as the bear ages. It may also be inherited.

CLEAN CARNIVORE
The raccoon's name comes from a North American word meaning "he who scratches with his hands." It rubs and dunks its food in water, washing it with its forepaws.

But giant pandas became endangered in the twentieth century because their habitat was destroyed for farmland, and they were hunted for their skins and meat. Today there are only between 500 and 1,000 giant pandas left in the world.

Masked Marauder

The raccoon is a member of the procyonid family, which is closely related to bears. Other members of this family include coatis, ringtails, and kinkajous.

The raccoon lives in dens in hollow trees or rock crevices in forested areas from southern Canada to Panama. Inquisitive yet solitary, it ventures out after dark to find aquatic prey such as frogs, fish, and crayfish. It also eats small rodents, birds, nuts, seeds, fruit, and turtle and birds' eggs—and doesn't mind raiding trash cans, either. Unlike its cousin the coati,

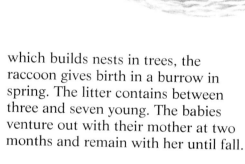

which builds nests in trees, the raccoon gives birth in a burrow in spring. The litter contains between three and seven young. The babies venture out with their mother at two months and remain with her until fall.

SNOUT SCOUT

Coatis search the forest floor with their flexible snout for roots and insects. They use their tail to balance while they are climbing in trees.

COLD CYCLE

In spring, polar bear cubs emerge with their mother from their den. In summer they mate. In the fall, they eat seals to store up fat for winter, and pregnant females dig dens. In winter their cubs are born.

THE KINKA-WHO?

The kinkajou is related to the coati. Although carnivorous, it eats mostly fruit and nectar. It lives in tropical forests from Mexico to Brazil. The kinkajou is one of the few carnivores that have a prehensile tail, which it uses when climbing or hanging from trees, collecting food. It often feeds in the same trees used by monkeys. No wonder it is sometimes mistaken for a primate!

The Dogs

Carnivora is divided into two suborders. One suborder, the doglike carnivores (Caniformia), evolved in North America 54 to 39 million years ago. Caniformia includes bears and wild dogs, which have now spread to almost every part of the world. Today's pet dogs are thought to have evolved from a wolflike ancestor.

Canine Collection

There are about 35 species of dogs, such as foxes, and wolves, coyotes, and jackals. Highly adaptable, these mammals evolved to chase prey across grassland, and almost all have lithe bodies built for speed and stamina. They all have scissor-like carnassial teeth; sharp canine teeth; and keen sight, smell, and hearing. Wild dogs are efficient hunters because their uniquely formed internal ear is tuned to the frequency of the sounds made by their prey.

Dog Dinners

Wild dogs are mainly carnivorous, but their adaptable digestive system allows them to also eat fruits, insects, snails, worms, and carrion. Some foxes eat fish; dingoes, descendants of Indian wolves that arrived in Australia about 4,000 years ago, eat everything from grasshoppers to kangaroos. The gray fox of North America even climbs trees in search of food.

Loyal to the Leader

Wolves, African hunting dogs, dholes, and coyotes are the most social dog species. They live in structured groups, led by a dominant breeding pair, which can contain up to 20 members. Each dog knows its place and defers to the authority of the leader of the pack.

Intelligent and efficient, pack dogs cooperate to catch their prey. Using their acute hearing and smell, the dogs find a victim and sneak up on it until, sensing danger, the prey flees. The pack then rushes to attack. Some chase and torment the prey to tire it. Then one dog, usually the pack leader, darts up to seize its nose while others rip its flanks and throat. Within minutes, the dogs are tearing into their meal.

Bright-Eyed, Bushy-Tailed

Foxes are relatively solitary mammals. They are nocturnal and rest during the day in dens, hollow trees, or even drains. They hunt by springing about 3 feet (1 m) off the ground and diving, front paws first, to squash their small victims—usually rodents.

The desert foxes are the smallest species. The pale coat of the cat-sized fennec fox, of Arabia

CALL OF THE WILD
The howling chorus of a wolf pack can be heard for about 6 miles (10 km) and warns other packs to stay away. Packs also howl at the end of a successful hunt, perhaps to celebrate.

CITY SURVIVOR
Red foxes have learnt to survive in urban habitats, feeding on trash and denning in disused buildings.

and North Africa, blends with its sandy habitat, and its gigantic ears radiate excess heat and help it to detect its prey. Its cousin, the bat-eared fox, also has large ears. But unlike all other carnivores, it has four to eight extra molars to help it chew through the exoskeleton (outer shell) of insects.

The Arctic fox is larger and has either a brown or steel-gray coat in summer. Both color types change to a white winter coat for camouflage in the snow. This species is now threatened by the red fox, the most widely dispersed of all carnivores, which competes with the Arctic fox for food.

Friend or Foe?

Many cultures have legends about wild dogs. Wolves are usually cast as crafty characters in fairy tales, such as *Little Red Riding Hood*, trying to lure unsuspecting children and adults to their death. Other legends credit wolves with adopting human infants and caring for them in the wild. Nevertheless, wild dogs are regarded by many farmers as a threat to their livestock. Hunting, combined with habitat destruction, now threatens the survival of some wild dog species.

CLOAK AND DAGGER
The blotched coat of the African hunting dog provides camouflage while the dog is resting under shady trees, or hunting at night. Packs of 6 to 12 dogs prey on zebra or antelope.

TATTLE-TAIL

Wolves and dogs use sounds and body language to tell others about their moods, intentions, or rank. Their tails are very expressive.

TOP DOG
A high, fluffed tail is a sign of authority and dominance. By making himself look bigger, this wolf is showing how powerful he is.

WATCH IT!
A wolf carrying its tail straight out behind it is aggressive and planning to attack. It will appear stiff-legged, with its body leaning forward.

DON'T HURT ME
A terrified wolf adopts a humble pose. It makes itself as small as possible by crouching with its tail touching its belly.

I'M NO THREAT
A low-ranking wolf, perhaps approaching a dominant member of the pack to greet him or to beg for food, will crouch with its tail close to its body. The tail tip will be curved back.

The Cats

FELIFORMIA, or catlike carnivores, is the other suborder of Carnivora. Of all carnivores, cats eat the most meat. The large cats are called the pantherines; the small cats are called felines. Besides size, the main difference between them is that the small cats purr, but don't roar, and the large cats can roar, but not purr.

MEAT LOCKER
Leopards like to rest in trees, but they hunt on the ground. They often drag their food up a tree to keep it out of the reach of lions and scavengers.

Meow Mix

Early cats lived in the Northern Hemisphere 54 million years ago. Today there are about 36 species. They range from the South American oncilla, which is half the size of a domestic cat, to the 12-foot (3.7-m) long Siberian tiger, but they have many features in common. All species are hunters, most eat only meat, and most are shy and live alone.

Steak Knives

With their strong jaws, piercing claws, and supple body, cats are designed to hunt. But their deadliest

TUFT STUFF
The caracal is one of the five lynx species. It is as small as a spaniel, but can take prey as large as impalas. It threatens other caracals by flicking its ear tufts at them.

weapons are their teeth. Bears have flat surfaces on their teeth for crushing food, but cats' teeth consist almost entirely of razor-sharp blades. Their canines stab and hold like knives; their molars slice flesh. Serrated-edged incisors shear the last shreds from the bones.

Cats' eyesight also helps them in their quest for prey. Like primates, cats have binocular vision and are able to accurately judge distance. This means they can sneak up on prey to just the right distance before making a final charge. The structure of cats' eyes also means that their night vision is acute. Since most cats are nocturnal, this adaptation has enabled them to survive in a variety of habitats.

Pussy Footing

Only hunger keeps most cats from sleeping their life away. Lions may rest for up to 19 hours a day! But

SWITCH-BLADE

Cats use their claws to catch their prey. A claw works like a switchblade. The blade's usual position is folded into a knifecase, but it springs out with a flick of a wrist. In the same way, a cat's claws usually remain retracted (pulled in), protected in sheaths of skin. They emerge from their sheaths only when the cat needs them.

retracted

ready for action

The Cats

when hunger strikes, most cats go on the prowl. They ambush their prey and use their canines to paralyze or strangle it.

One exception is the athletic cheetah—the only cat that catches its prey by pursuit. Unlike the claws of other cats, which retract to prevent them from getting blunt, the cheetah's claws remain exposed to provide grip during fast turns and rapid acceleration. Another unusual cat is the fishing cat of Southeast Asia and India. It scoops fish out of streams with its webbed paws and even dives into water, headfirst, to catch prey!

But despite their reputations as fierce hunters, large cats (leopards, lions, tigers, and jaguars) fail to catch prey more times than they succeed. Lions rely on rodents and carrion to make ends meet; the cheetah has little stamina. It gives up most chases after about 20 seconds because it is too hot and exhausted to run any farther.

LICK OF DIFFERENCE
Cats can change the surface of their tongue. They groom themselves or their young with a smooth tongue and scrape the skin off their prey with a rough tongue.

Cat's Cradle

Most cats are solitary, the common exception being females with cubs. Cats seek out sheltered dens, away from other predators, in which to give birth. Newborn cubs are blind and helpless, and stay in the den while their mother hunts. Their eyes open at about two weeks of age. As they grow, the cubs spend their time learning about their environment. They stalk, chase, and wrestle one another, practicing the skills they'll later use when hunting.

However, lions are the most social of the cats and live in prides of up to 30 animals. Most of these are females, all of which are related—mothers, daughters, cousins, aunts—and their cubs. They feed and care for each other's cubs until the cubs are six months old. Female cubs often stay with the pride, but males leave when they are three years old and live alone until they are older and stronger. Then they challenge the dominant males of another pride and try to take their place.

JUNGLE LOOK
The jaguar looks like a heavily built leopard, but its coat pattern is slightly different. It lives in forests from Mexico to South America.

FAST FOOD
Slowly and silently, a lioness stalks a gazelle. Then, with a sudden burst of speed, she rushes at her prey, drags it to the ground, and kills it with a piercing bite to the neck.

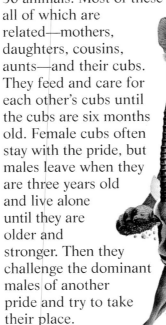

79

Carnivorous Relatives

THERE ARE ABOUT 270 SPECIES OF CARNIVORE. They are found on every continent in most habitat types: oceans, polar regions, rain forests, prairies, deserts, mountains, and even the urban environment. While most eat some meat, many species specialize in eating insects, worms, berries, fish, crustaceans, seeds—even fruit.

RIVER LIVER
River otters use their muscular tail to propel them while swimming. But unlike their cousin, the sea otter, they always den on land.

Animal Ambassadors

With nearly double the number of species of any other carnivore family, the mustelids are the most successful. Mustelids are doglike carnivores. They are distinguished by the musk gland near their anus and their unique way of breeding. They can delay the development of a fertilized egg, so they can mate and give birth at the most suitable times. Fur-bearing mustelids such as otters have played a major role in the exploration of many parts of the world.

Soft Gold

The 12 species of otter spend most of their life in fresh or salt water. Some freshwater otters are solitary, but sea otters are very sociable animals. They form separate groups of females and males and often sleep together, with their paws covering their eyes.

Sea otters grow to 4 feet (1.2 m) long. They come ashore only during heavy storms, or sometimes to give birth to their pups. But most females give birth at sea, then snuggle their single pup high on their chest as they swim on their back.

Unlike other sea mammals, such as whales, sea otters are not insulated against the cold water by a layer of fat. Instead, they depend on the layer of air trapped in their dense coat for warmth. They constantly groom and blow air onto their fur to keep it clean and waterproof—dirty fur becomes waterlogged and leads to chills and death. Sea otters use so much energy keeping warm that they must eat the equivalent of about 25 percent of their body weight each day!

FLOATING RESTAURANT

The sea otter is the only mammal besides primates to use tools to gather food. It fetches a flat rock from the seabed and, while floating on the surface, balances the rock on its chest. Gripping a mussel, sea urchin, or abalone in its forepaws, it smashes its prey against the rock until the shell breaks open. Some otters eat so many sea urchins that the dye from this food turns their skeleton purple!

WATER BED

The sea otter lives in coastal waters. It dives for food, using its stiff whiskers to sense its prey on the ocean floor. It sleeps on the surface, entangled in kelp to stop it from drifting.

PINT-SIZE PREDATOR

Weasels have short, round ears, a long, tube-shaped body, and short legs. They feed at night, mostly below ground, chasing mice, rats, and other rodents into their burrows.

Bald eagles and sharks are enemies of the sea otter, but the most dangerous predators are humans. Sea otter fur is so highly valued that it was once called "soft gold." By 1911 these mammals had been hunted almost to extinction, but are now protected.

Furred Fraternity

Weasels, martens, minks, and wolverines are also mustelids. Martens are large weasels that live in trees. The largest marten, the fisher, feeds on spined, tree-dwelling porcupines. The marten skillfully attacks the porcupine's head, where there are no quills. When the prey is dead, the marten flips it over and feeds from its underside.

The mink spends a lot of its time foraging in the water for mollusks, crustaceans, and fish. But not all mustelids eat meat—the weasel-like tayra of South America lives in trees, rather than the ground, and feeds mainly on fruit.

The wolverine is a ground-dwelling animal, but it can and does climb trees. It lives in forests and tundra in North America, Scandinavia, and Siberia. The wolverine is about 1,000 times heavier than the smallest species of musteline, the least weasel, which weighs 3 ounces (100 g). It is a solitary hunter and capable of killing animals larger than itself, such as caribou in winter. Its large feet give it a speed advantage in soft snow, when hoofed mammals are slowed down.

In summer the wolverine hunts small mammals and birds, and also eats carrion, berries, and plants. Its main enemies are wolves, grizzly bears, pumas, and humans, who kill it for its thick fur.

The black-footed ferret has also suffered at the hands of humans. Farming practices, such

EARTH WORKER

Eurasian badgers live in groups of up to 12, and feed mainly on grubs and earthworms. Burrows are constantly expanded and may be used by many generations.

RED BARON

The fossa is Madagascar's largest carnivore—around 2½ feet (70 to 80 cm) long. Its sharp, retractable claws and excellent vision help it to hunt on the ground and in trees.

as the poisoning of the prairie dog, have robbed it of its prey. Once found from Canada to Texas, the black-footed ferret survived only in captivity until a few were successfully reintroduced to the wild.

Poison Gas

The striped skunk is one of the best known mustelids. Its vivid black and white coat warns enemies not to come too close, but its most successful defense is the liquid that it sprays from its anal gland when threatened. It aims at the intruders' face. Apart from the awful smell—which temporarily stops the victim breathing—the fluid can cause temporary blindness!

Striped skunks live from southern Canada to northern Mexico, in woods, semi-open country, and grassland. They are nocturnal omnivores and eat small animals such as mice, as well as eggs, insects, berries, and carrion.

Female striped skunks produce five to six young in a den lined with vegetation. Male skunks take no part in the rearing of the young. In fact, they are aggressive to mothers and will sometimes kill the babies.

Perfumed Predators

Civets and genets are members of a family of catlike carnivores, the viverrids. They are the least studied of carnivores, possibly because, being nocturnal and solitary, they are difficult to observe. There are about 35 species of viverrids, which live in southern Europe, Africa, and southern Asia. Oil from a special gland near their anus has been used for centuries for making perfume!

LOVELY LINSANG

The banded palm civet, or banded linsang, is named for the markings on its body. It lives in the rain forests of Southeast Asia and eats small vertebrates such as rats, plus insects and snails.

Most civets and genets have a rather long face, and a tail as long as, or sometimes longer than, their body length. Most civets and genets eat small vertebrates and invertebrates, such as insects. But the common palm civet, which is notorious for raiding coffee plantations, is sometimes called the toddy cat because it loves to eat fermented palm sap (toddy). Another species of palm civets, which spend nearly all their time in trees, is known to eat up to 30 different kinds of fruit.

African and Indian civets are some of the few members of this group that live on the ground. African civets rest during the day in thickets and burrows. At night they hunt prey such as birds, reptiles, frogs, insects, and mammals up to the size of young antelopes. Unlike their cat relatives, African civets cannot retract their claws.

Quick and Clever

The 37 or so species of mongoose are found from deserts to tropical rain forest in Africa, the Middle East, India, and Southeast Asia. These small, solitary carnivores are active during the day. Their long, slender, agile body is well adapted for chasing prey down burrows. But like African civets, they don't have retractable claws and cannot climb well—except for the ring-tailed mongoose of Madagascar, which hunts in trees for birds, reptiles, and small mammals.

Meerkats, also called suricates, are related to mongooses but have four, rather than five, toes on each foot. These social animals live in packs in open country and savanna from Angola to South Africa. Meerkats have thin belly fur, which helps them to regulate their body temperature. They warm up by sitting erect and sunning themselves; they cool off by resting stomach-down in burrows or on shaded surfaces.

Garbage Guts

Hyenas grow to 4½ feet (1.4 m) long and can weigh as much as 175 pounds (80 kg). Females are larger than males, but all hyenas have long, powerful forelegs, short hindlegs, and a mane along their back. Their teeth are adapted for crushing bones, and their large head and massive jaw muscle give them one of the strongest bites of all carnivores. Hyenas range across the open plains of Africa. They hunt live prey at night, but spend most of their days scavenging the remains of prey killed by big cats, such as lions. They vomit up hooves, antlers, and anything else they can't digest. Few who have heard the cry of the hyena will forget the presence of this fearsome mammal.

FACE-OFF
Mongooses eat lizards, frogs, rodents, birds, insects, and even venomous snakes! Some build up an immunity to venom, and can survive a cobra bite that would kill a human.

CURIOUS CAT
The African civet is the largest "true" civet. It lives in forests, savanna, plains, and farmlands, from south of the Sahara Desert to South Africa.

REALITY BITES

Although they look like dogs, hyenas are more closely related to cats! They are members of the suborder Feliformia, believed to have evolved from a civet-like ancestor 54 million years ago. At night hyenas use pack tactics to kill large prey such as wildebeests or young rhinoceroses. A group of 38 hyenas has been observed tearing apart a full-grown zebra in 15 minutes! Some hyenas also store prey for other meals by burying it in muddy pools.

Whales, Dolphins, and Porpoises

THE ORDER CETACEA is thought to have evolved from an ancestor of the hippo 50 to 60 million years ago. While early cetaceans had legs, whales, dolphins, and porpoises are now perfectly adapted to underwater life. They are found in all oceans and in some rivers and lakes. Like all mammals, they feed their young on milk.

PRECIOUS MINKE
The minke whale has 230–360 baleen plates, each 8 inches (20 cm) long. In spite of international bans and public opinion, Norway and Japan continue to kill this graceful whale.

THE RIGHT STUFF
Named because it was considered "right" for hunting, the right whale has up to 540 baleen plates in its upper jaw. It has areas of rough, thick skin on its head and body.

Denizens of the Deep

The 80 or so species of cetacean are the only mammals that are fully aquatic. Their streamlined body, smooth, almost hairless skin, and lack of external ears allow water to flow over them with little friction or drag. They swim by flexing their flattened tail up and down, rather like the movements of a running land mammal. Their front flippers (called pectoral fins), which are actually modified hands, act as stiff paddles to help them steer and keep their balance. A fat layer up to 20 inches (50 cm) thick, called blubber, keeps them warm in even the coldest seas.

Like all mammals, cetaceans breathe with lungs, so they must swim to the surface to take breaths through a nostril—a blowhole—on the top of their head. (The blowhole closes when underwater.) When the cetacean surfaces, it breathes out, producing a spout or "blow" of moist air, mist, small droplets of oil, and mucus.

Although cetaceans have no sense of smell, their eyesight both above and underwater is good. Some species, such as orcas, even "spyhop": They raise their head vertically out of the water, have a look around, then

sink below the surface. Cetaceans also have a highly developed sense of touch all over their body. Mothers and their young, called calves, caress each other constantly.

Just Browsing

Baleen whales are generally large animals. The blue whale can grow to 100 feet (30 m) and weighs more than 2,300 people. The blue whale's heart is the size of a small car. Its mouth can be 20 feet (6 m) long. It is the largest animal ever known to have lived—yet its preferred food is just inches long.

Like other baleen whales, the blue whale has no teeth. It uses its baleen—the long, bristly, comblike plates in its upper jaw—to sieve tiny animals called zooplankton out of the water. Baleen is sometimes called "whalebone," but it is more like human

BODY OF EVIDENCE
The color patterns on the humpback whale's tail are unique, so individual animals can be identified and tracked as they migrate. This monitoring has provided the evidence that humpback numbers are rising.

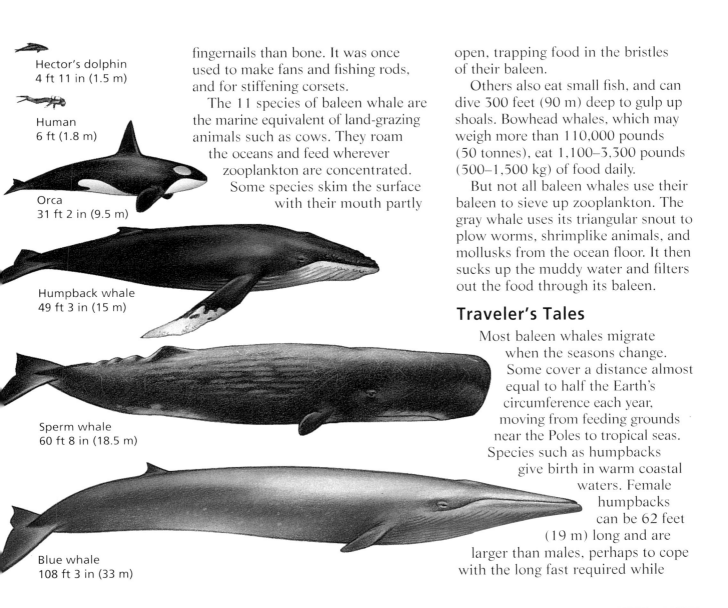

Hector's dolphin
4 ft 11 in (1.5 m)

Human
6 ft (1.8 m)

Orca
31 ft 2 in (9.5 m)

Humpback whale
49 ft 3 in (15 m)

Sperm whale
60 ft 8 in (18.5 m)

Blue whale
108 ft 3 in (33 m)

fingernails than bone. It was once used to make fans and fishing rods, and for stiffening corsets.

The 11 species of baleen whale are the marine equivalent of land-grazing animals such as cows. They roam the oceans and feed wherever zooplankton are concentrated. Some species skim the surface with their mouth partly open, trapping food in the bristles of their baleen.

Others also eat small fish, and can dive 300 feet (90 m) deep to gulp up shoals. Bowhead whales, which may weigh more than 110,000 pounds (50 tonnes), eat 1,100–3,300 pounds (500–1,500 kg) of food daily.

But not all baleen whales use their baleen to sieve up zooplankton. The gray whale uses its triangular snout to plow worms, shrimplike animals, and mollusks from the ocean floor. It then sucks up the muddy water and filters out the food through its baleen.

Traveler's Tales

Most baleen whales migrate when the seasons change. Some cover a distance almost equal to half the Earth's circumference each year, moving from feeding grounds near the Poles to tropical seas. Species such as humpbacks give birth in warm coastal waters. Female humpbacks can be 62 feet (19 m) long and are larger than males, perhaps to cope with the long fast required while

TINY AND TITANIC
The size of cetaceans reflects adaptions to their environments. Toothed whales are small and fast to hunt prey, but baleen whales can grow to an enormous size, since they don't need to chase prey.

SOUNDING OUT

Mammals make sounds with their vocal cords in their larynx but it is still not clear how, or even if, cetaceans use the larynx to produce sound. Baleen whales don't even have vocal cords! Still, humpbacks "sing" long, complex songs that can be heard 750 miles (1,200 km) away. Toothed whales produce high-frequency whistles, clicks, and pulses, and the whistles of belugas (right) earn them the nickname of "sea canaries."

nasal air sacs
blowhole
melon may focus sound
"vocal folds" may create sound

BRAIN POWER
The sperm whale, largest of the toothed whales, has up to 50 teeth in its lower jaw. It also has the largest brain of any animal—about six times heavier than an adult human brain!

MAN'S BEST FRIEND?
Dolphin species like the bottlenose dolphin enjoy human company. Stories about dolphins rescuing swimmers in distress or protecting them from sharks are common.

BLOWING BUBBLES
Humpbacks often catch their prey by "bubblenetting." They circle below a fish shoal and rise to the surface, blowing columns of bubbles to trap them.

bearing and feeding their calves during the migration.

The gestation period for most species is 11 to 16 months. When a calf is born it is about one-third the size of its mother, who pushes it to the surface for its first breath. It grows quickly because its mother's milk is rich in fat and protein. Newborn blue whales weigh about 5,300 pounds (2.4 tonnes)—one-third the size of an adult African Bush elephant—and can gain 180 pounds (85 kg) each day! Baleen whales feed their calves for about a year, but the calves of toothed whale species can suckle from 2 to 15 years.

Toothed Torpedoes

The 70 species of toothed whale evolved from the earliest cetaceans more than 45 million years ago. They use their cone-shaped teeth to seize and hold prey, but not for chewing. Since most toothed whales hunt mobile prey such as fish, squid, and octopus, they are generally fast swimmers. Some dolphins have been recorded traveling at 25 miles (40 km) per hour for several hours!

Some highly evolved species have developed specialized teeth. The male narwhal, which lives in Arctic waters, has an overgrown left incisor tooth growing in a spiral from its snout. This tusk can measure up to 8 feet (2.5 m) long. Narwhal tusks used to be sold as the horns of the mythical unicorn. Scientists now believe that males use these weird teeth to joust for females.

Sound Waves

Like bats, toothed whales navigate and find their prey using echolocation. A dolphin searching for food will send out long- and short-range sound signals or "clicks." The returning echoes tell the dolphin where prey can be found. As the dolphin closes in on the prey, it uses much shorter "clicks" to help it to gather more data about the size, shape, and structure of its target.

The power of echolocation means that the sperm whale can travel nearly 2 miles (3 km) beneath the ocean's

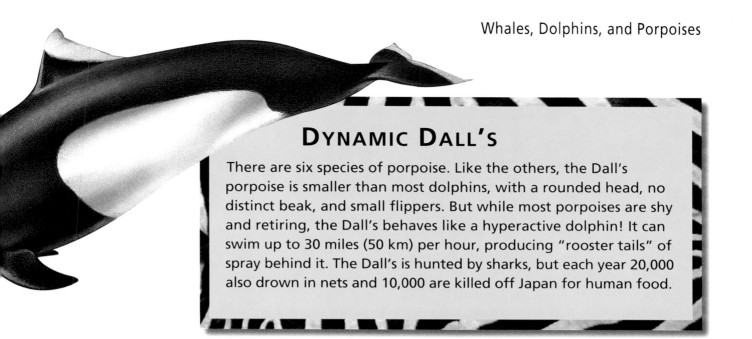

DYNAMIC DALL'S

There are six species of porpoise. Like the others, the Dall's porpoise is smaller than most dolphins, with a rounded head, no distinct beak, and small flippers. But while most porpoises are shy and retiring, the Dall's behaves like a hyperactive dolphin! It can swim up to 30 miles (50 km) per hour, producing "rooster tails" of spray behind it. The Dall's is hunted by sharks, but each year 20,000 also drown in nets and 10,000 are killed off Japan for human food.

surface—often in total darkness—to catch its prey of giant squid. The longest recorded sperm whale dive lasted 2 hours and 18 minutes!

Wolves of the Sea

Most toothed whales gather into large groups, called pods, to hunt more efficiently and for safety. In most species adult females form the basis of the group; males leave at puberty to join other groups.

Orcas live in close-knit family pods of up to 50 animals. They use distinctive calls to keep in touch with each other. Common dolphins form pods of tens to many hundreds to hunt anchovies, sardines, herring, and squid. Spinner dolphins rest in groups of about 20 during the day, but form pods of several hundred to go hunting at night. Before heading off they spend time swimming in zigzags, possibly to make sure each member is synchronized with the others.

The Ties That Bind

Cetaceans seem to be able to receive information from the Earth's magnetic field. They can sense areas of force and use this information to navigate, in the same way that humans use a compass. But it seems that sometimes

cetaceans make navigational mistakes. Confused, they become stranded on the shore. There they are burned by the wind and Sun. Without water to support their heavy weight, they can suffocate and die.

The strong social bonds of many toothed whale species can mean that an error by even one whale can cause its concerned companions to follow it into danger. They will refuse to leave the sick or trapped whale and, tragically, may also become stranded.

KILLERS ON THE LOOSE
Orcas, or killer whales, are the largest and most intelligent dolphins. They swim close to a seal colony, and the seals flee into the surf—where other orcas are waiting to catch them.

Seals, Walruses, and Sea Cows

ABOUT 50 MILLION YEARS AGO, mammals that resembled today's weasels were amphibious. Gradually, they began to spend more time in the sea. Their front and back legs became flippers. They grew larger and developed a thick layer of fat to protect them from cold oceans. By 10 million years ago, they had evolved into pinnipeds.

FATAL FUR

Fur seals were killed by the millions for their soft underfur. By the 1820s, some seals were nearly extinct. Today, some species are slowly recovering.

Flipper Slippers

Seals, sea lions, and walruses are all pinnipeds—a word derived from Latin roots meaning "winged feet." Pinnipeds are carnivores: Their closest living relatives are bears, raccoons, and weasels. Most pinnipeds eat crabs, fish, octopus, and squid. The leopard seal of Antarctic waters also hunts penguins. Walruses, which live in the Arctic, use their sensitive whiskers and tusks to find and gather worms, mollusks, and shellfish buried in the sand on the seafloor. Pinnipeds are in turn the prey of sharks, orcas, and polar bears.

WATER WINGS

Sea lions are social. They gather on the shore in large, noisy colonies to rest or to have their pups. Pups can swim a month or so after being born.

Partners in Brine

Fur seals and sea lions are "eared seals." They have small but visible ears, and can bend their hind flippers forward at the ankle to walk on land.

Fur seals are found in the Southern Hemisphere, except for the northern fur seal, which lives on the Pribilof Islands in the Bering Sea. All fur seals have dense, insulating fur beneath a sleek covering of long guard hairs. Pups have a soft black coat, which is shed when they are three months old.

Fur seals are mostly solitary outside breeding seasons. Superb swimmers, they can dive to 660 feet (200 m) in search of prey. When the seals are gathered together, adult males guard a territory, using their massive neck and shoulders and large canine teeth in battles for breeding females. Adult males, depending on the species, are 5 to 7 feet (1.5 to 2.1 m) in length.

The five species of sea lion are found only in the Southern Hemisphere, around the shores of the Pacific Ocean. Unlike fur seals, they have blunt noses and thinly furred coats. Their skin is light-colored, rather than black. On adult males, the muscular neck has a mane; females are always smaller. The largest species is the northern sea lion, which can measure up to 10 feet (3 m) long.

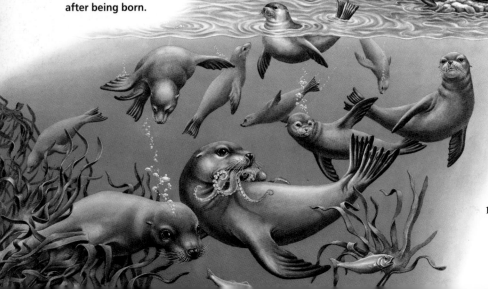

UNDERWATER MEADOW
The only herbivorous marine mammals, the dugong (right) and the manatee are called sea cows because they graze on underwater vegetation.

3,000'S A CROWD
Walruses gather in colonies of up to 3,000 in the mating season. A mature male walrus, which can reach 12 feet (more than 3.5 m) in length, may have a harem of as many as 50 females!

Tooth Picks

The bulky, cinnamon brown, wrinkled, and sparsely haired body of the walrus can weigh 2,600 pounds (1.2 tonnes). Its thick skin creases and folds at every bend of the body and is a protective armor against injury from tusks. Both males and females have tusks, which are actually overgrown canine teeth. A male's tusks can grow to over 2 feet (60 cm) long. The tusks are used to gather food, to haul the walrus out of the water, or to battle other males for control of females. Like eared seals, the walrus can bend its flippers forward to move about on land or on ice floes.

Sirens' Songs

Manatees and dugongs are not seals. They are Sirenians, or sea cows—their closest living relatives are elephants. Manatees are found in the rivers and coastal waters of the Americas, and in the rivers of West Africa. Dugongs live in the warm, shallow waters of the western Pacific and Indian oceans.

The dugong's body shape and tail are like those of a dolphin. It weighs around 660 pounds (300 kg). The manatee is almost twice as heavy and its tail is paddle-shaped, like that of a platypus. Both mammals give birth in water. The females communicate with their calves with squeaks and birdlike chirps. A calf stays close to its mother and often rides on her back.

SEAL STORIES

The 19 species of "true seal" lack external ears. They can't turn their hind flippers, so they move on land like caterpillars. The elephant seal is the largest—it can weigh 7,940 pounds (3.6 tonnes). The Weddell seal can dive to 2,000 feet (600 m) and stay under for more than an hour! The crabeater seal eats only zooplankton, like a baleen whale. Harp seals (right) breed on ice. Their milk is almost 50 percent fat!

Elephants

ELEPHANTS ARE THE LARGEST LIVING LAND MAMMALS. They are classed in the order Proboscidea, after their most distinguishing feature—the proboscis, or trunk. The word *proboscis* comes from Greek and means "before the mouth." Today there are only three species of elephant: two African elephants, and the Asian elephant.

BIG BALLERINA

An elephant has five toes on its front feet. Despite its great weight, it walks almost on tiptoe. Its toes are supported behind by a fibrous fatty cushion and enclosed in a tough skin.

Pillars of Wisdom

The Asian elephant can be found from Nepal across Indochina, and in southern India, Sumatra, and Sri Lanka. African elephants live from Senegal in west Africa, across central, east, and southern Africa.

All species are different to each other in a number of ways, but they also have many features in common. Their most obvious feature is their size—an adult African Bush elephant is equal to the weight of 190 children! The size of these mammals means they eat enormous amounts of vegetation. Elephants spend 18 to 20 hours a day either feeding, or moving toward a food or water source. Most elephants eat 165–330 pounds (75–150 kg) of food and 27–30 gallons (100–115 L) of water per day.

The elephant's body has developed some adaptations to cope with its size and weight. Mammals such as dogs have legs that are positioned at an angle, but the elephant's pillar-like legs are in an almost vertical position under the body—like the legs of a table. This arrangement provides a strong support for the elephant's mostly heavy skeleton and internal organs. Another adaptation is the skull, which is honeycombed with air cells and hollow cavities. These cavities make the skull lighter, yet strong enough to carry the weight of the trunk. An African elephant's trunk can weigh as much as 330–440 pounds (150–200 kg)!

Ear-Conditioning

An animal the size of an elephant has a small surface area, compared with its body weight, and cannot easily get rid of excessive heat. But the elephant has developed some clever ways to

MINI JUMBO

The earliest elephant ancestors were pig-sized mammals, without tusks or trunks, that lived 55 million years ago. With the exception of Antarctica and Australia, they inhabited every continent on Earth, in every kind of habitat: from swamps and deserts to rain forests and mountains. Gradually their legs, trunks, and tusks became longer—some species had three tusks! About 352 species have been identified; today, just two remain.

keep its cool. For example, it is almost hairless (although Asian elephants are a little hairier than African elephants, especially when young). This relative lack of body hair means the elephant isn't bothered by a hot, sweaty coat.

An elephant's skin can be more than 1-inch (2.5-cm) thick around its back, but is paper-thin around its mouth and on the inside of its ears. These thin-skinned ears, which contain blood vessels close to the surface, act as huge radiators to help control body temperature. When the elephant flaps its ears, the vessels become engorged and the heat flows through the skin. This is why the African species, which originated close to the equator and have remained in the hotter parts of Africa, have the larger ears—the bigger the fan, the cooler the body!

But even the thickest skin has a rich nerve supply and remains highly sensitive. To keep its skin moist, and to protect it against the harsh rays of the Sun, the elephant plasters itself with mud and dust. A thick mud pack also protects it against insect bites. African elephants often appear brown from wallowing in mudholes of colored soil, although all species of elephant are usually gray in color.

Nose Hose

The elephant's trunk is its single most important feature. Early naturalists described it as "the elephant's hand" or "the snake hand." The trunk is used

for smelling; touching; lifting; as a weapon of attack or defense; for protecting any young elephants in danger; and for communicating with other animals.

An elephant's trunk is sensitive, flexible, and strong. It can pull a whole tree out of the ground or pick up a single twig. For cooling, it can spray water, dust, or mud to almost any part of the elephant's body. In the mating season, male (bull) elephants wrestle each other with their trunk to decide which will mate with the females. The trunk is also used for feeding and drinking—an adult Asian

TREETOP TREATS
African elephants feed largely on tree leaves, bark, and branches. Asian elephants prefer to graze on grasses and shrubs, plus juicy leaves and fruit.

SUPER SOAKERS
Elephants stay cool by spending several hours each day in water, or by sucking water into their trunk and spraying it over their body.

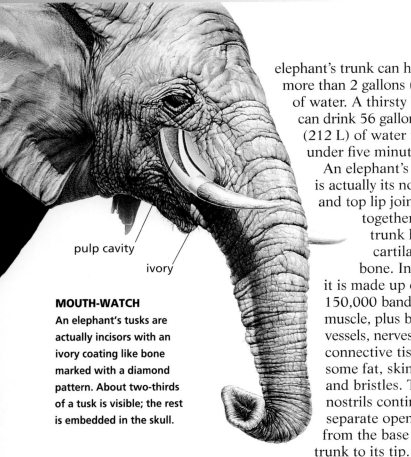

pulp cavity

ivory

MOUTH-WATCH

An elephant's tusks are actually incisors with an ivory coating like bone marked with a diamond pattern. About two-thirds of a tusk is visible; the rest is embedded in the skull.

elephant's trunk can hold more than 2 gallons (7.5 L) of water. A thirsty bull can drink 56 gallons (212 L) of water in just under five minutes! An elephant's trunk is actually its nose and top lip joined together. The trunk has no cartilage or bone. Instead, it is made up of 150,000 bands of muscle, plus blood vessels, nerves, connective tissues, some fat, skin, hair, and bristles. The nostrils continue as separate openings from the base of the trunk to its tip.

Gray Matter

Elephants are very social animals. The basic group is made up of five to ten family members led by an old female, called a matriarch. Sometimes several family groups join to form herds of hundreds of animals.

Elephants are intelligent animals with good memories, and the wise old matriarch passes on what she has learned to younger elephants. For example, during a drought she will lead her family to the best places to find food. This way the group learns her secrets and gives this information to their young, called calves.

A female elephant, called a cow, may give birth to about seven calves in her 60–70 year life span. An elephant is pregnant for about 22 months—the longest pregnancy of any mammal. A newborn elephant weighs about 165–255 pounds (75–115 kg). It is quite hairy, compared with mature elephants, but loses much of this hair as it gets older. The calf drinks up to 3 gallons (12 L) of milk a day for as long as ten months, although some calves continue to nurse for three years or more. It gets its permanent tusks when it is 6 to 12 months old. These tusks grow continuously at the rate of about 7 inches (17 cm) a year.

During its long childhood, a calf is protected and taught how to survive by the others in the group. They communicate by trumpeting and by making sounds that are too low for humans to hear. Elephants also communicate by smell and touch, and watch each other's body language. For example, an elephant's ears are not just for cooling and hearing—they are

TOOTH AND NAIL

Tusks are used to dig for water, salt, and roots; to strip bark from trees; as levers to move fallen trees about; for marking trees; for display; for work (in domesticated animals); as weapons; as trunk-rests; and as protection for the trunk. They may even be "status symbols." Just as humans are right- or left-handed, elephants are right- or left-tusked. The favored tusk is generally shorter and worn down at the tip.

HANDICRAFT
An African elephant grasps an object with the two "fingers" of its trunk, while the Asian elephant, which has one "finger," curls its trunk around an object, "squeezes" it, then lifts it.

African Bush elephant

WHO'S WHAT?

The most obvious difference between African and Asian elephants is the size of their ears—the Africans' are twice as big. Another important difference is the structure of the chewing surfaces of the teeth. Asians' teeth have close, narrow loops, but Africans have wider, diamond-shaped surfaces.

also a good indicator of its mood. An elephant raises and flaps its ears when it is alarmed, angry, or excited.

When male elephants are between 10 and 15 years old, they leave and join an all-male group. They meet with cows only during the mating season.

Chain Reaction

Asian and African elephants are endangered because humans take over their habitats for farming and poachers kill them for their tusks. But elephants play a vital role in their environment. They disperse seeds; distribute nutrients in their dung; and provide water by digging waterholes that are also used by other animals. When they walk they disturb insects, reptiles, and other small creatures, providing food for birds. The paths they tramp through forests and grasslands create firebreaks. Because they are tall they can spot danger far away and alert other, smaller animals. So killing elephants not only destroys close-knit families, but has a terrible impact upon the lives and habitat of many other living things.

African Bush elephants can grow to 13 feet (4 m) high at the shoulder; bulls can weigh 15,500 pounds (7 tonnes) or more. Their back curves downward, and they have three toes on each hind foot. Their trunk has more folds, or "rings," than that of the Asian, and it appears floppy. The trunk also has two "fingers" at the end. Both males and females have tusks.

Asian elephants can be 11 feet (3.5 m) high at the shoulder and may weigh 12,000 pounds (5.5 tonnes). Their back is either humped or level, and they have four toes on each hind foot. Their trunk is slightly more rigid, and it has just one "finger." Only males have tusks.

PAMPERED PROBOSCIS
Elephants have been used for thousands of years to carry various burdens. For religious processions in India, elephants are painted, and then draped in silks and jewels.

Asian elephant

Odd-Toed Ungulates

THERE ARE ABOUT 220 SPECIES OF UNGULATE, or hoofed mammal. These animals have a certain number of toes under a horny covering (the hoof). One group, the perissodactyls, have three toes (tapirs and rhinos) or one toe (horses and their relatives) on each foot. Perissodactyls are also called odd-toed ungulates.

A Class Apart

While it is clear that equids—horses, asses, and zebras—are related, their association with the rare and strange tapir and the lumbering rhinoceros is more surprising. What these mammals have in common is not only their odd number of toes, but also the relatively simple system they have evolved for digesting fibrous plant material.

Near Neigh-bors

About 20 million years ago, when early equids began to take advantage of grassy plains, they found that the only way they could escape predators was to run. Because it was easier to run on their toes than with a flatter foot, their claws gradually turned into hard hoofs, and toes that were not needed for support became smaller or vanished.

Horses and asses evolved in North America, but the ancestor of all domesticated horses became extinct about 12,000 years ago. The closest living relative of the ancestor of today's horses is the stocky, hairy Przewalski's horse of Mongolia. Two kinds of wild ass still exist today—the African wild ass of northeast Africa and the several species of Asiatic asses of the Middle East and Central Asia. Well adapted to their dry desert habitats, both species need little water and can tolerate extremes of temperature. But both species are now rare in the wild.

Horses are the largest of the equids. They can weigh up to 1,540 pounds (700 kg), although males, called stallions, are not much larger than the females, or mares. This is because the stallions' fighting technique involves trying to bite the legs of the opponent, requiring agility rather than strength.

The domestication of the horse was an important stage in the history of human civilization. Horses enabled

TIP-TOE
One large toe supports the equid's weight, and the other toes are just stumps of bone. Heavier ungulates, such as rhinos, have three short, wide toes to spread their weight.

THE STARS OF STRIPES

Zebras are black or brown, with white stripes. These rather conspicuous stripes are actually camouflage. A dark-colored animal has a definite outline, but the zebra's stripes cause it to blur or "fade" at the edges, making it harder for a predator to spot a zebra alone, or in a herd. A zebra's stripes are like a fingerprint—no other zebra looks the same. A mother licks her foal at birth to learn its unique pattern, but it takes a week for the foal to remember its mother's design.

cecum

colon

stomach

small
intestine

A SIMPLE PLAN
Odd-toed ungulates break down
their food in a simple stomach. The
food is then processed by bacteria
the cecum. This system is not very
efficient, so they have to eat a lot
to get the nutrients they need.

WILD AT HEART
The burro, donkey, or
domestic ass is a direct
descendant of the African
wild ass. It has been used
as a beast of burden since
4000 BC. Burros now roam
in feral herds in many
parts of the world.

humans to explore and
settle new territory; to hunt
more efficiently; and to overwhelm
foot soldiers during armed conflict.

Zebras do not have much stamina
and can easily be run down when
chased on horseback, which explains
why they are not tamed for riding.
There are three species of zebra—the
plains or Burchell's zebra, Grévy's
zebra, and the mountain zebra. The
880-pound (400-kg) plains zebra is
common and ranges across the
grasslands and savanna of East Africa.
The other two species, which
have asslike bodies, live
in semidesert areas and
are endangered.

Like all equids, zebras
have keen senses of
smell and hearing, and
can rotate their ears to
locate sounds. The plains
and mountain zebras live
in social groups of
several mares and

a stallion. They will often form mixed
herds with antelope to give them extra
protection against predators. Because
they graze coarse grasses they do not
compete with the antelope, which eat
other vegetation. Zebras must also
drink regularly and rarely stray far
from water. They can sniff out
water underground and will dig
for this water during droughts.

Crown of Horns

Rhinoceroses evolved about 40 million
years ago. More than 50 extinct species
are known, and they have always
been large. An ancient hornless
rhino, *Indricotherium*, was
18 feet (5.5 m) tall at the
shoulder and weighed
over 40,000 pounds
(20 tonnes)—the largest
land mammal ever!
Today there are only
five species left in
the world.
Rhinos have
poor vision,
but an

JAWBREAKER
Adult zebras are hunted
by lions; foals are preyed
upon by hyenas and wild
dogs. Stallions try to
protect foals in their
herd by kicking out with
their sharp hoofs.

PICKY EATERS

The black rhino browses, mostly at night, plucking leaves with its hooklike upper lip. Oxpecker birds often settle on rhinos and pick ticks and lice from their skin.

SKIN AND BONE

Unlike the smooth hide of the African rhinos, the hide of the Javan rhino is heavily folded. Sumatran rhinos are covered in red to black bristles; the Indian rhino has bony studs.

excellent sense of smell and good hearing. They have short, thick legs to support their huge weight, which ranges from the 990-pound (450-kg) Sumatran rhino to the African white rhino, which can reach 5,000 pounds (2.3 tonnes). The length of their horns also varies: Male Javan rhinos have one horn up to 11 inches (28 cm) long; the front horn of the white rhino can measure over 5 feet (1.5 m).

All rhinos are herbivores. The white rhino and the Indian rhino eat mainly grass, and the other species browse on leaves. They can survive for four to five days without water.

The two species of two-horned African rhinoceros, the black rhino and the white rhino, evolved from a common ancestor about 10 million years ago. The 5-foot (1.5-m) high white rhino is taller than the black rhino, and almost twice as heavy. Fossil remains indicate that the white rhino once lived throughout east and north Africa, but it now lives in the savanna of southern and northeastern Africa. Black rhinos can be found from South Africa to Somalia. Black rhino calves have a 15-month gestation; white rhino calves a month longer.

Rhinos are basically solitary animals but white rhinos are the most sociable

DEADLY DILEMMA

Female rhinos use their horns to protect their calves from predators. Scientists dehorned some black rhinos to stop poachers killing them—but the rhinos then could not defend their calves.

of the five species. While males live alone, females with calves sometimes team up in small groups. If predators threaten their calves, they form a circle to protect them. Although these groups move independently, they will approach another group for playful horn wrestles.

All species of rhino are in danger of extinction. In some parts of the world, such as Asia and the Middle East, rhino horns are carved into dagger handles, or ground into powder and taken as medicine. Although horns are made of keratin—the same material that our fingernails are made of—they are more valuable than gold. Between 1970 and 1993, poachers in Africa slaughtered more than 60,000 black rhinos! Under careful protection, white rhino numbers have slowly risen to 7,500. But there is only a remote chance of saving the Sumatran and Javan species. Most of the 60 Javan rhinoceroses alive today survive in a single reserve

Javan rhinoceros

Indian rhinoceros

Sumatran rhinoceros

White rhinoceros

Black rhinoceros

TAPIR-ING NOSE
Like all tapirs, this Malayan tapir uses the flexible trunk on the tip of its nose to forage for grasses, leaves, shoots, fruits, and seeds.

STAR GRAZER
The white rhino grazes with its wide lips. All rhinos are actually gray. The color of their hide depends on the color of the soil in which they roll to keep cool and rid themselves of insects.

on the island of Java, in Indonesia—and all because of human vanity and greed.

Friends of the Forest

The life of the tapir has changed little in 20 million years. Unlike early equids, they have remained in their swampy woodland habitats.

Tapirs are squat creatures that weigh about 660 pounds (300 kg). They measure about 6 feet to almost 8½ feet (1.8–2.5 m) from nose to tail. They are excellent swimmers and divers, can move quickly on land, and are able to climb well.

There are three South American species and one Asian species. While the American species are a dull brown, the Malayan tapir is a striking black and white. All young tapirs have a dark coat marked with pale stripes and flecks, making them hard to spot in the dappled light of the forest.

Tapirs are largely nocturnal and difficult to observe. They are usually solitary, except for mothers with young. Females give birth to one or two young in a secure lair.

By feeding on large fruits, tapirs play an important role in scattering the seeds of many forest trees. However, they are endangered because the forests they help to rejuvenate—and in turn rely on for survival—are being logged or else flooded by dam developments. Tapirs are also hunted extensively for food, sport, or for their thick hide. Unfortunately for tapirs, their hide provides fine leather for bridles and whips.

Even-Toed Ungulates

THE OTHER ORDER OF UNGULATES IS THE ARTIODACTYLS, or even-toed ungulates. These cloven-hoofed mammals carry their weight on two toes (pigs and camels) or four toes (deer, cattle, hippos, sheep, goats, antelopes, and giraffes) on each foot. The Artiodactyla are very diverse and far outnumber the species of odd-toed ungulates.

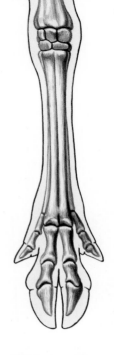

FOUR-LEAF CLOVEN
A deer's two middle toes bear its weight. The second and fifth toes are much smaller; the first toe (our "big toe") is missing.

Run for Your Life

Even-toed ungulates live in a variety of habitats, from tropical to polar, and are widely distributed across all continents except Antarctica. They are herbivores (although some pigs are omnivores) and all are the prey of carnivores. For this reason their body and behavioral adaptations are dominated by means of escaping predators. They are sprinters, and the bones of the soles of their feet are large to absorb the stress of running. Their hoofs give them a good grip on almost any surface. They have a large heart and lungs, and a large chest to contain them; their legs are slim and light. Only hippos use water to shelter from predators, so their build is different to that of other artiodactyls.

ONE HUMP, OR TWO?
The Bactrian camel lives in Mongolia. Unlike other ungulates, the camel does not walk on its hoofs. Its toes rest on fleshy cushions, which stop it from sinking into the sand.

A Cud Above

Even-toed ungulates also have a very sophisticated system for digesting plant material. Unlike odd-toed ungulates, most artiodactyls have a complex three- or four-chambered stomach. They regurgitate partially processed food from one chamber, called the rumen, to the mouth, where they break it down even more with their specialized grinding teeth. This food is swallowed again and passes on to another chamber, the omasum, and so on. By thoroughly processing food in this way the maximum amount of nutrients is absorbed.

Piga-ma-jigs

Giant species of pig emerged in Africa during the ice ages. While not related, the three species of peccary and about 20 species of pig have evolved in similar ways.

Peccaries are herbivorous and have a more complex stomach than pigs, which are the most omnivorous of the ungulates. Both mammals dig up roots and tubers that grow underground. Pigs also eat nuts, insect larvae, birds' nests, carrion, and small animals.

Peccaries live in close-knit groups and jointly defend their territories. Since defense is a priority, males and females have evolved similar physiques designed for fighting, including sharp canine teeth. An individual chacoan

COILED COIFFURE
The tusks of the male 200-pound (90-kg) babirusa of Indonesia curl backward from its snout. All male pigs generally use their tusks in fights, to hold and control their opponent's head.

HANDSOME HOG

Red river hogs of Africa and Madagascar come in several colors—not all of them red! They live in groups of 12, led by an old male, and eat almost anything.

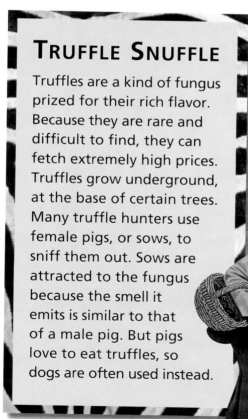

peccary will confront a puma or jaguar, risking its own life, to allow the rest of the group to escape.

Peccaries bear few young, but wild boars may have ten piglets a litter and bear several litters a year. The females shelter the piglets from cold or rain by building domed nests. The piglets' coats are striped with white to provide camouflage.

Wild boar males tend to be solitary. The dominant males control access to breeding females; the smaller males roam in bachelor groups. Females live in mother-daughter groups on large home ranges. As with all pigs, the males are larger than the females and can weigh up to 440 pounds (200 kg).

Unlike peccaries, pigs do not defend territories. But they do share resources, making them ideal for domestication. All domestic pigs are descendants of the wild boar of Eurasia and north Africa. Escaped domestic pigs have reinvaded

RIVER RAGE

Fighting male hippos clash their lower jaws together. They lock their upper incisor teeth and push each other for as long as an hour and a half—bellowing all the while.

natural habitats as feral populations in North America, New Zealand, and Australia.

Horses for Watercourses

The hippopotamus was once thought to be related to pigs. But new findings suggest that its closest relatives are whales! The four broad, webbed toes on each of the hippo's feet allow it to walk on the bottom of African lakes and swamps and live up to its Greek name, which means "river horse."

The average hippo measures about $11\frac{1}{2}$ feet (3.5 m) long. Its weight is equal to the combined weights of 90 ten-year-old children! It spends its days wallowing about in large groups, which may help to protect the young from crocodiles. At sunset it moves out to a grazing area along an established path, marked at intervals by piles of its dung. The hippo clips grasses with its thick lips to leave what looks like a mowed lawn.

TRUFFLE SNUFFLE

Truffles are a kind of fungus prized for their rich flavor. Because they are rare and difficult to find, they can fetch extremely high prices. Truffles grow underground, at the base of certain trees. Many truffle hunters use female pigs, or sows, to sniff them out. Sows are attracted to the fungus because the smell it emits is similar to that of a male pig. But pigs love to eat truffles, so dogs are often used instead.

HOW DO YOU PUDU?
The pudu of South America is only 15 inches (38 cm) high at the shoulder. It is one hundred times lighter than the 1,760-pound (800-kg) moose.

TUNDRA TUSSLE
Bull caribou lock antlers and push to see which is stronger. The winner mates with the females of the herd; the loser waits for another chance to prove his strength.

Males often fight viciously to protect food and to control breeding females. Young hippos suckle for about eight months and ride piggyback on their mother in deep water. Females are fiercely protective of their young, but hippos will rarely attack humans unless they are provoked or disturbed on their paths.

Fossils show that hippos used to live as far north as England. Dwarf hippos colonized Mediterranean islands! The only other species that survives today is the pygmy hippo. A tenth of the size of the "true" hippo, it is found in dense rain forest and swamps from Guinea to Nigeria. It has longer legs, and may be less aquatic than its larger relative.

HALF GIRAFFE
The okapi of Zaire is similar to prehistoric giraffes. Like its larger relative, it gathers food with its black tongue, which is so long that the okapi can use it to clean its eyes!

Hat Racks

Deer have long fascinated humankind and were painted on cave walls as much as 14,000 years ago. Today there are more than 40 species of deer. All are herbivores and most eat grasses, leaves and fruit, although caribou (reindeer) eat lichen and moss.

Although the water deer of Asia has tusks, most male deer grow a new set of antlers each year. Antlers become bigger and heavier as the animal gets older. The larger the species, the more complex the antlers: They range from simple spikes to racks with many branches, and are designed so that they rarely become accidentally entangled. The caribou is the only species of deer in which both sexes have antlers.

Deer live in most parts of the world. For example the wapiti, or American elk, was once common across North America, but now occurs naturally only in the western United States and Canada. The wapiti lives in large herds in winter, breaking into smaller groups for the summer. During the breeding season it makes a whistling sound. By contrast its relative, the nocturnal muntjac, lives in the thick forests of India, Sri Lanka, Tibet, China, and Southeast Asia. It is either solitary or moves about in pairs or small family

SCENTED GENT

The musk ox, which lives in the Arctic, is so called because of the musky smell emitted from glands in the faces of bull oxen during the mating season.

groups. Because of its cry, it is also called the barking deer. Like most species of deer, the muntjac is hunted by humans and other predators, such as tigers. It is always on guard, using its acute sight, hearing, and smell to detect danger. If it hears or sees movement, it flees.

Divine Bovines

Bovids first appeared about 23 million years ago. These even-toed ungulates graze, chew their cud, and live in herds. The 140 or so species of bovid include cattle, goats, buffalo, gnu (wildebeest), gazelles, and antelopes. Most farm animals are bovids; sheep and goats were first tamed around 10,000 years ago.

Bovids' bone horns are hollow and covered with a layer of keratin. They are not branched, but come in a range of styles. They also have many functions: Whereas the Barbary sheep's wide horns are used like clubs to batter rivals in the herd, the bongo's lyre-shaped horns are used to break down branches for food. The oryx uses its prong-like horns for defense against predators.

The shape and use of bovids' horns reflect, and are possibly influenced by, their body and behavioral adaptations. For example, the agile duikers of South Africa are too small to have large horns. Since they can't rely on their short horns for defense, they dive into undergrowth and lie low when they are scared.

A musk ox is too heavy to run fast, so it stands its ground with its herd and forms a protective circle around the calves, its mighty horns ready to strike out at any predator.

THIS YEAR'S MODEL

Horns are permanent, but the antlers of deer, elk, and moose are temporary. Each year, the animal loses its antlers and grows more. In early spring, the antlers bud from beneath the fur of the deer's head. They are covered in soft skin called velvet.

By late summer the antlers have grown to their full extent, nourished by blood vessels inside the velvet. New points, or tines, are added every year or so.

Antlers are signs of a male deer's status and dominance in contests for females and food. In fall, the velvet dries and is rubbed off against rocks and tree trunks. These shiny antlers demonstrate to other males that the deer is ready to fight for control of the herd.

In winter, after the mating season, the antlers become brittle at the base. They are easily knocked off against trees. New antlers start to bud.

Rodents

RODENTS ARE THE WORLD'S MOST SUCCESSFUL MAMMALS. From the pygmy jerboa, which could fit into a matchbox, to the capybara, which grows to 4 feet (1.25 m) long and weighs 146 pounds (66 kg), rodents live in almost every environment, from the Arctic tundra to deserts, forests, mountains—even the most isolated islands.

RODENT RUNNER
The 20-pound (9-kg) Patagonian mara mates for life. It rears its pups in a communal crèche. It sprints to safety on its long legs.

Mighty Mice

More than one-third of all mammals are rodents. Most of the estimated 2,000 or more species weigh less than 5 ounces (150 g), enabling them to make use of a wide range of habitats. They also look very similar—they all have a mouse-like body with modifications mainly in the digestive system, teeth, legs, and tail. Some species that spend almost all their life in trees, such as squirrels, have excellent eyesight and sharp claws that allow them to move easily about the canopy. Climbers including the palm mouse have opposable big toes to help them to grip stems. The elongated hindfeet of jumping rodents, such as jerboas, enable them to move quickly over long distances. Pocket gophers have external, fur-lined cheek pouches for carrying food.

Mole-rats and other underground rodents are blind, tailless, and have either small or no external ears. Other rodents are adapted for a semiaquatic life: The beaver's sleek body, webbed hindfeet, and flattened tail propel it through the water.

SLEEPS AND BOUNDS
The black giant squirrel is found in dense forest from Nepal to Indonesia. Its tail serves as a balance, a rudder, a signal flag, and a blanket.

Boom or Bust

A rodent's skull can be identified by a pair of chisel-like incisors in the upper and lower jaws. These teeth grow

LOGGER HEAD
Beavers use their incisors to fell trees for building dams across streams. They build lodges in the dams, with access to the living chamber through an underwater tunnel to avoid predators.

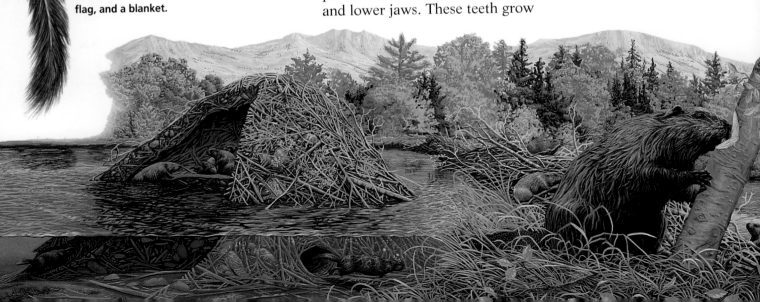

SOME LIKE IT HOT
Gerbils live in the deserts of Africa and western Asia. They get moisture from their food and never need to drink. Dense fur insulates the soles of their feet, and their white underbelly reflects radiated heat.

constantly, ready to gnaw through hard nutshells, or seeds, bulbs, shoots, leaves, and bark. A row of molars at the back of the mouth are used for grinding food. Some rodents, such as the speckled harsh-furred rat and fish-eating rats, have also adapted digestive systems suitable for their diet of insects or vertebrates.

Rodents have many predators, but few species can protect themselves. When threatened by land predators such as martens, flying squirrels glide away using a furry membrane down each side of their body. But they are less successful at avoiding flying threats such as owls. The crested porcupine has a more effective defense—when approached, it grunts, stamps its hindfeet, then raises its sharp quills and attacks!

But most rodents are largely defenseless. The survival of their species is instead ensured by their high rates of reproduction. Many rats and mice have gestation periods of less than 30 days! After the litters of three to seven pups are born the parents immediately breed again. Typically, the pups are born blind and naked, but in a few months they, too, can breed.

Taking the Rap

Rodents and humans have a close, and often unhappy, relationship. Some rat species spread fatal diseases such as the

bubonic plague (Black Death) and typhus. Rodent populations can also build to huge levels and wreak havoc on crops and stored grain. But rodents also make invaluable contributions to their environment. For example, European red squirrels collect and bury acorns to eat during winter. But sometimes they either forget where they stored the acorns, or else have enough and don't need the extra food. The acorns left behind grow into oak trees.

POND-EROUS
The largest living rodent, the capybara of South America is adapted for a semiaquatic life by having nostrils, eyes, and ears set high on its head.

URBAN PLANNING

The black-tailed prairie dog, a species of ground squirrel, lives on the treeless plains of North America. They shelter in "towns," huge networks of burrows that can cover 160 acres (65 hectares) and house 1,000 animals. Each burrow is occupied by one social unit—a coterie—of a male, several females, and their pups. An adult always keeps a lookout at the entrance to warn others of approaching predators.

Rabbits, Hares, Pikas, and Hyraxes

RABBITS, HARES, AND PIKAS belong to an order called Lagomorpha. The oldest known lagomorphs evolved 50 million years ago in Asia and North America. Hyraxes are not related to lagomorphs, and their history goes back even further. Forty to fifty million years ago, hyraxes were the dominant grazing mammals of North Africa.

Feral Peril

Today the 80 or more species of lagomorph live in most habitats in Africa, Europe, Asia, and the Americas. They have also been introduced to other parts of the world by humans, often with devastating consequences. The European rabbit was brought to Australia by settlers in the eighteenth and nineteenth centuries and has plagued the country ever since, damaging crops and the environment. Some Australian marsupials and native rodents are near extinction, or have been killed off, as a result of competition with rabbits for food and water.

Lagomorphs provide food for many predators, including lynxes, coyotes, hawks, and humans. Rabbits give birth to many young—sometimes up to 30 a year—so that at least some will survive to breed. Although young are born blind and almost furless, species such as the eastern cottontail rabbit can breed at just ten weeks of age.

Bunny Business

Lagomorphs have a slit between the upper lip and the nostrils—the "hare lip"—and two pairs of chisel-like upper incisors that bite against one pair in the lower jaw. Like those of rodents, these teeth continue to grow throughout the lagomorphs' life, and are used to gnaw grasses, buds, twigs, bark, and leaves. Most lagomorphs emerge from their burrows at sunset to feed, and their large eyes see well in the dark. The position of their eyes, at the sides of their head, also help them to spot predators approaching from above and behind.

EARS TO YOU
The black-tailed jackrabbit is a type of hare. Its very long ears are used to regulate its temperature in its desert habitat.

HARE-RAISING
Before mating, hares test the mettle of their potential mate. Their antics have given rise to the phrase "mad as a March hare."

FLOWER POWER
In the fall, pikas collect vegetation and dry it in the sun to provide food through the winter. They whistle warnings to intruders who get too close to their hoard.

WORKING MOTHER
A female European rabbit keeps her many young warm in special chambers lined with grass, and fur plucked from her belly.

Rabbits are generally smaller than hares and have shorter ears. Their keen senses of smell and hearing and their protective coloring are their main defenses against their enemies. They thump their hindfeet in aggression or alarm; the white underside of their tail, which flashes as they run, also warns others of danger. When threatened, most species scamper to their burrows, called warrens. Rabbits are usually silent, but squeal when frightened or hurt.

A hare's hindlegs are longer than those of a rabbit, and give it greater agility and speed. Some species escape danger by running in zigzags—a useful tactic when pursued by birds of prey, which cannot twist and turn as quickly. Unlike rabbits, which live in highly organized groups, hares are relatively solitary. They do not burrow much and give birth to fewer, furry, active young in their bed, called a form. One of the few species that will dig a burrow—into snow or earth—is the Arctic hare. In winter its brown or gray coat changes to white, giving it greater camouflage in snowy conditions.

Whistling Pixie

The 30 or so species of pika have a plump body, short legs, prominent rounded ears, and no tail. Most look like rodents, but pikas are the smallest kind of lagomorph, weighing from 3 to 11 ounces (80 to 300 g).

Pikas are found in rocky, mountainous areas in western North America and northeastern Asia. They live in colonies and rely upon individuals to warn the group of danger. Pikas are sometimes called whistling hares or piping hares for the shrill sounds they make.

Pikas sleep in burrows or rock crevices, depending on the terrain. They spend their days gathering food, digging or cleaning out their burrows, or sunning themselves. They produce litters of up to six furless young in the spring and summer after a gestation period of about one month.

BROTHERLY GLOVE

The Masai tribe of east Africa call the hyrax the "little brother of the elephant." Although often mistaken for a rabbit, the hyrax really is the elephant's closest relative on land. Both animals have five toes on each front foot. But the hyrax's feet are unusual. They have rubbery pads, kept moist by special glands, that give the hyrax a firm grip on dry rocks and trees. The eight or so species eat mostly plants and live in large colonies. They keep in touch using 20 or more sounds, including screams!

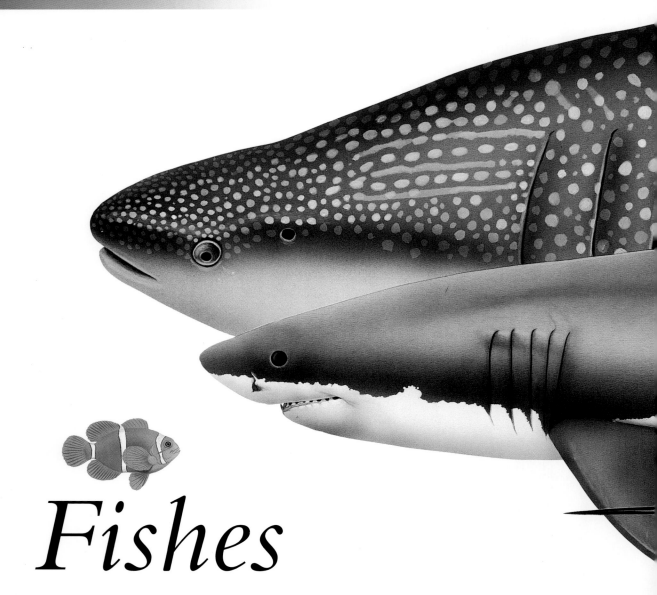

Fishes

With seas and oceans covering more than two-thirds of its surface, planet Earth should perhaps be called planet Water. The seas, oceans, rivers, and lakes contain many different habitats, including mangrove swamps, coral reefs, kelp forests, and quiet shallows. From boiling desert springs to supercooled Antarctic depths, fishes make their home just about anywhere there is water.

Over half of all fishes live in salt water. The remainder mostly prefer fresh water, and a few kinds can live in either. Most fishes live only where there is some sunlight, but some swim at such extreme depths that the Sun's rays never reach them. Some fishes can even survive for brief periods out of water!

The 24,000 or so species of fishes come in an almost infinite variety of shapes, sizes, and colors. Some look like boxes; others look like weeds. They can have horns like rhinos or bills like birds. Some fishes build nests and grow food, while others have their own lights or produce bolts of electricity. There are fishes which travel thousands of miles, and fishes which live more than 50 years. From the ⅖-inch (1-cm) long goby to the mighty whale shark, the world is all the richer for its fishes.

Classifying Fishes

FISHES ARE COLD-BLOODED VERTEBRATES that are superbly adapted for life in water. They are differentiated from other vertebrates by their fins, which they use to propel themselves through their environment. They are also characterized by their scales and by their gills, which they use to extract oxygen from the water.

IN THE SWIM
Flexible fins allow typical bony fishes (top) and cartilaginous fishes (bottom) to perform a range of precise movements, including hovering and swimming backward.

Fish Fin-gers

There are two main superclasses of fishes: jawless fishes (Agnatha) and jawed fishes (Gnathostomata). The jawless fishes, hagfishes and lampreys, have sucking mouths with horny teeth instead of true jaws. The jawed fishes are classified into cartilaginous fishes and bony fishes. The cartilaginous fishes, such as sharks and rays, have body frames made from cartilage, a substance like the flexible tip of our own nose, but the bony fishes have skeletons of bone.

While fishes range widely in their body shape and the arrangement of their fins, most have a streamlined body, rounded in the middle and tapering toward the head and tail. By contracting muscles on either side of their backbone, fishes sway and bend their caudal (tail) fin and body surface to produce a backward thrust that propels the fish forward. Because swimming movements require large muscles, swimming muscles make up to 65 percent of a fish's weight.

But many fishes swim in different ways. Pipefishes use their dorsal and anal fins for forward and backward thrusts. Wrasses and parrotfishes use their pectoral fins as oars, with the caudal fin acting as a rudder. Sharks

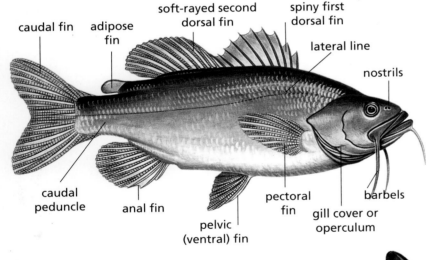

caudal fin · adipose fin · soft-rayed second dorsal fin · spiny first dorsal fin · lateral line · nostrils · caudal peduncle · anal fin · pelvic (ventral) fin · pectoral fin · gill cover or operculum · barbels

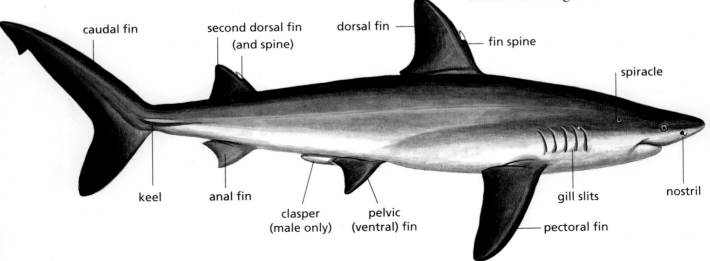

caudal fin · second dorsal fin (and spine) · dorsal fin · fin spine · spiracle · keel · anal fin · clasper (male only) · pelvic (ventral) fin · gill slits · pectoral fin · nostril

use their pectoral fins like wings to provide lift as they swim; this offsets their tendency to sink, because a shark's body is heavier than sea water.

Gills and Thrills

Some fishes have lungs, but most breathe by taking in water through their mouth. Water flows over the gills, where the oxygen is extracted and passed into the blood. The water is then forced out through the gill slits. During this process, up to 95 percent of the oxygen in the water is extracted. Such efficiency is vital, because water contains only $\frac{1}{30}$ of the oxygen in air.

Fishes have also developed sense organs that take advantage of the properties of water. Located in canals along the body and around the head, lateral line organs detect moving objects by registering disturbances in the water. Since water also conducts electrical currents, many fishes have modified lateral line organs that can detect even the weakest electrical fields, such as those generated by the muscles and heartbeat of prey. A fish's inner ear can also sense pressure changes caused by sound waves.

Fishes use a combination of these senses in their daily activities. For example, sharks rely not only on their sensitive electroreceptors, but also on their highly developed sense of smell to avoid danger or to find food.

TILE STYLES

Most fishes have scales—even eels, whose scales are so tiny that they are virtually invisible. Scales are made of a protein called keratin, and they protect the fishes from predators and harsh environments.

There are four kinds of fish scales. Tooth-like placoid scales are characteristic of sharks. Small and light, they probably help sharks to swim more quickly by reducing the amount of friction they cause. Fast-moving fishes such as marlin and mackerel have also developed fine, closely-fitting, flexible scales to allow greater freedom of movement.

Most bony fishes have tough scales that overlap like roof tiles. Depending on the lifestyle of the fish, the scales may have either roughened (ctenoid) or smooth (cycloid) edges. Armored fishes like sturgeons have horny ganoid scales, for extra protection.

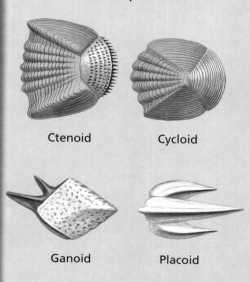

Ctenoid

Cycloid

Ganoid

Placoid

Fishes through the Ages

THE FIRST FISHES appeared in the oceans some 500 million years ago—100 million years before the earliest known animals with limbs. Fossils tell us that fishes rapidly spread from freshwater lakes and rivers to lagoons and then to open seas. Almost all major groups survive today, although older groups are smaller in number.

HELMET HEAD
Hemicyclaspis lived around 408 million years ago. A kind of cephalaspidiform, this jawless bottom-dweller had a solid bony shield around its head and grew to about 7 inches (18 cm) long. It may be related to lampreys.

Sedimentary, Dear Watson

Nearly all fossils are found in sedimentary rocks that have been formed in water, such as limestone or shale. For this reason the fossil record of fishes is generally better than that of non-aquatic vertebrates; it is more likely that a fish will end up being fossilised in fairly good condition than a bird or land animal.

What would be left of a fish after millions of years? The soft parts of an animal, such as skin or organs, are more likely to decay than bone. So a fish with little bony structure, like the first jawless species, is not so likely to survive in fossil form. Fish teeth and the skeletons of bony fishes, on the

other hand, may in rare cases be found preserved whole in certain types of limestone. These examples provide a glimpse of the evolution of fishes from their ancestral to their modern form.

The Role of Rock

After the fish dies, the soft parts (guts, muscles, and skin) rot away, leaving the teeth and bones behind. Soon after the animal has been reduced to its hard parts, it is buried by sediment—in soft mud on the bottom of a lake, in silt dropped by a flooding river, or in sand at the bottom of the sea. Once buried, the remains become soaked with water carrying dissolved minerals such as quartz or lime. These minerals slowly replace the organic material, turning the fish's remains to stone.

Over many millions of years, the sea may retreat, exposing the rocks in which the fossil lies. Movements in the Earth's crust may raise what was once the seabed and form a mountain range. Once near the surface, the fossil may be eroded out of its rocky tomb for humans to find.

Tales From the Crypt

The earliest fishes belong to a group called the Agnatha, which means "jawless." Armor-like plates and scales covered their body, and their head was protected by a bony shield. Thousands of their little skull helmets have been found, buried deep in sandstone. Today, hagfishes and

STONE BONES
The fossils of bony fishes, like *Priscacara*, are likely to be spread through a variety of rocks. Shales deposited in freshwater lakes, or marine black shales, can provide the collector with rich pickings.

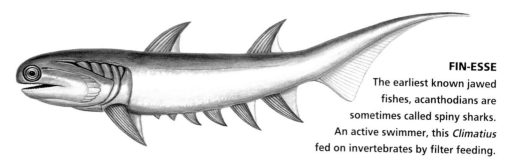

FIN-ESSE
The earliest known jawed fishes, acanthodians are sometimes called spiny sharks. An active swimmer, this *Climatius* fed on invertebrates by filter feeding.

Stage 1

Stage 2

Stage 3

Stage 4

FACES IN THE DUST
Transformed over millions of years to stone, the bones of an ancient fish are gradually revealed by the slow movements of the surrounding terrain and the effects of erosion.

lampreys are all that remain of the agnathans, but these fishes no longer have head shields.

The first jawed fishes appeared about 100 million years after the agnathans. The placoderms were one of the largest groups. Their name, which means "plate-skinned," refers to their heavily armored head and shoulder girdles. Most species are known only by these plates, which have been found in rock deposits from the early Silurian Period, 435 to 410 million years ago.

Another group of jawed fishes are the cartilaginous Chondrichthyians. This group first appeared in the late Silurian Period, and survives today with rays, skates, and sharks. These fishes had toothlike bones in their scales and these, and their teeth, are common fossils. One family of sharks, *Carcharodon*, became the largest fishes in the ocean. They grew up to 40 feet (12 m) long, and their huge mouth was armed with many rows of 8-inch (20-cm) teeth. While only half this size, the great white shark is a descendant of these ancient monsters.

Catch of the Devonian

The largest group of fishes, the bony fishes, or Osteichthyes, also have a large fossil record. Included in this

group are the coelacanths and lungfishes. Fossils of coelacanths date back to the Middle Devonian Period, 355 million years ago. By 320 million years ago, coelacanths had evolved marine, freshwater, and shallow water varieties.

Coelacanths were thought to have been extinct for 65 million years. But in 1938 a deepwater marine fish with strong, muscular fins was caught in the sea off South Africa. This species is the sole survivor of a once widespread and diverse group. However, several lungfish species can be found in Australia, Africa, and South America. Like coelacanths they have leg-like fins. They are able to breathe air, spending their summer in a special burrow.

Body Language

Today's fishes are an incredibly diverse group of animals. Some of them share many of the characteristics of their primitive relatives. But in order

MONSTER MASHER
Placoderms became quite diverse and widespread, with over 35 families. One, known as *Dunkleosteus*, was a predator which grew to more than 6½ feet (2 m) long.

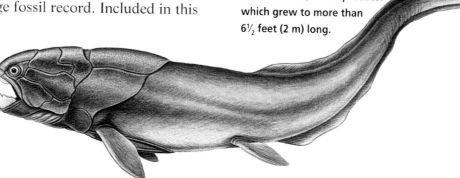

to exploit almost every type of aquatic habitat—from alpine lakes and tropical reefs to the deep oceans—other fishes have evolved different body shapes and colors. Many of these body adaptations have been in response to the need to eat.

For example, fishes which actively hunt for their prey, such as barracuda and sharks, combine strength and speed with a flexible, streamlined body capable of lightning-fast reactions. Pufferfishes, on the other hand, browse with their parrot-like beak and do not need to chase other fishes. Neither do they need to escape predators, because they can look frightening when threatened. Because they don't need to swim fast for long periods, they have a more rounded

figure and a smaller, less powerful caudal fin.

In order to survive on the river bottom in a fast current, fishes such as the Garra species of Africa have developed expanded lips which act as a sucker to help them hold onto rocks. Other bottom-dwellers, such as codfishes and catfishes, have evolved fleshy, sensitive feelers, called barbels. Best known as sense organs, barbels are covered with taste buds that allow the fishes to find, explore, and test food before they eat it.

Now You See It ...

If you lived at the bottom of an ocean or a lake, having a flat body and eyes on the top of your head would be an advantage. Halibut, plaice, flounders, and other flatfishes have developed these features. They enable the fishes to lie hidden in the sand, with only

REEF TEETH
Most parrotfishes are herbivores, and their specially adapted jaw structure allows them to graze on plants. But other parrotfishes prefer coral. Divers often hear them crunching on their favorite food before they see them.

LIFE IN THE FAST LANE
Thanks to its sucker-like pectoral fins, this saddled hillstream loach can live in fast-flowing water without being swept away.

Eyes at the side ...

move ...

to the top of the head

CROSSED-EYE
Like other fishes, young flatfishes have an eye on each side of their head. But as they grow older, one eye moves across their head to join the other.

LURE OF THE SEA

The gulper eel lives in the deepest oceans, more than 3,280 feet (1,000 m) below the surface. One of its adaptations to life in total darkness is a luminous bait at the end of its tail to attract its prey. Food is scarce in the deep oceans, so the eel is not a fussy feeder. Its huge, umbrella-like jaws enable it to swallow fishes of all sizes, from this small hatchetfish to prey larger than itself.

their eyes showing, as they scan the area for predators or prey.

Other fishes also use camouflage to helps them to ambush their prey. The stonefish, as its name suggests, is almost impossible to see in shallow waters. Algae and other growths on its body add the finishing touch. But these fishes are not the only masters of disguise. To protect themselves, some species change color to match the pattern and color of their habitat. For example, scorpionfishes mimic the growths on dead coral. If a predator persists, these fishes can also inflict wounds with their venomous spines.

Other fishes use reverse psychology: They either scare attackers away, or lure them close— then surprise them. The bright red colors of the aggressive lionfish warn enemies that it is venomous. Others, such as butterflyfishes, have false eye spots near their tail. These markings can trick a predator into striking away from the head.

... Now You Don't

Fishes eat almost any plant or animal found in water. The specialised jaws of many species allow them to feed on a particular type of food. For example, the spinynose sculpin selects a specific size of snail, fits the shell into its mouth, and then punches a hole in the shell with special teeth on the roof of its mouth. Halfbeaks, so named for their long, slender, protruding lower jaw, neatly slurp up pieces of floating seagrass like spaghetti. The jaws of the basking shark, the second-largest fish in the world, expand sideways like a net to take in large gulps of tiny plankton. Water passes into its mouth and across its gills, which strain out the plankton.

SPECIAL BRANCH
The long-nose hawkfish lives in rocky and coral reef habitats of tropical and subtropical waters. Its red and white markings help it to look like the branched coral where it hides.

WOBBE-GONE
The dark coloring, blotchy markings, and leaf-like mouth of the wobbegong shark make it difficult to spot among the seaweeds of the ocean floor.

Fish Behavior

WATER CANNON
Archerfishes spit well-aimed jets of water at insects hanging from overhead foliage, knocking them into the water, where they are quickly eaten.

F ISH BEHAVIOR, like all animal behavior, is governed by the need to find food and mates and balanced by the need to avoid predators. Fishes have evolved a remarkable range of behaviors and strategies for survival, many of which are achieved by the use of their specialized sensory systems.

Extra Sensory Perception

As with most vertebrates, vision plays a key role in enabling fishes to process information about their surroundings. But although sunlight can penetrate to 3,280 feet (1,000 m), 75 percent of the ocean is sunless. Most water also contains tiny particles of mud and debris, making it cloudy. Perhaps because vision is often so difficult, fishes have extremely well-developed senses of smell and hearing. They can smell even small concentrations of chemicals, and because sound waves travel much farther in water than they do in the air, fishes can hear noises from a considerable distance.

In addition to these basic senses, a fish's lateral line gives it the sense of "distant touch." Somewhat as humans feel wind against their cheeks, fishes can feel the wake left by a swimming neighbor through vibrations and changing pressure. Sharks, rays, and their relatives also have specialized electroreceptors that sense the tiny electrical currents that project from every living animal. The electric fish of South America and Africa also have electroreceptors, which help them to navigate and warn them of approaching predators.

The Medium is the Message

The senses of sight, hearing, "distant touch," and electroreception allow fishes to understand fully and survive in their watery world. For example, sharks use electroreception to line up their downward-pointing jaws with their prey. Electric fishes can also create pulses of electricity to stun prey, to deter predators, and to signal their identity, location, and "ownership" of a hunting territory. Midshipmen use the water to broadcast their froglike grunts and groans to attract mates.

While some fishes gather in large groups to spawn on full-moon nights, allowing their eggs and sperm to drift

GENDER BENDER

In most fish species, males and females are born as such. But many reef fishes have the ability to change their sex. Parrotfishes and wrasses go through up to three sex/color changes en route to maturity. In fact, the color patterns of the sexes are so different that for more than 200 years males and females were thought to be separate species!

Juvenile—not sexually active

The female seahorse lays her eggs into the male's pouch

The mother then leaves her eggs in the care of the male

The eggs are incubated in his pouch until they are ready to hatch

The babies are pumped out through a hole at the front of the pouch

on the current, other species select and defend nest sites and attract mates with courtship dances. A male cichlid, for example, performs a variety of body postures and fin movements, also appealing to the female's sense of sight with his intense coloration.

Infant-ry

Fishes display several types of parental care toward their young. In general, the amount of care provided is in direct proportion to the number of eggs produced. So fishes which release thousands of eggs, such as the ocean sunfish, tend not to be doting parents, while fishes which produce only a few young will be more protective toward them. The male of the South African lungfish even grows extra gills on his pelvic fins in order to improve the oxygen supply to his eggs.

In habitats with many predators, nest-building and egg-guarding become necessary. Male sticklebacks build algae nests, then guard the eggs from gangs of hungry predators by pretending to pick for food at the ocean floor nearby. By making believe the eggs are elsewhere, he may succeed in distracting the predators.

Other fishes care for their young by taking them wherever they go. Weedy seadragon males can carry up to

Initial phase—usually female

Terminal phase—always a mature male

115

FICKLE PRICKLE

When disturbed, a pufferfish can inflate itself with water or air, making it difficult for most predators to swallow. The fish's body also contains concentrates of a toxin more powerful than cyanide!

120 eggs safely on their tail until they hatch. Some cichlids brood their eggs in their mouth. After the eggs have hatched, the parent releases the brood into the water. But if danger threatens, the parents snap up their offspring and keep them in the safety of their mouth until the danger passes.

Follow Your Nose

Although most fishes spend their life in the waters in which they were born, a few, such as salmon and eels, travel vast distances back to their spawning grounds. Eels navigate by using their electroreceptors to perceive the Earth's electromagnetic field. Salmon, on the other hand, smell their way home. Following chemical cues too subtle for humans to detect, they migrate across open ocean to the streams where they hatched. Sockeye salmon can swim up to 2,300 miles

(3,500 km)! They stop eating when they enter fresh water, relying on fat reserves to finish the arduous journey.

Hunters and Gatherers

Finding a meal is often a difficult task for fishes. Food is usually not spread evenly across a habitat, but occurs in patches. This means that a hungry fish must either know where to look for food, or already have it on hand. Dusky damselfishes, for example, have developed a form of "farming." They defend territories within which they grow gardens of algae, providing a constant source of dinner.

Predatory fishes have developed a wide range of hunting methods. Camouflaged flounders sit and wait for prey, pike stalk their victims, and anglerfishes wave a lure, attached to the top of their head, to tempt small fishes close. But to save time and energy, species such as barracuda group together to attack smaller schools. They create such a panic that individuals are easily captured. The largest predators, such as marlin, hunt alone, slashing through schools of tuna with their bill and returning to pick off injured victims.

Mutual Benefit

Over the ages, different species have developed relationships from which both partners benefit. For example,

THE FEELING'S MUTUAL

The stinging tentacles of the anemone can kill intruders, but anemonefishes can live safely within the anemone's embrace. The fishes produce a skin secretion that mimics the substance that prevents the anemone from stinging itself. They can then shelter among the tentacles. In return for this protection, the fishes preen and keep the tentacles free of debris.

SCHOOL OF LIFE
There is safety in numbers for blackbar soldierfishes. Faced with a moving mass of identical fishes, their predators will find it hard to focus on a single target.

cleaner fishes such as wrasse form partnerships with larger fishes. The wrasse will swim near particular places, such as conspicuous rocks or coral heads, to signal that they are available. When a "client" approaches, it is thoroughly groomed of parasites that have attached themselves to its body and gills. These parasites provide the cleaner fish with a tasty meal.

Some fishes take advantage of this relationship by mimicking cleaners in color and behavior. A sabre-toothed blenny copies the cleaner wrasse to fool its potential prey into thinking it will be cleaned. Instead, the client receives a painful nip!

Synchronized Swimming

Fishes have also developed ingenious behavior to avoid danger. Many fishes use camouflage, while others seek protection in rock and coral crevices. The triggerfish hides in a narrow opening in the coral reef, erecting its spiny dorsal fin to lock it into place. Young cardinalfishes even hide among the sharp quills of the long-spined sea urchin.

Other fishes have other methods of warding off enemies. To startle or divert a predator, the warty prowfish squirts a smokelike cloud of toxic fluid, while lanternfishes flash bright lights. Parrotfishes spend the night in the safety of a sleeping bag made of foul-tasting mucus. But a quarter of all adult fishes (and over half of young fishes) seek protection in large groups called schools. Such fishes can outwit attackers with an impressive set of maneuvers. Schooling herring, for example, can clear the path of an approaching barracuda by performing a shimmering wave of movement. Each fish has to move at the same time as all the rest—one wrong move can lead to immediate attack.

FALSE IMPRESSION
Yellow is one of the few colors visible in deep water. Combined with black spots or bars, it creates a warning that is well understood. This mimic filefish (top) copies the poisonous black-saddled puffer (bottom) for safety.

Endangered Species

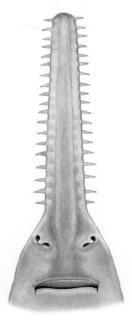

FISHES ARE UNDER PRESSURE right around the planet, with species from every continent being listed as threatened. All kinds of fishes are at risk, big and small—over 700 species are currently known to be in danger. Unless we take important steps to protect endangered species and environments, we will lose them forever.

People Pressure

Every year there are 90 million more people on Earth to feed and shelter. Since most of the world's population lives on the coasts, it is not surprising that the seas are suffering from the effects of increasing human activity.

People have gathered food from the oceans since prehistoric times, but it is only in the past 200 years or so that pollution has become a serious problem. People once believed that sea water could kill germs, so they used the ocean as a tip and dumped human and industrial waste there.

Inland waters are threatened, too. Industrial waste and agricultural runoff, such as topsoil, insecticides, and phosphates, affect the health of river systems. (Since rivers ultimately drain into the sea, this pollution can have a widespread impact.) The destruction of tropical rain forest deprives river fishes of habitats and food, like the fruits, seeds, and leaves of the trees. Urban development and canal and dam construction can block fish migration paths. The draining of

SOUPY SEAS
There is less oxygen in warm water than cold water. For this reason, the delicate ecosystems of coral reefs will be harmed by any increase in sea temperature as a result of global warming.

SAW LOSER
Cartilaginous fishes tend to be longer-lived than other types of fishes, and produce fewer offspring. Overfishing has depleted the population of sawfishes, leaving few to mature and breed.

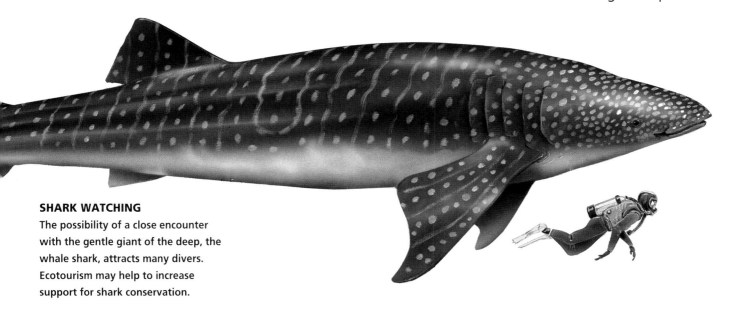

SHARK WATCHING
The possibility of a close encounter with the gentle giant of the deep, the whale shark, attracts many divers. Ecotourism may help to increase support for shark conservation.

LONG LIVE THE QUEEN
At least 118 marine species of fishes are globally threatened. On the danger list are wide-ranging coral reef species such as this beautiful queen triggerfish.

wetlands and streams has also meant the loss of fishes' spawning, feeding, and nursery grounds.

Reef Grief

The United Nations began to take marine pollution seriously in the 1970s but by that time, parts of some seas were already dying. Another problem is now taking its toll: coral bleaching.

Coral is a colony of microorganisms called polyps. The polyps use tentacles to catch their zooplankton prey. They have also formed a relationship with algae called zooxanthellae which live within the walls of the polyps. The algae create food for themselves and for the coral using carbon dioxide and light. The algae also give the polyps their distinctive colors.

But when corals are subjected to high sea temperatures, agricultural runoff, and chemical spills, they become stressed and eject the algae from their tissues. Not only do corals lose their color (thus the term "coral bleaching"), but their increased exposure to harmful ultraviolet rays and reduced supply of nutrients may cause them to weaken or even die.

Global warming and the effects of the periodic weather pattern known as El Niño are thought to be the main causes of coral bleaching. The death of coral colonies has ramifications for

NO TOAD ABODE?
Coral bleaching may soon threaten the survival of reef-dwelling fishes such as this splendid toadfish of Central America.

RAY OF LIGHT
Fishing practices and changes to their habitat have contributed to a decline in ray populations. The spotted eagle ray, once common, is now legally protected in some countries.

the entire reef ecosystem, as many species either eat coral or the animals that shelter within it, or rely on it for nests or shelter. Marine parks can only help so much—to stop the atmosphere from increasing in temperature, we must reduce our dependence on fossil fuels and stop clearing forests.

Appalling Trawling

In the past, netting, spearing, and other simple methods of catching fishes were not a threat to world fish populations. But nowadays fishing ships with modern equipment and techniques can take millions of tons of fishes such as herring, tuna, and mackerel from the sea each year, reducing the number of fishes left to breed. An example of wasteful overfishing is the use of the bottom trawl, a large net that is towed behind a boat and used to catch fishes that live on the seabed. Floats and weights keep the mouth of the trawl open so that everything in its path is scooped up. Many fishes are killed indiscriminately, and those with no market value are tossed overboard.

The population of fishes in enclosed or specialized habitats, such as lakes,

SAD IRONY
The rare and fascinating coelacanth is unfortunately in demand from museums and scientific collections for research.

GULP FICTION

Sharks are often portrayed as vicious killers, but more humans kill sharks than sharks kill humans. Many are slaughtered out of fear or prejudice, but most are killed for food and other resources. From Roman times, when dried shark brains were rubbed on teeth to treat toothaches, to the use of shark corneas in modern transplant operations, humans have found ways to exploit almost every part of a shark.

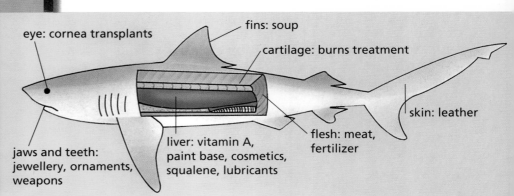

eye: cornea transplants

fins: soup

cartilage: burns treatment

jaws and teeth: jewellery, ornaments, weapons

liver: vitamin A, paint base, cosmetics, squalene, lubricants

flesh: meat, fertilizer

skin: leather

Sport fishers pay a lot of money for the chance to hunt a great white shark. Luckily, fishing restrictions have been imposed by some countries to protect this magnificent fish.

can also be disturbed by the release of introduced species. These species compete with native fishes for food and living space, as well as preying on them. For example, when the Nile perch was introduced into Africa's Lake Victoria, it decimated the population of native cichlids, upsetting the natural balance.

Think Global, Act Local

There are many things that we can do to help to safeguard the future of fishes and their habitats. Visiting marine parks and aquariums is a good way to increase our awareness of vulnerable species and to support the research being carried out to protect them.

We can avoid polluting waterways by recycling plastics and similar materials. We can also pressure our governments to prevent ships with harmful cargoes, such as oil tankers and nuclear-powered vessels, from going near sensitive marine areas. We can support the efforts of conservation organizations to place bans or limits on wasteful methods of fishing, write to companies that use these methods, and even stop buying their products. Alternatives to products made from endangered fishes can also be used. For example, the vitamin A in shark oil, thought to prevent heart attacks and cancer, can be made artificially.

One way of increasing the abundance of fishes in damaged areas is to build artificial reefs. Made of concrete, rubber tires, and even car wrecks or sunken ships, they provide shelter for animals just like real reefs. As fishes and invertebrates move in to colonize them, they gradually become part of the natural environment.

IN POOR HEALTH
Seahorses are now at risk, as for many years they have been used as an ingredient in traditional medicines. Seahorse farming may be a solution to the problem.

Jawless Fishes

THE FIRST FISHES to evolve, the agnathans, had a backbone but no jaws. They first appeared during the late Cambrian Period, over 500 million years ago, but by the end of the Devonian Period (360 million years ago) most of them had died out. Today, hagfishes and lampreys are their only surviving relatives.

Squishy Fishes

Unlike their ancient relatives, which had bony external plates, lampreys and hagfishes have soft outer tissue. For this reason, it was not until 1968 that the first fossil of either a lamprey or a hagfish was described. This beautifully preserved specimen from about 280 million years ago looks very much like present-day lampreys. Its soft, scaleless, eel-like body lacked paired fins, and it breathed through pore-like gill openings. Its backbone consisted of an elongated, rodlike structure with no cartilaginous or bony vertebrae.

But unlike modern adult lampreys, the fossilized specimen did not have well-developed teeth. Since these teeth are used to attach the lamprey to a food source, the fossilized specimen may have obtained its food by another method—possibly scavenging.

Jawless fishes are today found in the temperate waters of the northern and southern hemispheres, and in cool, deep waters in certain regions of the tropics. So far, a total of about 43 species of hagfish and 40 species of lamprey have been described.

Knot a Problem

Hagfishes live only in the depths of the sea, making them difficult to study. They tunnel into the soft sediment of the ocean floor, leaving only their snout protruding in order to breathe and to smell out food. Little is known about their breeding behavior, but it is thought that they lay their eggs in burrows. The large eggs are enclosed in a tough case and anchored by threadlike structures to keep them from drifting away. Hagfishes hatch into tiny versions of their parents.

Hagfishes are scavengers, eating bottom-dwelling invertebrates and dead and dying fishes. The two plates on their mouthpart are used to cut and tear away flesh. Their ability to tie themselves into a knot, and run the knot through the length of their body to work as a lever, helps with feeding.

This feature is also useful in other situations. For example, if a hagfish is grabbed by a predator it uses the extra strength obtained by knotting to free itself. It also produces lots of slimy mucus, making it hard for the enemy to keep a firm grip. Once the danger is past, the fish can run a knot down its body to scrape off excess mucus.

MIXED MENU
Unlike lampreys, hagfishes eat carrion. When feeding, the hagfish (top) enters its prey through the gills or underbelly. While many adult lampreys (bottom) are parasitic, others don't feed after their larval stage.

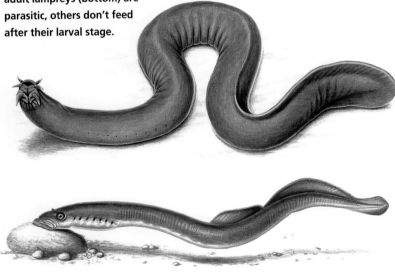

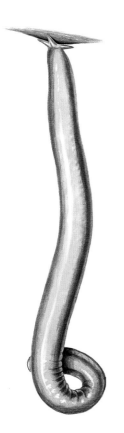
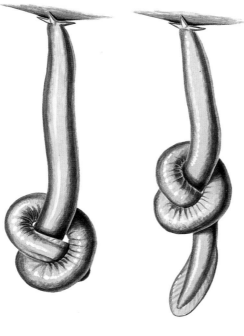

SMALL HITCH

The contortionists of the fish world, hagfishes can tie their body into a knot. When feeding, the knot helps to brace them against a carcass so that they can tear off flesh.

Have Teeth, Will Travel

Lampreys are found in both fresh and salt water. Unlike hagfishes, many go through a larval stage. The eyeless larvae lie buried in the soft bottoms of streams and rivers, feeding on algae and microorganisms.

After about three years, most species transform into young adults. They develop eyes and a sucking disk, complete with teeth with which to feed as parasites on unwitting animals. When this change is complete, they swim downstream from their freshwater home to the sea. During this marine phase, they grow rapidly—the sea lamprey, for example, grows from 5 inches (13 cm) to about 32 inches (80 cm) in two years.

After the marine phase, lampreys stop eating and migrate to upstream rivers to spawn. This journey can be as short as two weeks or, as in the pouched lamprey, an epic 15 to 16 months. The lampreys make a hollow in the river bed, using their sucker disk to move large pebbles to the rim of the nest. In a flurry of activity, the eggs are laid and lightly covered with sand. The larvae hatch less than two weeks later.

COMPACT DISK

Lampreys and hagfishes were once placed together in a single class, Cyclostomata. This name, which means "round mouths," refers to the bizarre sucker disk of hagfishes and adult lampreys. A lamprey (right) uses the many horny teeth lining its disk and mouth to attach itself to its host. It then uses its tongue, which is also toothed, to rasp a hole in its host, and feeds on its muscle tissue, blood, and other body fluids.

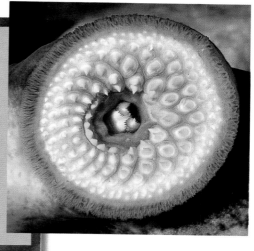

Stage 1

Stage 2

Stage 3

Stage 4

QUICK-DRAW JAW
It was once thought that sharks had to swim upside down to bite their prey. But the jaws of this great white show how it has adapted to cope with its diet.

124

Cartilaginous Fishes

Sharks, rays, and chimaeras are cartilaginous fishes. While there are relatively few cartilaginous fishes compared to the number of bony fishes, some have gained a bad reputation for their attacks on humans. As a result they are often regarded as stupid, vicious eating machines—but nothing could be further from the truth.

Respect Your Elders

Before dinosaurs walked the Earth, there were sharks. By the time the first amphibians had crawled onto land and the first insects had appeared in primitive plant forests, sharks had developed their streamlined shape.

Sharks evolved from a group of bony fishes around 450 million years ago. The strange and little-known chimaeras probably developed from prehistoric sharks during the late Carboniferous Period, about 350 million years ago, with the first rays appearing 150 million years later, during the Triassic.

Among the most ancient and primitive sharks was *Cladoselache*, which lived about 375 million years ago. It was only about 3 feet (1 m) long, with long, slender jaws and stiff, triangular dorsal fins. Some fossils also contain the remains of whole fishes, swallowed tail first. This, plus the fact that its tail was similar in shape to that of powerful modern-day mako sharks, suggests that *Cladoselache* had great speed and agility. This characteristic probably helped it to avoid being eaten by arthrodires, the giant armored fishes with which it shared the ocean.

Flexi-Fish

The agility of *Cladoselache* may also have been due to the fact that, unlike arthrodires, its body was supported by a light, flexible frame. In the race to survive, sharks and their relatives had

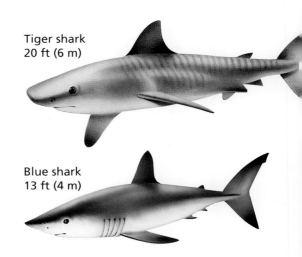

Tiger shark
20 ft (6 m)

Blue shark
13 ft (4 m)

Bronze whaler shark
6½ ft (2 m)

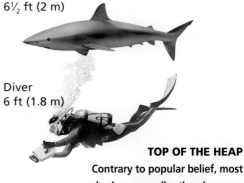

Diver
6 ft (1.8 m)

TOP OF THE HEAP
Contrary to popular belief, most sharks are smaller than humans. Eighty-two percent do not reach 6½ feet (2 m), and only 4 percent measure 13 to 40 feet (4 to 12 m).

developed a skeleton entirely of cartilage. In humans, cartilage is mostly found covering the ends of some bones, but in sharks, rays, and chimaeras this firm yet elastic body tissue also forms the skull and jaw.

The development of a cartilaginous skeleton reduced the fishes' weight. This adaptation was vital, because rays and sharks are heavier than water and do not have a swim bladder for buoyancy as bony fishes do. They evolved additional adaptations to control their buoyancy, including a large, oil-rich liver. Since oil, or squalene, is lighter than water, the liver acts as a float. The greater the depth at which a shark lives, the denser the water, so the liver of deepsea sharks contains more oil. Deepsea species such as the goblin shark have a liver that comprises about 25 percent of their body weight, and contains up to 90 percent oil.

The Great Divide

The 370 or so species of sharks make up only a tiny fraction of the fish population. While they share most of the general features of bony fishes, their flexible skeleton is not their only unique feature. For example, all of a shark's or ray's five to seven gill slits can be seen, while the gills of most other fishes are protected by a bony plate known as a gill cover, or operculum, with a single opening. Their fins are thick and relatively stiff, and lack the delicate spines and rays found in the fins of most bony fishes. Most other fishes have large, flattened scales, but a shark's skin has a layer of tiny, tough, and toothlike placoid scales, or denticles, that allow the water to flow smoothly over the body, reducing drag. Sharks can cruise at 3 mph (5 kmph), although some of the fastest sharks, such as the mako, are capable of bursts of up to 22 mph (35 kmph).

Another major difference between a shark and a bony fish is the design of a shark's jaw. In most living sharks, the upper jaw is loosely attached to the underside of the skull in a way that enables it to be thrust out from the skull during feeding. This means the

CABLE AND WIRELESS
Sharks and rays have groups of modified pores on their head. These link to sensory cells in jelly-filled tubes. The cells detect electrical signals, then relay this information, via nerves, to the brain.

INNOCENT MISTAKE
Sharks' evil reputations are exaggerated. We are more likely to be struck by lightning than to be attacked. Still, it is easy to see how this great white shark can mistake a person for its prey of seals.

SEEING IN STEREO
The location of a hammerhead's eyes gives it an excellent field of vision, in practically all directions. Sharks' retinas are also packed with sensory cells, giving them color vision and good detail in daylight.

shark can take big, powerful bites from relatively large prey. Their teeth, which are formed from skin tissue, are arranged in ordered rows on both jaws. Tooth replacement continues throughout a shark's life, with new teeth emerging from behind lost or broken ones. Some sharks may shed as many as 30,000 teeth in a lifetime!

Power Grid

Cartilaginous fishes have large brains. In fact, the relative size of their brain rivals that of some mammals. Lemon and nurse sharks have been taught to pick up objects and to respond when they hear and see certain signals. They have also been trained to push buttons for food, and can remember the right choice over long periods of time.

Sophisticated sensory organs channel messages into the fishes' brain to keep them fully informed about what is going on within and around them. Their organs of balance and hearing are especially advanced, and some cartilaginous fishes can smell another fish at concentrations of about 1 part per 10 billion parts of water! They can also detect even the tiniest of water vibrations through the sensory cells along their lateral line. But perhaps their most remarkable adaptation is their electrosensory system. No other fishes have it.

Sharks, rays and chimaeras are sensitive to electrical fields, detected by specialized electroreceptors seen as tiny pores clustered on the head and

FIN TALES

A shark's tail tells a lot about its lifestyle and prey. The nurse shark uses broad sweeps of its long tail to propel it slowly in search of crustaceans. Tiger sharks and other active hunters, which need to twist and turn rapidly to catch fast prey, have a tail with a large upper lobe. This enables the shark to produce sudden bursts of speed when necessary.

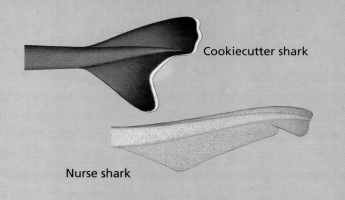

Cookiecutter shark

Nurse shark

SLEEPING BEAUTY
Sluggish swimmers, nurse sharks are often seen resting comfortably on the sandy floor of shallow reefs and mangrove flats.

THRESHING FLESH
The thresher shark has the longest tail of any known shark. It uses it to slap the water surface, frightening prey into tight groups to make capture easier.

lower jaw. Each pore is connected by insulated tubes filled with conductive jelly to electroreceptors (known as ampullae of Lorenzini) just below the skin. These electroreceptors pick up the electrical aura produced by another animal near the fish's head. Used in combination with the other senses, they are able to pinpoint the exact location of live prey—

or predators. From the strength and frequency of the signal, the fish may even be able to tell whether its prey is healthy, wounded, or dying.

The electrosensory system is also used for migration. By detecting ocean currents, the Earth's magnetic field, and even magnetic differences in the structure of the seabed, they can successfully navigate thousands of miles of seemingly empty ocean. The electrosensory system may also play a role in social behavior—it is used by some rays to find potential mates during the breeding season.

Custom Built

Sharks live in oceans throughout the world, from cold polar waters to tropical seas. They inhabit almost every marine ecosystem, from the coastal fringes to the ocean depths.

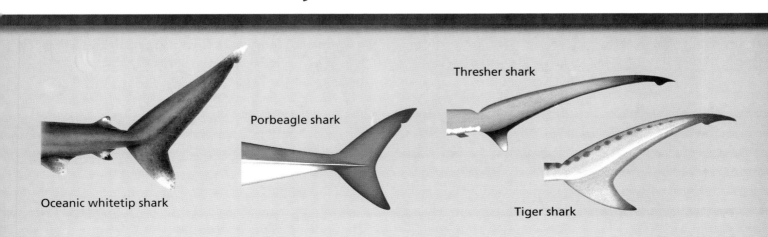

Oceanic whitetip shark

Porbeagle shark

Thresher shark

Tiger shark

FLOOR COVERING
Like other species that live on the bottom, this necklace carpetshark has a flattened body shape. Barbels help it to find food on the seabed, and its beautiful coloration provides camouflage.

The bull shark can even be found in tropical lakes and rivers. Others are extremely wide-ranging: Blue sharks tagged in English waters have been recovered off Brazil!

Sharks show adaptations to their lifestyle and habitats in a variety of ways, but the most telling evidence is body shape. For example the mako, an ocean-going shark that eats squid, bony fishes, whales, dolphins, and other sharks, is shaped like a torpedo. Its snout and head are fused into a missile-like nose cone, its body is stout and muscular, and its pectoral fins are short (to reduce drag) and stiff (for rapid maneuverability). By contrast, bottom-dwelling species such as angelsharks have a greatly flattened body and broad, fleshy pectoral fins. Other bottom-dwellers, including blind, nurse, and bullhead sharks, may use their specially adapted pectoral fins to clamber over the seabed.

The size and shape of a shark's teeth are good indicators of its diet, and one of the most spectacular specializations is to be found in basking sharks and whale sharks. These species have just tiny teeth, so they cruise slowly, their enormous mouth wide open, filtering plankton, shrimps, and other small prey using a sieving mechanism inside their gills.

Scare Tactics

Some sharks have sophisticated camouflage to help them find a meal. These ambushing predators, such as wobbegongs, lie concealed among the algae and weeds on the bottom until an unsuspecting small fish or crustacean comes close enough for a strike. Others use strategic behavior to lure prey close. The nurse shark rolls its pectoral fins under its body so that it resembles a small reef crevice—a supposedly safe haven for unsuspecting bony fishes.

ON THE PROWL
Some species, such as the great white, are solitary hunters. But this blacktip reef shark moves in a group over coral reef flats during the day, searching for surgeonfishes and mullet.

Bullhead

Blue

Mako

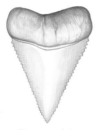

Great white

TOOLS OF THE TRADE
The bullhead's flat teeth crush crustaceans. Blue sharks saw up fishes with serrated teeth. The mako's "needles" grasp large fish. The great white can cut huge chunks from mammals.

Many sharks are pursuit predators that actively chase down their fleeing prey. Hammerheads commonly roam sandy reef flats in search of stingrays, which they pin to the bottom with their head and devour. The slim body of reef hunters, such as epaulette and whitetip reef sharks, is flexible enough to slip in and out of small holes in the coral in search of fish and crustacean prey.

COOKIE MONSTER

The cookiecutter shark has specialized sucking jaws and lips, and sharp, saw-like upper teeth. It uses its lips to form a suction cap on the skin of its prey, then bites and swivels around to cut out a plug of tissue— just like a cookiecutter in pastry. Although this shark grows to only 20 inches (50 cm), its victims include large billfishes, dolphins, whales, and seals. It has even been known to bite the rubber dome of a nuclear submarine!

ORIGINAL FIN
Fossils of the bullhead shark show that its skeletal structure has remained virtually unchanged for 160 million years. It forages over wide areas of the reef or seabed in search of invertebrates.

The diet of great whites and tiger sharks includes large fishes, seabirds, turtles, elephant seals, and sealions. The hunting method of these sharks is often termed "bite and spit." During close encounters with large prey, the shark attacks by taking just one quick, powerful bite. This is usually enough to cause a major, often fatal wound to the prey. Then, when the victim is weakened and unlikely to strike back, the shark moves in for its feed.

This behavior is thought to have developed in response to the risks of tackling such opponents as a 1,000-pound (500-kg) elephant seal. The great white uses the "bite and spit" method to avoid prolonged contact with the teeth and claws of this formidable mammal.

Feast or Famine
Food can be scarce in the ocean, particularly in winter, so sharks have to eat when they can. This is usually every couple of days, with an average meal weighing 3 to 5 percent of their body weight. But during lean times,

RAY RELAY
Unlike sharks, rays are basically sociable animals and occur in large groups. They will often rest on top of each other. Their skin is sensitive to touch, and they seem to go into a trance if stroked.

they are capable of surviving without food for several months. During this time, they live off fat reserves in their liver.

Blue sharks, which prey on mating squid, have been known to binge feed when the opportunity presents itself. On moonless winter nights, the squid gather in their millions to spawn. At this time they are particularly vulnerable, and the sharks are able to swim, mouth agape, through the enormous shoals. They continue to eat until their stomach is completely full and it is impossible to cram any more squid into their mouth. At this point, they vomit, to create more room so that they can continue to gorge and maximize their chances of nutrition.

Circular Saw

Sharks seem to spend much of their lives as solitary animals. However, a few species are known to form large schools, most notably hammerheads. Hammerheads have been seen off the coast of Mexico in schools of up to 225 individuals. When together, each fish remains a set distance from its neighbor, and all fishes move in the same direction.

It is not known why these big sharks school, because (unlike smaller fishes) they do not need to gather together to avoid being eaten by predators. However, species such as the 10-foot (3-m) long sevengill shark has been known to hunt in packs, and the reason for this is clear. Their prey is large fur seals, which, at up to 775 pounds (350 kg), are more than twice the weight of the largest sevengill. By hunting as a group, the sharks can overpower and eat an animal that a lone sevengill could never manage. One pack was observed off the coast of Namibia, in southern Africa, forming a loose circle around a fur seal. The sharks slowly moved inward, tightening the circle to prevent the seal from escaping. Eventually one of the sharks attacked the seal, signaling for the remaining sharks to start feeding.

Sharks feeding together have also been found to have a dominance

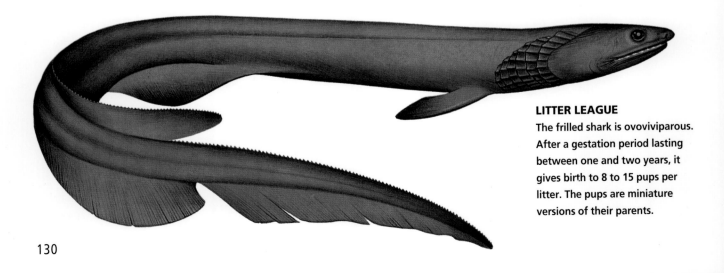

LITTER LEAGUE
The frilled shark is ovoviviparous. After a gestation period lasting between one and two years, it gives birth to 8 to 15 pups per litter. The pups are miniature versions of their parents.

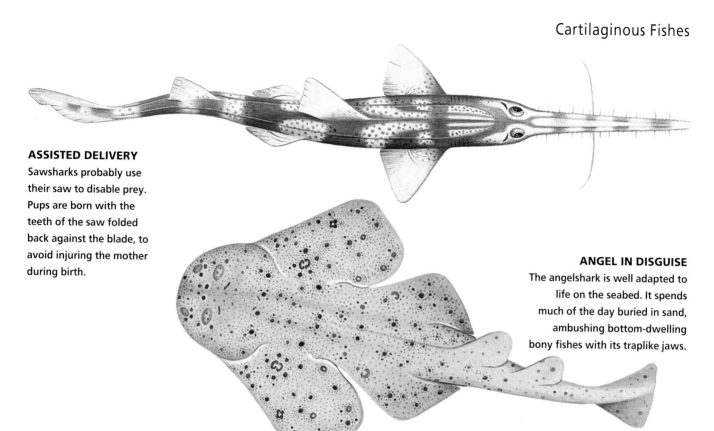

ASSISTED DELIVERY
Sawsharks probably use their saw to disable prey. Pups are born with the teeth of the saw folded back against the blade, to avoid injuring the mother during birth.

ANGEL IN DISGUISE
The angelshark is well adapted to life on the seabed. It spends much of the day buried in sand, ambushing bottom-dwelling bony fishes with its traplike jaws.

Jaw below skull

Jaw stays close to skull

Jaw detaches from skull

NO NIBBLING
Thanks to their unique jaw structure, sharks can bite off parts of prey that are too large to gulp whole. A great white can tear a 22-pound (10 kg) chunk off in one bite.

hierarchy. While feeding on whale carcasses, large white sharks will often chase away or even severely bite smaller sharks of the same species, and will ultimately get most of the food. This "pecking order" is also observed when sharks of different species gather over food. For example, whitetip sharks make way for gray reef sharks, which in turn give up food for the more dominant silvertip shark.

Shark-Witted

This kind of aggressive or submissive behavior is actually a kind of defense. Many sharks avoid trouble by staying out of the way, but others will protect themselves or their food by biting.

In order to avoid a physical attack, most frightened or angry sharks will first signal their intentions. For example, before attacking, a gray reef shark will swim in an exaggerated fashion with its pectoral fins lowered and its back arched. If the threatening object, fish, or human backs off, the shark will not attack. Other sharks show their intentions by swimming directly at the threat, then suddenly turning away. As the sharks turn, they flick their tail. This creates a loud cracking sound that no doubt scares off potential predators.

Other sharks have physical means of defending themselves. The hard, pointed spines on the dorsal fins of dogfish sharks and bullhead sharks make them painful for predators to swallow. A threatened swellshark can even increase its size by swallowing water, making it more difficult—and frightening—to attack.

Mermaid's Purses

Most female fishes eject thousands—or millions—of small eggs to be fertilized outside the body by males. But female sharks produce relatively few, large eggs that are fertilized inside the body. The majority of sharks are viviparous, which means they give birth to live young. In some species the embryos are nourished via a placenta, not unlike that of mammals, while in others they are nourished by

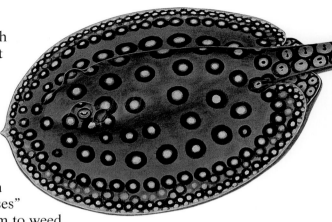

yolk sacs. But in species such as sand tiger sharks, the first fully-formed embryo will eat its own siblings as extra nourishment before it is born!

The eggs of oviparous species such as catsharks are encased in a hard, horny container known as a mermaid's purse. The "purses" have tendrils to anchor them to weed at the bottom. Bullhead sharks' eggs are shaped like large screws, which wedge into sand or rock crevices. The baby sharks, or pups, hatch up to 15 months later and must immediately fend for themselves.

Some sharks are ovoviviparous. This means they give birth to young that have developed from eggs that hatch within the mother's body. A whale shark can carry several hundred eggs, each of which produces a pup about 2 feet (60 cm) long.

Fishes Like Dishes

Sharks' cartilaginous cousins, the rays, are some of the most intriguing of all fishes. Their body is so flat that it is almost two-dimensional. Their well-developed pectoral fins form most of the body disk which, rather than the tail, is used for swimming.

The first rays are thought to have evolved from flattened sharks around the time of the dinosaurs. There are now 600 or so living species of ray. They range from the 4-inch (10-cm) long shortnose electric ray, which weighs less than 1 pound (500 g), to the gigantic manta ray, which may be more than 22 feet (6.7 m) across and weigh several tons.

On a Wing and a Lair

While it is known that most rays live and feed on or near the bottom, other knowledge of rays is relatively limited. In the past decade, more than 50 new species have been discovered in the Indo-Pacific region alone.

Most rays live only in the sea, from shallows to depths of over 10,000 feet (3,000 m). But some, like shorttailed electric rays, prefer sheltered habitats like muddy bays and estuaries. Tidal flats and mangrove swamps are also important feeding areas for many tropical rays, such as the Atlantic guitarfish. Some rays also live in fresh water: Ocellated stingrays can be found 1,000 miles (1,600 km) from the sea.

WATCH YOUR STEP
The stinging spines on a stingray's tail are used in defense. The closer the sting is to the tail tip, the more useful it is as a weapon. In South America, this ocellated freshwater stingray is feared more than the piranha.

WALL FLOWER
The bluespotted ribbontail ray is often seen by divers in the Indo-Pacific region. If approached, this timid ray will usually swim away. But others, such as the manta ray, seem to enjoy company.

TUNNEL FUNNEL
The cavernous mouth of the manta ray is located at the front of its snout. Since it feeds on plankton, it has no teeth in its upper jaw, and only tiny, skin-covered stumps in its lower jaw.

Shock Treatment

Most rays use their sense of smell and their electroreceptors to find food. They trap prey against the sea floor with their disk, then move themselves over the prey to direct it between their compact rows of strong teeth. But rays can be quite selective feeders, and the various mouth and teeth adaptations indicate their choice of food. For example, cownose and eagle rays have a series of flattened tooth plates, rather like beaks, to crush crabs and mollusks. Torpedo rays have a very arched lower jaw, studded with small spiny teeth, which can be thrust forward to suck up small fishes.

Electric rays use the kidney-shaped electric organs near the middle of each side of their disk to stun their prey. Among the most powerful found in fishes, these organs are also used for defense against sharks, and to communicate. Large torpedo rays can produce shocks of more than 200 volts—enough to knock a human off their feet!

NOSE PICK
The snout of the sixgill stingray is covered in sensory pores to detect food. Its highly flexible tip can move like a human finger.

RAY RANGE

Rays come in all shapes and sizes, but they do share features in common. Since most are bottom-dwellers, their mouth, gill slits and nostrils are on their underside. Their eyes and spiracles are placed on top of their head.

Members of the major orders can be recognized by their features and behavior. In rajiforms, for example, the pelvic fin is divided into two lobes. Torpediniforms use electric shocks for catching prey and for communication.

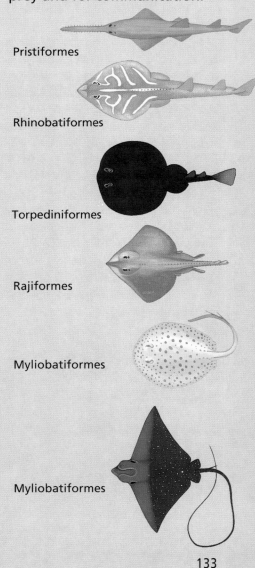

Pristiformes

Rhinobatiformes

Torpediniformes

Rajiformes

Myliobatiformes

Myliobatiformes

133

Bony Fishes

OST FISHES in the world today belong to Class Osteichthyes. These fishes have a bony skeleton and evolved from jawless fishes about 400 million years ago. Bony fishes live in almost every kind of aquatic environment, from the tropics to the polar regions. There are at least 20,000 species in existence.

JUMBO JAW
Despite its common name, the African elephantnose has an enlarged chin, rather than a big nose. It uses its chin to probe mud for insect larvae or bottom-dwelling creatures such as mollusks.

MURKY LURKER
The camouflage of the freshwater butterflyfish enables it to lurk just below the surface, among floating vegetation, in wait for its insect prey.

Balloons with Bones

Although a seahorse would seem to be as different from a moray eel as an elephant from a bumblebee, they are in fact both bony fishes. Like all fishes in this group, they have certain features in common. For example, all bony fishes have jaws, unlike their more primitive relatives, the agnathans. All have gills with which to breathe, although some bony fishes also have other ways of breathing: As its name suggests, the lungfish possesses a lung, as well as gills. Most bony fishes also have nostrils.

Fins are another feature of bony fishes. These can be either thick and fleshy, like those of coelacanths, or reinforced with bony rays, such as those of paddlefishes.

Unlike cartilaginous fishes, most bony fishes have a sac in their body cavity, just under the spine, called a swim bladder. The bladder, which is filled with air or gas, makes the fish weightless in the water, like an astronaut in space, and enables it to move up or down with little effort.

The fish can control the amount of gas or air by expanding or contracting its swim bladder. Changes in the weather, which have an effect on air and water pressure, also have an effect on how much the swim bladder expands and contracts. In parts of Europe, a type of loach called a weatherfish was once kept and used as a living barometer. By observing changes in the fish's size (caused by changes to the swim bladder), people were able to predict the weather!

Elemental Dental

Bony fishes left behind many fossils. From studying these fossil records, we have learnt that the fishes' jaws may have evolved as an extension of the armor-like skull plates possessed by most primitive jawless fishes. But it is still not known whether the first bony fishes had teeth, or whether their teeth came later, after their jaws had formed.

The teeth of today's bony fishes are joined to the jawbone. They come in

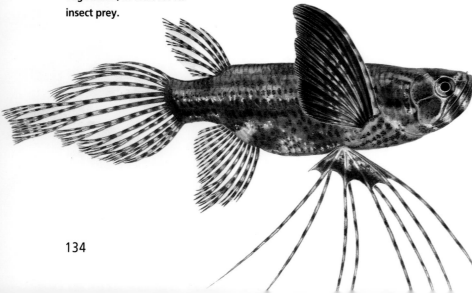

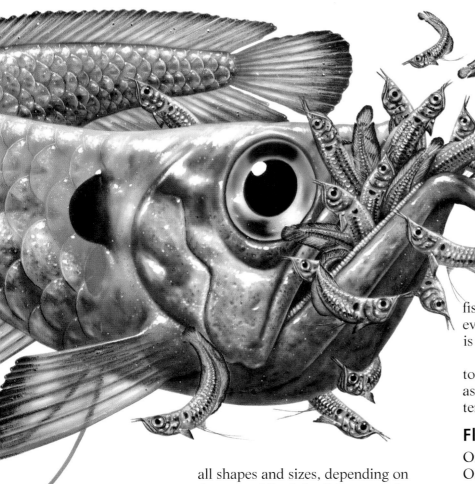

MOUTH HOUSE
In flooded Amazon rain forests, the male arawana sucks the female's eggs into a pocket near his mouth. The fry hatch and live inside this pocket until they can fend for themselves.

to amphibians, other fishes—and even the occasional warm-blooded vertebrate. In this way, bony fishes were able to colonize almost every part of the planet where water is found.

Jaws became useful in other ways, too—as weapons to protect the fish, as a means of attack, and even as a temporary home for young fishes.

Floating on Air

One order of bony fishes, called the Osteoglossiformes, or bonytongues, is named for the large and prominent tongue bone of its members. Fossils of the ancestors of these fishes, found all over the world, show that modern bonytongues have kept many of their primitive features, including the teeth on the tongue bone. It is thought that these teeth are useful for grinding their diet of small fishes and aquatic insects.

Some osteoglossiforms, such as the freshwater butterflyfish of tropical western Africa, have large pectoral fins controlled by a well-developed and complicated set of muscles. It

all shapes and sizes, depending on the type of food the fishes eat—from the powerful protruding teeth of the parrotfish, used to gnaw algae and crunch up coral, to the needle-sharp fangs of flesh-eating piranhas.

Essentially, the development of jaws ensured the bony fishes' survival. It meant that they were no longer limited to the restrictions of suction feeding, as the jawless agnathans were. With jaws they could move into new territories to take advantage of the huge menu available to them, from insects, worms, snails, and crustaceans

STARRED FISH
Once classified as a shark, the American paddlefish is in fact related to sturgeons. Covered in electroreceptors and held up by star-shaped bones, its snout is used to detect plankton.

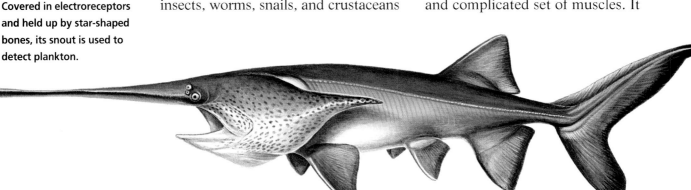

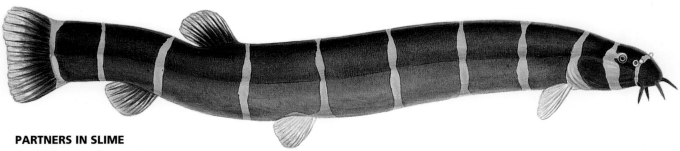

PARTNERS IN SLIME
The freshwater slimy loach lives in rivers and streams in Thailand. Its wormlike body and tiny scales make it look like an eel, but its barbels show that it is a member of the carp family.

uses these muscles to leap from the water in pursuit of low-flying insects. Since the first specimen ever captured had a dragonfly in its stomach, it is thought to be able to glide for short distances. However, there is no certain proof of this.

Eel Appeal

Among the number of fishes which don't look like fishes are the eels. To confuse matters, many animals which do look like eels, such as electric eels and Congo eels, are not true eels. (The electric eel belongs to the knifefish family, while the Congo eel is not a fish but an amphibian!)

Moray eels are some of the most widespread true eels, with more than 200 species distributed in all the world's tropical and subtropical seas. Common residents of coral reefs, many are endowed with bold color patterns, including stripes, spots, and bars. Others, such as the leaf-nosed moray, have strange anatomical features. The dragon moray of Hawaii even has prominent nose-tubes, which poke like little horns above its brow.

Morays are often feared because of their wicked-

looking teeth, which they occasionally use to bite divers. But this behavior can be explained by the fact that, to a short-sighted moray, human fingers can resemble a favorite food, octopus tentacles. The morays' real danger to humans can be much more serious. Although not considered delicious, morays are eaten in many parts of the

STRANGE SPROUT
Some eels live embedded in sandy burrows, usually where a current flows carrying the plankton on which they feed. With tails firmly anchored, they can retreat if threatened.

FEEDING FRENZY

Piranhas have a reputation for travelling in schools and eating any creature in their path, but many species eat aquatic plants, especially seeds. Nevertheless, certain species can be dangerous to humans, livestock, or other fishes. For example, the common red-bellied piranhas of the Amazon basin can reduce a bleeding animal to a skeleton in just minutes. Their short, strong jaws and sharp, interlocking teeth are ideal for stripping flesh from bone in clean bites.

world. On rare occasions, the chemicals in their flesh can cause ciguatera—tropical fish poisoning—which can be fatal.

Freshwater eels are also widely distributed. They have an amazing ability to detect fresh water through their sense of smell. Some actually slither over land for short distances to reach landlocked pools. These species are also unique among eels in that they practice reverse migration: They spend most of their adult life in lakes and rivers, but return to the sea to spawn, after which they die. To complete their life cycle they must travel immense distances. European freshwater eels swim more than 3,000 miles (5,000 km) across the North Atlantic Ocean to their spawning grounds in the Sargasso Sea.

Noisy Neighbors

Although fishes don't have external ears, some species have excellent hearing. The first few vertebrae of carp, for example, have over time become modified into a series of levers called the Weberian mechanism. This mechanism transmits sound waves, picked up by the swim bladder, to the fish's inner ear.

Fishes that can hear use sound to locate prey, to keep track of predators, and to communicate within their own species. Some fishes do this to great effect. Toadfishes have an impressive repertoire of frog-like croaks, grunts, and growls, plus a sound similar to that of a steam whistle. Particularly during courtship, the sounds may be so loud that people living nearby may find it

intolerable! On the east coast of North America, for example, people living on houseboats have been kept awake by oyster toadfishes bellowing for mates.

The flannel-mouthed characins of South America make a noise like a motorcycle to communicate with each other as they travel up streams to spawn. But a less well-known method of communication is also practiced by some species of carp. These fishes have a chemical in their skin which is released into the water if an individual is injured. As soon as this chemical is detected by other carp, they flee. This early warning system allows the others to escape if one fish is taken by a predator.

KOI POLLOI
The carp family forms about 30 percent of all living fish species. One of the hardiest of all fishes, the common freshwater carp, or koi, has been kept for centuries for food, display, and as a pet.

AQUATIC ACROBATICS
The striped headstander hides itself by swimming in a slanted position among aquatic vegetation. This colorful South American is also popular in aquariums.

HOOK AND SINKER
Sockeye salmon are usually sleek, silvery, trout-shaped fishes. Just before breeding, the male develops a humped back, bright coloring, and large hooked jaws with which to fight other males.

Doom in the Gloom

Stomiiforms—dragonfishes and their relatives—make up a significant part of the ocean's fishes. They are found in open waters of all temperate and subtropical areas, with some species even braving the cold subarctic and Antarctic waters.

Members of this order are known as scaly dragonfishes, black dragonfishes, snaggletooths, loosejaws, viperfishes, bristlemouths, and hatchetfishes. These names not only show their diversity, but also suggest that some are impressive predators! Indeed, many stomiids have extremely large and elaborately sculptured teeth—the lower jaw teeth of the deepsea viperfish often extend up over its head.

Regardless of their shape or size, all but one species of stomiiform have light organs with which to lure their prey and to communicate with each other. These organs range from tiny luminous dots scattered over the skin to elaborate arrangements of lenses, luminous material, and reflectors. The light produced can be either a steady glow or intense flashes, and the color varies from white and pale yellow to bright red and violet.

The combination of light organs and dark skin pigments makes some of these fishes virtually invisible to predators. The back of a marine hatchetfish, for example, is dark to match the dark water below it, so a predator above it would only see the dark of the ocean depths. But the light on the hatchetfish's stomach, seen by a predator below, would merge with any light coming from the sky.

Hanger-On

The use of light for luring prey is also practiced by female deepsea anglerfishes. They have a bulbous bait, called an esca, on their head. The esca contains luminous bacteria, and in many species it also features silvery light-guiding mirrors and tubes. The length of the esca varies—in some species it can be more than three times the length of the fish.

The comparatively small males, on the other hand, have no baits. Unlike the huge, gaping mouths of females, males have feeble, toothless jaws. They do not feed, instead following

GLOW WORM
Nearly all stomiids have a barbel hanging from their lower jaw. Its movement is controlled by muscles behind the jaw bones. This black dragonfish's barbel has a luminous tip.

PRETTY DISGUSTING
The brilliant coloration of the mandarin fish may serve as a warning to predators, because when attacked it gives off a stinky, foul-tasting mucus.

ZAPPY CAT
Using modified muscle tissue under its belly and on its sides, the electric catfish is able to send out and receive electrical impulses. It does this for self-defense and navigation.

scent trails to locate females. Males of a few families permanently attach themselves to females by means of hooks on their snout and chin, and live on their mates as parasites.

Cats on Crutches

The catfishes may be one of the most recognized groups in the world. This can be attributed to their widespread distribution, mostly in fresh water but also in estuaries and other coastal marine environments. They are also used for food in many parts of the world.

More than 2,200 species of catfish are known at present, but new species are being discovered at such a rate that their number may well exceed 3,000. They range in size from a

GILLED LIZARD
The slender profile of the 34 species of lizardfish gives them a reptilian appearance, but they are named for the way they sit on the seabed with their heads raised like lizards, waiting for prey.

South American species just $\frac{1}{2}$ inch (12 mm) long to the 16-foot (5-m) European wels. Nearly as large as the wels is the royal catfish of Thailand, which can weigh more than 440 pounds (200 kg).

A typical catfish has thread-like barbels around its mouth and retractable thorny spines at the front edge of the pectoral and dorsal fins. These spines sometimes contain venom, providing the catfish with a formidable weapon against predators. But in some species these spines have a more unusual purpose.

In tropical parts of the world, several catfishes are found in places that undergo dramatic seasonal changes in rainfall, with marked dry seasons. During these dry periods, the river channels and lakes dry up and become crowded with trapped fishes. Some catfishes that live in these

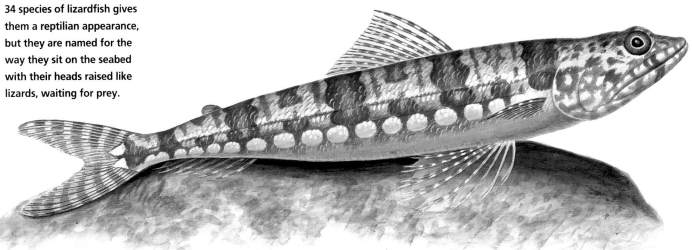

regions have extra air-breathing structures that allow them to take oxygen directly from the atmosphere until it rains again. They also use the sturdy spines on their pectoral fins like crutches to "walk" out of water.

The most famous of these air-breathing catfishes are the so-called walking catfishes of the Afro-Asian family Clariidae. Introduced into Florida fishponds by the aquarium fish industry, the fishes left their overcrowded ponds and walked to the natural waterways of southern Florida, where they have since succeeded in establishing many thriving colonies.

Sea Monsters Exposed!

With common names as fanciful as ribbonfishes, inkfishes, oarfishes, and tube-eyes, the members of the order Lampridiformes are a curious collection. Perhaps the most colorful of all ocean fishes, lampridiforms have fiery crimson fins and a body covered with brilliant white, brown, or red spots or bands. Their eggs, which incubate for up to three weeks on the sea surface, also have radiant hues, usually in shades of amber, pink, or red. The colors may help to shield the embryos from the harmful rays of the tropical sun.

Lampridiforms vary widely in shape, from the bulky, deep-bodied opah to the longest of all bony fishes, the oarfish. The maximum recorded length of an oarfish is 56 feet (17 m). These long fishes have an extremely

modified or reduced caudal fin, and swim slowly by making continuous, snakelike movements with their long dorsal fin. Sightings of oarfishes lolling in the surface waters of the open ocean are probably the basis of the scary accounts of sea monsters by early sailors.

Unlike other fishes, the upper jaws of lampridiforms are not connected to their cheekbones, allowing the fish's mouth to expand and the jaws to be carried far forward when feeding. This unusual advantage enables them to gulp large quantities of fishes and invertebrates such as krill and squid. In one species, the jaw can be elongated to as much as 40 times its usual length!

Cancers and Clones

Killifishes are also diverse in form and structure. Although their natural habitats are tropical and temperate

BIG BROTHER
The opah lives in all the world's oceans. A popular food fish, it can weigh up to 600 pounds (275 kg). Apart from its fin color, it does not look very much like its relative, the ribbonfish.

BY ROYAL COMMAND
In parts of its range the ribbonfish is known as king-of-the-salmon, from a Native American legend which tells that these fishes lead Pacific salmon back to their home rivers to spawn.

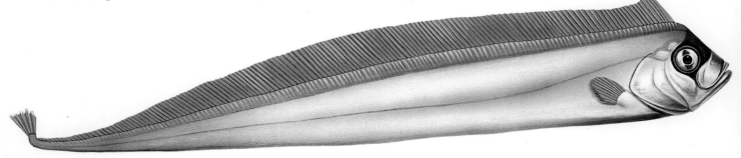

SEEING DOUBLE
The adaptation of the four-eyed killifish allows it to see above and below the surface at the same time. It can watch for enemies as it looks for food.

fresh and brackish waters, they are now the most widely used fishes in laboratory studies of genetics. For example, by studying the occurrence of melanomas (skin tumors) in a killifish species called the platyfish, scientists have learnt that some cancers may be inherited.

Killifishes are also notable for their varied methods of reproduction. Some species, such as guppies, not only give birth to live young but are able to carry two or more broods, each in a different stage of development, at the same time.

One fascinating species is the Amazon molly. Its common name comes not from its habitat (it lives in North America) but because it occurs naturally as all-female populations, suggesting the life of the legendary female Amazon warriors. Although the females mate with different male species to reproduce, the sperm of the males only provides a stimulus

CAUGHT JESTER
Species such as this clown killifish of west Africa are popular fishes in hobby aquariums. While most killifishes lay eggs, guppies, mollies, and swordtails give birth to live young.

for the egg's development and does not contribute genetic material. The eggs produce all-female clones, each daughter being a genetically identical copy of her mother.

The annual killifishes of tropical South America and Africa are also named for their reproductive method. The adults spawn at the end of the rainy season, as their habitat is drying out, leaving fertilized eggs in the mud. The adults then die and the eggs enter a resting stage until the rains return. The rain stimulates the eggs to develop and hatch.

FLY OR DIE

Flyingfishes, which live close to the surface of tropical seas, are thought to be related to killifishes. To escape predators, they can leave the water and glide on their winglike pectoral fins, building up speed by sweeping their caudal fin rapidly from side to side. Flyingfishes can travel over 650 feet (200 m) from their starting point, reaching speeds of more than 37 mph (60 kmph)!

PIED PIPER
Like seahorses, pipefishes such as this banded pipefish swim not by flexing their body, but by rapidly fanning their fins. This restricts their speed, but allows them to make precise movements.

Slurp and Burp

Pipefishes, seahorses, seamoths, cornetfishes, and trumpetfishes belong to the order Syngnathiformes. Most members of this diverse and often bizarre-looking order share the instantly recognizable characteristics of a long snout and a body encased in thick "armor."

Pipefishes and their close cousins, the seahorses, use their snout and other modifications in bone structure to suck in water containing small invertebrate prey. Both are also notable for the fact that it is the male who incubates the eggs. But seahorses differ from pipefishes in that they have a prehensile (gripping) tail.

The five species of seamoths are bottom-dwellers found in shallow, tropical, coastal waters. While their body is also covered with bony armor, they are named for their enlarged, winglike pectoral fins, which they use to "walk" across the seabed. Most seamoths also have a shorter snout with a tubelike mouth, which they use to slurp worms and other small creatures from their burrows.

The larger fishes in this order, such as trumpetfishes and the 6½-foot (2-m) long cornetfishes, are most often found in tropical and subtropical waters. Both are active predators of other fishes. Cornetfishes lurk in open areas, such as sand flats, where they attack passing schools of small fishes. Their very long tail—which is often as long as their body—is lined with sensory pores that may be used to detect prey over long distances.

Stickler for Tradition

Less exotic, but just as fascinating in behavior, is the stickleback of the order Gasterosteiformes. Named for

NO THANKSGIVING
The turkeyfish is related to the stonefish. While stonefishes only cause harm if stepped on by mistake, some turkeyfishes are aggressive and have been known to threaten humans in the water.

ROCK SHOCKER
The purple stonefish escapes attention by sitting amongst similar-colored rocks on the seabed and staying very still. The venom in its spines can kill humans.

FLASH OF INSPIRATION
The lights under the eyes of flashlight fishes contain luminous bacteria. The fishes can turn the lights on and off by covering them with a screen of dark tissue.

the strong spines in their dorsal fins, these little fishes are familiar to anyone in the Northern Hemisphere who has explored ponds, streams, and marshes. Male sticklebacks are unusual for their habit of building a nest of vegetation using secretions from their kidneys. They then attract females to their nest. If the nests meet with the females' approval, they lay their eggs for the males to guard.

Yikes! Spikes!

The many members of the order Scorpaeniformes share a unique feature: They all have a bony strut across the cheek that connects bones under the eye with the front of the gill cover. In many species, this strut is the

TRUMP CARD
Some long, thin trumpetfishes hide behind coral or larger fishes in order to ambush prey. This spiny-back trumpetfish lies still, looking like a drifting stick. But if small fishes stray too close it can move surprisingly quickly.

site of the head spines that may protect the fishes' eyes.

Most of the 1,200 or so species of scorpaeniforms have spiny heads, but they vary enormously in body shape. The coral crouchers of the tropical Indo-Pacific are oval, flat, and have soft, velvety skin. The pigfishes of cool southern and subantarctic seas have a projecting snout with a small mouth, while the spiny or ghost flatheads of Japan and Australia have a head so flattened that it looks as if it has been run over by a steamroller!

The majority of scorpionfishes are found living at the bottom in shallow water, although the idiotfishes live in depths of approximately 7,000 feet (2,200 m). They are predators of other fishes and crustaceans. Some species can defend themselves by

NIGHT LIGHT
Active at night, the Australian pineapplefish uses the light-producing organs on its lower jaws to find prey. These look orange during the day, but glow blue-green at night.

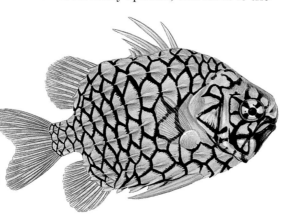

SKILLED KILLER
Found in warm seas around the world, dolphinfishes are thought to be closely related to remoras. Fast-swimming predators, they can catch speedy flyingfishes as they re-enter the sea.

using venom from glands leading to their fin spines. The stonefishes of the Indo-Pacific region are notorious for this feature. Their skin color can match the coral-covered rocks on the seabed, and to ambush prey they will often hide in sand or mud, leaving only the top of their head and their spines exposed. The fishes are in fact so difficult to see that most people only become aware of their presence when they step on them.

Stonefishes cannot deliberately inject poison; it is forced into the wound when the victim presses down on the fish's spine. At best, a "sting" is extremely painful—at worst it can kill. But although stonefishes are the most poisonous of all fishes, placing the affected limb in hot water renders the venom powerless.

Another poisonous member of the order, the turkeyfishes (also known as lionfishes or firefishes), do not hide but swim in open water. They rely on their brilliantly colored pectoral fins, which they spread out like wings, to make themselves look large and frightening. This tactic must work well, because they are rarely found in the stomach contents of other fishes—apart from other turkeyfishes, which have a lower response to venom from their own species.

Water Bugs

Probably the best known of all the reef fishes, the 115 or so species of butterflyfishes are found throughout tropical, subtropical, and temperate marine waters. These fishes are fairly small, ranging from 3½ inches to

THERE'S A SUCKER BORN EVERY MINUTE

The word *remora* is Latin for "hindrance," for it was once thought that these fishes had the power to slow ships. While remoras do attach themselves to large aquatic objects, they prefer sharks, rays, sea turtles, and whales to ships. Their dorsal fin is modified into a flat sucking disk. Ridges on this disk operate like slats in a venetian blind to create a vacuum, which the remoras use to attach themselves for free rides and access to scraps from their host's meals. They also clean skin parasites from their host.

12 inches (9 cm to 30 cm), but their bright and varied color patterns have long inspired artists and designers. Many species confuse predators by having a false eye spot near the tail. Their real eyes are often concealed by a dark bar or another marking.

Butterflyfishes have a disk-shaped body, but their jaws vary widely in size and shape, depending on what they eat. Some, such as the ornate butterflyfish, have short jaws used in nipping off live coral polyps. Others, such as the long-nosed butterflyfish, have elongated jaws, which they use like delicate forceps to pluck small invertebrates from among sea urchin spines and coral crevices.

Blue Fins, White Blood

Butterflyfishes belong to Perciformes, an order containing more species than any other group of fishes. The name "perciform," which means perch-like, is quite misleading because many of the 9,500 or so species of this diverse group look nothing like small, spiny-finned perches. They range from tiny gobies that mature at less than $\frac{1}{2}$ inch (1 cm), to mighty ocean-going tunas and billfishes that grow more than 13 feet (4 m) long.

The vast majority of coral reef fish species belong to this order, including cardinalfishes, angelfishes, and dottybacks. Perciforms such as

BUBBLE WRAP
Gouramies are freshwater perciforms from Africa and Southeast Asia. The males of some species brood their eggs in their mouth, while others, such as this splendid licorice gourami, build floating bubble nests.

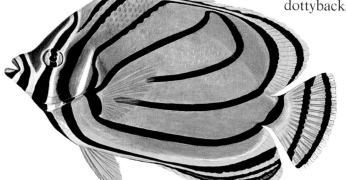

LET'S GET MEYER-RIED
Although pair-bonding is rare among fishes, butterflyfishes such as this Meyer's butterflyfish form exclusive partnerships which may last for several years.

SEND IN THE CLOWNS
Anemonefishes, or clownfishes, are a species of damselfish. Their bright colors make them popular with aquarium keepers.

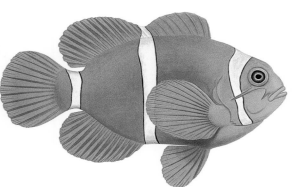

HEIR TO THE THRONE
This purplequeen is a species of fairy basslet. These fishes start life as females but can change sex. When a male dies, the dominant female in the group becomes the male and takes over his role.

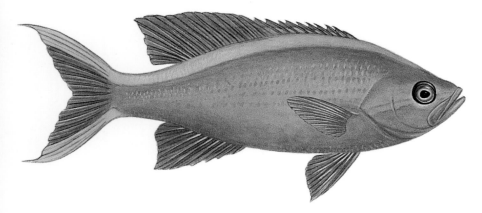

BAD TASTE
The rainbow cale is related to wrasses. It is one of the few fishes able to stomach the widespread but foul-tasting kelps of the colder reef waters of the Southern Hemisphere.

clocked at speeds of more than 68 mph (110 kmph) over short distances. Tagging programs have also revealed the speed and stamina of tunas. One tagged and recaptured bluefin tuna was found to have swum at least 4,770 miles (7,700 km) across the Atlantic Ocean in just 119 days.

Perciforms are found in almost every kind of aquatic habitat, from high-mountain freshwater streams to the deep ocean, and from the tropics to the Antarctic. Species in Antarctic waters range from 4-inch (10-cm) bottom-dwelling species which feed on invertebrates to $6\frac{1}{2}$-foot (2-m) predators that live in the open ocean. Some can even survive temperatures close to the freezing point of sea water (28.6°F, or −1.9°C). This is because of a substance in their blood called glycopeptide, which acts as a kind of "antifreeze." Strangely enough, crocodile icefishes lack red blood cells. Their blood is white!

Farms and Fandangos

Damselfishes are also perciforms. Most live close to the seabed and guard well-defined territories. If a diver dares to enter their domain they unleash an attack accompanied by biting and loud grunting noises.

Experiments have shown that in keeping away rivals and predators from their patch, the fishes not

snappers, bass, cod, tuna, mackerel, mullet, barracuda, and, of course, perch are all important food fishes.

Other perciforms, such as swordfishes, sailfishes, and marlins, are popular game for sports fishing. These species are literally swimming machines, with every aspect of their external body structure designed for maximum efficiency in the water. Not only do they have a streamlined body shape, but they also have grooves and depressions into which various fins can be tucked to reduce drag. No other fish is known to swim faster than the sailfish, which has been

only protect their eggs but are able to encourage the growth of a thick "garden" of algae. While algae outside their territory is cropped to a stubble by parrotfishes and surgeonfishes, inside it the damselfishes are able to enjoy their own private food supply.

Several days before spawning, male damselfishes begin preparing nest sites. They choose a rocky surface and use their mouth to pick it clean of algae and any invertebrates, such as starfishes, which may be attached. One large damselfish, the garibaldi, cultures a patch of red algae for a nest by selectively weeding out other kinds.

In between bouts of nest-building, male damselfishes display their courtship dance to potential mates. As complicated as any ballet, the dance includes chasing, nipping, hovering, swimming bursts, and a rapid up-and-down movement, as if the fishes were riding a rollercoaster.

Sea Chameleons

Groupers are among the largest of reef fishes. The giant grouper of inshore warm temperate waters can grow to at least 8 feet (2.5 m) and weigh more than 660 pounds (300 kg). Groupers are also among the most valuable food fishes, and their main predators are not other fishes, but humans. They are readily caught by hook and line, and since many of the species are readily

approached underwater, they are easy targets for spearfishers.

Groupers feed primarily on fishes and crustaceans. Those that eat fishes are recognizable by their very large canine teeth. Since groupers are at or near the upper end of food chains, there are usually only a few at any one place. Therefore, any one reef may have only one or two very large groupers in residence. These species are among the first fishes to have their populations drastically reduced as a result of overfishing. Because large groupers are believed to be very old, perhaps more than 50 years, it takes a long time for them to be replaced.

There is another important reason why groupers are so vulnerable to

overfishing. Like parrotfishes, they start out life as females but switch sex when they are much older. If they are all caught before they become males, there will be very few males, with a drastic effect on the population.

Groupers also have the unusual—and useful—ability to change their color. If one moves from a reef to open sand, for example, its skin will become paler. Color change is also used by groupers to communicate with others of their own species, and the colors of many become more intense during courtship, spawning, and aggressive behavior. Indeed, a fish's color could be considered a good indicator of its mood. Some groupers turn a different shade when they are relaxed and enjoying the attentions of a cleaner shrimp or fish.

Trigs of the Trade

Triggerfishes are named for the long, strong first spine on their dorsal fin that can be locked into an upright position by the action of the much shorter spine behind it—like a trigger. They use this to wedge themselves securely into a crevice or hole when under attack.

FIRE ALARM
Being small, gobies are often eaten by larger fishes, sea snakes, and birds. The stunning fire-goby is always found near its burrow, into which it darts when threatened.

BASKING BEHEMOTH
The ocean sunfish, or mola mola, can weigh more than 4,410 pounds (2 tonnes). It is often sighted on the surface, nibbling at jellyfishes or lying quietly on its side, perhaps basking in the sun.

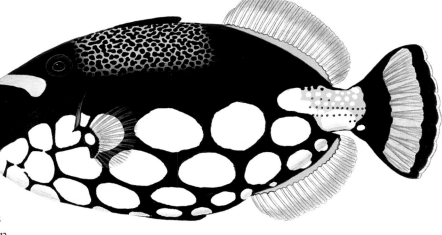

A predator would have difficulty dislodging such a meal, while the triggerfishes' thick or prickly scales also protect them from bites while in their refuge.

Triggerfishes use their massive teeth to feed on mollusks, starfishes, sea cucumbers, and crustaceans. Several species can even defeat the spiny defenses of the sea urchin by blowing a stream of water at it. This tricky maneuver overturns the urchin, exposing its vulnerable underside.

Air Bags and Armor

Triggerfishes belong to the order Tetraodontiformes. This order also features weird and wonderful species such as the 10-foot (3-m) long ocean sunfish, which appears to have been cut in half; porcupinefishes, which can resemble spiky golfballs; and cowfishes, which have a long horn above each eye.

Boxfishes are also tetraodontiforms. Their thick scale plates, which encase most of their body, are as complete as those of the armored fishes of the Paleozoic Era, 245 million years ago. This "box" keeps adult boxfishes relatively safe from all but the largest predators. However, young boxfishes live in the open seas and are easy prey for billfishes and tunas. At least some are able to protect themselves by secreting a poisonous substance from their skin into the surrounding water.

Pufferfishes also use this defensive mechanism, but they are best known for their habit of puffing up their body when under threat. The flesh of many species is highly poisonous and is responsible for the death of a number of people each year. The problem is that toxic species such as *Takifugu* look similar to harmless, edible fishes; it takes an expert chef to know the difference! The explorer Captain James Cook almost died on the second of his three voyages of exploration after just a small taste of a pufferfish.

Many pufferfishes spawn in large groups. Huge schools of some species of *Takifugu* arrive at the Japanese coast from May to July. After each full and new moon, thousands of fishes ride the rising tides, then rush up on to pebbly beaches to spawn.

TRIGGER-HAPPY
Triggerfishes are common in shallow tropical areas near coral reefs. Unlike filefishes, which may live in pairs, they are generally solitary. This clown triggerfish is a large and aggressive species.

WHIPPERSNIPPER

Blennies are mostly small fishes found in warm, shallow waters. They may look cute, but some are also crafty! Saber-toothed blennies, for example, copy the colors of the cleaner wrasse. They dart out of their holes and snip skin, mucus, or scales off passing fishes with their large lower canine teeth. The victim, fooled into thinking it is going to be cleaned, is surprised to receive a painful bite instead.

Birds

Birds have been a source of envy and inspiration for humans since the Stone Age. Today there are about 9,300 species, and their diverse sizes, striking colors, and beautiful voices continue to delight us. Birds range from the bee hummingbird, which could fit inside a matchbox, to the ostrich, which weighs over 300 pounds (136 kg). But whether a soaring eagle, zooming hummingbird, or diving penguin, birds share one feature that makes them different from other animals. All birds have feathers.

Although birds must return to land to rear their young and to rest, their feathers and the flying ability of most mean they can fish in the farthest seas and find food amidst the cliffs and cacti of the driest deserts. No other living creatures can travel so far and so fast under their own power. These features, plus the fact that they are warm-blooded, have enabled birds to colonize most of the Earth. Step outside almost anywhere and, within minutes, you will find a feathered friend.

Classifying Birds

AMONG THE BIRDS there are remarkable variations in weight and size. They also come in a kaleidoscope of colors and patterns. But despite their external diversity, birds vary far less in basic body structure and function than most other groups of animals. These similarities are due mainly to the adaptations associated with flight.

Flying Machines

Birds are the only living creatures that have feathers. They are also vertebrates, but their skeleton is highly modified to support powered flight. For example, the bones of the hand have fused to form a single "finger," which supports the main flight feathers. In most birds, the collarbones have also fused into a rigid brace for the wings: the U-shaped furcula, or "wishbone."

Other typical features are the hooklike extensions on each rib, and a keel-like structure on the sternum, or breastbone, which serves to anchor the enormous muscles used to flap the wings. In most birds, these muscles make up about one-third of their total weight. They are used to "row" the bird through the air. First they push the wings down and back, then they lift the wings up for another stroke.

Soft Scales

Of course, a bird could not fly without feathers. Feathers are modified scales and are made almost entirely of keratin, the same substance as scales (and human hair and fingernails). Birds have many different kinds of feathers, but most of them are either contour feathers or flight feathers. Contour feathers are small, curved, fluffy feathers that cover the body and keep the bird warm. The flight feathers on the wings are aerodynamically shaped, being much longer, stiffer, smoother, and less curved than contour feathers. Birds also have a soft underlayer of down feathers, for extra insulation.

shaft
barb
barbule

LIGHTWEIGHT LATTICE
Structures called barbs branch out on each side of the shaft of a flight feather. Along the sides of each barb are hooked barbules, which lock onto the barbules of the neighboring barb.

THE LIGHT FANTASTIC

Birds' feathers come in almost every color of the rainbow. Some colors are the result of pigments such as melanin, the pigment that colors human hair, skin, and eyes. But other colors are created by a trick of the light. The feathers are colorless, but their barbs and barbules have structures that reflect or scatter certain colors in the light spectrum. This is why iridescent feathers change color according to the angle at which you see them.

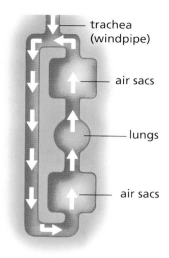

trachea (windpipe)

air sacs

lungs

air sacs

UNITED AIRWAYS

Air flows through a bird's body, rather than in and out. Because a bird extracts oxygen while inhaling and exhaling, it can fly even at high altitudes, where there is less oxygen in the air.

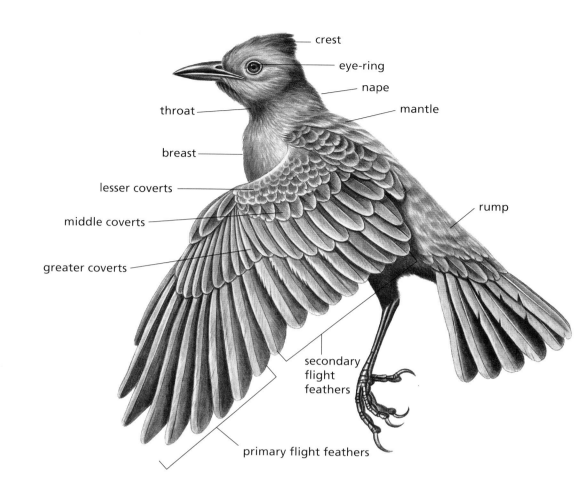

crest

eye-ring

nape

mantle

throat

breast

lesser coverts

middle coverts

greater coverts

rump

secondary flight feathers

primary flight feathers

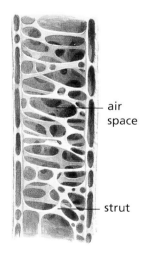

air space

strut

BUBBLE BONES

Many of the larger bones in a bird's skeleton are thin-walled and hollow. They are reinforced with struts. This design makes the bones light but strong.

A bird's feathers, or plumage, also streamline the body to reduce friction during flight, or when moving on the ground or through water. Their colors and patterns also help the bird to recognize others of its own species, find a mate, or provide camouflage. Small species such as hummingbirds have about 1,000 feathers, whereas a big swan has more than 20 times as many. Plumage makes up a large proportion of a bird's total body weight: A typical songbird's feathers are about one-third its body weight.

Common Senses

Some birds have a poor sense of smell, but their hearing is rather like that of humans. Some species have amazing abilities: A barn owl can catch a mouse in total darkness, guided only by the tiny sounds made by its prey as it breathes and moves.

FEATHER FEATURES

The primary flight feathers pull the bird forward, and the rest of the wing generates the lift. The wings change shape as they flap: They are broad and extended on the downstroke, but tucked in tight on the upstroke.

Since almost all birds have extremely well-developed eyes, their vision is thought to be very important to them. A unique feature of birds' eyes is the pecten, a structure that emerges from the retina. It may play a role in improving the supply of oxygen and nutrients to the light-sensitive cells of the retina.

A bird's eyesight is like a human's, although again there are exceptions. The eye of a large eagle, for example, is about the same size as a human eye, but can see perhaps three times better!

Birds through the Ages

THE EXACT ORIGIN OF BIRDS IS UNCERTAIN, but it is believed they evolved from reptiles. One theory links birds to theropods, a subgroup of dinosaurs common about 200 million years ago. The theropods' scales became feathers, enabling them to escape predators on land, or, like flying lizards, glide from tree to tree.

Dinosaur Design?

Birds today still show signs of their reptile heritage—they have scales on their legs and feet, and they lay eggs with shells. But our understanding of how birds came to be is still developing. This is because there are relatively few bird fossils. Since many bird bones are hollow, they are easily broken into fragments. Also,

MARCHING ORDERS
This coelurosaur was a theropod. A hollow-boned, fast-moving predator, it hunted insects, reptiles, and small mammals on foot, like the modern-day secretary bird of Africa.

few landbirds die where their remains can be buried in waterlaid sediments, the best source of fossils. It also seems likely that many ancient birds, like birds today, were eaten by carnivores.

Feathered Fossil

Archaeopteryx, the earliest known bird, lived about 150 million years ago. The first *Archaeopteryx* fossil was discovered in Germany in 1861. *Archaeopteryx* is the most important evidence of the link between birds and dinosaurs because of its furcula. This "wishbone" is found both in birds and in some theropods—a group of two-legged dinosaurs that included *Tyrannosaurus rex*. In birds, the bone plays a vital role in flight. In the dinosaurs it probably evolved as a support for their short forelegs, which they used for catching prey.

Archaeopteryx was certainly a bird, since its fossil shows that it also had feathers. But it had reptilian characteristics as well, including teeth in its beak and claws on its wings. Scientists are unsure whether it lived in trees or on the ground, and how well it could fly.

Air Force

Although only slightly younger than *Archaeopteryx*, birds of the Cretaceous Period (145 to 65 million years ago) were much more like birds today. Most were strong fliers. At the same time, their skeletons still looked like those of dinosaurs. Two fossils discovered near Las Hoyas, Spain, had forelegs and shoulder bones like those found in modern birds, but a pelvis and hindlegs similar to those of theropods and *Archaeopteryx*.

TERROR-SAUR
Pterosaurs, such as this *Pteranodon*, lived at the same time as the dinosaurs. They were flying reptiles, not birds, and glided on wings of skin instead of feathers.

DIVE BOMBER
Hesperornis lived in the late Cretaceous Period. This fish-eating bird may be the ancestor of grebes. It could not fly and, like *Archaeopteryx*, it had teeth.

Hesperornis and *Ichthyornis* lived in North America about 70 million years ago, although *Hesperornis*-like fossils have also been found in England and South America. Like their dinosaur ancestors, both had teeth, but they had also developed adaptations for their habitats. Whereas the diving bird *Hesperornis* had heavy bones, tiny wings, and powerful feet designed for swimming, *Ichthyornis* was a strong flier a little like modern-day gulls—although it is not related to them.

Flock Shockers

Most orders and many families of living birds had their origins during the Cretaceous Period. By the Eocene Period (57 to 37 million years ago), birds such as ducks, geese, chickens, and quails were distributed worldwide. Some of these early species were flightless and measured about 7 feet (2.1 m) tall. Some albatross-like gliders had 20-foot (6-m) wingspans—larger than that of any albatross today. They skimmed the ocean, using the bony projections in their jaws to snag prey.

By 45 million years ago, penguins were already specialized for "flying" through the water. Flamingos, storks, and ibises, plus owls and other birds of prey, were also present by this time.

The most spectacular vulture-like birds were the teratorns ("wonder birds"). They lived from 25 to 5 million years ago in South America and from 2 million to 10,000 years ago in North America. One kind of teratorn had a wingspan of 24½ feet (7.5 m) and weighed 176 pounds (80 kg). It was the largest flying bird ever known!

Inner Space

About 11,500 species emerged in the Pleistocene Period, 2 million to 10,000 years ago. Most of these birds are still

BRAIN CASE

In barn owls, the ears are different sizes and shapes. By enhancing the "stereo" effect of sound signals, they enable the bird to pinpoint its prey.

FINE TUNING

Below is an image as it may been seen by most animals, then how an eagle would see it. Eagles' retinas are densely packed with sensory cells, so they are able to see things in greater definition.

around today. Because, like mammals, they can maintain their internal body temperature, birds have come to occupy almost all habitats, from swamps to rain forests, from ice flows to deserts, and even the ocean.

Birds have adapted to their habitats both with internal body processes and external body forms. Birds that live in hot climates, for example, conserve water that would otherwise be used to keep cool by letting their temperature rise several degrees above normal during the hottest hours. This means that they don't gain as much heat because of the narrow difference between their body temperature and the air temperature. Birds of cold climates, such as the tundra-dwelling ptarmigans, reduce heat loss by having very short, feathered legs and feet.

To survive, birds have specialized to such an extent that not only do they favor a particular habitat but also a specific slot, or "ecological niche," within that habitat. This niche is often associated with the means of gathering food. One species might forage for insects on the ground, another in tree bark, and yet another might snap up prey while flying. These birds occupy

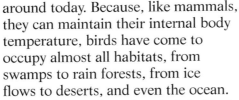

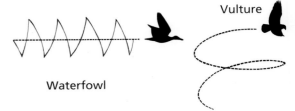

Vulture

Waterfowl

FLIGHT PATTERNS

Waterfowl fly fast in a line, flapping at a steady rate to maintain speed. Vultures use rising air currents to propel them in an upward spiral. Woodpeckers flap to gain speed, then glide to save energy.

the same habitat and share the same diet—insects—but they have different tools and techniques to get their food. These differences define each bird's niche within its habitat.

Mission Control

Birds' body parts have been adapted to suit their feeding behavior and the niches they occupy. One of the most obvious characteristics is the size and shape of the bill. The feet, too, are an important indication of a bird's lifestyle: The great talons of eagles are for gripping large prey, while the webbed feet of ducks are for paddling.

GLOW IN THE DARK

Owls such as this eagle owl combine sensitive night vision with forward-facing eyes. This gives them wide binocular vision, enabling them to accurately judge depth and distance.

Woodpecker

Tree-creeping birds have long toes and claws to keep a firm grip on branches. Birds that spend most of their life in the air, such as swallows and swifts, have very small feet.

A bird's wings and tail are also designed to suit its needs. A long, narrow wing is generally more efficient than a short, blunt wing, so birds that spend time in open skies, such as albatrosses, have long, narrow wings that provide maximum efficiency.

But large birds of prey ride thermals all day to conserve energy. Since they have little need to flap their wings, their wings tend to be long and broad, providing maximum lift.

But flapping long wings is hard work. Many birds that live on the ground, such as quail, need flight for little more than escape from predators. Therefore the best design for them is a short, blunt wing that enables them to build speed very quickly over a short distance, without using a lot of energy. A hummingbird also has small wings, but they are stiff and narrow, like the rotors of a helicopter. These give the control they need to hover above the flowers that provide their favorite food, nectar.

A bird's tail is used like a rudder for steering. It, too, has a bearing on flight performance. A short tail is more aerodynamically efficient, but a long tail can improve maneuverability. For this reason, most flycatching birds have long tails. Some hawks that hunt in cluttered woodlands have broad wings as well as a long tail. These features give them the speed and control to catch their prey by surprise.

flight muscle

WING SPRING
A bird flies by keeping a constant flow of air over the wings' surface. It does this by soaring on the wind, or by muscle power. Muscles on the breast flap the wings to maintain airflow.

BILLS OF FARE

Birds' bills demonstrate adaptations to their feeding behavior and environment. Indeed, bill shape often shows what and how a bird eats more clearly than any other feature.

KERNEL CRACKER
Finches such as this cardinal have thick, cone-shaped bills for crushing the husks of seeds and grains. They also eat fruits, and occasionally insects.

KNIFE AND FORK
Birds of prey such as this Swainson's hawk have hooked bills that are ideal for tearing fur, skin, and chunks of flesh.

DRINKING STRAW
Insects are a vital source of protein for a hummingbird, but it eats mostly nectar. Its long bill enables it to probe deep into the trumpet-shaped flowers of its habitat and drain them of their sweet nectar.

SHRIMP PICK
If you guess from its bill shape that whatever the avocet feeds on, it must be very small and agile, you would be right—it eats tiny shrimps living in shallow water.

Bird Behavior

THE ELABORATE BEHAVIOR of birds is governed primarily by their senses of vision and hearing. These play an important role in activities including attracting mates, setting up territories, and finding food. The power of flight also influences bird behavior.

Dressed to Impress

Like humans, birds respond strongly to visual signals. Therefore much of their communication involves showing off their plumage. These displays can convey a range of messages, including greetings, threats, and warnings. For example, when dark-eyed juncos fly up, they flash their white outer tail feathers. This says "follow me" to other birds in the flock.

But some of the most elaborate plumage displays are designed to attract mates, and in the spring breeding season many birds grow beautifully colored and patterned feathers. Since males generally take the initiative, they usually have more colorful plumage and perform most of the display routines. One extravagant display is that of the peacock, which fans his train of shimmering feathers and shakes them so that they rattle.

The more impressive a male's feathers, the more likely he'll attract the females' attention. Since it takes a lot of energy to grow and maintain such plumage—and to escape the predators it attracts—mature males with flashy feathers have proven their ability to survive. Females may choose to mate with a male with the fanciest feathers because their chicks will inherit his superior genetic qualities.

IN THE SPOTLIGHT
Male bowerbirds build intricate structures as part of their courtship ritual. The satin bowerbird decorates his "stage" with bright blue objects and dances with one of them to attract a mate.

CUSTOM PACK
Eggs laid in open nests on or near the ground are usually camouflaged to blend with the surroundings. Eggs laid in hollows or burrows, out of sight from predators, are mostly white or near-white.

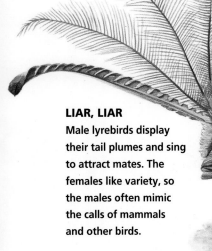

LIAR, LIAR
Male lyrebirds display their tail plumes and sing to attract mates. The females like variety, so the males often mimic the calls of mammals and other birds.

Dinner Dance

In some 90 percent of bird species, a male and female will pair off for the entire breeding season, if not for life. Both male and female usually help to feed and care for their chicks. In these species, the courtship rituals are quite different. Apart from plumage displays, some birds exchange "gifts." A male tern's gift of a fish, for example, shows the female how well he will be able to feed the chicks. Birds of prey also present food and nesting materials to females in midair to show off their hunting and flying abilities. This way the females can judge the males, then take their pick.

Courtship isn't always a one-sided affair. In many species, both males and females perform displays, either to attract their mate, or to cement their bond. Western grebes run across the water together in a display called "rushing." They also fill their bill with weeds and perform a "weed dance." Species such as albatrosses court each other with synchronized flying, while cranes perform dances of graceful bows and leaps.

Arias and Architects

Hummingbirds, woodcock, snipe, and larks often accompany their flight displays with singing. Song is a vital part of courtship in many species, and in some it is more important than plumage displays. For example, the rich songs of warblers are a stark contrast to their plain feathers.

Song is used in courtship rituals to announce territory and warn rival males to keep away. By advertising his territory, the male is showing that he controls resources, such as food, shelter, and a nesting site, to support a "family." The song's message attracts females to his territory for breeding.

As soon as a breeding pair forms, work begins on building a nest to cradle the eggs and house the growing

BEST NEST
Weaver birds build woven nests of grass. They must be well crafted, since weavers' courtship is conducted after nest-building, not before. A female selects her mate only if his nest is of high quality.

IN FULL PLUME
Raggiana birds of paradise form groups to posture and dance in unison. They quiver their lacy plumes and call hysterically to the females.

BIRD BALLOONS

Albatrosses "renew their vows" by clacking their bills together. Tiny manakins of Central America perform tumbling acrobatics. But the frigatebird pulls out all stops. Sitting in a bush, he opens and shuts his beak, waves his wings wildly about, squeals and croaks, and inflates a patch of red skin on his throat into a huge pouch—all to coax females flying overhead to mate with him!

FLUFFY FLOTILLA

"Precocial" chicks hatch with their eyes open, are covered with down, and leave the nest within days of hatching. Some are fed by their parents; others feed themselves. Like swans, some grebes carry their chicks.

chicks. Birds use a huge range of techniques to create nests. While some use a simple scrape on the ground—or build no nest at all—most construct cup-shaped nests of twigs and grass firmly wedged into the fork of a tree or bush. The materials are either threaded or twisted together to prevent the nest from falling apart. Sticky spider web is sometimes used to glue the nest together, and an outer layer of lichen can camouflage it from predators.

Other building materials are also used. Swallows and martins plaster their nests with mud, while some penguins nest on piles of stones—even stealing stones from their neighbors' piles to complete their own. Brush turkeys create mounds of vegetation, then use the heat of the rotting plants to incubate the eggs. Some birds, such as great horned owls, reuse the nests of other birds or mammals. Cuckoos also lay their eggs in the nests of other birds, but they leave these eggs to be hatched and the chicks to be reared by the unwitting foster parents.

A batch of eggs laid in a single breeding attempt is called a clutch. A clutch may take up to a week to lay. It may comprise a single egg, as in some seabirds and vultures, or more than a dozen in the case of waterfowl.

The eggs may be incubated by the female, by the male, or by both. The incubation period varies from a couple of weeks in smaller birds to more than eight weeks in gannets, vultures, and eagles. Either or both parents may care for the chicks.

Home Security

Birds have developed behavior to keep their eggs or chicks safe. Some use special alarm calls to warn their mate and chicks to keep quiet and still until the danger has passed. Burrowing owls and some small birds on the nest scare off potential predators by hissing like snakes.

Other small birds bravely fly at larger carnivorous birds to chase them away. Skuas and magpies dive-bomb large animals that stray too close. Fulmars defend their nest by spitting oily, half-digested food at intruders!

Of course, birds without chicks or eggs are also vulnerable to attack. Most fly away, but others try to avoid detection by becoming "invisible." A bittern will adopt a "sky-pointing"

HIGH CHAIR

In some species, such as this phainopepla, chicks are born blind and helpless. These "altricial" chicks are fed and cared for by their parents until they are able to fly.

COSY TOES

The emperor penguin builds no nest. Instead, the male balances the egg on his toes and covers it with his brood pouch. The chick spends the first two months of its life snuggled in the pouch.

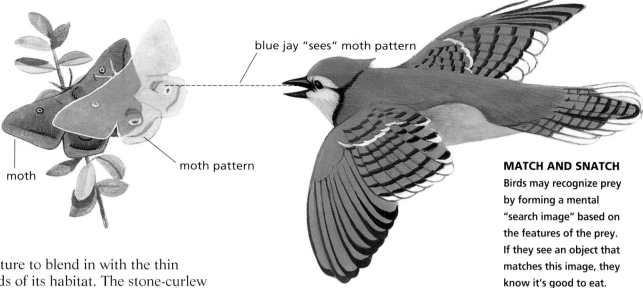

blue jay "sees" moth pattern

moth

moth pattern

MATCH AND SNATCH
Birds may recognize prey by forming a mental "search image" based on the features of the prey. If they see an object that matches this image, they know it's good to eat.

posture to blend in with the thin reeds of its habitat. The stone-curlew stretches out close to the ground to avoid detection. Tawny frogmouths imitate dead tree stumps.

Table Manners

Birds are warm-blooded animals, and need a great deal of energy to maintain their body temperature. Flying also uses up a lot of energy. Whether they are probing for crabs, diving for fish, or scratching for seeds, most birds spend a large part of their waking hours searching for food.

Birds need to find food quickly, using as little energy as possible—especially if they feed in the open where predators lurk. For this reason, many small species feed in a flock, where there are more pairs of eyes to look out for enemies. Different species may also join forces. Some flush out food for others, while the more noisy and alert species, such as chickadees and antshrikes, give an early warning of predators to the other members of the group.

Catch of the Day

While many species enjoy safety in numbers while they feed, few actually work together to catch food. One exception is Harris's hawk, which often hunts in family groups of four to six. Together they will chase or harass prey until it is exhausted. Cooperation allows the hawks to catch large prey, such as jackrabbits, more often. The group members share the kill.

Some birds let others do the work—then steal their catch! Frigatebirds and skuas are aerial pirates, bullying

TOXIC TOUCH

Most birds either fly from danger, or use camouflage or threatening behavior. But in 1991, scientists found that the skin and feathers of New Guinea's pitohuis contain a poison similar to that found in the toxic skin secretions of poison frogs. Pitohuis are the first birds discovered to be poisonous.

TRICKY TACTICS
Birds such as this killdeer distract predators from their eggs or chicks by pretending to be injured. When the predator has been tempted to chase it far from the nest, the killdeer flies away.

THE LONG HAUL
Wandering albatross parents take turns to incubate their single egg. One adult may fly up to 9,300 miles (15,000 km) in a single foraging trip during its partner's shift.

smaller seabirds into giving up their fish. Blackheaded gulls rob lapwings of earthworms. Other resourceful species use tools to gather food. The woodpecker finch of the Galápagos Islands uses a cactus spine, held in its bill, to pick grubs from holes in trees. Song thrushes smash snail shells on stones until the shells break open.

Some birds develop useful relationships with other animals to find food. Cattle egrets, oxpeckers, and piapiacs eat insects disturbed by grazing mammals, such as zebras or elephants. They also pick lice and ticks from mammals' bodies. The cleaner bird is not afraid to enter the mouths of hippos and crocodiles to eat the parasites and food scraps within, and the honeyguide deliberately leads humans to beehives that it cannot open itself. When the hive is broken open, the humans gain access to the rich honey, while the birds eat the wax.

Sun Seekers

For centuries, humans were puzzled by the annual disappearance of some bird species. Many people thought it was a sign from the spirit world. Others believed the birds went into hibernation. We now know that species in colder climates do not have

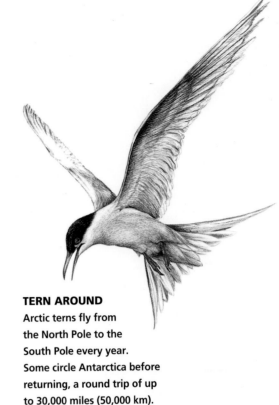

TERN AROUND
Arctic terns fly from the North Pole to the South Pole every year. Some circle Antarctica before returning, a round trip of up to 30,000 miles (50,000 km).

to hibernate or otherwise endure the short and cold winter days, when there is little food. Instead, they travel to warmer places where the living is easier. Nearly half the world's birds divide their year between two main locations. That's about 50,000 million individual birds migrating every year!

Bird Brains

Since flight uses up a lot of energy and water, many species stock up on food before departure, converting it into fat that will provide energy during the

CARVING A PATH
On a long flight, geese fly in a V-formation. The lead bird pushes against the air, making it easier for the other birds to fly. When the bird tires, another takes its place.

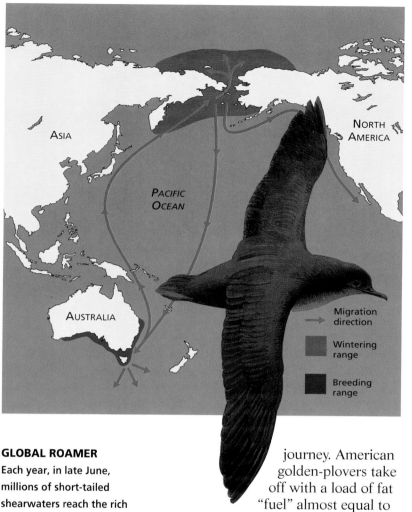

GLOBAL ROAMER
Each year, in late June, millions of short-tailed shearwaters reach the rich feeding areas of the North Pacific. They return to their nesting colonies in southern Australia in late September.

Sun and stars to guide them. In cloudy conditions, they may use the Earth's magnetic field as a map. Birds also have a "chronometer," or innate time sense, that tells them when it is time to leave and how long the journey will take. But while they have these senses and abilities when they are born, migrants also become familiar with territories and flyways. They learn to follow air and sea currents, to look for landmarks, and to use temperature changes as guides. Seabirds and some pigeons may also use their strong sense of smell to trace an odor "map."

Birds use many migration strategies. Most songbirds break their journey into short hops of 200 miles (320 km) or so. They may also delay their trip if the weather is bad. Cranes travel mainly overland. But some migrations span entire oceans or continents in a single flight. For example, the swallow breeds across North America and Europe, but winters in Southeast Asia, Africa, or South America. This means it flies up to 7,000 miles (11,300 km)!

journey. American golden-plovers take off with a load of fat "fuel" almost equal to their own weight to fly nonstop from the Canadian Atlantic coast to South America.

While most birds migrate alone, some travel in flocks of one or several species. Flocks provide protection against predators, particularly for birds traveling by day. For young geese and cranes, traveling in a flock also means they are guided by more experienced birds.

It is thought that most birds navigate by sight, using the

HUMMING ALONG
In winter, the ruby-throated hummingbird flies up to 500 miles nonstop across the Gulf of Mexico to find warm weather and nectar.

Endangered Species

Throughout history, birds have been used to symbolize certain qualities and states: the wise owl, the bluebird of happiness, the dove of peace, and so on. But humans do not always value birds so highly. Today, more than 1,000 species are threatened with extinction, and many more are in severe decline.

Empty Skies

At least 100 species have died out during the last 400 years. More than 30 disappeared during the twentieth century. Extinction is a natural process: Birds have always died out, and others have changed in response to changing environments. But the big difference between the birds that disappeared in ancient times, and those that have become extinct more recently, is that recent extinctions were caused almost entirely by humans.

Stranger Danger

The greatest cause of extinctions has been the effect of introduced species, especially predators such as cats, rats, and mongooses, on island birds. Many of these birds evolved without any predator pressure, so were unable to protect themselves against these animals, which stole eggs and ate chicks and adults. One such bird was the Stephen Island wren, which became extinct in 1894. Stephen Island is a tiny speck of land in the Cook Strait of New Zealand. The lighthouse keeper's cat killed the entire population of wrens in a few months!

Rabbits and goats can be as deadly as predators because they often destroy natural vegetation and leave little for native herbivorous birds to eat. Fish, too, can cause problems: In Madagascar, exotic fish have caused

DEAD AS A ...
Confined to Mauritius, the dodo was discovered by explorers in 1507. This defenseless bird was killed for food and sport, and because it was considered ugly. By 1680 it was extinct.

GOOD LUCK?
In Asia, cranes symbolize long life and good luck. Close to extinction in much of Southeast Asia, sarus cranes are now being bred in captivity. Young cranes are reintroduced into the wild crane population.

PASSING THROUGH

The passenger pigeon was once so numerous that flocks of millions were a common sight in North America. Hunting competitions were organized in which more than 30,000 dead pigeons were needed for hunters to claim a prize. The supply of birds seemed inexhaustible, yet within a century the species was reduced to small bands. The last passenger pigeon died in Cincinnati Zoo in 1914.

The bait on these lines, which stretch for enormous distances behind the fishing boats, appear to be a free meal for albatrosses. But the hooks in the baits are lethal. More than 40,000 birds are drowned each year when they are hooked and dragged beneath the surface.

Deadly Doses

In the early 1960s, it became clear that wildlife was being poisoned through widespread use of pesticides such as DDT. These "miracle" sprays were great for growing insect-free crops, but were devastating to such species as birds of prey and brown pelicans. This is because these birds absorb the pesticides in the bodies of their prey. With each link in the food chain—say, from sprayed grass, to insect, to starling, to falcon—the pesticides become more concentrated. The falcon gets the biggest dose of all.

The absorption of DDT caused the birds to lay eggs with thin shells that broke when the parent tried to incubate them, or eggs with no shells at all. As a result, their chicks died and some species disappeared from vast areas of the world.

DDT use is now banned or restricted in many parts of the world, and some populations of affected species are recovering. But new chemicals have taken the place of DDT. These

CHEMICAL REACTION
The plight of the peregrine falcon drew attention to the effects of pesticides. The species was rescued in some areas by the release of captive-bred birds into the wild.

a decline in waterlilies and other aquatic plants, thus endangering the little grebe.

Baits and Bullets

Hunting has also been a major cause of extinction. Island birds were easy targets because they were unafraid of humans. But thousands of other species have also been hunted for food, for sport, and for feathers, which were used to decorate clothing and hats. Sometimes whole birds were used as decoration. At the height of this destruction, in the 1880s, a survey of 700 hats in New York found that 542 sported at least 20 species of bird!

Hunting for other animals also affects birds. Thousands of seabirds die annually in gill and drift nets on the open ocean. Perhaps even more dangerous is longline tuna fishing.

FORMER GLORY
A large, flightless seabird, the great auk lived on islands in the Atlantic Ocean. It was hunted for food and oil. The last known pair were killed by a fisherman in 1844.

HOPE FOR THE HARPY?
A pair of harpy eagles need an area of up to 77 square miles (200 square km) to satisfy their requirements. Only a network of forest reserves can save them now.

now pollute the air, the land, and the water, and are likely to be harmful to birds—and to other animals, including humans. Plastics, too, are harmful: Seabirds can peck up plastic in one form or another from the ocean surface. Oil is also a killer. Even a small amount of drifting oil strips the waterproofing from feathers. Birds are poisoned when they swallow oil as they try to clean their feathers. Without their waterproofing, they are exposed to the cold and freeze to death.

Killer Cages

The pet trade is a major threat. The rarer some birds become—especially parrots—the higher their value. It is very difficult to control the trade in prized birds because trappers and dealers are tempted by rich rewards. Worse still, the birds are often transported in cruelly cramped conditions. Many do not survive the journey to their new homes.

Parrots are not the only species under threat. When it was discovered

LUCKY DUCK
The wood duck was once endangered through hunting and habitat loss. But thanks to habitat management and a ban on hunting, it is now common in eastern North America.

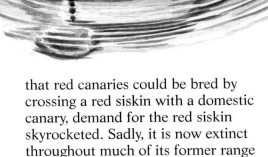

that red canaries could be bred by crossing a red siskin with a domestic canary, demand for the red siskin skyrocketed. Sadly, it is now extinct throughout much of its former range across Venezuela and Colombia.

Help the Homeless

The greatest overall threat to birds today is the destruction of their habitats. Grasslands have been plowed or overgrazed by livestock; wetlands have been drained; tropical rain forests have been cut down. It is estimated that up to 78,700 square miles (20.4 million hectares) of tropical forest are lost each year. So it's no surprise that this habitat is home to the highest number of threatened species, including birds of prey, parrots, pigeons, pheasants, hornbills, the antbirds of Central and South America, the broadbills

FAMILY AFFAIR
The Siberian crane is highly endangered, mainly due to the loss of its wintering grounds in Asia. Without the conservation of these areas cranes will not live to breed in the following spring.

HUNGRY HUNTER
The Great Philippine eagle eats flying lemurs, squirrels, monkeys, deer, palm civets, and reptiles. Destruction of its habitat denies this eagle not only its nesting trees but its food, too.

of Africa and Asia, and the birds of paradise of Indonesia, New Guinea, and Australia. Even numbers of many migratory species have dropped dramatically as their summer and winter habitats have been cleared for agriculture and urban development.

A Combined Effort

Although the problems can seem overwhelming, much can be done to help birds in danger. Different species have different conservation needs, but some combination of saving habitat, preventing pollution, getting rid of introduced species, controlling the trade in wild birds, and encouraging responsible hunting will help to ensure the survival of threatened species.

Such measures have already been put into effect in many countries. Organizations continue to campaign effectively for endangered species, and many private groups are buying property to protect habitats. In the United States, for example, the setting up of wildlife sanctuaries has saved a number of species, and a remarkable US–Canadian conservation effort has also brought the whooping crane back from the brink of extinction.

But the majority of threatened birds live in developing countries, where funding for conservation takes second place to the needs of people. Here action to help protect key sites, where several threatened species occur together, needs to be combined with projects to aid the local people so they have no need to destroy the forest. Such projects can benefit not only the birds, but the other creatures with whom they share their habitats—including humans.

NO MORE MACAW?
Poaching and habitat destruction threaten more than 80 species of parrot, including the largest species, the magnificent hyacinth macaw of South America.

Land Birds

THERE ARE APPROXIMATELY 9,000 SPECIES of birds, grouped into 24 orders. More than half are classified by the way they perch. Most spend a significant amount of their time roosting, nesting, feeding, or socializing on land. But even a few land species, such as some kingfishers, find their food in water.

Foot Lockers

No bird has more than four toes. Most species have three toes of almost equal length pointing forward and one toe pointing backward. When the bird lands on a perch, the tendons leading to the toes force them to tighten their grip. With their toes locked into position, birds never fall off their perch when they are sleeping! Many of the birds that have this kind of "locking" system of perching are called passerines, or songbirds. The birds that either lack this system, or have one that is less developed, are known as non-passerines. These species are extremely varied. Some non-passerines are waterbirds; others live on land, and some are flightless. Birds of prey are non-passerines, too.

Planet Poultry

Gamebirds are also non-passerines. These birds are familiar to almost everyone: Chickens, which are the domesticated forms of central Asia's jungle fowl, can be found on virtually every part of the planet. Turkeys from North America are also featured on menus around the world. Other gamebirds, such as partridge, quail, and grouse, are known to hunters. Although they vary in size, gamebirds

EARLY WARNING
Sociable birds, the turacos of Africa communicate with harsh, loud, barking calls that may be recognized by other animals as alarm signals.

BALD SPOT
The vulturine guineafowl lives in arid scrublands in east Africa. Its largely naked head is thought to help it to regulate its brain temperature.

PRETTY BOY
Nearly turkey-sized, the crowned pigeons of New Guinea are the largest of all pigeons. Males use their glorious crests in bowing displays during courtship.

have a small head, a plump body, and short, broad wings.

Pheasants also have a close association with humans. In ancient China, the pheasant was regarded as a symbol of harmony and its feathers were used as decorative, ceremonial, or religious symbols. A number of the most beautiful species have been released by (or escaped from) collectors. For example, the golden pheasant, originally from Asia, has established feral colonies in Britain.

Peafowl are famous for their train of decorated feathers. Blue peafowl have adapted easily to living with humans, not only in their native India—male peacocks and female peahens are also found in parks throughout Europe. However, the even more beautiful green peafowl is threatened by hunting and the destruction of its forest habitat in Southeast Asia.

Milk Ilk

Pigeons and sandgrouse belong to the order Columbiformes. Both are non-passerines, but they may not be related to each other. Pigeons and their smaller cousins, doves, eat seeds and fruits and live mainly in trees, although some species feed in huge flocks on the ground. Most of the 304 species of pigeon and dove live in tropical and subtropical regions of the world. But the 16 species of sandgrouse are desert-dwellers of Africa and Eurasia.

Unlike most birds, sandgrouse and pigeons drink by sucking. Sandgrouse have glands which produce an oil used to preen their feathers, but pigeons have powder down—special plumes that disintegrate into a powder that cleans the feathers. When pigeons are breeding, glands in the crop (a saclike extension of the gullet) of both sexes enlarge and secrete a

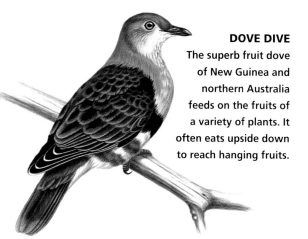

DOVE DIVE
The superb fruit dove of New Guinea and northern Australia feeds on the fruits of a variety of plants. It often eats upside down to reach hanging fruits.

QUAIL TALE
The plump, rounded little California quail can actually be found from Vancouver Island to the tip of Baja California. Hunters shoot more than two million of these birds every year.

Puff Daddies

To court females, male tragopan pheasants erect the fleshy blue horns on their head and inflate their throat flap. A Temminck's tragopan (right, with speckled flap) first peeks at a hen from behind a rock. Slowly, he shows her his flap and horns, then beats his wings, making the horns vibrate. He also spreads his tail and calls in time to his wingbeats. Finally he rises up, puffs his flap up to its fullest, and hisses!

thick, milky substance which is fed to the young. Sandgrouse cannot produce crop milk, but they do have a unique way of watering their chicks. The male wades into a waterhole and lets his feathers soak up water. He then flies back to his nest, where the chicks drink from his wet feathers.

Split Personalities

Turacos, cuckoos, and mousebirds are also non-passerines. Turacos, which live in Africa, have a fourth toe at right angles to the foot. This toe can be directed forward or backward.

BUZZ OFF!
Before eating a bee, the rainbow bee-eater rubs off the insect's sting on a branch, or squeezes out the venom with its bill.

Mousebirds, so called because of the way they creep and crawl among bushes, perch with their feet almost level with their shoulders—they look as if they're doing the splits!

Cuckoos are notorious for laying their eggs in the nests of other birds, but of the 130 or so species, only about 50 are truly parasitic. But they all have zygodactylous feet: two toes pointing forward, and two pointing backward. Hairy caterpillars form most of their diet, although the roadrunner—the inspiration for the cartoon character—eats lizards, snakes, and other small animals.

Bright and Beautiful

Trogons live in tropical woodlands and forests in Central America, Asia, the West Indies, and Africa. Secretive and territorial, trogons such as the resplendent quetzal will perch quietly scanning their surroundings for insects or small lizards. Some also eat fruit.

Like cuckoos and trogons, parrots have zygodactylous feet. Parrots are remarkably skillful, using their feet for climbing or as a "hand" for holding up food to their bill. Short and blunt, the unique design of the bill enables them to expertly extract kernels from the seeds and nuts that form the diet

HEAVEN SENT
The national bird of Guatemala, the resplendent quetzal was worshipped by the Aztecs. Anyone who killed the bird was also sentenced to death.

HOLDING COURT

The kakapo or owl parrot of New Zealand is unique. It is nocturnal; it is heavier than other parrots; and it can't fly. It extracts juices from foliage and stems, then leaves behind balls of chewed material hanging on the plant. But its courtship behavior is weirdest of all: Males display in hollows in the ground, called "courts," and make booming sounds from inflated air-sacs in their throat!

of most species. Their muscular tongue is prehensile, and in lorikeets it is brush-tipped to lick pollen and nectar from blossoms.

Parrots live mainly in the Southern Hemisphere, and most have striking plumage. Green feathers are common, and provide good camouflage amidst the rain forest canopy where many live. Cockatoos also have colorful crests, and other parrots may also have longer feathers on their necks.

RUFF STUFF
The hawk-headed parrot of Amazonia raises its ruff when it is excited or angry. It is sometimes kept as a pet, but it can be aggressive in the breeding season, even killing its mate!

DIRT DIET
In Peru, macaws flock to rain forest river banks most days to eat clay. The clay is rich in minerals that are lacking in the birds' diet. It may also neutralize the toxic effects of the fruits and seeds eaten by the birds.

Parrots usually nest in holes dug in termite mounds, in tree hollows, or in rock crevices. Monk parrots from South America gather twigs to build a huge communal nest in a tree, and each pair has its own breeding chamber. The lovely hanging parrots of Indonesia, which roost upside down like bats, carry nesting material among the feathers on their rump.

Royal Flush

Kingfishers, bee-eaters, rollers, todies, motmots, hornbills, and the hoopoes are all non-passerines belonging to the order Coraciiformes. Many have toes fused together along part of their length. They also have a large, robust bill, generally long and straight, with a sharply pointed or slightly hooked tip.

In some kingfishers, the pointed bill is used for striking at and grasping prey, especially fishes, while those with a hook-tipped bill crush prey. Not all kingfishers eat fish: The shovel-billed kingfisher from New Guinea uses its short, wide bill to dig for worms, and the laughing kookaburra of Australia is renowned for its taste for snakes! The birds sit and wait for prey, then dive or swoop down to seize it. The

SCHOOL OF FISH
Belted kingfishers are taught to fish by their parents, which drop dead fish into the water for the young to retrieve.

prey is then killed by being struck repeatedly against a branch. Rollers use similar dive-hunting techniques, or else descend like parachutes to snatch their next meal.

Drum Majors

Woodpeckers are also well known for their bill. Strong, tapering, and often chisel-tipped, the bill is used to batter, pry, and probe tree trunks for insects. Prey is then extracted with the woodpecker's long, frill-edged, and very sticky tongue. The bird's tongue is so long that, enclosed in a membrane extending from the right nostril, it loops right over the skull to anchor points in the back of the jaw!

Woodpeckers also drum on tree trunks to establish and maintain their territory, and to excavate roosting and nesting cavities. Since the cavities are later taken over by other hole-nesting birds, many species depend on woodpeckers for their survival.

Sugar and Spice

The 320 species of hummingbird are unmistakable. They are small—most weigh less than 1/3 of an ounce (3.5 to 9 g)—and have gorgeous, iridescent plumage. They also beat their wings so rapidly (up to 78 beats per second) that the wings vibrate with a humming sound.

Hummingbirds can hover and fly in all directions without needing to turn in that direction first. To fly forward, they flap their wings up and down. They hover by flapping in a figure-8 shape,

and fly backward by flapping above and behind their head. This uses up an enormous amount of energy, and some species need to drink the sugary nectar of about 2,000 flowers a day to survive. This is equal to a human eating 99 pounds (45 kg) of sugar each day!

With their cigar-shaped body and narrow, scythe-like wings, swifts are also superb fliers. They spend almost all of their time in the air, catching flying insects. Some species, such as the chimney swift of eastern North America, make long migration flights across the ocean to breeding grounds in the Southern Hemisphere.

Many swifts use their saliva to glue small sticks together to form a nest; in the smaller cave-dwelling swiftlets of Southeast Asia, saliva makes up the bulk of the nest. Men climb rickety bamboo scaffolding or vine ladders to collect the nests from cave ceilings, where tens of thousands of the swiftlets nest. As the main ingredient of bird's nest soup, the nests have become a major economic resource.

FAIRY MAGIC
Australian fairy-wrens hold their tail high when courting or feeding. But when their chicks are in danger, adults distract predators by holding their tail and head low and running like mice.

BILL SKILL
The hornbill uses its bill for feeding, fighting, preening, and for sealing the entrance to its nest. Unlike the Asian species, this yellow-billed hornbill feeds largely on insects rather than fruit.

Reptile Relic?

With its long neck and tail, frizzled crest, blue face, and red eyes, the hoatzin of tropical South America is a weird-looking bird. Strangest of all, its chicks are able to clamber in the trees just a few days after hatching using

PITTA-PATTER

Pittas and broadbills are passerines. Despite its brilliant plumage, the banded pitta is hard to see when it is hunting insects in the gloom of the rain forest floor.

their feet, bill, and specially adapted wings that have two claws. These claws disappear as the chick grows.

The hoatzin's bizarre appearance suggests that it is the "missing link" between the reptiles and the birds, especially since the claws of the chicks are similar to those of *Archaeopteryx*. But the hoatzin's highly specialized crop, which grinds up the fruits, buds, leaves, and flowers of only a few plant species, suggests that it is not a primitive species at all. Even its claws may have evolved recently.

Wise Words

Owls, frogmouths, and nightjars share many features and are thought to be distantly related. Most take live animal prey and hunt at night, so they are often termed nocturnal birds of prey. They live on every continent except Antarctica and are more often heard than seen; their calls, described as spooky, startling, or strangely beautiful, often carry across the countryside.

Life in dim light has led to some remarkable sensory adaptations. Owls have large, forward-facing eyes with binocular vision, like those of humans but unlike most other birds. Barn owls have smaller eyes, but exceptional hearing. These owls also have "face masks" of contoured feathers to catch sound. The oilbird (a kind of nightjar) also uses sound: In complete darkness it navigates by echolocation, making audible clicks and listening to the returning echoes to find its way.

Nightjars sweep insects out of the air with their wide, gaping mouth, but owls drop on larger mammals, snatching prey with their sharp, hooked talons. A barn owl can kill up to 20 rodents in a single night! Frogmouths pounce from a perch to catch prey with their heavy

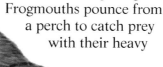

WHO CAN? TOUCAN!

Toucans are related to woodpeckers. They use their "frilled" tongue and often serrated bill to eat fruits, but they can also pluck untended eggs and chicks out of nests.

GREEN SCHEME

The green broadbill is a master of disguise. Its nest is usually attached to a vine hanging above a stream. Decorated with lichen and spider webs, it looks just like debris caught by high water.

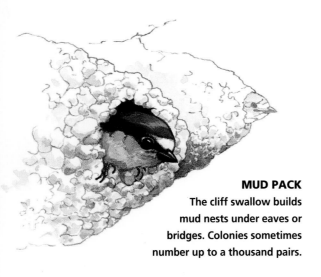

MUD PACK
The cliff swallow builds mud nests under eaves or bridges. Colonies sometimes number up to a thousand pairs.

bill. They batter prey to soften it before swallowing it whole. Almost all of these birds have soft-edged flight feathers to muffle hunting flight. The exceptions are the fruit-eating oilbirds of South America and the fishing owls of Africa. Since they have no need for silent flight, their feathers are firmer.

Some owls lay a similar-sized clutch during a regular breeding season; in other species, the size of the clutch is influenced by seasonal conditions. For example, a snowy owl can lay up to 14 eggs in a year when its lemming prey is plentiful, but only two to four when times are tough. Incubation can last more than a month, and in some species the chicks and parents will stay together for several months more.

Name Brands

The order Passeriformes, or passerines, contains more than half the known species of bird. Many have names that echo their songs, such as warblers and babblers, while the mockingbird is a talented mimic of other birds. Other birds are named for their appearance or habits. For example, the waxwings of Europe, northeast Asia, and

North America have red, waxlike droplets on the tip of each secondary wing feather, just for decoration. The antbirds of South America cling to stems just out of the reach of army ant swarms, picking off fleeing insects and other prey. Treecreepers are the only small birds that creep up tree trunks. The West Indies trembler is noted for its habit of shivering and shaking. Pink-legged acrobats swing from high twigs in shade trees over cocoa plantations in Brazil. Dippers feed underwater on aquatic insects, using their wings to maneuver and bobbing up like corks when surfacing. The noisy scrub-bird is renowned for its ear-splitting call.

The rufous hornero and its relatives of Central and South America are familiar birds near houses, stalking about lawns and singing in noisy duets. They are commonly referred to as ovenbirds because they build mud nests that look like traditional clay

FLORA ADORER
This regal sunbird lives in mountain ranges in central Africa. Many plants rely on these small, glittering birds for pollination, and males often defend their favorite flowers from other sunbirds.

TINY TRAVELERS
White-eyes can be found in Africa and across southern Asia to Australasia, north to Japan and east to Samoa. This Cape white-eye is about to feed on nectar with its brush-tipped tongue.

ovens. These closed nests are hard to build, but they do protect against sun, cold, and predators. The nests' narrow entrance poses no problem for these birds, since they are adapted to creep into narrow places as they hunt for insects and spiders.

Individual ovenbird species also have unusual names. Leaftossers toss or rake leaves on the forest floor to uncover insects, as does the streamcreeper along the edge of creeks. But a few streamcreepers at sewer outlets above Rio de Janeiro in Brazil have given the entire species the local name "President of Filth."

Snack Attack

Like some ovenbirds, the lyrebirds of Australia also rake leaf litter to find food. They also use their large, clawed feet to turn over stones and rip apart rotten logs. But other passerines take to the skies for a meal. Swallows and martins catch insects in midair, more or less sucking them up as they fly in graceful swoops and glides, with seemingly little effort, for hours on end. As they fly, they also dip down to the surface of lakes and rivers to drink and bathe. The tyrant flycatchers of the Americas also eat flying insects, perching bolt upright on some vantage

ROCK CONCERT
The cock-of-the-rock is related to tyrant flycatchers. Males gather at a "lek," or display area, to show off for the females. After mating, females depart alone to build nests in rock crevices.

point before rushing out to snatch prey with an audible snap of the bill.

Other passerines also have the gift of the grab. The shrikes of Africa, Europe, Asia, and North America seem like a songbird version of a hawk. Solitary and aggressive, they use the highest perches available in open country from which to look for

BREAKFAST BANDITS

Many birds learn to exploit new environments and food supplies by copying or imitating each another. One example is the blue tit's habit of pecking through the foil tops of milk bottles left on doorsteps and eating the cream. The habit spread from one part of Britain to another for several years. Humans at first thought this was an endearing example of adaptation. But now humans themselves are adapting, by designing bird-proof bottle tops!

large insects, mice, or small birds. Many shrikes have the habit of impaling left-over food on the thorns of bushes or barbed wire fencing. Because its feet are not strong enough to grasp prey, the butcherbird of Australia also impales its larger victims, or wedges them in a tree fork, before tearing into them. Tame butcherbirds are notorious for their habit of using clotheslines as perches and storing meaty snacks in the washing.

FINCH FAMILY AFFAIR
A thick-billed finch, the painted bunting is related to the cardinals and grosbeaks. It breeds in thickets and weedy tangles across the southeastern United States.

Gobble, Gobble

Big, bold, and versatile, the 117 species of jay, magpie, and crow (including jackdaws, rooks, and ravens) probably originated in Australia, but are now found almost everywhere. Crows have been seen fighting their own reflection in the gilded domes of the Kremlin, in Russia, and peering into bicycle baskets in Mombassa, Kenya! Crows and jays don't mind pulling meat from a carcass, but they also enjoy insects, berries, and seeds. The true jays of Europe and Asia are particularly fond of acorns, which they store to provide food in winter.

Many other passerines eat fruit. A flock of figbirds, a kind of oriole found

RARE JEWEL
The Gouldian finch is confined to tropical northern Australia. Illegal trapping for the pet trade, habitat loss, predators, and parasitic mites have all led to the decline of this species.

in Indonesia, New Guinea, and Australia, can almost strip a tree of fruit. The mistletoebird of Australia, a kind of flowerpecker, feeds almost entirely on the berries of various species of mistletoe. The plant relies on the bird as heavily as the bird relies on the plant: While the bird absorbs the fruit pulp, the seeds pass through its body undamaged, stick to tree branches, and germinate. So close is this partnership that the bird is seldom found where the plant does not occur, and vice versa.

The colorful tanagers of the Americas are primarily fruit eaters, although species like flower-piercers and honeycreepers have long, thin bills for extracting nectar. The honeyeaters, wattlebirds, miners, and friarbirds of Australasia have a tongue custom-built for nectar: Deeply grooved, it is delicately fringed at the tip so that it forms four parallel brushes.

Finches prefer to eat seeds, but in Malaysia the white-rumped munia feeds in irrigated rice paddies on the rice and protein-rich green algae that grow there. It even times its breeding seasons to correspond with each crop.

FEATHERED THIEF
Scrub jays are often found perching on roadside wires, keeping an eye out for insects and lizards. They are also notorious nest raiders, snatching eggs and chicks.

Most grain- and fruit-eating passerines switch to an insect diet while nesting. The bill length of crowned sparrows and juncos (two species of bunting) even change with the seasons, being shorter for eating seeds during the colder months. But finches such as canaries, greenfinches, siskins, and linnets feed their chicks a mix of predigested seeds and buds.

Chorus Lines

Most passerines have a complex syrinx, a specialized organ situated at the base of the windpipe, or trachea. The syrinx has two chambers, which the bird can use simultaneously to produce its characteristic song. Some songs are more pleasing to the human ear than others: Drongos have grating, metallic or harsh, scolding calls, while the lark has a lovely, musical song. The call of the crimson sunbird of India and Southeast Asia has been likened to a pair of scissors being snapped open and shut, but thrushes are compensated for their drab color with their beautiful, evocative songs.

Passerines sing to attract mates and to advertise territory. In some species, males and females duet to strengthen their pair bond. Birds recognize the calls of their own species and those of others, and some take advantage of this knowledge. When the euphonia (a kind of tanager) sees a potential predator, it imitates the alarm calls of other passerines. This attracts those other birds to come and mob the enemy, leaving the crafty euphonia to go about its business.

While some birds are born with their songs, others learn them from their parents—or each other. Some mimic others to improve their chances of mating success. In the whydah, a kind of African finch, one male in the neighborhood is the favorite of most females. When he changes his song, other males copy him.

WHAT A RACKET
The twisted tips of the tail feathers of the greater racket-tailed drongo cause a distinctive humming noise in flight.

STAR OF THE SPECIES
Some starlings, such as the Indian mynahs, are mainly dull brown with patches of naked yellow skin on the head. But Africa is home to some gorgeous starlings, such as this blue-eared glossy starling.

Waterbirds

Two-thirds of the Earth's surface is covered by water. Rivers, swamps, mangroves, and lagoons support a huge array of birds. Some, like ducks, spend most of their time on lakes and ponds; others have adapted to life on the greatest waterway of all, the sea. Yet there are also waterbirds that seldom go near water!

Aqua Spectacular

Waterbirds are a diverse group, and their body and behavioral adaptations reflect this. Long-legged herons and spoonbills wade into deep water for food, while small, narrow-bodied rails stick to the reeds at the water's edge. Ruddy turnstones use their short, wedge-shaped bill to turn over stones, seaweed, and other beach debris to find prey. The heavy bones of auks and puffins enable them to dive deeply and catch food underwater.

Despite their differences, many species also have features in common. For example, birds that swim have webbed toes that serve as propellers, and many diving birds have a special air-sac system across their chest that cushions the bird against impact with the water. Since oily feathers improve buoyancy, almost all species also have waterproof plumage.

Quack Pack

Known as waterfowl, the 160 species of duck, goose, and swan are among the most beautiful of all birds. They are members of the family Anatidae, so they are often referred to as anatids. While most live in the Northern Hemisphere, they can be found worldwide except in Antarctica. Ducks and geese have been raised for food for more than 4,500 years.

Most species are powerful fliers—although some are flightless—and many northern species migrate in winter. Some can fly at speeds of over 68 mph (110 kmph). Mountain ranges and oceans are no barrier, since most species can fly over them. Bar-headed geese have been seen flying near the summit of Mount Everest, at an altitude of 28,000 feet (8.5 km)!

Most waterfowl are excellent swimmers, although species such as the magpie goose of Australia and the Hawaiian nene goose have adapted to life on land and have less-webbed feet. Some species come ashore to roost, but stifftails and sea ducks, such as scoters and mergansers, generally doze on the water. The stifftails are so well adapted to their aquatic, diving lifestyle that they can hardly walk.

Most waterfowl have relatively long necks and flattened, broad bills. The exceptions are the six species of

FAIREST OF THE FOWL
The snow goose nests in colonies of thousands of pairs in the Arctic tundra. It flies south for the winter, sometimes traveling as far as the Gulf of Mexico.

LONG DISTANCE CALL
Screamers of South America are the closest surviving relatives of anatids. They are strong fliers and excellent swimmers, and their long toes enable them to walk over floating vegetation.

HEAVY CARGO
Before a swan can take off, it has to run along the water to build up enough speed to support its weight in the air, like a plane gathering speed on a runway.

material sieved from the water surface, although they also upend to get juicy morsels from bottom mud. True geese spend a great deal of time ashore, grazing. Diving ducks rarely dive beyond 10 to 20 feet (3 to 6 m), although sea ducks such as the king eider and oldsquaw can dive at least 180 feet (55 m). Since sea ducks feed mainly in salt water, they have evolved glands above their eyes to remove excess salt from their body.

Feather Fashion

All anatids are densely feathered with compact waterproof plumage, as well as an undercoat of insulating down. Unlike most birds, which replace old feathers with a new set

WARM ON WATER
The down of the eider duck is thick and heavy, with the best thermal quality of any natural substance. In some regions, such as Iceland, eiders are still "farmed" for their down.

merganser, which have a long and slender bill with sharp, jagged edges used to grasp slippery fish. In general, waterfowl feed on a variety of foods. Some eat grass, seeds, grain, and aquatic plants, while others prefer fish, mollusks, crustaceans, and insects. Aquatic insects are important for many ducklings and goslings (young geese), although as adults they may feed mostly on plants.

There are three main methods of foraging. Dabbling ducks eat mostly

EQUAL OPPORTUNITY
Some anatids are dull-colored, while others are brightly colored and patterned. Males are generally more ornate, but in species such as this Siberian red-breasted goose both sexes are colorful.

once a year, most waterfowl molt twice: once for courtship plumage, and again after the breeding season. During this second molt most anatids shed all their wing feathers at once, leaving them flightless for up to a month while the new feathers grow.

Waterfowl have elaborate courtship behaviors, including bowing, dancing, and calling. Male ducks often have striking courtship plumage. Most anatids mate for the duration of the breeding season, if not for life; swans are famous for their lifelong pair bonds. The nests of waterfowl tend to be simple, although most swans build huge nests, and those of the trumpeter swan may even float. Some geese nest in colonies, while the black-headed duck of South America lays eggs in the nest of other birds. In almost all species the female incubates the eggs, which hatch after an average of four weeks. Most young waterfowl must feed themselves from the moment they hatch.

Tall Order

Herons, storks, ibises, and spoonbills, together with the cranes, are known as the large waders. In addition to their long legs, these birds are easily recognized by their feeding behavior and bill shapes. Some herons use their short, straight bill to spear prey that comes close; others chase prey or fly and pounce onto prey on the water surface. Ibises have a sickle-shaped, downcurved bill to probe into water or soft mud. Storks have a very long bill to match their very long legs. The well-named spoonbills are easy to identify.

RAIL WAYS
The purple gallinule is a kind of rail. These hen-like marsh birds are related to cranes. A lack of land predators has led some island rails to become flightless.

STORK FORK
The painted stork is often seen in marshland reserves in Asia. Storks eat a variety of foods, including insects, amphibians, crustaceans, fish, mammals, and carrion.

PRETTY IN PINK

Flamingos are instantly recognized by their bright feathers and crooked bill. To feed, they drag their bill upside down through the water. Water flows into the half-open bill, and the tongue pumps it out through a mesh of hooks along the inner edges of the jaw, trapping shrimps inside. The birds eat so many shrimps that they turn pink—in the same way that a person who ate only carrots would eventually turn orange!

Large waders are found throughout the world, except near the poles, and in all habitats. Many species, such as ibises, feed, roost, and nest together in large colonies. Others, such as the yellow-billed stork of Africa, are mostly solitary.

Most species travel long distances to escape cold weather, probably because their food is scarce in winter, and also because their large body uses a lot of energy to keep warm. The migratory habits of the white stork of Eurasia have made it a popular symbol in folklore. Its habit of nesting on buildings, and its return to the breeding grounds in spring after wintering in Africa, have long been associated with fertility and birth.

CROWNING GLORY
The crowned crane of Africa is considered a living fossil of the crane family. Unlike other cranes, it roosts in trees. Its relatively short beak and magnificent crest are also unique.

POWDER PUFF
Like other herons, the green heron has specialized feathers which are never molted. Instead, the tips fray into fine powder, which is used to remove slime from the feathers.

Top Hat and Tails

Egrets are also considered wading birds; in fact, they are a smaller type of heron. Some, such as the cattle egret, are more likely to be seen on farmlands than in wetlands, catching insects disturbed by plows and large grazing animals. Their name comes from "aigrettes," the term used by hat makers to describe the bird's beautiful plumes. (The plumes were used to decorate hats.) These feathers are grown only in the breeding season,

and courting egrets posture to show themselves to best effect.

Cranes, too, perform courtship rituals, including trumpet-like calls and elaborate dances. Crowned cranes dance all year round, leaping with half-open wings, bowing, and running around in circles to cement their lifelong bond with their partner.

The 15 species of crane are also known for the care they lavish on their young. They usually nest on the ground, or build platforms in shallow water. Both parents incubate their

SPOON FED
The roseate spoonbill sweeps its partly opened bill through water until nerve endings lining the bill sense vibrations from prey. The bird snaps up the food, then tosses it down its throat.

SUPER-SCOOPER
The black skimmer flies just above the water, dragging its lower bill a little below the surface. When prey is touched, it is snapped up.

two eggs and take care of the chicks, which are active as soon as they hatch. The chicks stay with their parents until the next breeding season. Northern species learn the route to wintering areas by following their parents throughout the fall migration.

Scaredy-Coots

Cranes are found in Europe, North America, Africa, Asia, and Australia. A close relative is the water-loving limpkin of South America. But the best-known relatives are perhaps the 133 species of rail, gallinule or moorhen, and coot. Just about every major wetland on almost every continent—and on many islands—is home to these long-legged birds. Their short, rounded wings reflect their ground-living habits.

These cautious birds hide their nests of reed stems among vegetation. Some of the young moorhens stay with their parents to take care of chicks from subsequent broods.

Loony Tunes

Scientists think that rails may be distantly related to grebes. Like loons (called divers in Europe), grebes are slim, streamlined birds about the size of a small goose. They spend almost their entire life in water, even nesting on floating platforms of plant

BEAK CHIC
During the breeding season, male puffins grow a colorful bill sheath. It is shed when the season is over. Some Native Americans use the sheaths to adorn their ceremonial clothing.

material hidden in the reeds of their freshwater habitat. The chicks can swim immediately but, being sensitive to cold, prefer to be tucked under their parents' wings.

Loons are shy birds which spend some of their time at sea, and the rest of their time in lakes in northern forests and tundra. Their loud, yodelling calls conjure up for many people the essence of these lonely wildernesses. Like grebes, they have flexible, semi-webbed feet that work like propellers. These give them speed and maneuverability when chasing prey in the water.

While some small-billed grebes pick insects from waterweeds, the western grebe spears fish with its slender bill. It also eats its own feathers, even feeding them to its chicks! Grebes regurgitate pellets of things they can't digest, such as fish bones. Feathers may pad the pellets, making them easier—and less painful—to vomit.

Wading Game

The shallow coastal and inland shores seem always to have been rich in tiny animals. Waders and shorebirds, the Charadriiformes, emerged to exploit these valuable habitats. These birds have evolved to wade or swim after food. Since the shallow waters are prone to either freezing over or drying up, the birds are also able to fly far and fast should the need arise.

Charadriiformes includes waders such as curlews, sandpipers, snipe,

BILL BAG
This brown pelican is using its bill and pouch like a net to scoop up fish swimming near the surface. To reach fish deeper down, it will dive headfirst into the sea.

dotterels, stilts, avocets, jacanas, and pranticoles. Most have long, slender legs for wading, equally long and slender necks for feeding, and long, narrow wings for fast flight. Species that prefer estuaries and seashores, such as oystercatchers, tend to be a little heavier in build, with a wider range of bill sizes and shapes for snatching, probing, or prizing open prey. One small plover, the New Zealand wrybill, is unique among birds in having a bill that bends sideways, to the right. It seems to be an adaptation for picking insects from under stones in riverbeds. Least wader-like are the two sheathbills of Antarctic shores. They look like large white pigeons, although the skin around their eyes is bare. They use their stout bill to scavenge in the breeding colonies of birds and seals, eating eggs, carrion, and droppings.

CLOWNING AROUND
The blue-footed booby's name may come from the Spanish *bobo*, meaning clown or fool. Since courtship can involve head-tossing, bill-fencing, and parading around, the name seems appropriate.

GIRL POWER

Jacanas, or lotus birds, are sometimes called lilytrotters because of the way they walk across lily pads with their long toes and claws. Females, which are larger than males, often fight vigorously with other females over males. They usually mate with several males, which are left to build the nests, incubate the eggs, and look after the chicks.

Waders build nests in a variety of styles, ranging from the curlew's scrapes in the ground to the sand mounds of the Egyptian plover. The sand incubates the plover's eggs, but when it becomes too warm, the plover cools the eggs with wet belly feathers. It cools its chicks in the same way and buries them, too, if danger threatens!

SHEER SKILL
Shearwaters get their name from some species' habit of skimming just over the surface of the sea. This short-tailed shearwater, or muttonbird, nests in colonies of burrows.

The order Charadriiformes also contains gulls and gull-like birds, such as skuas or jaegers, skimmers, and terns. These birds live mainly by the sea, although some are found by fresh water. Their feet are webbed for swimming and the tip of their bill is generally hooked, since they are scavengers as well as predators.

Auks—guillemots or murres and puffins—also belong to this order. They fly offshore to exploit deeper seas; in fact, they seem to fill the same role as that of penguins in the Southern Hemisphere, using their wings as flippers to swim underwater for their food. But unlike penguins, auks can fly, although their stumpy wings and heavy body give their flight a "buzzy" appearance, low to the water.

anhingas, frigatebirds, tropicbirds, and pelicans. Many species dive like darts, often from amazing heights, to catch their prey. Squid and even other birds' eggs and chicks may be eaten, but the birds' primary food is fish. Gannets may even pursue fish underwater, moving with powerful feet and half-open wings. A few boobies will chase other birds until they regurgitate, then steal their food!

WIND SURFING
Albatrosses use strong gusts of wind, deflected upward by the waves, to soar for thousands of miles across the open ocean. This requires great skill, but wastes little energy.

Dart Attack

Flying is no problem for members of the order Pelecaniformes, such as gannets and boobies, cormorants and

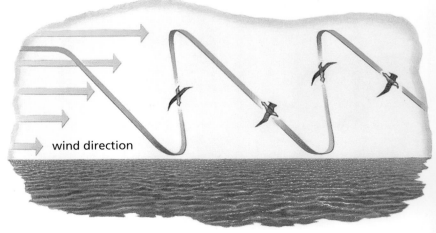

wind direction

SEA SWALLOWS
Terns are related to gulls.
But with their smaller feet,
forked tail, and longer,
more pointed wings, terns
are adapted for catching
prey by plunge-diving
into the ocean.

FREE SPIRIT
When fifteenth-century
Portuguese sailors sailed
into the South Atlantic they
called the birds they saw
alcatraz—"large seabirds."
English sailors later changed
alcatraz to *albatross*.

Cormorants are so skilled that some fishermen in Asia keep trained flocks. A collar is tied around the neck of each bird to stop it from swallowing its catch. The men let the birds dive, then take the fish when they resurface.

Pelecaniforms are found from the open ocean and sea coasts to lakes, swamps, and rivers. Most live in tropical and temperate areas, but some gannets and cormorants brave the subantarctic chill. Pelecaniforms can live more than 20 years, and many return to the same nest site each year to breed with the same mate. Some nest in huge, noisy, crowded colonies on isolated islands, and fights often break out as neighbors attempt to defend a space around their own nest. These colonies also produce enormous quantities of droppings, which in some countries is mined for fertilizer.

Both parents incubate the eggs by wrapping them in their large, webbed feet, or tucking them under their breast feathers. While one bird sits, the other feeds. If the incubating bird does not relinquish its duty when the other returns, the returning bird may push it off the nest!

Sky Sailors

Albatrosses, shearwaters, storm-petrels, and diving petrels are often called tubenoses because their nostrils are set in tubes on top of their bill. This feature is linked with the birds' well-developed sense of smell, which they use to find food, nesting sites, and each other.

Many tubenoses are recognized by their huge size: The average wingspan of the largest albatrosses is 10 feet (3 m). Other tubenoses are smaller— some prions measure 2 feet (60 cm) across—but many are handsomely marked with black and shades of gray.

Tubenoses live all over the world's oceans, using their hooked bill to catch squid and fish. Prions also use comblike growths in their bill to filter zooplankton (tiny animals) from the water. Most fulmars are scavengers, often flying around fishing boats. Giant petrels behave like vultures, cleaning subantarctic shores of the carcasses of seals and whales.

Albatrosses seldom approach land except to nest. They mate for life, and greet their partner on their return with spectacular displays that include bowing, braying, and wing-waving. Most albatrosses lay a single egg on nests of heaped soil and vegetation in dense colonies. They care for the chick for months until it can fend for itself.

DRY DOCK
Cormorants' plumage is not waterproof, reducing the energy needed to stay in the water, fishing. But it soon becomes waterlogged and heavy, so the birds spend much of the day drying out.

Birds of Prey

MEMBERS OF THE ORDER FALCONIFORMES are also known as raptors. "Raptor" comes from the Latin word *raptare*, which means "to seize and carry away." This term calls to mind eagles, the most powerful of avian predators. Yet this order includes a wide range of birds, from swift falcons to ungainly vultures.

Power and Privilege

Raptors' great strength and amazing abilities of flight and sight have inspired, enthralled, and terrified humans for thousands of years. So potent are they as symbols of power and freedom that even today they appear on the crests of many nations, and terms such as "eagle-eyed" have universal meaning.

Raptors are thought to have evolved from a waterbird ancestor during the Eocene Period, about 55 million years ago. Today, there are approximately 300 species. The smallest are the tiny falconets of Southeast Asia, which weigh only 2 ounces (55 g) and have a total length of 5½ to 6½ inches (14 to 17 cm). Among the largest is the Andean condor, which weighs up to 25 pounds (11.3 kg). Only albatrosses have longer wings.

The Jet Set

Raptors live on all continents except Antarctica, on many islands, and in almost any habitat: from tropical rain forest to Arctic tundra; dry desert to damp marshland; farmland to city.

Some raptors can live in a wide range of habitats, as long as there is suitable prey to catch. Other species are highly specialized and dependent on a particular type of habitat. For example, the snail kite eats only snails, which it picks out of the freshwater marshes of Florida, Cuba, and Mexico, south to Argentina. Some habitats support raptors only at certain times of the year. In winter, the Eleonora's falcon deserts its arid, rocky nesting

GLIDING HIGH
Condors and vultures can ride columns of air called thermals. These are caused when the Sun heats open ground, such as a field. This warms the air above, which then starts to rise.

WING SPAN
Raptor size ranges from the Andean condor, with wings spanning 11½ feet (3.5 m), to the 16-inch (40-cm) wide little sparrowhawk. Their proportions, wings, and tail shape reflect their lifestyle.

AIR FORCE
Raptors such as this bald eagle locate prey with their amazing eyesight. Some can spot a rabbit one mile (1.6 km) away. A human would need to be as close as 550 yards (500 m) away to see it!

islands in the Mediterranean and coastal Morocco and migrates to the humid forests of Madagascar.

Habitat and body shape are linked. Forest-dwellers such as goshawks tend to have short, rounded wings for flight among trees, while open-country species have either long, broad wings for soaring, like buzzards and eagles, or long, pointed wings for rapid flight, like falcons. The peregrine falcon can dive at speeds of up to 178 mph (288 kmph)! But despite their variety of shapes and sizes, lifestyles, and habitats, raptors share a common characteristic: They all eat meat.

Meat Hooks

Like most raptors, owls hunt live prey. But while owls are birds of prey, they are not considered raptors. This is because raptors typically hunt during the day; owls hunt at night. Raptors are also characterized by their sharply curved talons, hooked bills, and crop—a fleshy, pouchlike extension of the gullet, which is used to store and to partly digest food. Also, their large eyes are positioned at the front of their head. Unlike other birds, which have eyes in the sides of their head and see mostly through one eye at a time, raptors' eyes have some binocular

GYM-NASTICS
The remarkably flexible legs of the African gymnogene enable it to grope in awkward tree hollows for its prey of nestling birds and other small animals.

TALON TECHNIQUE

A raptor's feet are its most powerful weapons. The size, thickness, and curvature of its talons, and the length and thickness of its legs, are designed to match the bird's hunting habits.

ROUGH TROT
The osprey's curved talons, reversible outer toe, and spiny scales on the toe pads help it to clutch slippery fish and eels.

NEEDLE NAILS
Long, sinewy toes enable sparrowhawks and falcons to snare small, agile birds in midair. Their needle-sharp and well-curved claws offer maximum reach and grasping ability.

KING HIT
The powerful, grasping feet of the harpy eagle, with a dagger-like rear talon, can subdue large mammal prey not already killed by the impact of the bird's strike.

STRAIGHT AND NARROW
Scavenging species, such as vultures, have long, slender toes with limited gripping ability. Their almost straight talons are used to hold prey already dead, not to kill.

vision, allowing accurate judgment of depth and distance.

Some raptors are generalists: The versatile brown falcon eats rabbits, birds, insects, shrimps, and many other creatures, found dead and alive. Others, like the honey buzzard, are specialized feeders on honey and grubs. Harpy eagles use feet as large as a man's hands to snatch mammal prey from the trees of the Amazon rain forest. All raptors use their bill to tear off chunks of flesh, which they swallow whole with their muscular tongue. Most also regurgitate pellets made from parts of their prey that they can't digest, such as fur or scales.

Raptor Rapture

In a few species, such as harriers, the male may mate with several females, while in the Galápagos hawk and Harris's hawk several males may attend one female. But most raptors mate for life. Almost all species have courtship displays, often with mock aerial battles. For example, the male bald eagle commonly dives at the

HOVER CRAFT
The American kestrel, or sparrowhawk, is often seen hovering in search of ground prey. As with many raptors, males are smaller than females.

SMALL GAME
The generic name for falcons, *Falco*, means "sickle." It refers to the birds' curved claws. This African pygmy falcon takes insects and birds on the wing.

female flying below. In response, she rolls over in midair and raises her legs to him. Occasionally the pair may lock talons and somersault spectacularly across the sky. Male raptors also offer the females gifts of food, and both birds may bow and call. Harriers, which have a featherless yellow face, blush pink with excitement!

Most raptors build a nest of sticks, lined with feathers and similar soft materials, including, in some areas, clothing snatched from washing lines. Others return to the same nest year after year and need to make only minor repairs before settling in. But falcons use a tree hollow or a cliff edge, or take over the nest of another species. For example, the African pygmy falcon depends on weaver birds to provide it with a place to roost and nest. The weaver and the falcon breed

CHICK PICNIC
These red-shouldered hawks are waiting for their parents to return from hunting. They will then be fed pieces of meat torn up by their mother. The chicks will fledge at seven weeks.

at different times, so there is little conflict over the nest. Perhaps the weaver is helped by the aggressive little falcon who guards its nest. However, the falcon is not always so grateful—it occasionally eats weavers!

Raptor pairs split nest duties. The female incubates the eggs and broods the chicks. The male hunts and brings prey to the nest, where it is fed to the chicks. Honey buzzards, vultures, and the secretary bird also regurgitate food from their crop to feed their nestlings.

Small species tend to have larger clutches, and shorter incubation and nestling periods than those of larger species. A kestrel may lay four eggs and incubate them for four weeks; the chicks may leave the nest when they are five weeks old. But the Eurasian black vulture incubates its single egg for eight weeks, and the chick remains in the nest for more than four months.

Coaching Clinic

Most birds provide their chicks with food, shelter, warmth, and protection from predators. But young raptors must also be taught to hunt. After peregrine falcons have learnt to fly, they spend two months training in their parents' territory. The adults lead the young in mock chases, and

HUNTER'S HELPER

For centuries, raptors have been trained to catch food for humans. Falconry is now a sport in some countries. The hood is used to calm an excited or fearful falcon.

MOUSE TRAP

More than most raptors, kites seem to use their hearing to find their rodent prey. When food is plentiful, this black-shouldered kite may raise two or three broods of chicks in one year.

SAVANNA STOMPER

The secretary bird is more than 4 feet (1.2 m) tall. When excited or threatened, it raises the stiff, dark feathers on the back of its head. These make it look like a nineteenth-century lawyer's secretary, with a bundle of quill pens behind its ear. The secretary bird has no close relatives, and differs from other raptors in that it hunts on the ground. It rarely flies, instead striding across the African grasslands and stomping small prey to death with its stout toes.

South America are also Falconidae. Their name describes their cackling call. One species, the red-throated caracara, eats wasps, wasp nests, and forest fruits. Others are scavengers; the straited caracara of the Falkland Islands cleans dead chicks from seabird rookeries. Unlike true falcons, caracaras are sluggish fliers with a weak bill and talons designed for walking. Also unusual for Falconidae, they build nests.

WASTE DISPOSAL
Before sewerage systems were invented humans were grateful to have their trash removed before it started to spread disease. Old World lappet-faced vultures still provide this service today.

drop prey from above for them to catch. The young also learn by observation and imitation, catching insects and pretending to attack their siblings. But even with this training, the first few months alone are hard for a young peregrine. Many die before their first birthday.

Falcon Affiliates

Scientists classify raptors into four families. Family Sagittariidae has only one living representative, the secretary bird. Family Falconidae includes true falcons, such as the smaller kestrels, the gyrfalcons of the Arctic tundra, and the peregrine falcon, the fastest of all birds. The caracaras of Central and

The Nose Knows

The family name for the New World vultures, Cathartidae, comes from the Greek word *kathartes*. This means "a cleanser or purifier," and refers to the birds' habit of cleaning up carcasses, human waste, and other garbage. New World vultures—which also include two species of condor—are found only in North and South America.

But New World vultures are in fact related to storks, not to other raptors. Like storks, they have a "perforate" nostril running through the bill. Also like storks, they squirt their white excreta onto their legs to keep cool. However, they are commonly grouped with raptors because they share some

MOB RULE
Vultures push and shove to get the best bits of a carcass. But younger or weaker birds give way to those that are older or more powerful, and birds that have fed make room for hungry birds.

GROUP SWOOP
Eurasian griffons are some of the most sociable of vultures. They fly in flocks, spreading out and watching each other. When one spots a carcass, they all fly down for a feed.

and buzzards. These birds are varied in appearance and habits. The osprey can close its nostrils as it dives into the sea or lakes for fish. The bat hawks of Myanmar (Burma) to New Guinea catch bats at dusk. Black kites have a taste for carrion and can mass in hundreds around abattoirs. Sea eagles are known to steal prey from other raptors. Long-winged and long-tailed, harriers fly low and slow over open country and drop on birds, reptiles, and mammals. Goshawks, too, are powerful predators, but the palm nut vulture of Africa is almost vegetarian!

CRACKING CODE
Bearded vultures collect bones with their feet, then drop them from a height onto bare rock or rubble. They then eat the bone fragments, and extract the marrow with their tongue.

features. For example, like Old World vultures, these large, long-winged birds have long necks for reaching into carcasses, and a bare head that is easier to keep clean.

Old World vultures find food by sight, but some New World vultures find hidden carcasses using their excellent sense of smell. When not feeding, some smaller species roost together at night. They lay their eggs in caves, on the ground, or on ledges.

Squadron Leaders

Old World vultures are classified in Accipitridae. This family also includes honey buzzards and white-tailed kites; true kites and fish eagles; snake eagles; harpy eagles; booted eagles; goshawks and sparrowhawks; opreys; harriers;

DIVINE INTERVENTION
The Andean condor is the national symbol of Peru. Believed to have supernatural powers, condors were often sacrificed to the gods. They are now protected.

Flightless Birds

SOME FLYING BIRDS BECOME FLIGHTLESS when they are isolated on an island, away from predators. But "true" flightless birds evolved from flying birds to overcome challenges similar to those faced by early ungulates, such as horses. Penguins, too, have adapted their wings to take advantage of life at sea.

Why Fly?

Flying costs energy. A bird that flies must develop huge muscles to work its wings. In order for these flight muscles to work properly, the bird must also eat a lot of food to provide energy to power the muscles.

The ancestors of today's "true" flightless birds are thought to have emerged when the dinosaurs became extinct, 65 million years ago. Since they no longer had to fly to escape dinosaur predators, they ate less, enabling them to survive famines. As their wings and flight muscles shrank, their energy was used to grow taller and heavier. Their sternum, originally pointed to anchor the flight muscles, became flatter. In fact, most flightless birds belong to a group called ratites because of the shape of their sternum. "Ratite" comes from the Latin word *ratis*, meaning "raft."

But when large mammal predators evolved, many flightless birds died out. Others survived by becoming fast runners. Birds on islands without predators were also safe—for a time. New Zealand was home to the moas, wingless birds that first appeared about 2 million years ago. But when humans arrived, they overhunted the moas and burned their habitat. The very last moa was killed about 250 years ago.

Amazing Grazers

Ratites have several features in common. The structure of their palate is different to that of other birds, and their feathers are also unusual. The emu of Australia and cassowaries have plumage that hangs like hair from their body; each feather has two shafts. The ostrich of Africa, the rheas of South America, and the kiwis of New Zealand all have feathers with one shaft, but since the feathers are not used for flight, the barbules no longer "zip" together. This gives their plumage a loose, shaggy appearance.

STRANGE FRUIT
The hen-sized kiwi sleeps in a burrow during the day. At night, it probes the forest floor with its bill, sniffing out prey. Its rudimentary wings are hidden beneath its feathers.

TALL ORDER
About 12 species of moas are known. The largest moa, *Dinornis maximus*, was 10 feet (3 m) tall and weighed up to 440 pounds (200 kg).

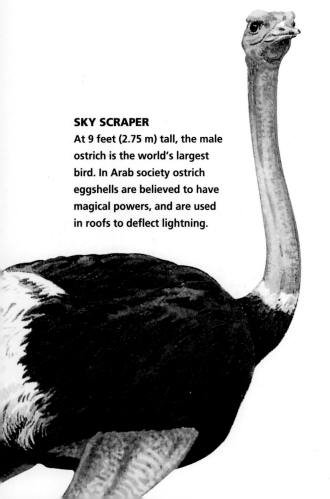

SKY SCRAPER
At 9 feet (2.75 m) tall, the male ostrich is the world's largest bird. In Arab society ostrich eggshells are believed to have magical powers, and are used in roofs to deflect lightning.

Ratites are running birds—an ostrich can sprint up to 40 mph (65 kmph). Their long, thin legs support their body's weight above the ground in a way similar to ungulates. The toes of some ratites have also modified for running. Most birds have four toes on each foot, but the emu and rheas have three toes, and the ostrich has only two.

Like some ungulates, emus lead a nomadic life. They feed wherever their food of flowers, seeds, leaves, grasses, and shoots grows, and move on when the supply runs out. Ostriches gather in large herds around waterholes, or wherever food is abundant. They also eat plants, and small vertebrates. Cassowaries depend on forest fruits, and move around a territory of up to two square miles (five km²) to gather food as different trees ripen. All ratites swallow grit and stones to help grind up plant food in their gizzard.

Role Reversal

Most ratite nests are a scrape in the ground lined with leaves and grass; the male kiwi digs a burrow. While emus form a pair bond for the breeding season, the male rhea attracts small flocks of females to his nest. Each hen lays an egg until the male drives the flock away. Once he begins incubating the eggs, the hens go off to attend another male!

Male kiwis and emus also incubate their eggs. The emu neither eats nor

DOTING DAD

As with most ratites, the male emu incubates the eggs. He then protects his chicks from predators and shows them what to eat. The chicks are striped for camouflage in long grass.

BE WARY OF THE CASSOWARY

Cassowaries are tall birds native to New Guinea and northeast Australia. Their powerful kicking legs have stiletto-like toes that can easily cut off a person's arm. Nevertheless, many people in the rain forests of New Guinea capture and raise young cassowaries. The people slaughter the cassowaries for food when the birds reach maturity to supply the protein that their diet lacks.

BIRD BULLETS

Leopard seals eat penguins. To avoid seals lurking under the ice, the birds accelerate as they near the surface, catapulting into the air. These Adélies are falling on each other in their rush.

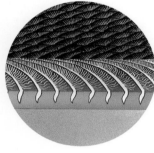

TILE STYLE

The penguin's efficient plumage combines a warm, downy inner layer of feathers with a smooth, waterproof outer layer. These overlap, much like the tiles on a roof.

drinks during the eight weeks of incubation, instead living on reserves of fat. In ostriches, the hen incubates during the day, while the male takes the night shift.

Most ratites lay large eggs, but a kiwi's egg, equivalent to 25 percent of the female's total body weight, is proportionately the largest egg laid by any bird! Kiwi chicks are independent almost from the time they leave the burrow. But emu males guard their chicks for their first seven months, while ostriches can remain in family groups for a year or more.

Feathered Fins

Penguins have remained essentially unchanged for at least 45 million years. The most aquatic of all birds,

some may spend up to three-quarters of their life in the sea, coming ashore only to breed and molt.

Penguins use their stiff, flattened, paddle-like wings to "fly" underwater. Covered with tiny feathers, their wings feel like felt-covered boomerangs to the touch. Their short legs and feet are set back on their body and act like rudders. Although ridiculously clumsy on land—some penguins toddle as if their knees are tied together—they are the most accomplished of avian divers. Most other seabirds are confined to the top 65 feet (20 m)

PENGUIN PARADE

The 18 species of penguin range in size from the 4-foot (1.2-m) tall emperor penguin to the fairy penguin, which is smaller than a chicken.

Emperor   Chinstrap   Yellow-eyed   Magellanic   Fjordland   Little (Fairy)

TAKING THE PLUNGE
On land, the rockhopper often bounds with its feet together, like someone in a sack race. But it is a supreme swimmer, reaching speeds of up to 15 mph (24 kmph) during brief stints.

of ocean, but the emperor penguin can dive to 1,772 feet (540 m) and stay under for more than 20 minutes. Their bones, which are heavier than those of other birds, enable them to dive deeper, while their blubber-like fat layer provides warmth and "neutral buoyancy" to stop them sinking too deep. Even the smaller gentoo penguin can dive to depths of 500 feet (150 m) as it hunts for krill, fish, and squid.

Southern Comfort

Penguins are often associated with the icy wastes of Antarctica, but only the emperor and the Adélie penguins live in Antarctica all year round. Other species are found in the cooler waters of the southern oceans, especially in the subantarctic areas around New Zealand and the Falkland Islands. They also live in eastern and southern Argentina and Chile, extending north to Peru; on the mainland coasts and offshore islands of Australia; and in

southwestern Africa. Although the Galápagos penguin lives almost exactly on the Equator, there are no penguins in the Northern Hemisphere.

Many penguins make nests out of stones, although species in warmer areas, such as the Magellanic penguins of Patagonia, nest under bushes or dig burrows in sand. But emperors breed in the dead of winter, the female going off to the sea to feed while the male incubates the egg on his feet. By the time she returns to give her chick its first feed, two months later, the male may have lost half his body weight.

Penguins are hunted by such aquatic predators as leopard seals and orcas. Skilled aerial predators such as skuas can also snatch chicks and eggs. But humans have taken the greatest toll. For example, in the nineteenth century thousands of king penguins were boiled down for oil. Thanks to legal protection, the population of these wonderful birds is now recovering.

USE 'EM OR LOSE 'EM
The flightless cormorant of the Galápagos Islands has no natural enemies. It has evolved only tiny wings, so it hops in and out of water, scrambling up rocks to get to its nest—like a penguin.

MOONLIGHT VIGIL
Emperor penguins gather in colonies that can number up to 60,000 birds. During blizzards, they huddle in huge circles, which slowly spiral so that each bird gets a turn out of the wind.

Reptiles and Amphibians

The ancestors of today's amphibians were the first vertebrates to leave the water and spend some of their time on land. Early reptiles evolved from these amphibians. Today there are 4,950 living species of amphibian and 7,400 species of reptile. They vary enormously in size and structure, from tiny frogs only half an inch (1.3 cm) long to snakes that can reach nearly 30 feet (10 m)! Many species are dull to look at, but others rival the birds with their bold, bright patterns and gaudy colors.

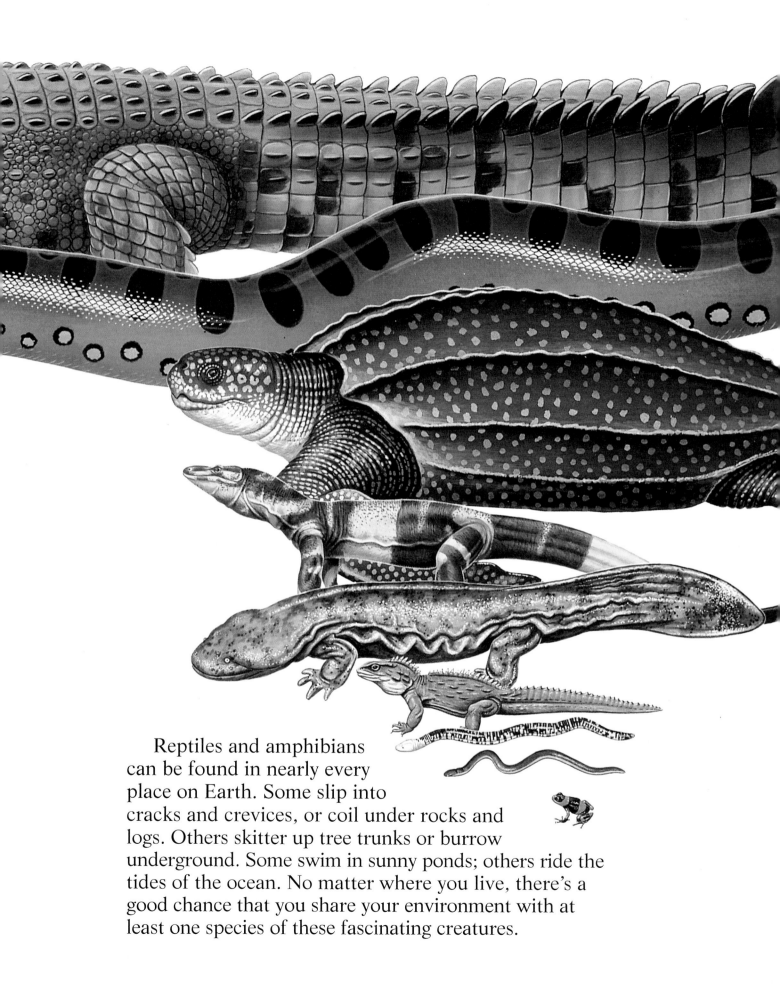

Reptiles and amphibians can be found in nearly every place on Earth. Some slip into cracks and crevices, or coil under rocks and logs. Others skitter up tree trunks or burrow underground. Some swim in sunny ponds; others ride the tides of the ocean. No matter where you live, there's a good chance that you share your environment with at least one species of these fascinating creatures.

Classifying Reptiles and Amphibians

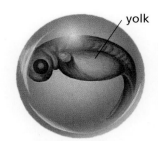

yolk

AMPHIBIAN EGG

L IKE FISH, MAMMALS, AND BIRDS, reptiles and amphibians are vertebrates—backboned animals. But unlike mammals and birds, reptiles and amphibians are "cold-blooded," and also differ from each other in many ways. Still, they are often studied together in the field of herpetology (from the Greek *herpo*, to creep or crawl).

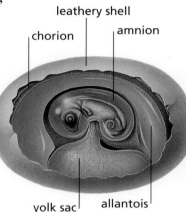

leathery shell

chorion — amnion

yolk sac — allantois

REPTILE EGG

Hatched Batch

There are three orders of living amphibians and four orders of reptiles. Most amphibians and reptiles hatch from eggs, but the life cycle of amphibians, which include newts, frogs, and toads, is quite different from that of reptiles.

Amphibians lay eggs varying in number, from a single egg to many thousands. Since the eggs do not have a waterproof covering, they are always laid in water or damp places so they do not dry out. Most species fertilize the eggs outside their body. Water carries the sperm to the eggs.

Each fertilized egg is surrounded by dense protective jelly, and contains yolk to nourish the developing young. The waste products simply pass out

through the jelly. The eggs hatch out into aquatic larvae, such as tadpoles, which eventually develop into adults which breathe air and live mostly on land.

A reptile egg is more complex. Most reptiles produce eggs within which the embryo develops into a miniature version of the adult, then hatches. The eggs are fertilized inside the female reptiles by the males.

The egg is typically covered with a hard or leathery shell. This waterproof shell prevents the young from drying out and enables it to develop on land. Oxygen enters the egg through a sac called the chorion, just beneath the shell. The yolk sac nourishes the embryo and its waste is stored in another sac called the allantois.

SELF-CONTAINED UNIT

An amphibian embryo develops inside a jelly capsule. A reptile grows within a closed system, cushioned by the amnion, a fluid-filled sac which also prevents it from drying out.

DOUBLE LIFE

"Amphibian" comes from the Greek word *amphibios*, meaning "a being with a double life." Most amphibians do indeed live two lives—in water as larvae, and on land as adults. Even when mature, species such as this red-eyed leaf-frog cannot survive far from a damp environment. A reptile's watertight skin stops its body from drying out and enables it to live in dry habitats. But most amphibians' thin, porous skin must be kept moist to function well.

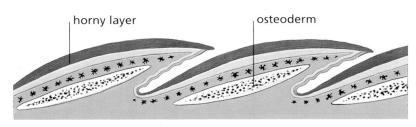

horny layer   osteoderm

SKIN AND BONE
A reptile's outer skin layer, made of dry, coarse scales or scutes, protects it from enemies and the rough ground. Some species have osteoderms—bony plates under the skin—for extra strength.

Clever Cover

A reptile's skin is watertight, but amphibians absorb and expel water through their skin. Although most amphibians have lungs, their skin also absorbs oxygen and releases carbon dioxide. Glands secrete mucus to keep the skin moist, fats to waterproof the skin, or poisons with which many species defend themselves.

Many reptiles and amphibians can also protect themselves by changing their skin color, using pigment cells just below the skin surface. Skin color is also used to attract a mate and to regulate temperature.

DRESSED FOR DINNER
Mammals and birds shed and replace their skin constantly. But reptiles and amphibians, like this spotted salamander, typically shed their skin either in large fragments or all at once.

The Taste Test

Amphibians and reptiles have good eyesight to capture prey and avoid predators. Many also have color vision, used to recognize mates. Hearing is acute in those species that use sound to communicate, such as frogs.

The senses of smell and taste are also well developed in most reptiles and amphibians. Many species "taste" food caught by their muscular, flexible tongue with the Jacobson's organ in the roof of their mouth. The tongue also collects scent particles and passes them to the Jacobson's organ for identification. In this way such species can sense prey—or predators.

Efficient Feeders

Most amphibians have simple teeth to grasp their food, but reptiles' teeth vary in structure and form. Some lizards have blunt teeth to crush prey, while some snakes use specialized teeth called fangs to inject venom.

"Warm-blooded" animals must eat a great deal just to create the energy to maintain their body temperature. But because reptiles and amphibians draw heat from the environment, they do not need to eat as much and use the energy from food more efficiently.

CATCHING SOME RAYS
Reptiles and amphibians are ectothermic—they depend on external sources of heat to create energy. They adopt different positions during the day to regulate their body temperature.

12 noon

10 am

6 pm

5 am

Reptiles and Amphibians through the Ages

ABOUT 300 MILLION YEARS AGO, during the Carboniferous Period, some amphibians developed a dry, scaly skin and eggs with a waterproof shell that protected the growing young from drying out. These adaptations allowed them to move away from water and evolve into a variety of reptiles living in many environments.

A Breath of Fresh Air

The first vertebrates evolved in the sea about 500 million years ago. During the next 150 million years, they continued to develop into amazingly diverse groups of fishes. But to take advantage of the new habitats available on land, these animals had to develop ways of obtaining oxygen from the air, rather than water, and modify their skeleton to support their body weight without the buoyancy offered by water. They also needed a way to propel themselves along the ground.

The first animals with four jointed legs were the amphibians. They made the transition from water to land about 350 million years ago.

FISH OUT OF WATER
Euthenopteron lived 360 million years ago. It had lungs as well as gills, and its muscular fins were the forerunners of amphibian leg bones.

From Fish to Flesh

The earliest known amphibians were *Ichthyostega* and *Acanthostega*. They had a skull like that of their ancestors and other fishlike features, such as a tail fin and scales on the belly and tail. But unlike fish they had a short neck, and four legs, a thickened spine, and a well-developed rib cage to support them on land. Over the next 100 million years, the amphibians evolved into many diverse forms and became the dominant animals of the day. Some were enormous, reaching 13 feet (4 m) in length! But their eggs lacked a protective shell, so they still needed water—or at least a very moist environment—to complete their life cycle.

About 50 million years after the first amphibians appeared, the first reptiles emerged. Unlike their ancestor, they hatched from eggs with a waterproof shell that could be laid on land. As their survival rate improved, new species flourished. This was the beginning of the Age of the Reptiles (250 to 65 million

EGG CUP
Dinosaurs laid hard-shelled eggs, increasing their chances of survival. By the Triassic Period, 225 million years ago, they had replaced the amphibians as the dominant land animals.

DASH AND SLASH
Deinonychus, a saurischian, was an energetic, agile predator. It grabbed its prey with its long forelegs and disemboweled it with the sharp claws on its hindlegs.

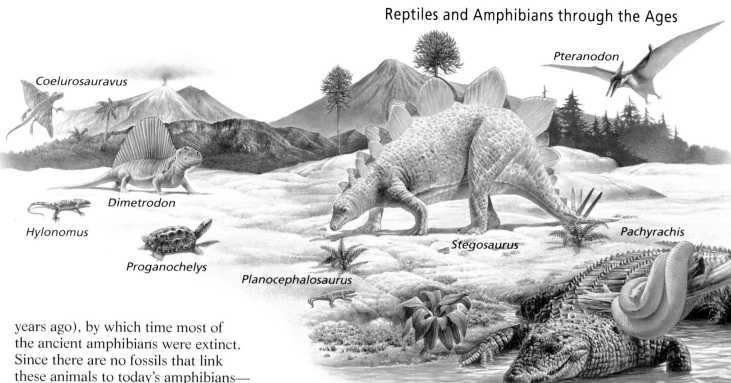

Coelurosauravus

Pteranodon

Dimetrodon

Hylonomus

Stegosaurus

Pachyrachis

Proganochelys

Planocephalosaurus

Deinosuchus

Archelon

Ichthyosaurus

Elasmosaurus

years ago), by which time most of the ancient amphibians were extinct. Since there are no fossils that link these animals to today's amphibians— the earliest known frog fossil, from Madagascar, is 245 million years old— the direct ancestors of modern species are unknown.

Reptiles Rule, OK

One early reptile was *Hylonomus*, a little lizard-like animal that hunted small amphibians and insects. Some later reptiles, such as the 10-foot (3-m) long *Dimetrodon*, were related to the ancestors of mammals. Another species, *Coelurosauravus*, had flaps of skin attached to its ribs, which enabled it to glide from tree to tree like a modern-day flying lizard. The 3-foot (1-m) long *Proganochelys*, from the late Triassic Period (245 to 208 million years ago) had much in common with living tortoises. The smaller *Planocephalosaurus*, which also lived during that time, resembled the New Zealand tuatara.

Dinosaurs first appeared in the Triassic Period. Some were the size of chickens; others may have been as long as a jumbo jet. Scientists divide dinosaurs into two groups, depending on how their hip bones were arranged: The Saurischia had a reptile-like pelvis, while the

Ornithischia had a birdlike pelvis. Some of the Saurischia evolved into the biggest carnivores the world has ever known, fierce predators such as *Tyrannosaurus* and *Allosaurus*. Others became giant herbivores: *Brachiosaurus* stood 40 feet (12 m) high, and *Diplodocus* was 100 feet (30 m) long. Some of the Ornithischia, which were all plant-eaters, also became giants. *Stegosaurus*, from the late Jurassic Period, was 30 feet (10 m) long. It had rows of plates along its back and sharp spikes, probably used for defense, on its tail.

While dinosaurs ruled the land, marine reptiles such as plesiosaurs and ichthyosaurs dominated the sea. One species from the Cretaceous Period, the 3-foot (1-m) long *Pachyrachis*, may be related to the ancestor of today's snakes. The sky was the domain of pterosaurs, the largest animals that ever took to active flight. They had wings of skin, which were supported by their greatly

SEA MONSTERS
Elasmosaurus was a 46-foot (14-m) long plesiosaur. The toothless 13-foot (4-m) long *Archelon* may have eaten jellyfish. *Deinosuchus was* 49 feet (15 m) long—maybe the largest crocodile ever!

201

elongated fourth fingers and attached to their body at thigh level. The best known pterosaur, *Pteranodon,* had a 23-foot (7-m) wingspan. It soared far out to sea, gulping fish caught in its pouch like a modern-day pelican.

'Saur Losers

Dinosaurs dominated the Earth for 180 million years. Their reign came to an end when, about 65 million years ago, a catastrophic event suddenly killed them off, along with most of the other large reptiles, such as plesiosaurs and ichthyosaurs. While the ancestors of today's reptiles survived to evolve into thousands of different species, the only living representatives of those original reptiles are the turtles and crocodiles.

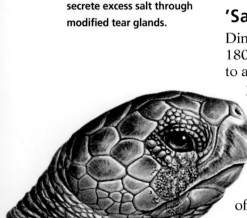

Smooth Moves

Today, reptiles and amphibians are found throughout much of the world, even in the Andes and the Himalayas above 15,000 feet (4,500 m). But because they rely on external sources for their body heat, most species are found in the warmer parts of the world, especially tropical and desert areas.

Reptiles and amphibians have developed special features to suit their different habitats. For example, most lizards have four well-developed legs, and toes with strong claws for digging or climbing, fringes for shimmying through sand, or even webbing for gliding or swimming. A few species, like geckos, have evolved adhesive toe pads that enable them to scale smooth vertical surfaces and even walk upside down! Other tree-dwelling lizards, such as chameleons, have opposable toes (like the thumb and fingers of a human) and a

prehensile tail that enables them to grasp twigs and branches, monkey-style. But other lizards have reduced limbs or no limbs at all. These lizards usually burrow underground, or live in habitats where limbs would be of little use, such as areas with many narrow crevices or low, dense vegetation.

In the same way, a snake's body shape will also reflect its lifestyle. For example, a ground-dwelling snake has an almost circular body. It moves by using its strong muscles to push backward against slippery sand and soil, or rough rocks. Some tree snakes have a ridge running along each side of their belly to help them grip small crevices and notches on the branches.

Eye Contact

Many tree snakes and lizards also have eyes directed forward so that they can see in three dimensions and judge distances. But since eyes have no useful purpose in a dark burrow, reptiles that live underground have only rudimentary eyes.

To keep soil out of their ears, burrow-dwellers also have reduced ear openings. Projecting scales over the ears make the openings even smaller. Other species that dive into soil to escape predators, such as the Mohave fringe-toed lizard, also keep dirt out of their eyes and mouth with interlocking scales on their upper and lower eyelids, and an upper jaw that overlaps the lower one. They can also close their nostrils.

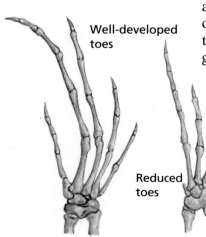

Well-developed toes

Reduced toes

No toes

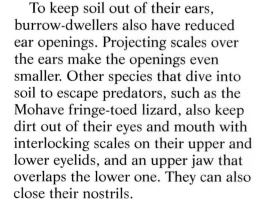

Wet Ones

Due to their greater dependence on moisture, amphibians tend to be less diverse in shape and size than reptiles. Nevertheless, they also have adapted to meet the challenges of their environment. Burrowing amphibians such as caecilians have a heavy skull useful for plowing tunnels. Some burrowing toads and frogs have bony, spadelike growths on their hindfeet so they can scoop holes into soft dirt. Pond frogs have powerful hindlegs and fully webbed feet for leaping from land to water, where they are excellent swimmers.

Tree frogs have adapted to life among the leaves by becoming much flatter than ground-dwelling species. This distributes the weight evenly over their whole body, enabling them to balance and move with great agility. Special finger and toe pads help them stick to smooth surfaces as they move

WATER TOWERS
The thorny devil of central Australia is well adapted to desert life. Its sharp, spiny scales are arranged so that they collect rainwater, which is channeled along fine grooves to its mouth.

VINE ENTWINED
The green colors of the vine snake of Central and South America blend in with leaves. Its long, slender body enables it to bridge gaps between branches.

FLYING SQUAD

Perhaps the most unusual adaptation of tree-dwelling lizards is the ability to glide. Some Asian species have extended ribs that support a membrane to form gliding "wings." These lizards can escape predators by gliding up to 65 yards (60 m), either to the ground or onto another tree trunk. The "gliding" gecko of Southeast Asia (above) also parachutes from tree to tree, using the fleshy flaps of skin along its sides and the webs between its toes.

about grasping branches or leaping from one perch to another.

The need for water for their tadpoles presents special challenges for those frogs that live in trees. This problem has been solved in some clever ways. For example, the female pygmy marsupial frog of South American highland rain forests carries her eggs in a moist pouch on her back.

Species such as the water-holding frog of Australia have even adapted to arid environments. Before the dry season, it fills its urinary bladder with water to stop itself from drying out. It then buries itself underground, shedding its loose, baggy skin and lining it with mucus. The skin dries and hardens to form a waterproof cocoon, within which the frog lies still until the rains come again.

Reptile and Amphibian Behavior

Every activity of an animal's life—hatching, feeding, reproducing, escaping from predators, even just moving about—depends on the maintenance of a body temperature that allows it to function normally. As a result, much of the behavior of reptiles and amphibians is aimed at temperature regulation.

Solar-Powered

The temperatures at which most reptiles and amphibians function best range from 68°F to 86°F (20°C to 30°C). They regulate their temperature by their behavior. Many lizards, for example, warm up by moving into the sun or onto a warm surface and exposing as much of their body as they can to the heat. To cool down, they expose as little of their body as possible to the heat, or they move into the shade or to a cool crevice or a burrow. These places often trap a little water, and the sheltering lizard can breathe moist air, which also helps to keep it cool.

Some species use different methods. The sand goanna of Australia opens its mouth and flutters its throat pouch to increase evaporation from its mouth. Crocodiles also cool themselves by evaporation by filling their gaping lower jaw with water. But not all reptiles are active during the day: Some tropical lizards and snakes are nocturnal because the nighttime temperatures are mild and constant.

Most amphibians are nocturnal, and are active only when their surroundings are moist enough to stop them becoming dehydrated. However, some frogs in cooler climates bask to raise their body temperature, but only if they live near water, since basking also dries them out. Tiger salamanders and tadpoles in many parts of the world raise their temperature by moving into shallower water on sunny days.

Cold Storage

Being "cold-blooded" can have its disadvantages. When the weather becomes cooler, so too do many reptiles and amphibians. Their heartbeat and breathing slow, and their movements become sluggish. This makes them vulnerable to predators. Low temperatures can also mean that they can't digest their food. But some species

RESTING UP
Crocodilians save energy by lying still, submerged in shallow water. This behavior, plus their efficient digestion, helps them to survive for months without a meal.

when tail is shaken, interlocking shells of hardened skin make a rattling sound

SUN TANS
In the morning and late afternoon, the skin of rhinoceros iguanas becomes dark to absorb the Sun's heat. In the middle of the day, it gets lighter to prevent overheating.

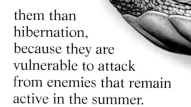

have devised some clever ways to overcome this problem. For example, marine iguanas of the Galápagos Islands huddle overnight in large piles to help stay warm and speed digestion.

But being "cold-blooded" also has its good points. A drop in body temperature that could kill a warm-blooded animal will merely render a lizard inactive. Also, reptiles and amphibians can "shut down" when conditions are unsuitable. In colder climates, lizards, snakes, and frogs head for safe retreats in burrows or under rocks and hibernate there until spring. Turtles also hibernate, either in or out of water. Hibernation not only conserves energy, but also helps keep these animals safe from predators. Alligators, too, can survive freezing conditions in shallow pools—as long as they keep their nose above the water so that a breathing hole forms when the water freezes.

Temperatures which are too high can be just as problematic as the cold, however. In desert regions, frogs are active during the cooler seasons but burrow underground to avoid the heat and drought of summer. They go into a state of inactivity, called estivation, until conditions improve. Estivation is like hibernation, but the animal goes into a lighter sleep. Turtles also estivate when ponds and rivers evaporate and become too warm. Estivation is more dangerous for

them than hibernation, because they are vulnerable to attack from enemies that remain active in the summer.

Lures and Sinkers

Most reptiles and amphibians are predators themselves. Many amphibians simply sit and wait for prey to come within reach before grabbing it in their long, sticky tongue. But some frogs, especially the small poison frogs in tropical America, actively forage for insects by day and find their prey by sight. The South American horned frogs lure prey by waving the long toes on their hind feet.

PERPETUAL MOTION
Turtles derive their body heat from warm water. Species that dive for food rely on an insulating layer of fat to help them cope with the lower temperature of deeper water.

DEATH RATTLE
Some scientists think that the rattlesnake's famous rattling tail distracts prey; it watches the snake's tail, and ignores its fangs—until it is too late.

HIGH SEAS DRIFTER

Marine turtles can spend more than a year building up the fat reserves they will need when they leave their feeding grounds. They can journey up to 3,000 miles (5,000 km) across oceans to reach their nesting beaches. Other species travel by accident, riding drifting logs and other debris to remote islands. Some castaways are washed ashore, where they may set up colonies.

MISTAKEN IDENTITY
The colors of the venomous Mayan coral snake (right), warn predators away. The almost identical colors of the harmless false coral snake (far right), trick enemies into avoiding it, too.

Some snakes, such as the death adder, the woma python, and vipers, also lure prey within striking range by wiggling the insect-like tip of their tail. The movement, and the rustling noise it makes in the grass or leaves, lures animals close. It is also thought that the twig snake uses its black-tipped red tongue to lure birds.

Other reptiles actively chase prey, while some species hunt by stealth. As an alligator approaches its victim, it submerges and swims beneath the surface until it is close enough to attack. It moves so quietly and smoothly that the vegetation on top of the water is not even disturbed. The saltwater crocodile can watch its prey for days beforehand, waiting for just the right moment. A split second of vulnerability, and the crocodile strikes—dragging its meal under the surface in a "death roll."

While crocodiles are always ready to take advantage of a ready-made meal in the form of a drowned zebra or wildebeest, they also occasionally cooperate to catch fish. The Nile crocodile gathers in groups in areas where water flow is restricted to a single outlet. This one-way water flow forces fish down the river straight into the jaws of the crocodiles. They form a semicircle around this area to reduce the chances of fish escaping between two crocodiles. Cooperative crocodiles catch more of the fish moving downstream than a solitary hunter could.

Hide or Seek

Amphibians and reptiles have many enemies, including wading birds, bats, spiders, fish, mammals—and other amphibians and reptiles! A good way to avoid being eaten is to avoid being seen—a camouflaged, motionless frog is difficult to spot. Many lizards have patterns and colors that blend in with their habitat, and some lizards are able to change their color and pattern. In only a few seconds, a chameleon can change dramatically by moving and expanding pigments in its skin.

Running away is sometimes the best form of defense, and lizards are renowned for their speedy

TONGUE TERROR
The slow-moving blue-tongued skink cannot run from danger. Instead it puffs itself up, sticks out its bright blue tongue and hisses at its attacker.

FRILLED TO MEET YOU
Some lizards try to frighten attackers by pretending to be bigger than they really are. The Australian frilled lizard startles a predator by opening its mouth, hissing, and flourishing the frill behind its neck.

escapes. They climb trees and walls, scuttle into crevices or even, in the case of the basilisks, run across water. A frog can also escape death with a great leap on its long, powerful hindlegs. But sometimes escape is not possible: An enemy has to be faced, and other defenses are necessary.

Fright or Fight

Reptiles and amphibians have devised numerous ways to defend themselves. These include secreting poisonous or foul-tasting substances from the skin. Salamanders that have poison glands in their tail may lash it at predators. One species of musk turtle is known as the stinkpot: When picked up it releases a very strong smell.

Biting is another effective deterrent. Many snakes are notorious for their venomous bite, but there are even some frogs that actually leap at predators and snap at them!

PRETTY BUT POISONOUS

Many frogs try to avoid detection by blending in with their surroundings. Others do the opposite: Their vivid coloring signals that they are dangerous. When disturbed, this oriental fire-bellied toad arches its back to show its colorful underside. Predators learn to avoid it, or risk a mouthful of a foul-tasting—and toxic—skin secretion.

Some lizards and snakes try to intimidate attackers by bluff. Some extend their neck or throat crest or inflate their neck in order to look bigger than an attacker—or too big to swallow. Some frogs and toads defend themselves by puffing up their body.

Other species attempt to startle a predator to give themselves a chance to escape. Some lizards and snakes flash brightly colored throats or tongues. A few South American frogs deter attackers with vivid eyespots on their rump. The regal horned lizard even bursts blood vessels in and around its eyes. It can then squirt a stream of blood up to 3 feet (1 m).

Many small lizards, especially geckos and skinks, are able to shed their tail if it is grabbed by a predator. While the predator is distracted by the writhing tail on the ground, the lizard escapes. It loses very little blood and a new tail grows back over the next few months. The chameleon gecko of Australia goes one step farther—its broken tail distracts enemies by making squeaking noises.

Some frogs scream loudly when seized. The noise may not only scare the predator into dropping the frog, but may also warn other frogs of danger.

Last Chance

Some reptiles defend themselves with armor. For example, the armadillo girdle-tailed lizard of Africa curls itself into a

MIRACLE WALKER
The basilisk escapes predators by going where they cannot follow. It runs on water, supporting itself with fringes on its toes, before diving in and swimming to safety.

HOT-HEADS
Male chameleons change their dull camouflage colors to bright hues to warn other males away from their territory. This species changes to a threatening red to intimidate a rival.

IT'S A WRAP
Pythons are some of the few species that incubate their eggs. But they do not care for the newly hatched young. Once snakes hatch, they must fend for themselves.

ball and protects its soft belly with a prickly fence. The long, spiky scales of species such as the Australian thorny devil and the horned lizards of North America make them hard for predators to swallow. But when all else fails, some species play dead in the hope that a predator will release them. Nicoll's toadlet of Australia will even lie on its back, perfectly still, with its legs in the air. The hognose snake also confuses predators by rolling onto its back, going limp, releasing a foul smell, opening its mouth and letting its tongue hang out!

Love and War

Some lizard species live in colonies, but many amphibians and reptiles live alone. They come in contact with other members of their species only for courtship and mating, and to fight over living areas. For this reason, it is important that individuals of the same species recognize each other.

The most obvious examples of this behavior in amphibians are the calls made by male frogs. Each species has its own distinctive call. Many frogs call not only to attract females, but also to advertise their territory. Some reptiles also use sound. During the breeding season, male crocodiles roar loudly. Geckos court mates or defend their hunting territories with chirping or clicking sounds or sharp barks.

Some lizards communicate with color. Male anole lizards have a brightly colored throat flap, called a dewlap, that they expand in a sudden flash of color to warn other males or to attract females. Male chameleons change skin color to threaten rivals, while other male

HAND SHAKE
During the spring breeding season, this male red-eared turtle courts a female by fluttering his claws in front of her face.

TRICK OR CHEAT

When mating is highly competitive, usually because there are more males than females, some males adopt alternative mating strategies—or cheat. In some frog and toad species, such as the natterjack toad, smaller males that cannot make the louder, more rapidly-repeated calls that are preferred by females stop calling. Instead, they sit near a larger, calling male and try to intercept females attracted to the calling male before they can reach him.

GOOD VIBRATIONS
American alligators can communicate without sound. They tell other alligators where they are by a kind of silent purring that sends vibrations through the water.

lizards change color to let females know they are ready to mate. Some females change as well. Collared and leopard lizard females develop red or orange markings on their sides, head and under their tail just before they lay eggs. This may let males know they are not interested in mating.

As male and female turtles usually look the same, they recognize each other through behavior rather than by appearance. Male turtles head-butt or bite females, or "dance" in the water to attract their attention. Other reptiles also use movement: Iguanas and dragon lizards wave one leg in the air, bob their head or do "push ups" to show that

they are ready to mate or to warn invaders to leave their territory. Other lizards send similar messages by raising their crest, or lashing their tail.

Some reptiles and amphibians, such as salamanders, can also send scent messages with pheromones, chemicals produced by glands in the skin. But sometimes peaceful communication gives way to battles to establish dominance and the right to mate with females. Male lace monitors wrestle each other for a mate, as do some snakes. Some green tree pythons in zoos have been known to kill each other. Tortoises may butt their shells together, while the bony "tusks" in the lower jaw of the male tusked frog may also be used to fight other males.

Mission Accomplished

Unlike mammals, parental care is almost unheard of in reptiles. Some species guard their eggs, but perhaps the only species that take care of their young are crocodiles and alligators. They help their young hatch and escape the nesting mound to the relative safety of the water.

It is also rare for amphibians to care for their young after birth, but there are some exceptions. Some South American pond frogs guard their tadpoles, and even leap at potential predators. The male marsupial or pouched frog of Australia carries his tadpoles in "pockets" near his hindlegs, where the tadpoles stay until they are mature.

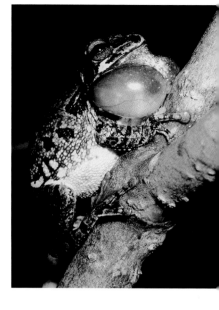

LOVE SERENADE
This Mexican tree frog is calling by forcing air from his lungs through his vocal cords into his vocal sacs. The sound is amplified in these bubble-like chambers.

SPIKY SWEETHEARTS
Galápagos marine iguanas are usually grayish-black. When the male's body turns rusty red and his spiny crests and front legs turn green, females know that he is ready to mate.

Endangered Species

REPTILES AND AMPHIBIANS are threatened when their habitats are destroyed; when they are hunted for body parts; when they are collected as "pets;" and when they are preyed on by introduced species such as pigs, cats, and rats. Humans are the main danger, but we have the power to stop the extinctions.

Decline and Fall

There have always been endangered species. Fossils tell us that clusters of species have died out during the course of millions of years. Perhaps one animal out-competed another for a limited resource, or became unable to adapt to a changing environment. This happened to many amphibian groups 285 to 200 million years ago. As each group died out, new species emerged to take its place.

But now the extinction of species is occurring faster than new ones can replace them. This rate will continue as some people struggle to meet the most basic needs of life while others pursue lives of excessive consumption.

Danger: Humans

Species are threatened by hunting for meat, skins, and other body parts. Crocodiles, alligators, snakes, and lizards are killed for leather for the fashion industry. As the demand from wealthy countries grows, so does the rate of the slaughter. For many people living in developing countries, a skin can be worth a month's wages.

Turtle eggs, too, are eaten in many countries, but young turtles already face many dangers. Harvesting eggs reduces even more the number of hatchlings that survive to maturity. But in developing countries, laws to control the trade in skins and eggs are difficult to enforce.

Disturbing the Peace

Introduction of predators such as foxes, cats, and mongooses have wreaked havoc on some species. Animals on islands or in other small areas are especially vulnerable because they often occur in small numbers. Also, they have evolved in relative safety and may not have developed the behavior or body adaptations needed to protect themselves against attack from intruders. Feral goats also ruin

THE COMMON GOOD
The gavial lives in rivers from Pakistan to Myanmar (Burma). It is threatened by drowning in fishing nets, hunting, and egg collection. Protected areas provide safe havens for the gavial and other animals.

BORN FREE
Gila monsters inhabit dry regions of Mexico and the American southwest. They are considered vulnerable because large numbers are taken from the wild for the pet trade.

SHELL SHOCK

The marbled upper shell of the Pacific hawksbill turtle is used in the production of items from hair brushes to spectacle frames. The use of sought-after "tortoiseshell" has put turtles at great risk.

vegetation, and even exotic plants can take their toll: On the Galápagos Islands, introduced trees and vines compete with native plants and deny the local tortoises food.

Land Is Life

Pollution is one of the greatest threats facing amphibians and reptiles today. For example, some turtles die when they choke on plastic bags, which they mistake for their food, jellyfish. Many others get tangled in fishing nets and drown. Frogs are especially sensitive to water pollution, and chemical run-off and detergents in water can stop frogs from breathing through their skin, or even poison them. Logging, farming, and grazing, as well as rapid increases in human populations, are responsible for the

BIG BULLY

The bullfrog is native to eastern North America. This predator competes with—and sometimes eats—other frogs, and its release in places such as Italy has caused the extermination of local frogs.

destruction of many species. Laws to "protect" a species will not work unless its habitat can also be saved. But this is a difficult task in some countries, where the need to feed hungry people takes precedence over the needs of other species.

There is no easy solution to this problem. But there are some ways to ease the crisis. If demand for skins cannot be reduced, for example, the farming of species such as crocodiles can at least let economic benefits flow to local people. It can also provide a reason for protecting the habitat of wild populations needed to replenish farmed stock. Tourism, too, can bring the money and impetus to save species and their habitats. For example, the Komodo dragon's notoriety as a potential man-eater, and consequent high status as a tourist attraction, offers hope that its numbers will be increased by careful management.

WORTH A SMILE

The land iguana of the Galápagos Islands is seriously endangered because of predatory dogs and cats. Programs to remove feral animals are now under way.

BOA CONSTRICTED

The anaconda is hunted because it is slow-moving—and easy to kill—and large enough to provide a valuable skin, as well as a meal for local people.

Caecilians

CAECILIANS ARE LONG, wormlike, mostly secretive, burrowing amphibians which are found only in the subtropical and tropical regions of the world. Although their name (pronounced "see-SIL-e-an") means "blind," most caecilians have small eyes, which in some species are hidden below the bones of the skull.

SAY THAT AGAIN?
Caecilians are so little known that most have no common name. *Dermophis mexicanus* of Mexico and Central America grows to more than 2 feet (60 cm).

Curious Creatures

Caecilians are the least known of the three orders of amphibians. The only living amphibians that are completely legless, they live mostly in moist soil in tropical forests and plantations. In Asia, they can be found in southern China, the southern Philippines, Sri Lanka, India, and Southeast Asia. They also live in equatorial east and west Africa, the Seychelles, and in tropical Central and South America.

No one is quite sure about the origins of caecilians. Some scientists believe that they evolved from microsaurs, salamander-like amphibians that became extinct 250 million years ago. Only two discoveries of caecilian fossils have been reported. One discovery, in northeastern Arizona, consisted of fossils that were at least 170 million years old. Unlike their modern relatives, these ancient caecilians had small but well-developed legs.

Tunnel Vision

The 156 species of caecilians vary in length from 3 inches (8 cm) to nearly 5 feet (1.5 m). They are capable of moving snakelike across land when forced to do so, but most live underground. This makes them very difficult to find and observe. They move through existing tunnels or create new ones by pushing their head through moist soil or loose mud. Even those that live in water are skilled at burrowing into the soft mud and gravel on the bottoms of streams and rivers.

Caecilians have many adaptations for burrowing. The skull is powerfully built, with a pointed snout and a recessed mouth or underslung lower jaw—features that allow the head to be used as a kind of battering ram to push through soil or mud. Their peculiar jaws also help them to burrow.

Because there is no light in their underground world, most caecilians have only rudimentary eyes. Instead they sense their environment with a unique pair of sensory organs called tentacles. The tentacles emerge from a groove on each side of the snout, between the eye and the nostril, and are thought to be used for tasting and smelling.

Caecilians also differ from other amphibians by having ringlike skin folds or segments, called annuli,

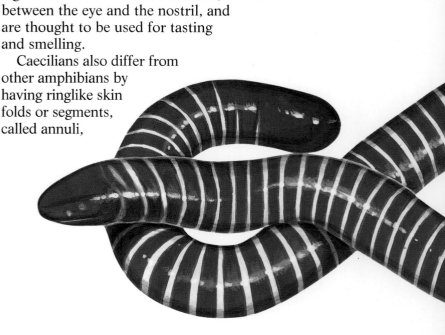

that partially or totally encircle their body. Many species also have small, fishlike scales under the skin.

WATER BABIES
The aquatic *Typhlonectes natans* from South America gives birth to small but fully developed young. Unlike most amphibians, all caecilians fertilize their eggs internally.

Tube on the Move

Land caecilians have a round body and move by undulating—like some snakes. Their muscles are arranged so the body can act like a rod moving within a tube. The "tube" is the skin and outer layer of muscles. The "rod" is the head, spine, and the muscles attached to the spine. With the tube fixed in position in a tunnel, the rod can be pushed slightly forward through the soil to extend the tunnel. When the tip of the rod—the head—has gone as far forward as it can, the tube is pulled forward and fixed in position so the rod can again be pushed through the soil.

The body of semiaquatic and aquatic caecilians is flattened from side to side. A fin running along the length of their back helps them to move through the water like eels.

Caecilian Supper

All caecilians are carnivorous. When they find prey, they approach it slowly, then seize it with their jaws. Land species feed mainly on earthworms, beetles, and other insects, and occasionally small frogs and lizards. Aquatic species eat earthworms, insects, and other invertebrates.

Like all amphibians, caecilians have poison glands in their skin. Most species are dull-colored, but some are brightly colored and boldly patterned, perhaps to warn enemies of their toxic skin secretions. Still, caecilians are often eaten by snakes and introduced predators, including pigs, chickens, and shrewlike tenrecs.

STRIPED PIPE
Ichthyophis kohtaoensis of Southeast Asia lays eggs in underground chambers. The female stays with her eggs until they hatch into larvae.

MUSCLE HEADS

Typical vertebrates have one set of jaw-closing muscles that pull on the lower jaw from a point in front of the jaw hinge. Caecilians have these muscles, too, but they are the only vertebrates with a second set of jaw-closing muscles. These pull back and down on a special extension behind the lower jaw hinge—in much the same way as pushing down one end of a seesaw causes the other end to swing up. These muscles improve burrowing efficiency.

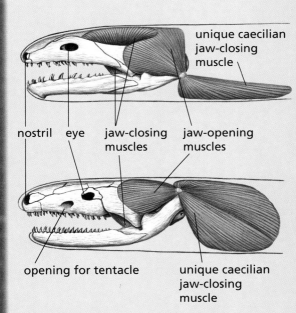

unique caecilian jaw-closing muscle

nostril   eye   jaw-closing muscles   jaw-opening muscles

opening for tentacle   unique caecilian jaw-closing muscle

Some caecilian species are better burrowers than others. The more efficient burrowers, such as the *Ichthyophis glutinosus* (bottom) make more use of the second set of muscles. This is why its muscles are larger than those of the relatively inefficient burrower, *Epicrionops petersi* (top).

Salamanders and Newts

SALAMANDERS BELONG TO THE ORDER CAUDATA (from the Latin word *caudatus*, meaning "provided with a tail"). Salamanders differ from other amphibians in that they keep their tail even after metamorphosis from the larval stage. Because they are easy to raise in captivity, salamanders have become popular as pets.

FINNED FIDO

The mudpuppy is so called because it is thought to be able to bark. Most salamanders have no vocal cords or larynx, but some can give a weak squeak or yelp if disturbed.

What's in a Name?

"Salamander" is a broad term used for any species in the order Caudata, but "newt" is more specific. Newts are mostly aquatic salamanders, spending at least half the year in water courting mates, laying eggs, and building up the fat reserves needed to survive the winter on land. Some salamanders are also mostly aquatic, while other salamanders live only in water, or only on land.

Most salamanders and newts live in the temperate parts of the Northern Hemisphere—in Europe, central and northern Asia, northwestern Africa, North America, and Mexico. A few species occur in Bolivia and southern Brazil, and also in Southeast Asia.

Life and Lungs

With their long tail, salamanders look more like lizards than amphibians. But unlike lizards, most salamanders have smooth skin. Salamanders usually have four legs, but species such as sirens, which have long, slender bodies, small forelegs, and no hindlegs, look rather like eels. Some lungless salamanders of southern Mexico measure only 1 inch (2.5 cm), while the Chinese giant salamander can grow nearly 6 feet (1.8 m) long!

Males court their mates with elaborate "dances." Most fertilize the female's eggs indirectly—they deposit a sperm capsule on a rock or branch, then position the female over the capsule. The female then takes it inside her cloaca. Other species, such as hellbenders, fertilize eggs externally, like frogs. Some species lay 5 or 6 eggs, while mole salamanders lay up to 5,000. But species such as the fire salamander give

SLY DISGUISE

The red salamander mimics the North American newt, whose poisonous skin repels birds and snakes. The red salamander is not toxic, but many enemies avoid it, just in case.

FROM EGGS TO LEGS

Larval development in salamanders varies greatly between species. In the most common amphibious life cycle, much of the development occurs outside the egg. But in many land-dwelling species, the young emerge from the egg as miniature adults, with no aquatic stage.

5. Land-dwelling adult

1. Eggs laid in water

4. Larva with fully developed limbs, gills, and fins

2. Larva develops gill buds

3. Gills and limbs start to form

birth to either live, well-developed larvae or fully-formed young.

Species such as the Mexican axolotl mature and become capable of reproducing while retaining many larval characteristics. These include its external gills, which stick out in bright red tufts on the sides of its head. It will metamorphose—change into an adult form—only when treated with hormones. Other species, such as the olm, never metamorphose.

Larvae and those species that retain larval features as adults breathe either through their skin or their gills. Hellbenders and giant salamanders breathe through their lungs, but they also have skin folds along their flanks that increase the surface area through which oxygen can be taken in from the water. Some other species are lungless, instead breathing only through their skin and the lining of their mouth.

Hard to Swallow

Most salamanders are active at dusk or at night, usually in the warmer seasons. When it is too cold or dry, many species take refuge in rock crevices, under rotting vegetation, or in mucous cocoons underground. Here they stay, often for long periods, until conditions are suitable again.

Salamanders are all carnivorous, at all stages in their life cycle. Usually they feed on small invertebrates such as insects, worms, and mollusks. The larger species also prey on small vertebrates, including fish, frogs, snakes, mice—or even each other! They lie in wait for their prey, relying on smell and touch to find it. They then snatch it up with a flick of their tongue or a snap of their mouth.

Salamanders in turn are hunted by other amphibians, reptiles, mammals, birds, fish, and even large beetles, spiders, and centipedes. They defend themselves by secreting

foul-tasting or toxic substances. Some have poison glands on the back of their neck. The spotted salamander, for example, bends its head down when threatened, thus presenting the attacker with the most distasteful part of its body. Some mole salamanders even head-butt their enemies. Other salamanders and newts display their brightly colored underside to warn that their skin is toxic. If seized, lungless salamanders can shed their tail, growing a new one later.

BACK IN THE SWIM
When newts return to ponds and streams in early spring, they grow back features they had as larvae. This alpine newt has developed finlike extensions on its tail and back.

NEWTS IN BOOTS
When living on land, newts shelter under logs, rocks, and leaf litter. During this phase, species like this marbled newt from Europe take on the features of typical salamanders.

215

Frogs and Toads

THE MOST NUMEROUS AND DIVERSE of the amphibians, frogs and toads can be found in nearly all habitats, from deserts and savannas to mountains and tropical rain forests. Most of the nearly 4,400 species live in water for at least part of their life, usually the tadpole stage.

NON-SLIP GRIP
This painted reed frog lives in Madagascar and Africa. Its expanded toe pads help it climb water reeds. At dusk, it begins calling and hunts for its prey of damselflies.

Leapers and Creepers

Frogs and toads belong to the order Anura. The words "frog" and "toad" were first used to identify two common European amphibians: a smooth-skinned, long-legged creature that jumps (the frog), and a warty, short-legged creature that walks (the toad). When new species were found in other parts of the world, they were named "frog" or "toad" depending on how closely they resembled the "first" frog or toad. But this distinction was not scientific, and became unworkable when new species were discovered that did not fit into one or the other category. Today, "frog" may be used for any member of the order Anura, whereas "toad" is used for species belonging to the group, or genus, *Bufo,* as well as for other frogs of similar body form.

Original Model

The earliest frog fossil dates from 245 million years ago. By 150 million years ago, there were frogs so similar to those that are alive today that they can be allocated to modern families. They outlived the dinosaurs and continued, largely unchanged, while mammals were undergoing their extraordinary evolution.

Today, there are frogs and toads on every continent except Antarctica. While many frogs and toads live in temperate regions, more than 80 percent of species are found in the tropics and subtropics. But three species—the common frog and the moor frog of Europe, and the wood frog of North America—even live north of the Arctic Circle.

DANGEROUS LIAISONS

It's not easy being green. Many frogs, such as this Pine Barren tree frog, are threatened by habitat loss and pesticide use. Other species face more traditional dangers. The calls of the túngara frog attract not only mates, but also eavesdropping bats. They can detect a frog's position by its calls and, gliding in on silent wings, pluck it off a branch with their jaws!

MAKING A SPLASH
A frog's hindlegs, including its long ankle bones, give it extra jumping strength. Webbed toes propel species such as this Australian green and golden bell frog through water.

such as within a rotten log or a burrow in the ground, or even in the base of plants that hold moisture. Some tree-dwellers, such as the glass frogs of Central and South America, lay their eggs on the underside of leaves overhanging running water. The male guards them from predators until they hatch and fall, as tadpoles, into the water below. In other species, development takes place within the egg, not in water, and the young that hatch are fully-formed froglets.

An unusual example of parental care is Darwin's frog of Chile. The male waits by the eggs and snaps the tadpoles up in his mouth as they hatch. They go into his vocal sac, where they stay until ready to emerge as froglets. Males of many poison

FAMILY CIRCLE
The eggs of most frogs are laid in water. Depending on the species, the eggs hatch after a period lasting from just a few days to weeks or even years.

Whether it burrows in desert sand, swims in a mountain lake, or lives in a rainforest tree, a frog needs to be kept moist because of its delicate and porous skin. Even land-dwelling frogs are to be found under logs, amongst the leaf litter on forest floors, or in damp rock crevices. Some burrow into soft dirt or mud, either for daytime retreats, or for long periods of estivation during very dry seasons.

Spawn Born

Almost all frogs fertilize their eggs externally, and the majority lay their eggs in water. There the eggs hatch into tadpoles that develop into adults.

But a large number of species—perhaps 30 percent or more—have a different life history. Some species of frogs in Africa and Puerto Rico miss the egg-laying stage completely, instead giving birth to live young. Other frogs lay relatively few, large eggs in a moist place out of water,

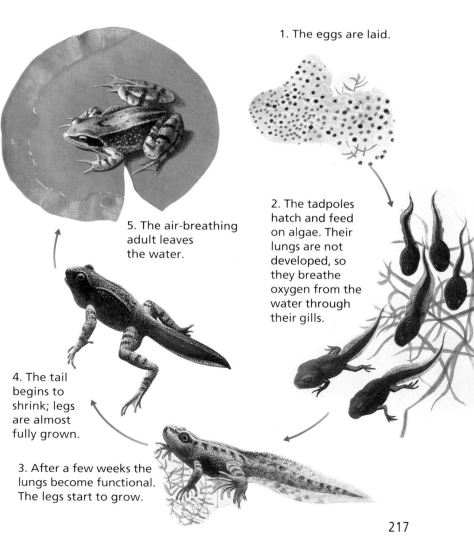

1. The eggs are laid.

2. The tadpoles hatch and feed on algae. Their lungs are not developed, so they breathe oxygen from the water through their gills.

3. After a few weeks the lungs become functional. The legs start to grow.

4. The tail begins to shrink; legs are almost fully grown.

5. The air-breathing adult leaves the water.

FANCY FOOTWORK
The Wallace's tree frog uses its toe "wings" to glide between branches, steer in midair, and slow its fall. Gliding is also used to escape predators.

But these frogs have not been seen in the wild since 1981, and it is feared that they are now extinct.

Read It, Read It

All frogs have adapted to particular ways of life, but they also share some features. Frogs rely on sight to interpret their world, and their eyes are generally large. Although their eyeballs cannot move around in their sockets, they protrude and give the frog a broad view. The eyeballs can also be retracted into their sockets, where they bulge against the roof of the mouth and help the frog to swallow!

Frogs have a keen sense of smell, used to identify breeding sites and possibly their prey. Hearing is also important to frogs. Their ears tend to be tuned to the frequency of their species' own unique call, so their hearing is not "jammed" by background noise. This is useful in places where thousands of frogs of different species may all call at once. Scientists as well as the frogs use these calls to identify species.

Frogs were the first animals to develop a true voice. Females are

frogs carry their tadpoles on their back, taking them from pond to pond. But perhaps the most amazing species are the gastric brooding frogs of Australia—the female swallows her fertilized eggs. Safe in her stomach, they develop as froglets, and are then spat out of her mouth. During this time, the female does not eat and her digestive processes are "turned off."

SAFETY FEATURES
The vivid pattern of the tiny corroboree frog is similar to that used by Aboriginal Australians for ceremonial dances, or corroborees. While non-toxic, its bright skin may scare off enemies.

SLIPPERY SUPPER
Few frogs are large enough to eat other vertebrates, so most feed on insects, spiders, and other invertebrates. This leopard frog of North America is enjoying a worm.

LEAPS AND BOUNCE
The red-banded crevice creeper lives in Africa, south of the Sahara. Because its smooth skin is rubbery in texture, it is sometimes called the rubber frog.

Some of the larger frogs, such as the North American bullfrog, can take birds and mice, small turtles and fish, young snakes and even smaller frogs of their own and other species.

Tadpoles are mostly vegetarian. They filter organisms from the water, or scrape algae from rocks. But some scavenge on carrion, or prey on invertebrates or other tadpoles. Even vegetarian larvae, such as meadow tree frog tadpoles, may occasionally make a meal of a dead sibling.

In turn, frogs are preyed upon by a host of enemies, from tarantulas to birds to humans. The larval stage, too, is a dangerous time—almost any meat-eating predator will find a tadpole a juicy morsel.

mostly silent, but males call to attract females ready to mate and to repel other males from their territory. In some species, one sort of call serves both purposes; other frogs may add extra notes for the territorial call or change the "tune" entirely.

Calls can range from long trills to faint underwater chirpings. Different calls have been described as plonks, honks and unks, whistles, warbles, chuckles, as well as bleats, barks, and quacks. The call frequency depends mainly on the frog's size. Most small frogs have high-pitched calls, while large frogs generally have low-pitched calls.

Male Tail

The order Anura is divided into four suborders. The members of one suborder, Archaeobatrachia, are

FINGER FOOD
The Cape clawed frog lives in rivers and stagnant pools in southern Africa. It has no tongue, so it waits with outstretched arms for prey to swim by, or digs it up with its long fingers and claws.

Tongue Twisters

All mature frogs are carnivores. Some species ambush their prey from hiding places, but many wait for prey to come within reach. In most frogs, the tongue is attached to the front of the mouth. It can be flicked forward and some distance with considerable speed, snapping up prey with the help of sticky mucus secreted from glands in the tongue. Frogs that cannot extend their tongue simply lunge forward and grab prey with their mouth or hands.

Most frogs aren't fussy and will eat whatever small animals share their habitat and fit into their huge mouths.

SEE-THROUGH SKIN
Glass frogs have very little pigment on their belly, and it is possible to see their internal organs through this transparent skin. In some species the heart can be seen beating!

thought to be the most primitive living frogs because of their "free" ribs—all other frogs have ribs attached to their spine. One such species is the tailed frog, which lives in cold, fast-flowing mountain streams in North America. It does not have a "true" tail; rather, males have a small attachment which they use to fertilize the female internally. This ensures that the sperm is not washed away in the rushing water. It is one of the few frog species to have internal fertilization.

Flat Freaks

Members of the suborder Pipoidea are among the most peculiar of frogs. They have a flattened body, and are tongueless (all other frogs have tongues). They use their sensitive fingers to probe the bottom of streams and lakes for insects, worms, and larvae. All species spend most of their life in water, and have large, fully webbed feet to help them swim. Some also have claws on three of the toes on each hind foot. They don't have vocal cords, but make clicking sounds underwater by using bony rods in their larynx.

One notable species is the Surinam toad of South America. It is almost 7 inches (18 cm) long and built like a square pancake with a leg at each corner. Its reproductive behavior is equally bizarre. The male deposits

ORNERY CRITTER
The ornate horned toad has been called a "mouth with legs." It lies partially buried on the forest floor and ambushes prey many times its own size.

RAIN LOVER
The Mexican burrowing toad spends most of its life underground. It emerges after heavy rains to call and breed in temporary ponds.

the fertilized eggs over the back of the female. The eggs then sink into individual pockets in the spongy tissue of the female's back. Here they develop into fully-formed froglets.

Other members of this suborder include the African clawed frogs, which are found south of the Sahara Desert. These frogs were once used to test for pregnancy—a female injected with the urine of a pregnant woman rapidly lays eggs. Development of chemical tests has since spared the frogs this indignity.

Warts and All

The third suborder, Pelobatoidea, includes species such as spadefoot toads, named for the digging "growth" they have on each hind foot. Most spadefoots live in dry areas of northwest Africa, North America, western Asia, and Europe. They spend the day and long, dry periods—most of the year if rain is scarce—in their deep, almost vertical burrows.

On warm, moist nights spadefoots may emerge to eat. The sound of rain falling will also prompt them to travel to puddles to breed. The tadpoles can develop in less than two weeks, but even this may not be fast enough if more rain doesn't fall to top up puddles evaporated in the desert heat. In the race to survive, they must make the most of available protein. Some develop enlarged jaw muscles and a "beak" and eat their pondmates.

Kermit's Cousins

The largest suborder, Neobatrachia, includes every other frog on Earth. The names of many members indicate their characteristics: tree frogs; reed and lily frogs; shovel-nosed frogs; poison frogs; squeakers (so called because of their voice); and burrowing frogs. This suborder also includes the genus *Bufo*—true toads—which range from 1 inch (2.5 cm) for some African

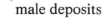

FATAL ATTRACTION
Poison frogs produce some of the most toxic substances known to humans. The Choco Indians of South America put the skin secretions of some poison frogs on their blow gun darts.

HOW ARE EWE?
The nocturnal eastern narrow-mouthed toad uses its slit-like mouth to eat insects such as ants. Its croak sounds like the weak bleat of a sheep.

species to South American toads as big as dinner plates!

Within the vast array of this suborder are virtually all modes of life open to frogs. Many spend their active hours in shrubs and trees; others forage in leaf litter on the forest floor; and those in dry areas remain below ground, encased in a protective cocoon, until rain falls. They have developed adaptations to help them to survive and exploit their habitats. For example, most frogs that climb or live in trees have enlarged pads on their fingers and toes, and forward-facing eyes that help them to judge distance. One African genus, *Chiromantis*, also has two inner fingers opposable to the outer two, providing a firm grip on twigs.

Frogs that live on the ground or in water generally have eyes atop their head and aimed less forward, enabling aquatic frogs to rest with only their eyes above water. But even some species that spend much of their time in water, such as the Asian genus *Amolops*, have enlarged finger and toe disks that enable them to cling to rocks beside fast-flowing streams. Their tadpoles avoid being swept away by fixing themselves in place with special suckers.

LEAF-ALIKE

Some frogs startle and confuse predators with color. As some tropical leaf frogs leap away they flash bright colors, on their belly or inner legs, that were hidden while they were at rest. But the Asian horned toad avoids trouble by trying not to be seen in the first place. Its "dead leaf" coloration and shape make it almost invisible among the leaf litter of its rainforest home.

Turtles and Tortoises

Land tortoise

Sea turtle

Pond turtle

scutes

carapace

THE INSIDE STORY
A tortoise's shell is fused to its spine and ribs. The upper shell is called the carapace; the lower shell is called the plastron.

retractable neck

plastron

CHELONIANS, OR TURTLES AND TORTOISES, are the oldest reptile forms on Earth. They have changed very little in the 230 million years since they first appeared. Chelonians are the only reptiles with a bony shell as part of their skeleton. Many can pull their head and legs inside their shell, making it difficult for predators to eat them.

Ahead By a Neck

Today's turtles are thought to be direct descendants of the first reptile group, the anapsids. The anapsids gave rise to two other groups: the synapsids—the ancestors of the mammals—and the diapsids, which included the dinosaurs, crocodiles, lizards and snakes, and rhynchocephalians, of which only the tuatara survives.

Chelonians are now divided into two suborders, according to the way they draw their head into their shell. The 200 or so hidden-necked, or straight-necked, species of turtle and tortoise can retract their neck straight into their shells. They are found on all continents except Antarctica, and in most oceans. The 70 or so species of side-necked turtle, which live only in central and southern Africa, South America, and Australasia, bend their necks sideways and curl their heads under the front of their upper shell.

SNORKEL SNOUT
The Sepik turtle is a side-necked species from New Guinea. Its long snout allows it to breathe at the water surface without exposing its body to predators.

Dome Homes

A chelonian's shell not only protects it from predators, but also prevents it from drying out when water is scarce, and absorbs heat to keep the animal warm. Both the carapace and the plastron are made of interconnected bony plates covered by a outer layer of large horny plates, or scutes. The scutes are made of keratin—the same material as our fingernails. Only the Papuan softshell turtle, the leatherback turtle, and the several softshell species do not have scutes on their shell.

The shape and structure of a chelonian's shell often point to how it moves

chelonians had small teeth, but modern turtles and tortoises have none. Instead, they have horny ridges which cover their upper and lower jaws. In carnivorous turtles, these ridges are knife-sharp and work like shears. Plant-eating species use their serrated jaw ridges to grasp and cut food.

Little Shell-ter

Like most reptiles, turtles lay eggs with shells. After mating, the females lay their eggs near the areas where they live and feed. But some sea and river turtles migrate vast distances to breed. Some green sea turtles migrate from the coast of Brazil to beaches on Ascension Island, a distance of 3,000 miles (5,000 km)!

Most species lay their eggs in nests scraped out of the sand or soil with their hindlegs. A few lay their eggs in burrows, or in the nests of other

SNEAKY SNAPPER
The brown, algae-covered shell of the alligator snapping turtle provides it with excellent camouflage. The turtle waves its wormlike tongue to lure fish into its jaws.

BIG SOFTIES
Softshell turtles have a lighter, more flexible shell instead of horny plates. They are fast swimmers and can hide from predators on the bottom of muddy ponds.

and the environment in which it lives. Pond turtles have a small, flattened, usually lighter, shells for swimming. Sea turtles also have a streamlined, light shell. But turtles that live on both land and water have a semi-domed shell to suit their semiaquatic life.

All chelonians have strong legs. Even the heaviest tortoise can lift its body off the ground when walking. In land turtles, the fingers and toes have more or less grown together to form solid "clump-feet" to support their heavy weight, whereas the fingers and toes of aquatic freshwater species are often webbed for extra power when swimming. In sea turtles, the fingers have fused to form paddle-like flippers. Unlike other turtles, their forelegs are more strongly developed than their hindlegs, and they are also the only group that have to drag their body across the ground when they come ashore.

Ripper Clippers

Like all other reptile species, turtles and tortoises are cold-blooded. Most soak up warmth from the Sun before setting off to hunt for food in cool water. Ancient

HEAD FOR HEIGHTS

The shell of the big-headed turtle of Asia is too small to enclose the fleshy parts of its body. For this reason, its huge head and long tail are well armored. A good climber, it is at times seen basking on the lower branches of bushes and trees at the water's edge. Turtles that escape indoor captivity have been found not on the floor, but in the curtains, near the ceiling!

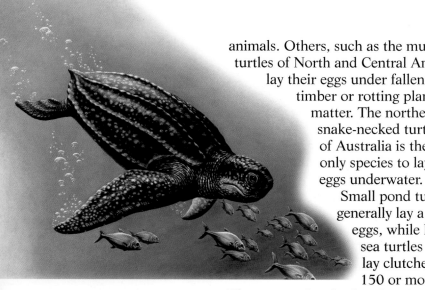

animals. Others, such as the musk turtles of North and Central America, lay their eggs under fallen timber or rotting plant matter. The northern snake-necked turtle of Australia is the only species to lay its eggs underwater.

Small pond turtles generally lay a few eggs, while large sea turtles can lay clutches of 150 or more. The average incubation time is two to three months, although the eggs of some larger species take a year or longer, depending on the nest temperature. In some species the temperature also determines the sex of the young.

Once the eggs are covered over, the young must fend for themselves. They use an "egg tooth"—a sharp bump on top of their snout—to break free of their shells. (This drops off later.) But the new generation faces great danger. Many predators, including humans, eat turtle eggs, and rats, pigs, fish, and other animals eat hatchlings. Only one turtle in 100 lives to become an adult.

In the Swim

Most chelonians live in or near fresh water such as lakes, rivers, swamps, and estuaries. There are 200 or so species of freshwater turtle, from pond turtles, softshell turtles, mud and musk turtles to river turtles.

Well adapted to an aquatic existence, many species, such as the softshell turtles, can take in oxygen from the water as well as from the air. They can also stay submerged for long periods while looking for food. They ambush their prey of aquatic insects, worms,

frogs, and fish. Some species also feed on mollusks and crustaceans, and a few, including the South American river turtles, eat fruits and plants.

In seasonally dry areas, species such as the helmeted side-necked turtles of Africa estivate by burrowing deep into the mud at the bottom of lagoons and swamps. There they will remain, dormant, until the rain comes again.

CREVICE CREEPER
Land tortoises usually have domed shells, but the African pancake tortoise has a flat, flexible shell that enables it to squeeze into crevices in its rocky habitat.

TOUGH ENOUGH?
Unlike other sea turtles, the 5-foot (1.5-m) long leatherback turtle has a shell covered by a leathery skin. But like the others, it is critically endangered by hunting and pollution.

BACK IN THE SADDLE
Plants grow tall on the smaller and drier of the Galápagos Islands. There, tortoises have a smaller "saddleback" shell so they can stretch their neck up to reach cactus stems.

After a long journey, female green sea turtles come ashore to lay their eggs.

Several clutches of 80 to 200 eggs may be laid at two- or three-week intervals.

Closely related to freshwater turtles, semiaquatic turtles include some beautiful species, such as the painted terrapin. They hunt on land and in water, and eat both animal and plant food. They may also estivate in holes on land or in mud underwater.

Land Luggers

There are about 40 species of land tortoise. These straight-necked species can be found in Europe, Africa, Asia, and North and South America, and on islands such as the Seychelles, and the Galápagos. They range from the 4-inch (10-cm) long Madagascan spider tortoises to the wheelbarrow-sized giants of Aldabra. Large species can live for 100 years or more.

Many have a high-domed shell that provides protection and room for their long necks and large lungs. In the giant species, the shell is honeycombed with small air chambers so that it is not too heavy to carry. Nevertheless, some land tortoises can travel at just 295 feet (90 m) per hour.

Most species are mainly vegetarian, but they will also eat insects, worms, crustaceans, mollusks, and even the dung of hoofed animals! In hot areas, they are active only early and late in the day, lying in the shade of shrubs and trees during the heat of the day. Species such as the gopher tortoise retreat into a burrow for protection from extreme heat and cold.

OBSTACLE COURSE
With their streamlined shells and large front flippers, the seven species of sea turtle are built for life in the ocean. Female sea turtles leave the sea only to lay eggs, and males never come ashore.

The hatchlings emerge from the sand.

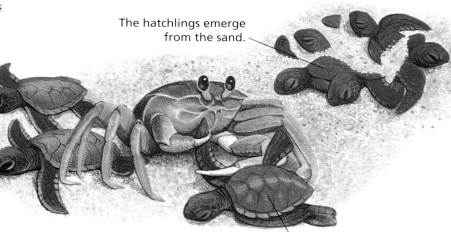

The newborn green turtles race for the sea, relying on safety in numbers to escape predators such as birds and crabs.

Offshore Explorers

Sea turtles can swim at speeds of up to 18 miles (29 km) per hour to escape predators such as sharks. They use the currents to search for their food of crustaceans, fish, jellyfish, sponges, sea urchins, and sometimes seagrasses. They are mostly found in temperate and tropical oceans. They often sunbathe at the surface on fields of seaweed, or in shallow water left by the tide on coral reefs.

Lizards

N O OTHER GROUP OF REPTILES has evolved into as many different forms as the lizards. They range from tiny, legless creatures to giant monitors. Some are brightly colored, while others are dull and blend into the background. Perhaps the only thing all species have in common is their scaly skin, which stops them from drying out.

Squirming Squamates

Lizards, snakes, and amphisbaenians, which make up the majority of modern reptiles, belong to the order Squamata. Their ancestors date back at least 200 million years, although modern species do not appear until about 20 million years ago. Lizards appeared first, with amphisbaenians and snakes coming later. These later animals probably evolved from lizards.

Today there are about 4,300 species of lizard. They come in all shapes and sizes, from the Virgin Islands gecko, which is only 1½ inches (4 cm) long when fully grown, to the 10-foot (3-m) long Komodo dragon. Because of their size diversity, lizards are found in almost all habitats: A region can support a greater number of smaller animals than it can of large animals.

Most lizards live on the ground or in trees. A few are semiaquatic, retreating to water when disturbed, but the marine iguana of the Galápagos Islands is the only lizard that takes to the sea.

Talking Tongues

Regardless of their different habitats, lizards have many features in common. For example, all lizards have scaly skin. Most geckos, and some other lizards, also have a transparent scale "spectacle" over each eye. The scale is probably to prevent the eye from losing water from its surface, and to protect it from damage.

But lizards have also developed special features for their different habitats. Those that live above ground have external ear openings and large eyes. Lizards that live underground have tiny eyes, and their external ear openings are often covered by scaly skin. Most burrowing lizards also have smooth scales to reduce drag as they plow through the soil.

BOILED, OR FRIED?
Studies of the leopard gecko of southwestern Asia have shown that the sex of its offspring is determined by the temperature at which the eggs are incubated.

BABY BLUES
Some skinks, such as the Australian blue-tongue skink, give birth to live young instead of laying eggs. The young born in large litters are smaller than those born in small litters.

Lizards have a well-developed tongue, but it, too, varies greatly in structure. Monitor lizards and whiptails have a slender, deeply forked tongue which, like snakes, they use to "taste" scent particles in the air. The beaded lizards, including the Gila monster, use their tongue to track their underground prey.

In some lizards, like the flap-footed lizards, the tongue is fleshier and is used for lapping up water or nectar.

Geckos also use their tongue for "spectacle wiping"—cleaning the transparent scale over each eye.

Lizards such as the iguanas and the agamid lizards use their tongue to catch food, but it is the chameleons, with their long tongue, that have developed this ability to an amazing degree. They slowly stalk their prey, then shoot out their tongue, which is covered in sticky mucus. The tip of the tongue often travels at speeds of more than of 16 feet (5 m) per second! The chameleons then draw their tongue—and their meal—back into their mouth.

Egg Roles

Most lizards lay eggs. Some geckos lay only a couple, while larger lizards may lay as many as 40. A few guard their eggs against predators—some skinks, for example, coil their body around the eggs until they hatch—but most cover their eggs with soil and leaves, then abandon them.

The eggs usually take from two weeks to three months to hatch, depending on the temperature of the nest, although some take much longer. The eggs of most lizards have a leathery shell, but some geckos lay hard-shelled eggs that often stick to tree bark or leaves. If the eggs are on a branch that is washed out to sea, currents may carry them to another island. This partly explains why

Skink tail

Leaf-tailed gecko tail

Chameleon tail

Australian shingleback tail

geckos are found on many islands that other lizards have not reached.

In some dragon lizards, whiptail lizards, night lizards, wall lizards, chameleons, and geckos, the eggs do not need to be fertilized by males. Because a single egg is all that is needed to create a new population, these all-female lizards increase in number faster than those that have male and female parents. This allows them to colonize new habitats. But it also means that they lose the genetic diversity needed to adapt to new conditions. Perhaps this is why, out of the 900 gecko species for example, only six are all-female.

Other lizards, such as the northern alligator lizard of Canada, give birth to fully formed young. The eggs are protected inside the mother's body, and the developing young are nourished by the yolk in the same way as young that grow in eggs outside the body. In some species the method varies, depending on the climate: The European common lizard lays eggs in warm climates, but in cool mountain climates, where the temperature may not be high enough for eggs to develop properly, the female gives birth to live young. But in a few species, such as the night lizards, a placenta forms so the young obtain nourishment directly from their mother—just like the young of placental mammals.

All lizards fend for themselves as soon as they hatch, but many dangers await them. Spiders, insects, birds, snakes, and mammals—even other lizards—all eat hatchlings. Very few young lizards survive to breed.

ON THE LOOKOUT
Monitor lizards are fast runners that usually live in deserts or grasslands. They are found in Asia, Africa, and Australia, and include the largest of the lizards, the Komodo dragon.

Biting Words

Most lizards are predators. They eat mainly insects and other invertebrates, which they crush with their pointed teeth and swallow whole. A house gecko can eat half its own weight in insects in a single night! But lizards that eat snails have flat, rounded teeth for crushing shells, and the Komodo dragon of Indonesia uses its fanglike teeth and sharp claws to bring down prey such as deer, pigs, and even water buffalo.

Many other species are herbivorous. For example, the chuckwallas of American desert regions eat flowers, buds, leaves, and fruit, including the fruit of cactus. The marine iguana of the Galápagos Islands eats mostly algae. Many herbivorous lizards have long, narrow teeth with sharp edges for chopping their food.

CRUNCHY LUNCH
Collared lizards of North America and Mexico are fast runners with hearty appetites. When chasing prey, which can be anything from insects to small snakes, they often run on their hindlegs.

EXTENDED VACATION

The ancestors of this Fijian crested iguana may have rafted over from the Americas on floating vegetation, a journey of over 5,600 miles (9,000 km).

Hot Spots

Like all reptiles, lizards get their body heat from external sources, such as the Sun. This is why they are found mostly in temperate or tropical climates, although some can survive in mountain areas as high as 16,400 feet (5,000 m). Some Asian and North American skinks hibernate over winter in burrows beneath the snow, emerging in spring to feed on insects attracted to spring flowers.

Nevertheless, lizards are often thought of as desert animals, and they have adapted to live in such habitats in different ways. Many species are nocturnal. They hunt in the early evening, when the air is cooler but the ground is still warm enough for them to function. Their pupils—the transparent "holes" that let light into the eyes—are large, vertical slits that open wide at night to let in as much light as possible.

Diurnal species escape the intense heat of the midday sun by hiding in crevices and beneath rocks. Some dragon lizards of Australia avoid hot surfaces by raising their hind toes. The African Namib dune lizard keeps its cool with a "thermal dance," lifting one foreleg and the opposite hindleg, then balancing on

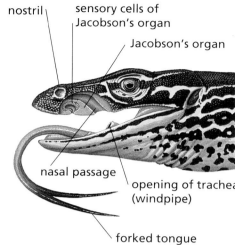

nostril
sensory cells of Jacobson's organ
Jacobson's organ
nasal passage
opening of trachea (windpipe)
forked tongue

TASTING THE AIR

Some lizards "test" their environment by using their tongue to pass scent particles to sensory cells of the Jacobson's organ in the roof of the mouth. The organ connects to the brain.

its other legs for a few moments. It also buries itself in cool sand, using its flattened, shovel-like snout.

Finding water is also a problem. Most desert lizards get the moisture they need from their food. Their body converts their prey into fat, which they store in their tail. When the fat is turned into energy, water is produced for the body.

Lizards' scales, which are made of keratin, prevent water loss through the skin. By producing droppings that are almost dry, desert lizards also reduce the loss of body water in their arid habitats.

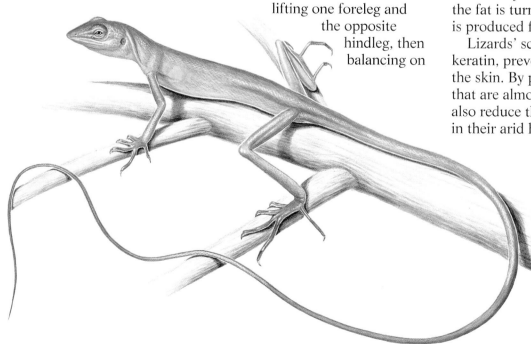

MAGIC DRAGON

The tree dragon of Australia has only been known to science since 1974. Its skin color and stick-like body and legs make it nearly invisible among narrow leaves.

Scale Squad

Modern lizards are divided into three major groups. One, the Iguania, comprises the iguanas, chameleons, and agamids. These lizards use their good eyesight and large tongue to ambush and capture their food. Body features such as crests, fans, and dewlaps are common in this group.

There are about 350 species of agamids living throughout the warmer regions of Europe, Africa, Asia, and Australia. One distinguishing feature is their teeth, which, rather than being anchored in sockets, sit on the rim of their jaws. Agamids are active by day, and all but a few species lay eggs. Some of the most bizarre agamids, such as the frilled lizard and the thorny devil, live in Australia.

The chameleons are perhaps the most distinctive of all lizards. There are about 135 species, most of which live in humid forests throughout much of Africa and eastward to India and Sri Lanka. They can also be found north to Spain. Chameleons can change the color of their skin for camouflage and communication. Their skin color also changes with air temperature. At night when it is cool, chameleons turn pale and look like white leaves when they sleep on the end of twigs. By sleeping in such spots, the lizards are protected from predators such as snakes, which are too heavy for the slender branches.

Iguanas are related to agamids and chameleons, but they have teeth on the inner edge of their jaw bones. More than 850 species are distributed from southwestern Canada to the southern tip of South America. Others live in Madagascar and on oceanic islands. They include anoles, sand lizards, horned lizards, and basilisks. One of the most familiar species is the green iguana of South and Central America, which can grow more than 6½ feet (2 m) long. Perhaps the most unusual species is the marine iguana, the only living lizard dependent on the sea. To get rid of excess salt swallowed while feeding on the seabed, it sneezes concentrated salt crystals from its nostrils!

Vacuum Clasp

Most of the species in the second group, the Gekkota, are geckos. They are found in all continents except Antarctica. The majority of geckos are nocturnal. Since other lizards sleep at night, geckos can take advantage of the lack of competition from other lizards for their mostly insect prey.

PURPLE PERIL
The Knysna dwarf chameleon is mostly green when at rest. But males develop this bright color pattern as a threat display to other males.

SNEAK PEEK
Many lizards have a small clear area on their lower eyelids. This allows them to watch for predators while their eyes are closed.

BIG BLUFF
If another lizard enters a collared lizard's territory, it threatens the invader by performing "push ups" that make it look bigger.

EYE-CATCHING
The blue-tailed day gecko lives on islands in the Indian Ocean. Unlike nocturnal geckos, which have vertical pupils, this diurnal species has round pupils.

They are characterized by their adaptations for nighttime hunting by sight, such as their huge eyes.

Although many geckos live on the ground, they can also climb well. Their toes have pads with thousands of fine, hairlike projections. These cling to invisible rough spots and allow a gecko to walk on almost every surface, at every angle—even upside down. These adaptations have made geckos some of the most successful species on the planet.

Mixed Breeds

FLAP OF HONOR
The color and shape of the dewlap in anoles varies from species to species. This Cuban brown anole is showing off his dewlap to warn off other males or to attract females.

The third group is the Autarchoglossa. These lizards—which include slow worms, monitors, beaded lizards, whiptails, night lizards, and skinks—live mostly on the ground, or in burrows or among rocks. They rely heavily on chemical cues, transmitted to their Jacobson's organ, to understand their world.

Many species, such as the alligator lizard, have osteoderms in their skin. Others, such as the glass lizards, can "break" off their tail when attacked. The beaded lizards, such as the Gila monster, use venom to repel enemies.

One odd species is the skinklike Malpelo galliwasp, which eats crabs and seabirds, as well as the birds' droppings. Stranger still, it mobs adult seabirds returning to nests with food intended for their chicks. It scares the birds into vomiting up the food, then eats the vomit. Tropical Asia is home to another unusual species, the green-blooded skink. Not only does this skink have green plasma—its bones and eggs are also green! Scientists are still not sure what the green pigment is used for.

TAILS OF SURVIVAL

The Australian red-tailed skink and the five-lined skink from North America are not related, but they protect themselves in a similar way. Since they are relatively small and cannot fight off attackers, they use their colorful tail to distract predators away from their vulnerable head and body. Their striped body also confuses predators. If attacked, the skinks shed their tail and make their escape.

Granular scales

Keeled scales

Smooth scales

A USEFUL SCALE
Many water and sea snakes have "granular" scales with a rough, grainy surface. Most freshwater and wetland snakes have keeled scales. Snakes that burrow usually have smooth scales.

Snakes

THERE ARE ALMOST 2,700 SPECIES of snake. From the tiny thread snakes no bigger than a pencil to the 30-foot (10-m) long anaconda, snakes come in a huge range of sizes, colors, and patterns. All snakes are carnivores and their methods of catching prey are diverse, requiring a range of techniques and weaponry.

Slinky Link

As snakes evolved from their lizard ancestors, they became long and slender, and lost their legs—perhaps to take advantage of narrow spaces where legs were not much use. As their body became elongated, so, too, did their internal organs. Unlike other vertebrates, which have two lungs, most snakes have just one functional lung that runs nearly the length of their body. In some species the second lung has even disappeared!

Several features suggest that snakes' ancestors may have been burrowing creatures. For example, snakes' eyes are covered by clear scales that are fixed in place. They give them an unblinking stare, but they protect the eyes from damage. Also, snakes do not have external ear openings, although their inner ear is well developed and able to detect even faint vibrations through the ground or water.

Snakes rely heavily on smell to hunt prey, recognize predators, and find a mate. Their forked tongue and Jacobson's organ are superbly adapted for "tasting" and "smelling" chemicals in the air.

From Seas to Trees

Snakes are found in almost all parts of Earth except the very coldest areas. Most live on the ground, but many live in trees, in underground burrows, or in fresh or sea water. To survive in their habitats, snakes have developed various adaptations. Their scales

provide clues about how and where they live. The keeled scales of many snakes help to balance side-to-side movement and provide a larger surface area for heating and cooling. The smooth scales of burrowing snakes make it easier for them to push through the soil. Granular scales, which feel like sandpaper, help water snakes to grip their slippery prey.

Body shapes and functions also reflect a snake's lifestyle. Many sea snakes have a paddle-shaped tail to help them swim quickly. Their nostrils are on top of their snout, so they can breathe when most of their head is underwater. The nostrils can be sealed by fleshy valves when the snake dives.

Some African and Asian sand boas also have eyes on the top of their head, but this is so they can see when they are partially buried in soil. Well adapted for their burrowing lifestyle, they dig through sand or loose soil

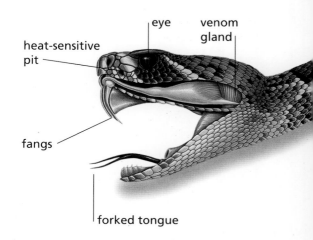

heat-sensitive pit

eye

venom gland

fangs

forked tongue

Horned viper

Python

Burrowing snake

Tree snake

EYES ON THE PRIZE

Diurnal snakes (active by day) have large eyes, since they rely mainly on sight to hunt. Nocturnal snakes use their heat-sensing organs and tongue to sense prey, so they have smaller eyes.

Diurnal

Nocturnal

with their blunt, shovel-shaped snout. Tree-dwelling snakes have evolved differently: Like the mangrove snake, they have a slender, compressed body, or, like the green tree python, a prehensile tail to grasp and hang from branches.

Slither Hither

Without limbs, snakes had to develop new ways of moving. Their spine provided the solution. We have 32 vertebrae in our spine, but some snakes have 400 or more! A system of interlocking muscles makes their strong spine very supple. They push with muscles attached to their ribs (which are, in turn, attached to the spine) to lever themselves along on the edge of their belly scales.

Snakes have developed four different ways to push their body along in their different habitats. They can move rapidly by a process called lateral undulation. Sea snakes, too, use lateral undulation, pushing against the water with the sides of their curved body.

If they are in confined spaces, such as narrow crevices and tunnels, snakes use concertina movement. They grip the side of the tunnel by bending the

SKULL SESSION

A python's large head holds its many teeth. A viper has a large head because it eats large prey. The blunt head of a burrowing snake pushes through soil. The slender head of a tree snake slips between twigs.

hind part of their body, then straighten out their front part, get a similar grip with this segment, then pull their hind part forward. Some heavy-bodied snakes use rectilinear movement (movement in a straight line) when they are moving slowly. Large boas, pythons, and vipers often use this kind of locomotion when creeping up to prey across open ground. Sidewinding movement is used only by a few snakes that live on loose, slippery surfaces, such as sand dunes.

GOING UNDERCOVER

Most of the internal organs of snakes are long and thin. The stomach and intestines are arranged one behind the other in the body.

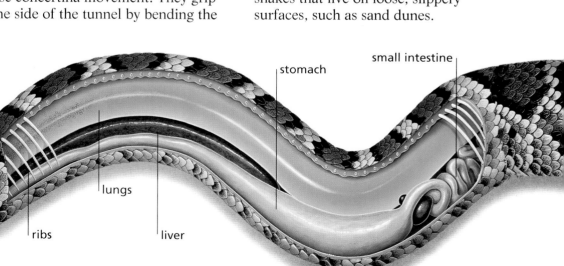

stomach

small intestine

lungs

ribs

liver

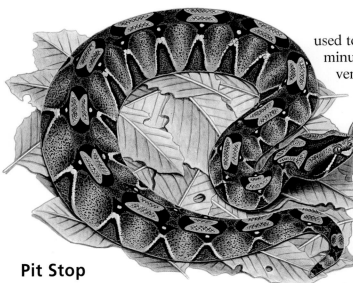

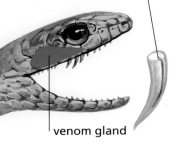

rear, grooved fang

venom gland

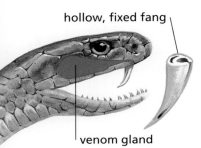

hollow, fixed fang

venom gland

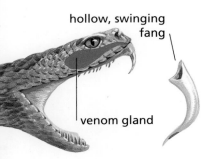

hollow, swinging fang

venom gland

TEETH OF GRIEF
Venom runs down grooves on the fangs of rear-fanged snakes. Cobras and their relatives have hollow, fixed fangs. The fangs of vipers and rattlesnakes swing to the front of the mouth.

Pit Stop

Some snakes have a broad diet, eating almost anything they can catch and subdue. Others will eat only one kind of prey, like snails, eggs, frogs and tadpoles, worms, or crabs. Snakes also have different ways of catching their food. Some stalk or pursue their prey. For example, the hognose snakes of North America and Mexico use their broad snout to dig toads out of burrows. Other species, such as the slow-moving boa constrictor, lie in wait for their prey or creep up on an unsuspecting animal.

Snakes have many adaptations for hunting. For example, rattlesnakes have small pits on the front of their face; many pythons and some boas have pits in their lip scales. These pits contain heat sensors that can detect even the smallest of temperature changes. The snake can tell how far away its prey is by comparing the input from the right and left pits. This enables it to strike its prey with deadly accuracy, even in total darkness.

Lethal Injection

Many snakes are venomous. In some species the venom acts only as a digestive juice, but in the most venomous snakes it is a lethal weapon used to subdue or kill prey within minutes—or even seconds. The venom of the small-scaled snake of Australia, a relative of the taipan, is so strong that a single bite can kill almost 250,000 mice!

Snake venoms affect their prey in one of two different ways. The neurotoxic venoms of the cobras and their relatives act on the nerves to stop the heart and damage the lungs. The hemotoxic venoms of vipers and rattlesnakes destroy blood. Most venomous snakes are highly resistant to their own venom. Amazingly, some non-venomous species, such as the king snake, are also resistant— anti-toxins in their blood make them immune to the venom of their prey, which includes rattlesnakes, coral snakes, and copperheads.

Venom is produced by highly evolved mouth glands and released through fangs—grooved or hollow teeth. Different venomous species

RAT SNATCHER
The Mandarin rat snake is found in mountainous areas of China. It kills its warm-blooded prey, especially rodents, by constriction.

have different kinds of fangs. Kraits, taipans, mambas, sea snakes, coral snakes, most cobras, and all Australian venomous snakes have hollow fangs, in the front of the mouth, which are firmly attached to the upper jaw. Most search and stalk their food, and when they strike, they use their fangs like hypodermic needles to inject venom into their victim's bloodstream.

FROG IN THE THROAT
A snake swallows prey headfirst so that the animal's legs don't get stuck in its throat. After a large meal, most snakes seek a sunny spot because heat helps them to digest their meal quickly.

But rather than stalking its prey, the yellow-bellied sea snake relies on the tendency of small fish to gather around the end of an object. To attract fish to its head, not its tail, the snake swims backward. A quick sideways strike, and it has its meal. Spitting cobras also kill their prey by biting it, but to defend themselves they use a different technique. They can blind a potential predator by spraying venom into its eyes.

Because much of their prey is not only large but also covered in fur or feathers, the fangs of vipers and rattlesnakes are very long, so that they penetrate deep into the

victim's body. For this reason, their hollow front fangs are not fixed in position; instead, they are hinged so they can be folded back into the mouth. When the snake opens its mouth, the fangs spring forward, ready for action.

A number of species, such as the African boomslang, have potent venom that oozes down grooved, fixed fangs at the back of their mouth. They hold their prey in the back of their mouth and chew on it so the venom enters the broken skin.

Get a Grip

Many non-venomous snakes, such as pythons and boa constrictors, kill their prey by constricting, or squeezing it. A python, for example, coils itself around an animal. Whenever the animal breathes out, the python squeezes a little tighter, until the animal suffocates.

Snakes without constricting coils or venom catch small prey in their mouth. Water snakes of North America

SEA SERPENT
Sea kraits live in the Indo-Pacific region. They bask, shelter, and lay their eggs on small coral islands. They have highly toxic venom, but are reluctant to bite, even in self-defense.

SPIT IN YOUR EYE
By exhaling forcefully, a spitting cobra can spray venom out in a jet, like water spraying from a puncture in a hose, and can hit a target nearly 10 feet (3 m) away!

A COLORFUL PAST
Green tree pythons, which live in northern Australia and New Guinea, are bright yellow or brick brown when they hatch. They become the green color of adults in one to three years.

have been seen with their mouth open to the current, grabbing fish swimming by. Some nonvenomous snakes use the enlarged teeth at the back of their mouth to puncture hard objects, such as eggs, or prey such as toads, that inflate themselves so they become hard to swallow. Other species, such as the agile racer of North and Central America, kill their prey by pressing it to the ground.

Since snakes cannot tear or bite pieces of flesh from their prey, they must swallow it whole. The bones of their jaws (and some of the bones in their skull) are attached by elastic connections that allow the bones to move apart and stretch the snake's entire mouth to swallow a large animal. In fact, a fully grown python can eat prey at least twice as big as its head, such as a pig or an antelope! Digesting such a meal can take weeks or months.

Little Wrigglers

Snakes are usually solitary animals. They come together briefly, either to mate, or when two males fight to test their strength. Some species begin to mate and reproduce each spring in mild climates, or just before the rainy season in the tropics. In most egg-laying species the female lays her eggs under a safe, warm, and slightly moist place—such as a rotting log. Some small tropical snakes lay only

a couple of eggs, while larger species can lay more than 100 eggs.

Once the female has laid the eggs, she leaves them to develop and hatch on their own. However, a few species do stay with their eggs until they have hatched: Female pythons coil themselves around the eggs, shivering their body to keep the eggs warm, and both male and female cobras guard their eggs. When they are ready, young snakes use the temporary "egg tooth" at the tip of their upper

lip to slit their shells, which have the texture of thick, strong paper.

Some snakes, such as most vipers and various water snakes, don't lay eggs. Instead, they give birth to live, fully developed young. Garter snakes can produce litters of four or five to up to a hundred young! "Live-bearing" snakes tend to live in cool climates or watery habitats. Scientists believe this type of birth occurs in cool climates

REVEALING PEEL
Snakes shed their old outer layer of skin when they grow too big for it. A snake rubs its snout against a hard surface to loosen the layer, then wriggles free, revealing a new skin underneath.

MEGA MOUTH

Snakes can extend the opening of their trachea, or windpipe, so they can keep breathing while swallowing prey. They then slowly "walk" their jaws forward to engulf the animal.

because the eggs would be generally warmer in the mother's body than in the soil. For example, the European adder, whose range extends into the icy Arctic Circle, spends most of her time basking so the embryos can develop quickly in the short warm period. Snakes in wet environments give birth to live young because eggs could drown in water or become moldy in soil.

Give a Snake a Break

Snakes have a bad reputation. Their slithering bodies fill many humans with revulsion and fear. So great is this fear that venomous snakes have been used as weapons of war. Many years ago, the famous Roman general Hannibal

defeated an attacking navy by tossing live, venomous snakes onto the decks of the enemy's ships!

But most snakes are not dangerous to humans, and in most areas they do more good—by controlling agricultural pests, for example—than harm. A high proportion of snake bites occur when people try to kill snakes, even when the snake poses no threat to human safety. Also, most people can't tell the difference between harmless snakes and venomous snakes, and kill the harmless species by mistake. If we respect snakes and allow them their space, they will do the same for us.

TINY TIDBITS

Most snakes eat one large prey item at each meal. But blind snakes, like lizards, eat small, soft prey, such as ant eggs, frequently. These little burrowing snakes resemble worms both in shape and, often, in color. Since their eyes are just small spots, they rely on scent to locate their food, flicking their tongue in and out to pick up any faint chemical traces left by foraging ants. They then follow the trail back to the ant nest.

Amphisbaenians

AMPHISBAENIANS (worm lizards) are some of the strangest reptiles in the world. All 140 amphisbaenian ("am-fizz-BEEN-ee-an") species spend most of their life underground, beneath soil and leaf litter in forests in the warmer parts of North, Central, and South America, the Middle East, Africa, Southeast Asia, and Europe.

Soil Toil

There are four families of worm lizard, or amphisbaenian, and three of these have no legs at all. These amphisbaenians burrow through tunnels with their hard, strong head and move like snakes in confined spaces. They inch their way through tunnels in a straight line, or in undulating waves, depending on the soil and the shape of the tunnel.

The exception is the fourth family, the Mexican worm lizards, which have two strong front legs that are flattened like paddles. These legs help them to move above ground, and are used to sweep soil back past their head when they are digging a tunnel beneath the surface.

Mud Wrestlers

Amphisbaenians live mostly in moist and sandy soil. They may emerge at night to feed on the surface, but they are usually only seen above ground if heavy rain floods their burrows. They have a variety of adaptations to enable them to take advantage of their earthy home. Most have a mouth that is tucked beneath the snout, or underslung, so dirt cannot get into it when the animal is burrowing. Since keen eyesight is not required in a tunnel, their eyes are very simple—and often not even visible—and are covered by clear skin. Amphisbaenians can barely see movement, and can distinguish only between light and dark.

Amphisbaenians' rather baggy skin is loosely attached to their body and is ringed with small scales. Some species have tubelike bodies, but others have rectangular or triangular body shapes to prevent the animal from spinning as it pushes soil from side to side with

EVEN KEEL
Keel-headed worm lizards have large, reinforced scales on their head. These help them to plow and compress the soil from side to side as they move forward.

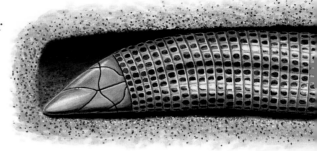

SCRAPING BY
Amphisbaenians have body scales arranged like tiles to help to keep dirt from building up on their body.

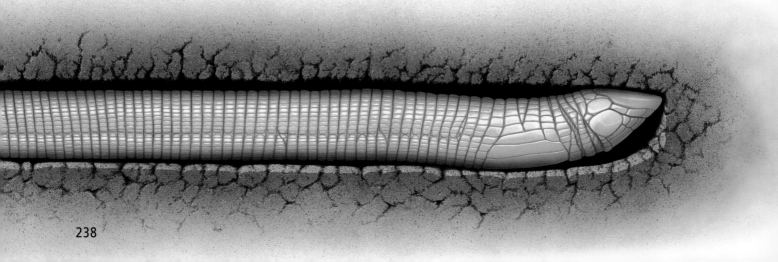

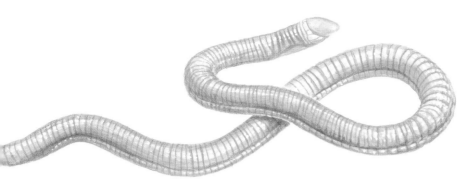

SMALL DETAIL
This amphisbaenian looks as if it has two heads, but one end is in fact its tail. Worm lizards can shed their tail if they are grabbed by a predator—but a new one doesn't always grow back.

LITTLE LEGS
The only amphisbaenian in Europe, *Blanus cinereus* is a member of a small group of little-known species that still have tiny hindlegs. Their mouth is also primitive, in that it is not underslung.

its head. The tail, which is pointed in some species and rounded in others, is plated with horny scales to provide protection from predators.

Amphisbaenians range in length from 4 to 30 inches (10 to 75 cm), with most being around 6 to 14 inches (15 to 35 cm). Most species lay eggs, with some nesting in ant or termite mounds. But at least three species are known to retain the eggs inside their body and give birth to live young.

Saw Jaws
Amphisbaenians have no external ear openings (these would be clogged by dirt), but they can sense vibrations in the soil. If they detect prey, such as a crawling insect or earthworm, they can dig very quickly and catch it with their sharp, interlocking teeth and powerful jaws. The larger species can also cut and tear pieces from larger prey, such as small vertebrates and carrion. But even these teeth are often no match for birds and mammals that forage on the surface, such as monkeys, which lift pieces of wood and rocks under which amphisbaenians may shelter. Pigs are also a danger, since they dig in the soil and root out any tasty treats.

HEAD QUARTERS

Amphisbaenians, or worm lizards, prefer moist habitats in which to build their tunnels, but some can dig through very hard soils. The way different groups of amphisbaenians burrow is reflected in the different shapes of their head.

WEDGE WORK
Chisel-headed species rotate their head in one direction and then in the other, carving a path through the soil.

DOZER NOSE
Keel-headed species use their wedge-shaped snout to scrape soil from the front of the tunnel.

DRILL BIT
Round-headed species push forward into the earth and turn their head in any direction to make the burrow, like a borer.

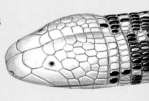

SPADE BLADE
Shovel-headed species push forward and then raise their broad, hard head, compressing soil into the roof of the tunnel.

239

Tuataras

THE TUATARA looks like an iguana, but it is not a lizard at all. The two species of tuatara are the only living members of a group of reptiles called Rhynchocephalia, or "beak-heads." These animals were common throughout the world around 225 to 120 million years ago, before many dinosaurs had appeared.

Sole Survivors

Rhynchocephalians were small to medium-sized reptiles that flourished during the Jurassic Period, but later their numbers declined. Then, 80 million years ago, New Zealand became separated from the other landmasses. While rhynchocephalians in other parts of the world died out about 60 million years ago, tuataras in New Zealand survived. They are now the closest living relatives of today's snakes and lizards.

Apart from birds, no big predators reached New Zealand until humans arrived a few thousand years ago. Humans brought with them dogs and Polynesian rats, and these animals began to eat the tuatara's eggs and hatchlings. Now tuataras can be found only on islands without rats.

Spiky Types

Often called a "living fossil," the tuatara seems to have changed little in 225 million years. Its Maori name means "lightning back" and refers to the spiky crest along the reptile's back and neck. Male tuataras have larger spikes than females.

Tuataras are gray, olive green, or occasionally rusty red. While they may look like lizards, they are in fact very different. For example, they have an extra bone in their skull, but no external ears. They also have hooklike extensions on some of their ribs—a feature shared by birds. Unlike the teeth of lizards, tuataras' sharp, triangular teeth are permanently fused to the jaw. Tuataras also have a "third eye," part of an organ on top of the brain. It has a lens, retina, and nerve connection to

BIG BOYS

At 2 pounds (1 kg), a male is twice the weight of a female (top). Males can also grow to 2 feet (60 cm) in length—6 inches (15 cm) longer than a female.

LAZY DAYS

Tuataras spend the day sleeping in their burrows or basking in the sunshine at their burrow entrances. They are active mostly at night, when they emerge to hunt.

the brain, but early in the growth of the reptile it is covered by scales. Many lizards also have a "third eye," which is involved in regulating temperature, but no one is sure what the tuatara's "third eye" is for.

Lizards have two penises, but tuataras have none. They mate by touching their cloacas together. The females gather in an open sunny spot to dig nests, in which they lay an average of eight eggs. They guard their nests for about a week, to prevent other females digging up the same site, then leave them.

The 12- to 15-month incubation period is one of the longest of any reptile. The young tuatara hatches using the egg-tooth on its snout, then burrows through the soil to the surface.

Rent-A-Burrow

Tuataras are found on islands off the coast of New Zealand. They prefer to live in areas of low forest and scrub, spending their day in burrows on the forest floor. They either use burrows that have been built by the petrels (seabirds) which share their habitat, or they excavate their own.

There are no ponds or streams on the islands, so tuataras are especially active on rainy nights, when they may often be found soaking in puddles.

Snatch and Grab

Tuataras come out to hunt at night. Since they are not fast runners, they usually wait for small prey such as insects, snails, and worms to come close before seizing it with their tongue. Larger animals are impaled on the tuatara's sharp front teeth. They also eat lizards, birds, and birds' eggs—and even their own young!

Crocodiles and Alligators

URING THE MESOZOIC ERA, 245 to 65 million years ago, the Archosauria, or "ruling reptiles," dominated the land. The only giant archosaurs to survive to modern times are the crocodilians. The order Crocodilia includes the largest and some of the most dangerous of the world's living reptiles.

Snap Dragons

Crocodilians are among the largest of the aquatic vertebrates that still venture onto land—although few stray far from water. Most species favor the warm, still water of lakes, ponds, swamps, or the lower reaches of rivers, while a few prefer the cool, clear water of running rivers. Most crocodilians live in freshwater habitats, but a few are at home in the more salty environments of mangrove swamps and estuaries.

Most of the 22 or so species of crocodilian—the crocodiles, alligators, gavials, caimans, and tomistoma—live in tropical regions in Australia, Africa, Asia, and North and South America. A few, such as the American and Chinese alligators, can also be found in temperate regions. Cuvier's dwarf caiman of South America, which grows to 5 feet (1.5 m), is the smallest species. The biggest, the Indopacific or saltwater crocodile, can grow to 23 feet (7 m) and weigh 3,300 pounds (1,500 kg).

Dental Records

The features that distinguish crocodilians from other reptiles are mainly adaptations to their watery lifestyle. For example, crocodiles can hold their breath underwater for as long as an hour. Their elongated head is also characteristic of many aquatic vertebrates, from fish to dolphins, but their snouts differ depending on the prey they catch. The gavial from India, the Southeast Asian tomistoma, and other fish-eating crocodiles have narrow teeth and long snouts to clamp their slippery prey. The broad snouts

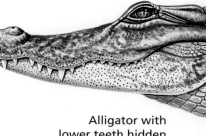

TELLING TEETH
An alligator's lower teeth fit into pits in the upper jaw. In a crocodile, one large lower tooth on each side slips into a notch on the outside of the upper jaw.

Alligator with lower teeth hidden

Crocodile with lower teeth showing

GENTLE JAWS
An alligator's jaws can be lethal, but this hatchling sits safely in its mother's mouth. It is being carried to a quiet pond, where the female alligator will protect it from predators.

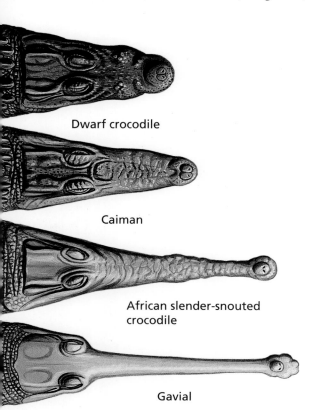

Dwarf crocodile

Caiman

African slender-snouted crocodile

Gavial

SNOUTS WITH CLOUT
The snout's width tells about a species' diet. Long, slender snouts snap quickly to catch fish. They are also useful for poking into burrows to find crabs. Shorter, wider snouts catch fish and larger mammals.

of other species are so powerful they can crush the skull of large animals!

Crocodilians' peg-like teeth are also similar to those of other aquatic animals, such as toothed whales. With up to 32 teeth in the upper jaw and 40 in the lower, crocodilians can puncture and grip prey. But they can't chew their food: Instead, they swallow prey whole or tear it into large pieces by twisting and spinning their body.

Crocodilians' teeth often break during hunting, and since the teeth do not have strong roots, they also fall out easily with wear. Luckily, for the crocodilian anyway, new teeth continually grow to replace the damaged and missing ones.

Crocodilians have well-developed eyesight. They can probably see color, and their eyes have a reflective area at the back to help them see at night. Their eyes also have a protective third eyelid. Like their nostrils, which have watertight valves, their eyes are set high on the head so that they remain at the surface of the water while the rest of the animal is completely submerged.

Hatch and Dispatch

Crocodilians are some of the most ferocious reptiles in the world, but females look after their eggs and young more carefully than most reptiles. This is essential if the young are to survive, as the eggs and hatchlings can be eaten by

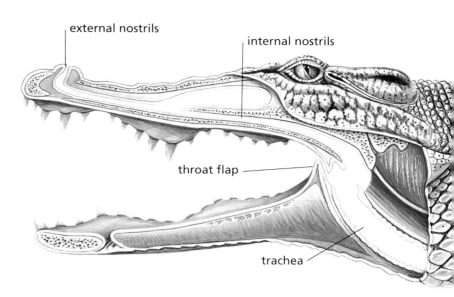

external nostrils

internal nostrils

throat flap

trachea

a host of predators, including turtles, lizards, fish, birds, or mammals, such as wild pigs, mongooses, or humans.

Some species make nests by scraping soil and vegetation into mounds with their clawed front feet. Others bury their eggs in holes in the sand or soil. In South America, Schneider's dwarf caimans make nests in shady rain forests. Because there is no heat from the Sun to warm the eggs, the female builds a nest beside a termite mound, scraping together plant material which she then uses to cover the eggs. Heat from the termite mound and the rotting vegetation incubates the eggs.

SCALY SUBMARINE
A crocodilian can breathe while half submerged, since its nostrils stay above water. A flap stops water entering the trachea, so it can also open its mouth underwater without drowning.

DEADLY DASH

Most crocodilians seem awkward on land. But when startled, the Johnston's crocodile can sprint at 10 miles (17 km) an hour!

Crawl

Walk

Gallop

All female crocodilians guard their nests and will attack any intruder. Sometimes the father will also remain near to defend the eggs. Some species rarely leave the nest except to drink. The Indopacific crocodile may dig out a wallow just beside her nest, where she can lie on guard, but unseen.

The eggs take 60 to 100 days to develop, depending on the species and the temperature of the nest. The sex of a hatchling is also determined by the nest temperature. In the American alligator, for example, temperatures of 82°–86°F (28°–30°C) produce females; temperatures of 90°–93°F (32°–34°C) produce males. Temperatures in between produce a mixture of males and females.

When young crocodilians first break through the shell, they begin calling with grunts, yelps, and croaks to attract their mother's attention. When they hear their babies crying, the females gently scrape away the nesting material to help free them. They then carefully pick the babies up in their mouth and carry them to the water. The Nile crocodile even picks up the unhatched eggs, rolling them between her tongue and the roof of her mouth until the shell breaks.

The mother and her hatchlings often stay together for several weeks or more—or years, in the case of some American alligators—until the young can fend for themselves. Sometimes other adults also help guard the young. During this dangerous time, the hatchlings often ride on their mother's back and head, where they can rest or bask, safe from attack.

Slip and Flip

Crocodilians spend much of their life lying motionless on riverbanks. Their generally large size and short legs mean that they can usually walk only for short distances, lifting their belly high and dragging their tail. When hard-pressed, they will revert to a typically reptilian crawl or slither

GREAT PRETENDER

The tomistoma was called the "false" gavial because it was thought to be part of the crocodile family. But DNA tests prove that it is related to the gavial.

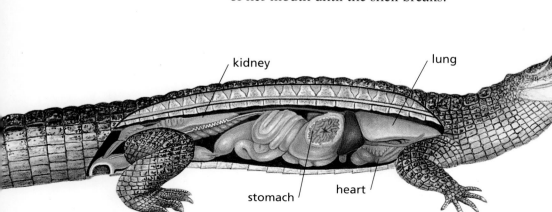

kidney

lung

stomach

heart

GUT GRINDERS

Crocodilians do not chew their food. Most species swallow stones and other hard objects, called gastroliths, which help mash up the food so that it can be digested.

on their belly, especially when they enter the water from a riverbank and do not want to alert prey by disturbing the water's surface. Their belly scales are thinner and lighter than those on their back, enabling them to slide along with little drag.

By contrast, crocodilians swim with ease, holding their legs against their body and using sideways S-shaped strokes of their powerful, paddle-like tail to propel them along. To conserve energy, they tread water and slowly drift toward their prey, such as an antelope drinking at the water's edge. They then explode into action, their webbed hind feet providing power for a sudden rush as they vault out of the water, seizing the antelope's muzzle in their teeth. They then flip or drag the prey underwater and drown it.

People Eaters

The Nile crocodile is the biggest and strongest freshwater predator in Africa. It can grow to 18 feet (5.5 m) long. When lying motionless in water, its drab green, brown, and black coloring makes it difficult to detect. It often hides itself even more by floating next to reeds or under an overhanging tree. From this sit-and-wait position, it

can lunge several times its own length up a riverbank!

Hatchlings eat insects, spiders, and frogs. Adults eat anything from fish and birds to zebras and humans. Although mostly solitary hunters, large numbers of crocodiles will gather to attack herds of wildebeest as they ford rivers on their annual migration across the Serengeti plains.

The Nile crocodile has few enemies apart from humans, which it will eat if necessary. Another species that strikes terror into the heart of many humans is the enormous Indopacific or saltwater crocodile. While people

are not usually on the Indopacific's menu, it will take advantage of any clumsy human that gets too close.

The Indopacific crocodile is the only species to enter the sea, and it has been seen swimming in the ocean 620 miles (1,000 km) from land. On the crocodile's tongue are glands that secrete excess salt, allowing it to maintain the correct salt balance in its body fluids and survive in a marine environment. However, it is often found in freshwater rivers and lakes

SMILE FROM THE NILE
An adult Nile crocodile has no enemies, apart from hippopotamuses—which probably only attack in defense of their calves—other crocodiles, and humans.

GREAT AND SMALL
The Cuvier's dwarf caiman is 5 feet (1.5 m) when fully grown. It is only half the size of the tomistoma, which itself is only about half the length of the Indopacific crocodile.

SCUTE SUIT
All crocodilians have osteoderms in the scutes on their back to protect them from predators. Cuvier's dwarf caiman is one of the most heavily armored—even its eyelids have bony plates.

in its range, which stretches from India to northern Australia and the Solomon Islands.

Buzz Words

Crocodilians have a social life quite unlike that of other reptiles. They communicate with sounds, such as grunts, coughs, and roars, and by vibrations made by rapidly squeezing their trunk muscles beneath the surface of the water. The American crocodile also relies on body language to signal its intentions, such as tail thrashing and a behavior known as headslapping. The headslap is performed by lifting the head partly out of the water, then closing the jaws as if biting the water surface. The sound is like the noise of a flat shovel being slapped on top of the water. A territorial crocodile will show his dominance by headslapping the water two or three times in a row.

By contrast, the tiny dwarf crocodile of tropical west and central Africa is a docile, timid creature. It is rarely seen during the day, unlike its neighbor, the African slender-snouted crocodile. This noisy species roars repeatedly, sounding like a truck exhaust backfiring! Since its slender snout is too fragile to take large prey on land, it instead seizes fish with a sideways sweep of its open jaws.

Fish are the main food of the gavial, but it also eats insects, frogs, and other small animals. One of the most distinctive crocodilians, the gavial gets its name from a Hindi

UP PERISCOPE

In winter, American and Chinese alligators either retreat into burrows under riverbanks and in mud holes, or move to shallow backwaters. They can survive freezing conditions by keeping their nose above the water so that breathing holes form when the water surface freezes. Here they remain dormant until spring.

LATER, ALLIGATOR?
The Chinese alligator is critically endangered because human population pressures and natural disasters such as floods threaten its habitat.

HANGING LOOSE
Crocodilians are "cold-blooded." This alligator is basking to warm itself. At night, as the temperature drops, it will retreat to the warmer water.

word meaning "pot." This refers to the knob on the male's snout. During the breeding season, the male snorts air through its knob, making a buzzing noise that warns rival males away. The gavial lives in rapid rivers and streams from Pakistan to Myanmar (Burma).

Broad-Casters

The two species of true alligator are found in widely separated regions of the world. The Chinese alligator lives in the muddy waters of the lower Yangtze River in China, and rarely grows longer than 7 feet (2 m). The 20-foot (6-m) long American alligator lives in ponds, swamps, and estuaries in southeastern North America. Both species have broad heads, perhaps an adaptation to living in thickly vegetated swamps—a heavy skull can catch prey by smashing through reeds.

The American alligator eats reptiles, amphibians, fish, birds, and mammals. Females occasionally attack people, but usually only when they are protecting their nests. When it spots prey, an alligator swims soundlessly through the water until it is close enough to attack. Yet this same silent hunter is also the noisiest of all the

crocodilians. During the breeding season, a territorial male utters bellowing roars that can be heard 500 feet (150 m) away. Its neighbors respond with choruses that may last half an hour or more.

Goggle Gators

Alligators and caimans are closely related, but all five species of caiman live in Central and South America. They are usually smaller than alligators and have bonier ridges, or "spectacles," between their eyes. The largest species, the black caiman, grows to 20 feet (6 m) and lives in the flooded forests around the Amazon and Orinoco rivers. Widespread in South America, the common caiman often lives in dams and cattle ponds, where it mainly eats snails and fish. If its pools dry out, it will walk long distances in search of new hunting territories.

JUMP SHOT
American alligators often hunt near waterbird colonies, where they eat the fish that feed on the birds' droppings. They can also blast straight out of the water to snatch birds!

Insects and Spiders

There are more than a million species of insect and spider. This means that they outnumber all the other animal species put together. Even more await discovery, and some scientists think that the total number may be as high as 30 million. Many people fear and hate insects and spiders, and it is true that some can either hurt us or destroy our food and crops. But the majority of these interesting and often beautiful animals play a vital role in the lives of humans, and of the other species with whom we share our planet.

Insects, spiders, and their relatives have adapted to living on Earth more successfully than any other type of animal. Most are less than ¼ inch (6 mm) long, enabling them to survive in an extraordinary range of environments. They live in icy lakes, searing deserts, poisonous pools, steaming springs—even on our own body! We could say that the world was made for them.

Classifying Insects

INSECTS BELONG TO A GROUP OF ANIMALS called arthropods. The name comes from the Greek *arthropoda* and means "jointed leg." Insects are well-named, because they all have three pairs of tubelike legs with joints that allow them to bend. While insects don't have a backbone, they are also characterized by their external skeleton.

Case Closed

All arthropods have a hard external skeleton. Called the exoskeleton, it encases the whole body and is made up of separate plates, arranged in segments, that meet at flexible joints. An insect's muscles are attached to the inside of its exoskeleton, and they pull against the plates to move the body.

The exoskeleton is made of a plastic-like material called chitin. It is usually covered with waxy substances that help prevent the insect from drying out. Unlike the skeleton of vertebrates, which grows in step with the rest of the body, the exoskeleton is rigid. In order to grow, the insect has to molt and replace its old exoskeleton with a larger one. Some insects molt just twice, but others molt more than 25 times. Once an insect matures, it usually stops molting.

An exoskeleton also serves as armor plating, shielding the insect from predators. But during molt an insect is vulnerable to attack, as well as disease and (if the insect lives on land) dehydration.

Scientists think that the dangers associated with molting may partially explain why most insects are small. If they were any larger, most would die before they could reach maturity and reproduce.

Wings, Springs, and Stings

An insect's body is divided into three basic parts: the head, the thorax, and the abdomen. In adult insects, the head consists of several interlocking plates and is one of the strongest parts of the body. It carries a pair of antennae and a set of mouthparts, which handle food and guide it into the insect's mouth. On the top of the head of most insects are small, simple eyes, called ocelli, which sense the amount of light in their surroundings. Adult insects also have compound eyes made up of tiny lenses packed together. The more lenses an insect has, the more clearly it can see.

EYE FOR A FLY
This horsefly relies mainly on vision to find her food of blood. Signals from the thousands of lenses in her eyes, combined by her brain, make up an image of her surroundings.

LAUNCH PAD
To jump, a flea squeezes rubbery pads in its thorax. When the pads are released, they spring back and fling the flea into the air. A flea can leap 100 times its height. This is equal to a person jumping a tall building!

FUZZY BUZZER
The honeybee is a typical flying insect, with two pairs of wings and six legs. Its exoskeleton is covered with hairs that detect the slightest air current. Each tiny hair sends messages to the brain.

A dragonfly can have up to 30,000 lenses per eye, but a worker ant that lives underground has only a few hundred lenses.

The thorax carries three pairs of legs and, usually, two pairs of wings, plus the muscles to operate them. The wings are made of chitin and braced with thickened veins. In some species, such as bees, the front wings are joined to the back wings by a row of hooks. Thus attached, the two pairs beat together.

Hooks, pads, and suckers on the feet allow insects to cling to surfaces or to catch food. Food is digested in the abdomen, which also contains the venom glands—if the insect can sting—and reproductive organs.

GASPING AT STRAWS
Many insects spend part of life underwater. To breathe, some species such as this water scorpion get oxygen from the air through a tube piercing the surface.

Breathing Space

Like all animals, insects must breathe. In humans, oxygen from the air flows through the lungs into tiny air sacs, called alveoli. From the alveoli the oxygen seeps into blood vessels and is pumped, along with nutrients and other necessities, through the body by the heart. But an insect has no lungs, and its circulatory system carries only food, not oxygen. Its blood is pumped forward by several hearts positioned along a muscular tube, but then flows out of the tube and back through open body spaces, bathing the tissues.

Because they have no lungs, most insects breathe with the help of tiny air tubes called tracheae. The openings of the tubes, called spiracles, are like portholes on the sides of the thorax and abdomen. The spiracles let air into the tracheae, which divide into branches that deliver oxygen into the body cells. Since this system wouldn't be able to meet the oxygen needs of a large body, this is one reason—despite all the horror movies—that there will never be insects as big as humans!

DEFT DETECTORS

All adult insects have antennae. These delicate organs carry sensors that smell the air, taste buds that sense food, and hairs that register temperature or touch. Insects also often use their antennae to hear, but they have other ways of detecting different sounds and other vibrations.

LISTENING LIMBS
Bush crickets have ears on their front legs, just below their knees. Each ear is a thin, oval membrane that moves when the air vibrates.

EARS TO THE REAR
Grasshoppers and locusts have ears on their abdomen. They are particularly sensitive to the calls made by their own species.

ANTS' PANTS
Like cockroaches, ants sense vibrations through their legs. They often respond to these vibrations by preparing to attack.

LOUD AND CLEAR
The transparent, delicate wings of a lacewing pick up vibrations in the air and sense movements.

Classifying Spiders

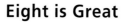

A S WELL AS INSECTS, arthropods include centipedes, millipedes, crustaceans, and arachnids. Spiders, scorpions, ticks, and mites are all arachnids. Like insects, arachnids have jointed legs and a hard body case. But arachnids are also unlike insects in many ways. One of the obvious differences is that spiders don't have wings!

Eight is Great

There are about 80,000 species of spider, and all have an exoskeleton, also known as a carapace, made of chitin. Like insects, the exoskeleton is inflexible and must be shed at regular intervals. But unlike insects, spiders lack antennae and wings. They have four pairs of jointed legs, and just two body regions instead of three.

The front part, or cephalothorax, consists of the head and thorax. The legs are also attached to this body part. The cephalothorax contains the eyes, jaws, venom glands, stomach, and brain. Unlike insects, most spiders have eight eyes (a few species have six) arranged in two or three rows. Each eye has only a single simple lens, and most species don't see very well.

Whereas many insects are vegetarian and have jaws, called mandibles, for grinding up plant food, all spiders are carnivorous. Their jaws, called chelicerae, have fangs for spearing insects, frogs, lizards, or even small birds and snakes. In some spiders, the fangs stab downward, pinning prey. Other species have fangs that come together, like pincers. Nearly all inject venom, passed from glands through ducts to the tip of each fang, to paralyze or kill their prey.

There's a Soup in My Fly

Once prey is caught, the spider injects it full of juices from a digestive gland in the rear part of the body, called the abdomen. These juices dissolve prey into a kind of liquid "soup," which is then sucked into the spider's mouth by the pumping action of the stomach.

The abdomen is relatively soft and usually rounded, not divided into segments like that of insects. As well

WAIST WATCHING
The abdomen is attached to the cephalothorax by a "waist" called the pedicel. The aorta, intestine, nerve cord, and some muscles pass through the pedicel, giving the spider flexibility.

HAIRY STARE
Many spiders sense the vibrations of moving prey with the hairs on their body and legs. But this jumping spider has relatively good vision. It can spot prey up to 8 inches (20 cm) away.

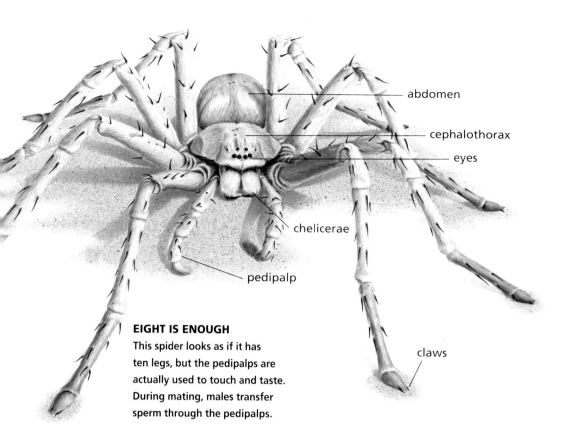

abdomen

cephalothorax

eyes

chelicerae

pedipalp

EIGHT IS ENOUGH
This spider looks as if it has ten legs, but the pedipalps are actually used to touch and taste. During mating, males transfer sperm through the pedipalps.

claws

Skin splits

as the digestive gland, it contains the heart, gut, reproductive organs, and lungs. Spiders have two different ways of breathing. Some have two pairs of "book lungs." In these gill-like lungs, air flows through thin, blood-carrying membranes that are arranged like the pages of a book. But other spiders have one set of book lungs and a set of tracheae, which work in a way similar to the tracheae of insects.

Glands on Demand

Some insects, such as the caterpillars of many moths, use silk from their mouth to spin shelters or cocoons. But a spider's silk comes from glands in the abdomen. Web-building spiders have between four and seven glands. Each gland makes silk for a different purpose: to build webs; to wrap prey; to create a safety line to lower the spider or to stop it from falling; to make sacs for their eggs; and so on.

Spider silk is made of protein. It is stored as a liquid inside the glands, but instantly becomes solid when it is drawn from the body by the spinnerets. The silk is stronger than steel and can be stretched by more than a quarter without breaking. The silk of the *Nephila* spiders is the strongest natural fiber known!

Legs pull out

SPIN OFF
The spinnerets are located on the underside of the abdomen. The silk comes from glands through the small nozzles on the spinnerets.

spinnerets

Skin dries and hardens

BUSTIN' LOOSE
A spider pulls its legs out of its old skin like someone pulling their fingers from a glove. When it is free, it expands to its new size.

Insects and Spiders through the Ages

INSECTS AND SPIDERS were some of the earliest animal life on Earth, but no one is really sure how they evolved. This is because there are relatively few fossilized specimens. What is known is that they had begun to colonize the continents long before vertebrates struggled onto land.

Crushed to Dust

Despite their abundance, insects and spiders rarely became fossils because of the delicacy of their exoskeleton and muscle tissue. The fossilized insects that are known are usually badly crushed. But the study of fossils of early arthropods, as well as animals trapped in amber, has allowed scientists to draw some conclusions.

It is thought that the first insects may have evolved from marine arthropods called trilobites. Fossils confirm that land-based insects were flourishing 395 million years ago, when trilobites started to decline.

But there is evidence of arthropods on land even before this date. For example, the earliest fossil scorpions, which are related to spiders, date back about 425 million years. These scorpions were amphibious, and some measured more than 3 feet (1 m) long.

Salad Days

During the Carboniferous Period, 360 to 285 million years ago, thousands of new species of arthropod emerged to exploit every inch of the humid forests, from the moist soil to the topmost branches. By 300 million years ago, diverse groups had developed new equipment and techniques to feed on different plant parts. Some insects plunged their beaks into branches to suck up sap. Some gnawed the edges of leaves or pierced into the veins; others drilled into the trunk; and still more caused plants to grow layers of abnormal tissue, called galls, to surround and protect their young.

The insects' success made possible the advance of vertebrates, since insects were a food source for these migrants to the land. But insects, too,

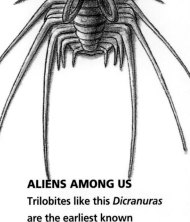

ALIENS AMONG US
Trilobites like this *Dicranuras* are the earliest known arthropods. They became extinct about 260 million years ago, when insects were well established.

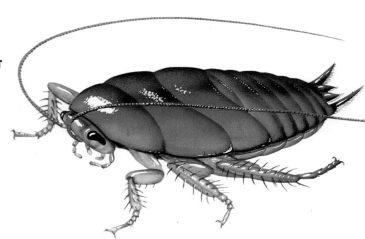

SURVIVAL OF THE FLATTEST
Cockroaches appeared about 320 million years ago. Some were 20 inches (50 cm) long. Today the largest species is just 6 inches (15 cm) long. By becoming smaller and flatter, they ensured their survival.

continued to adapt to environmental forces. One force was the evolution of flowering plants—a food supply which enhanced the chances of survival of any creature that could exploit it. Many insects developed the ability to see wavelengths of light invisible to humans, enabling them to find pollen and nectar more easily. Most important of all, insects became the first animals to fly. Flying allowed them to move to new food sources. As insects attacked plants, plants took advantage of the mobility of insects, which spread pollen as they fed.

Small World

Flying also enabled insects to escape danger and to search for a mate. As they evolved, they developed other features to aid flying, such as ocelli. But before they could fly efficiently, insects also had to shrink. A feature of many ancient insects was their size: *Meganeura monyi*, a dragonfly that lived 300 million years ago, had a wingspan of about 2¼ feet (70 cm)! By contrast, the largest damselfly alive today spans just 7½ inches (19 cm). The *Meganeura's* exoskeleton might have been too heavy to stay airborne, making it vulnerable to predators.

Today, most insects are smaller than a bean, and so light that they defy gravity. They can run up surfaces almost as easily as they run down them.

If they do fall, they are rarely injured when they hit the ground. Their size also means that they can exploit places that are too cramped for larger animals, such as gaps among particles of soil, or spaces between the upper and lower surfaces of leaves.

These body modifications were just one strategy for survival. Behavioral adaptations also help to explain the success of insects and spiders today.

SWAMP BUGGY

A 388-million-year-old bristletail—a creature like a silverfish—found in Quebec, Canada, is the oldest recorded fossilised insect. Silverfish remain primitive insects, having neither wings nor ocelli.

SET IN STONE

A few species, such as this snakefly, have been preserved in delicate layers of shale dating from the Carboniferous Period, about 345 million years ago.

TRAPPED IN TIME

Some people make jewellery out of amber, but for scientists it is a goldmine of information. Amber is fossilized sap, or resin, from pine trees that lived 40 million years ago. Some animals became caught in the sticky resin as it flowed down tree trunks. Eventually the resin (and its prisoner) hardened and was buried in soil. Millions of years later, it was washed down rivers and streams into the sea.

Sap oozes from wound in tree

Without amber, even less would be known about the evolution of insects and spiders. Some specimens are so perfectly preserved that even hairs on tiny insects can be seen. Muscle fibers and DNA fragments can also be extracted for study. But scientists have as yet been unable to extract DNA from the insects' food. So dinosaurs recreated with DNA found in the stomachs of fossilized mosquitoes remain in the realms of *Jurassic Park!*

Insect is trapped in sticky sap

Sap hardens, preserving insect

Insect Behavior

ALONG WITH PHYSICAL ADAPTATIONS, insects have evolved many other strategies of survival. Their behavior is some of the most fascinating and complex in the whole animal kingdom, and includes ingenious ways of solving the problems associated with their small size and relative fragility.

A Caste of Thousands

Many of the challenges faced by insects are solved by cooperation. Many insects, such as termites, and some bees, wasps, and ants, live in groups. By living together, many individuals can share the sometimes difficult tasks of finding food, building and repairing a nest, taking care of the young, and protecting themselves.

While some species of bee, for example, are solitary, others live in enormous colonies consisting of up to 100,000 individuals. The members of these colonies are structured into strictly defined "castes," such as queens, drones, and workers. The male drones mate with the queen,

who produces all the eggs. The worker bees collect food and care for the eggs and young. No bee directs the work of the others, yet all the bees know instinctively what task they must perform. Together, their efforts add up to a better chance of survival for the colony.

Worker bees are also responsible for the construction of their colony's hive. Worker ants, too, are engineers. The seed-eating ants of the southwestern United States tunnel up to 7 feet (2.1 m) into soil, while African weaver ants and Australian green ants build "woven" nests. Some workers form chains to pull leaf edges close, and others carry larvae from the existing nests and use the silk from the mouth of the larvae to glue the leaves together.

Army ants of South America don't use soil or silk for their nests; instead, they use a more convenient building material: their own body. Worker ants link their bodies together by their claws, creating a kind of chain mail with which they form temporary shelters as they search for food. By adjusting their body position, the ants can make ventilation spaces—which can be opened up to increase air flow or closed to retain heat—or a shield to protect the queen, eggs, and larvae.

GARDEN GOOD-GUYS
Ladybugs are common in gardens and orchards. While some are leaf-eating pests, the adults of other species are beneficial, eating 300 to 400 aphids a month.

IN THE BAG
Bagworm caterpillars live in cases like sleeping bags. Each species builds a different kind of bag. The left bag is made of silk and sticks; the right bag is made of shed skin and broken leaves.

ONE FOR THE POT
A potter wasp makes a pot out of mud. Inside it she puts a caterpillar that she has paralyzed. She then lays an egg on it, and seals the pot. When her grub hatches, it has fresh food to eat.

Bricks and Mortar

The purpose of a home is to protect its occupant, and solitary insects also build structures to shield them from an often hostile world. The cases of fresh-water caddis fly larvae protect against fish and sharp-jawed insects. Bagworms craft cases designed to resist attacks from birds. Since it can't outrun enemies, the case-bearing leaf beetle carries its home on its back.

Some caterpillars undergo the transformation to moth in silk cocoons. But other species use silk and their own droppings in their shelters. Since their droppings are mostly regular in shape, contain little water, and are odorless (and therefore don't attract predators), they make ideal building bricks. The caterpillar of one Australian moth even excretes its droppings in groups of three or four to form pillars. It then uses the pillars to build a corridor of archways, filling it in with curtains of silk.

Other insects, such as carpenter bees, prefer to build nests in trees. But some solitary wasps make nests of mud. As it spreads a fresh load, the wasp makes a buzzing sound. The vibrations turn the mud to liquid, allowing air bubbles to escape and the new load to stick easily to the dry nest.

Herbs and Herds

Of course, all this work requires energy. Many different insects eat plant food including roots, flowers, leaves, and stems. The hazelnut weevil uses its long, slender snout, with tiny jaws at the tip, like a drill to chew holes in nuts. Termites devour wood. The larvae of leaf-mining beetles burrow inside leaves to form narrow galleries, which provide not just a supply of food but physical protection, too.

Some insects even grow their own food. The leafcutter ants of South America cultivate fungus gardens. Other ants "milk" sap-sucking aphids for their sugar-rich excreta known as honeydew. In return for the honeydew, the ants protect the aphids. Some even store the aphid's eggs over winter and take the young out to pasture, like cattle, when they hatch.

MIDAIR MEAL
With its mouthpart, or proboscis, uncoiled, this hawk moth sips nectar from a flower. The proboscis of some hawk moths is more than 6 inches (15 cm) long!

SAY YOUR PRAYERS
A praying mantis surprises its victims by striking out with its forelegs. The spines on its legs grip the prey. The mantis often begins eating while its catch is still struggling to escape.

These orderly insects even plan ahead to make sure they have enough food in hard times. North American desert ants store food underground in granaries to feed them during times of drought. These larders are so huge that colonies are reported to have survived a drought which resulted in no seed crop for 12 years!

Meal-y Bugs

One third of all insects feed on other animals. Parasitic insects live on or inside another animal, called the host, and feed on its body or blood. Many lay their eggs on the larvae of other insects, or inject eggs through the victim's skin. When the eggs hatch, the larvae feed on the host. They start with the less essential parts of the host's body, so that it survives for as long as possible. Eventually, they burst out through the host's skin and turn into adults.

Many insects live off others in a less damaging way. Some dung beetles eat the droppings of herbivores, while carrion beetles bury dead animals, then feed themselves and their larvae on the remains.

Some predators catch their prey by hunting it actively. Dragonflies are the hawks of the insect world, patrolling the surface of quiet waters ready to swoop and snatch other flying insects

CAUTION PORTION

Instead of hiding, some insects use a different line of defense. The bright colors of this caterpillar make it extremely conspicuous, but they warn predators that it is foul-tasting or even toxic.

KICK BACK

When threatened, the giant weta of New Zealand raises its powerful back legs to demonstrate that it can fight back. The legs have large, sharp spines.

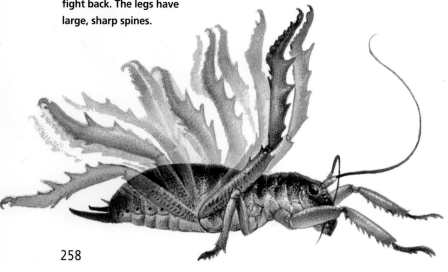

LYING EYES

Species such as this polyphemus moth have spots on their back wings. When they are disturbed, they reveal their spots, which look like the hungry eyes of an owl. Small birds fly for their life.

with their long legs. On the ground, tiger beetles chase ants at speeds of 1½ feet (45 cm) per second, crushing them in their jaws.

Other insects hunt by stealth or ambush. Assassin bugs lie in wait until food comes close, then use their sharp beak to stab their victims and suck out the body fluids. The larvae of fungus gnats, found in caves in New Zealand, catch prey by glowing in the dark. Each larva produces a thread of sticky mucus that traps insects as they fly toward the light.

Other predators use camouflage to avoid being seen by their prey. Many praying mantids have developed a plantlike body to enable them to hide on vegetation before striking at unwary prey. Flower mantids may even sway from side to side on their perches, mimicking the movements that plants make in a gentle breeze.

Don't Ant-Agonize

For creatures as small as insects, the world is full of danger. Camouflage is useful not only for protection against predators, but also for catching prey.

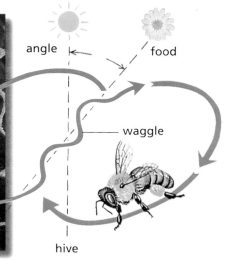

While many insects protect themselves by flying away or hiding, others stay still and make themselves look like the objects around them. For example, a leaf insect's flattened body and front wings mimic a single leaf, while the long-headed grasshopper's pointed head gives it a sticklike shape.

Some species use their appearance to scare predators away. The bright colors of many insects warn enemies that they will leave a bad taste in the mouth—or worse. Others have evolved body armor, such as the leg spines of weta crickets. Lily beetle larvae reinforce their exoskeleton with a coat of their own droppings.

Other species resort to chemical weapons. Bush crickets ooze droplets of a foul-smelling liquid; wood ants spray acid from their abdomen; and termite soldiers squirt "glue" from their mouth at high pressure and with great accuracy. This glue poisons predators as well as entangling them, and

works against even enemies as large as birds.

Many other species find safety—and strength—in numbers. In a locust swarm, the chances of one individual being picked off by a predator is tiny. On the other hand, the sting of one killer bee is no worse than any other

SNAP-HAPPY
A click-beetle avoids danger by lying still on its back (left). If attacked, its head suddenly snaps upwards hurling it out of harm's way and back on its feet.

Go Figure

When a worker honeybee finds a good food source, it returns to the hive to spread the news. It uses coded dances to tell the others where the food is. If the food is close by, the bee dances in tight circles. If it is far from the hive, the bee dances in a figure-8, waggling its abdomen. The size of the figure-8 shows the distance the others must fly. The angle of the waggle indicates the direction in relation to the Sun.

angle

food

waggle

hive

bee's sting, but when killer bees defend themselves in huge numbers, they can kill large animals—even humans.

Flowers and Candy

Bees and ants use chemical messages, or pheromones, to coordinate their attacks on predators. But scent is also used for peaceful purposes. The male tiger moth attracts females with pheromones released by two glands in his abdomen. Male orchid bees use perfume from flowers to attract mates.

For insects such as crickets and cicadas, sound provides a way to contact a mate. The male hissing cockroaches of Madagascar attract females by forcing air from tiny holes in their abdomen. Other insects use bright colors or patterns to identify themselves. After dark, most insects are hard to see, but the small beetles called fireflies use their pale greenish light to flash signals to attract their own kind. A female may cheat and flash the code of another firefly species. When the duped male lands, she eats him.

HAPLESS HOST

This ichneumon wasp has drilled into a branch. She stings the larva of a wood wasp and deposits an egg through a tube, the ovipositor, onto the larva. When the egg hatches, it will feed on its host.

PAMPERED PUPAE

Queen bees lay eggs in wax cells in the hive. The worker bees care for the hatched pupae. Those destined to become new queens are fed a diet of royal jelly, a special saliva made by the workers.

Taste is an important method of communication. When two ants meet, they touch each other with their antennae to find out if they are from the same nest, and to taste any food they have found. Food also plays an important role in courtship rituals, since many males present the females with a tasty gift. A dance-fly, for example, gives his partner a mosquito, which she eats as they mate. In some insects, the male has no organ for transferring sperm, so the sperm are passed to the female in a package called a spermatophore. In some species the spermatophore also contains nutrients, which the female eats while the sperm are transferred to her body. Female bush crickets may mate with several males to get extra food!

Offspring Offload

A few insects, such as aphids, can reproduce without having to mate. But most female insects do mate, after which time they must find a place for their eggs near a suitable source of food. Many species whose larvae eat plants must lay their eggs on the plant to which their larvae are adapted.

Monarch butterfly larvae, for example, are adapted

WHIPPERSNAPPER

The puss moth caterpillar relies initially on camouflage for protection. But if it is threatened, it waves a pair of whiplike threads from the "horns" on its abdomen. As a last resort, it squirts acid from glands on its thorax.

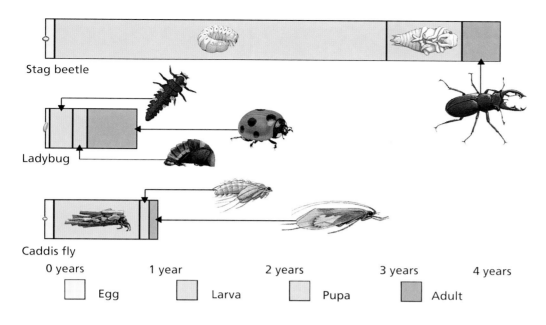

Stag beetle

Ladybug

Caddis fly

0 years	1 year	2 years	3 years	4 years

☐ Egg   ☐ Larva   ☐ Pupa   ☐ Adult

CYCLE PATH

Insects that change form completely as they mature have four stages in their life cycle. Each stage can last a different amount of time. A ladybug spends over half its life as an adult, but a caddis fly lives mostly as a larva in a special case.

to feed on the leaves of milkweed, which are poisonous to most other animals. Some dung beetles lay their eggs in dung, then bury it.

Eggs are sometimes laid singly, but many are laid in clusters of hundreds or even thousands. Some eggs hatch soon after, but others stay inactive during months of cold or dry weather, when all the adults may die. In most cases, the female insect abandons her eggs and makes no attempt to care for her

young. An exception is the female giant water bug, which glues her eggs onto the male's back. While carrying his cargo, the male can't use his wings. The female earwig also looks after her eggs by licking them clean. She stays and protects her eggs until they have hatched and the young earwigs are able to fend for themselves.

MAGIC DRAGONS

A dragonfly nymph spends up to five years developing underwater before it hauls itself up a plant stem, molts its skin for the last time, and emerges as an adult, able to fly.

On patrol for a meal

Wings expand and dry

Mating

Laying eggs

Leaving the water

Molting for the last time

Nymphs hatch

Hunting and growing

BACK PACK
Like all beetles, a ladybug packs its back wings away under its hardened front wings when they are not in use. During flight, the front wings provide lift that helps the insect stay airborne.

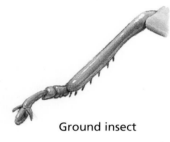

Ground insect

Water insect

SHOE, FLY
Ground-dwelling insects often have claws to grip rough surfaces, or flat pads if they live on sand. Many water insects have hairs along their legs that repel water and stop the animal from sinking.

Bag of Tricks

The eggs of insects, including wasps, bees, ants, flies, beetles, butterflies, and moths, hatch into larvae called grubs, caterpillars, or maggots. They don't have wings, and some don't even have legs. They have a softer body than their parents, and since most feed for many hours every day, they grow quickly and must shed their exoskeleton several times.

When mature, a larva's appetite suddenly vanishes. It stops moving and becomes a pupa, or chrysalis, with a tough outer case or silk cocoon. Inside the case, its body is dissolved and reassembled. When this change, or metamorphosis, is complete, the case splits open and the adult insect, complete with wings, flies away.

Budding Babies

The larvae of species such as earwigs, dragonflies, grasshoppers, true bugs, and praying mantids undergo an "incomplete" metamorphosis. As they grow, they become nymphs. A nymph doesn't have wings—although it does have wing buds and well-developed

legs—and it is usually a different color from its parents. It often lives in a different habitat and feeds on different food. Many cicada nymphs spend years underground before emerging as tree-dwelling adults. Damselfly nymphs live in ponds, using gills on their tail to get oxygen from the water.

Gradually, over a series of stages, the nymphs transform. With every molt, their body grows larger and their wing buds become longer. Eventually, they emerge as adults with functional wings. For some species this long lead-up has a short pay-off: Some female mayflies spend three years as nymphs, but live for one day as adults, mating and laying eggs, before dying.

Flying Colors

Although legless larvae wriggle to get around, adult insects normally move using their legs. Most either walk or

EASE AND SQUEEZE
Some caterpillars move by gripping the ground with their front legs, and pulling their body into a loop. They stretch forward to straighten the loop, then start the process again.

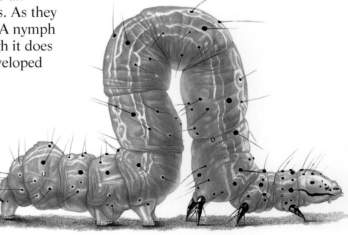

run, or leap into the air, where their wings carry them away. The fastest fliers are the dragonflies, which can reach speeds of up to 30 mph (50 kmph). By contrast, insects such as thrips and aphids are too small and slow to make much headway on their own. Instead, they are blown from one place to another by the wind.

While some ladybugs hibernate through winter, huddling together to stay warm beneath the snow, some insects travel long distances in search of food, or warmth, or both. Moths,

BEETLE BOOGIE
Insects walk by moving three legs at a time—one on one side, and two on the other. This makes their body zigzag as they move along.

WINTER VACATION
Many millions of monarch butterflies spend winter in the upland forests of Mexico and California. There they rest and relax, conserving energy, before flying back north in spring.

locusts, and dragonflies often migrate, but the star travelers are butterflies.

Painted lady butterflies fly from north Africa to Scandinavia, some even crossing the Arctic Circle—a distance of more than 1,800 miles (2,900 km). Each year, masses of monarch butterflies migrate from their homes in eastern North America to their winter roosts 2,500 miles (4,000 km) away. In spring, they head to Florida, where adults lay eggs on the fresh growth of milkweed. Many then die. As summer creeps north, the next generation of butterflies head north, too, some as far as Canada. Several generations may thrive before the days shorten. Then the adults, which have never been south, build up their fat stores and fly down to Mexico, where they use the same roosts as their ancestors before them.

WINGED THINGS
The back wings of a mantis fold like fans when not in use. Thrips' wings look like feathers. A wasp's wings connect to each other with hooks. The two pairs of a dragonfly's wings beat independently of each other.

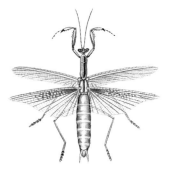

Mantis—pleated wings

Thrip—plumed wings

Wasp—hooked wings

Dragonfly—independent wings

Endangered Species

INSECTS AND SPIDERS are often thought of as "creepy-crawlies." They have less public appeal than, say, a majestic tiger or cuddly giant panda, and they receive less attention from conservationists. But insects and spiders play such a vital role in the ecosystem that dangers to them will ultimately impact upon the whole world.

Worth Saving

As living creatures, insects and spiders have an inherent value. They exist, and have the right to continue to exist. Many are also valuable because they are useful. For example, spiders and termites provide other animals with food, shelter, and nesting materials. Dung beetles use animal droppings as food for their larvae. These and other species also break down nutrients, enriching soil and promoting plant growth. Predators foster global diversity by keeping population levels balanced.

Humans also benefit from insects and spiders. Bees give us honey and beeswax; spiders provide venom for medical research; moth caterpillars make silk; and scale insects produce a red food coloring called cochineal. Ladybugs and wasps kill many of the insect pests that plague our homes and farms. Most importantly, bees, flies, and butterflies pollinate 90 percent of all flowering plants—including the world's food crops.

NATURAL REMEDY
Pyrethrum daisies are the source of pyrethrin, a potent insecticide. Unlike artificial chemical insecticides, pyrethrin breaks down quickly when exposed to the environment.

The War on Bugs

Of course, the relationship between arthropods and humans is not always beneficial. Mosquitoes, flies, and ticks transmit diseases. Termites demolish wooden structures. Weevils bore through stored grain, and caterpillars, beetles, and locusts destroy crops.

People have hit back with weapons such as chemical insecticides. But these kill not only the targeted species, but many harmless species and, eventually, the animals and plants that rely on them for survival. Even the spraying of "weeds" such as native milkweed destroys the food source of species such as the monarch butterfly.

BUSY BEE
Honeybees contribute enormously to the health of our planet. It is estimated that one in every three bites we eat was produced thanks to the services of an insect or other pollinator!

TIGER TROUBLE
Tiger beetles prey on a wide variety of insects, including those we consider pests. But some tiger beetles are under threat. Without the beetles to keep them in check, some pest species may multiply.

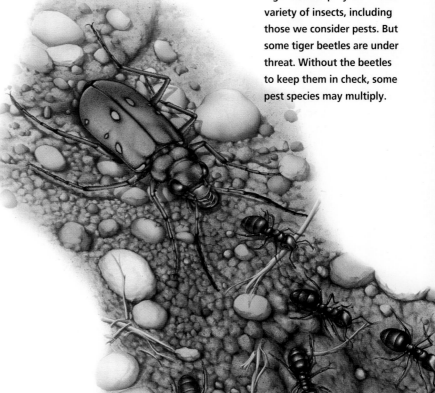

Insecticides, herbicides, and fertilizers also indirectly threaten biodiversity by contaminating groundwater and the air. The introduction of "exotic" species has also decimated some animals. For example, the introduced balsam woolly adelgid is destroying spruce-fir forests in the United States. The forest canopy shelters the moss mat home of the spruce-fir moss spider. Without the canopy, both the moss and the spider dry out and die.

The pressures of rural and urban development have also taken their toll. The Texas tooth cave spider is under threat because many of its caves have been filled in. The happy-faced spider of Hawaii is threatened by weeds and parasites introduced to control farm pests—contributing to the decline of its prey—and even by feral pigs.

Dreams and Schemes

There are so many insects and spiders, and they are so widely dispersed, that little is known about the extent of their destruction. But it seems logical that the widespread use of natural predatory species, instead of chemical pesticides, could help curb insect pests. The creation of "pollination corridors" of undisturbed land could also allow species to feed, roost, and pollinate in peace—ensuring the preservation of that entire ecosystem. Butterfly ranching is also an option in countries where natural resources are plentiful, but economic opportunities are few. The raising and exporting of butterflies for sale to collectors and zoos gives an incentive to protect wild butterflies and their rain forest homes.

TOUGH LOVE

The collection of spiders for pets has endangered some species. The absence of just a few individuals can affect the wild population and its habitat. This Mexican red-kneed tarantula is now protected by law.

Butterflies and Moths

THE 150,000 OR SO SPECIES OF BUTTERFLY AND MOTH belong to the order Lepidoptera. Meaning "scaly wing," the name refers to the insects' delicate rows of modified hairs, which cover not only their four wings but every part of their body. Their patterns and colors make Lepidopterans some of the most beautiful of all insects.

Moths mate

Brother Sun, Sister Moon

Fossil records tell us that the first moths lived during the Cretaceous Period, about 140 million years ago. Butterflies emerged about 100 million years later. While they are perhaps the most easily recognized insects, moths and butterflies have subtle differences.

Butterflies are usually more colorful than moths and fly during the day. Moths are often quite dull-colored and mostly active at dusk or after dark,

spending the day hidden on leaves or in dark corners. Their antennae also differ from those of butterflies, and many moths have thicker abdomens. When flying, the front and hind wings of moths link together with tiny hooks.

The larvae, or caterpillars, of many moths pupate in silk cocoons. Other species burrow under leaf litter or into the ground. The locust-bean moth uses hollowed-out thistle stems, and the Mexican jumping bean moth pupates in the seed of a small bush. By contrast, butterfly larvae pupate in a bare case called a chrysalis.

MAPPING A JOURNEY
Like all lepidopterans, the atlas moth goes through complete metamorphosis. The four stages in its life cycle are egg, larva, pupa, and adult.

SOLAR PANELS
Lepidopterans are only able to fly when they are warm enough. This swallowtail butterfly basks with its wings open, but night-flying moths must shiver to warm up.

Liquid Lunch

Lepidopterans also vary in size, from Queen Alexandra's birdwing butterfly of Papua New Guinea, which has a wingspan of 12½ inches (32 cm), to the fingernail-sized pygmy moths of North America. Nevertheless, they share many features. Their large, compound eyes are sensitive to movement and the color patterns of flowers and

NETTLE METTLE
Caterpillars make a tasty snack for many predators, so they defend themselves either with toxins, "horns" that release a foul smell, or stinging, hairlike spines, like those of this silk moth larva.

TRICK OF THE FLIGHT
The scales on lepidopterans' wings are actually flat, hollow hairs. Many scales are filled with pigments from the insect's food, while others reflect light to produce a metallic sheen.

Eggs glued to leaves of food plants

Larvae, or caterpillars, hatch and grow rapidly

Larvae become pupae

Adult moth breaks open pupal case

When its wing veins harden, moth flies away

other butterflies and moths. They also have taste organs on their back pair of legs. Some primitive moths have jaws for chewing pollen, spores, or wool, but the mouthparts of most adults form a long tube, or proboscis, which coils away when not in use.

Most species suck nectar, fruit juices, and tree sap. Others use their proboscis to pierce skin and drink blood. Tear moths drink from the eyes of large animals, and some butterflies suck mineral salts from mud puddles. But some adults spend their short life breeding, and do not feed at all.

Food Tubes

Most lepidopteran larvae use their powerful jaws to devour plant food. The larva of the polyphemus moth can eat 86,000 times its birth weight in just under two months! But not all larvae are vegetarian. North American harvester butterfly larvae eat aphids. The larva of the looper moth disguises itself as a stick and attacks small flies. Indian meal moth larvae enjoy candy.

Moth Maneuvers

Butterflies and moths are found on all continents except Antarctica. In alpine areas, where temperatures are too cold for night-flying, moths have adapted to fly and feed during the day. These species are more brightly colored than nocturnal moths.

Color is used as camouflage, and to regulate temperature. It is also vital for identifying and attracting a mate of the same species. But since color is less important for moths that are active at night, they find partners (and food) by smell. A male emperor moth can detect the pheromones of a female up to 6 miles (10 km) away.

Moths that are food for species such as bats use evasive action, not camouflage, to survive the night. If they detect a bat's echolocation clicks, they either drop suddenly to the ground, or mimic the bat's calls to jam or swamp its "radar." Confused, the bat may go hungry.

Butterfly

Moth

HEAD GEAR

Each butterfly antenna is a slender shaft ending with a knob. Moths have either simple or feathery antennae. The antennae are covered with hairs that detect air currents and scents.

FLAT OUT

Butterflies usually rest with their wings upright. But moths such as this yellow emperor rest with their wings spread flat, or held tentlike over the body, or curled around the body.

267

Beetles

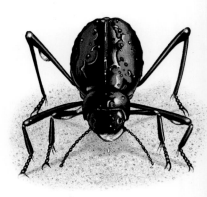

THERE ARE MORE BEETLES on Earth than any other kind of animal. Almost one in every three animal species is a beetle! From the 7½-inch (20-cm) long male hercules beetle to the microscopic feather-winged beetle, they come in every shape, size, and color. There are few places on the planet where beetles do not live.

Beetle Bevy

With more than 300,000 species, the order Coleoptera is the largest in the animal kingdom. The name Coleoptera means "sheath wings," and refers to the tough, rigid front wings that fit over the insects' back wings like a case. These front wings, called elytra, meet in the middle. They stop the beetle's spiracles and fragile back wings from being damaged as it clambers around in search of food.

As the beetle gets ready for lift-off, the elytra separate and spread wide apart to allow the transparent back wings to unfold and carry the insect away. Almost all beetles fly, although some are stronger fliers than others. Most beetles fly only short distances, such as to another food source or a different part of their habitat. But some species, such as auger beetles, can cross the globe inside furniture or containers of grain.

Beetles can be found in almost all habitats. Some crawl through searing desert sand, others shelter under lichen on rain forest trees; others swim in swamps and streams, or bore tunnels in logs and trunks. Some rove beetles live only in the fur of beavers; others live on birds or in the nests of bees and ants. Some clerid beetles of Australia live in termite nests, or on carrion. Many beetles make their home in damp leaf litter.

Common Senses

Although beetles come in all shapes and sizes, they do share some features in common. Most have large compound eyes, and antennae composed of ten or more segments. These vary in design, from the stumpy antennae of the African goliath beetle to the enormous "antlers" of longhorn beetles. Some of these antlers have several branches covered in tiny hairs, making them even more sensitive to vibrations and sounds. Scarab beetles such as the chafer beetle have fanlike antennae, which they spread out when flying to detect scents and wind direction.

DEW DRINK

In Africa's Namib Desert the only moisture comes from fog rolling in from the sea. To get water, this darkling beetle points its abdomen into the wind. It waits until fog condenses on its body and trickles to its mouth.

ODD BODS

The shape of some beetles is difficult to explain. The long head and thorax of the male giraffe weevil may attract females, but the purpose of the long front legs of the harlequin beetle is unknown.

Giraffe weevil

Over millions of years, many beetles have evolved body adaptations to suit their way of life. For example, weevils have an elongated snout, called a rostrum, equipped with a tiny pair of jaws used to drill deep into seeds and stems. Their head even swivels in their thorax, like a ball in a cup, allowing them to feed on foods other insects cannot reach.

Whirligigs, which live on pond surfaces, have developed divided compound eyes that can see above and below water at the same time. Other beetles have developed unusual body cases. For example, one African jewel beetle species has hairs on its elytra to help it to collect pollen. The flattened body of the violin beetle of Indonesia helps it to slip between the layers of fungi in which it lives. The transparent edges of the tortoise beetle's elytra may guard it against predators. When threatened, some pull their antennae under this edge, just as a tortoise pulls its head and legs into its shell.

Rugs and Drugs

Another reason beetles have been able to survive and prosper in so many places is their mouthparts. While the long, spiny jaws of species such as the stag beetle are mainly ornamental, and are used to threaten rivals, most beetles can deliver a powerful bite. Depending on the species, these well-developed jaws eat anything from hardwood to nectar. Flowers, leaves, fruit, roots, pollen, seeds, and sap are popular with many beetles. Tiger beetles and ground beetles, including the sinister-looking devil's coach-horse beetle, hunt insects. Carpet beetles feed not only on rugs but stored grain, upholstery, fur, and stuffed animals—including museum displays. The American spider beetle thrives on its strange diet of tobacco seeds, cayenne pepper, and opium.

TASTY LACE
Beetles undergo complete metamorphosis. Their eggs are laid under tree bark or stones, on dung or leaves, or in plant stems. While some larvae are agricultural pests, others pollinate flowers.

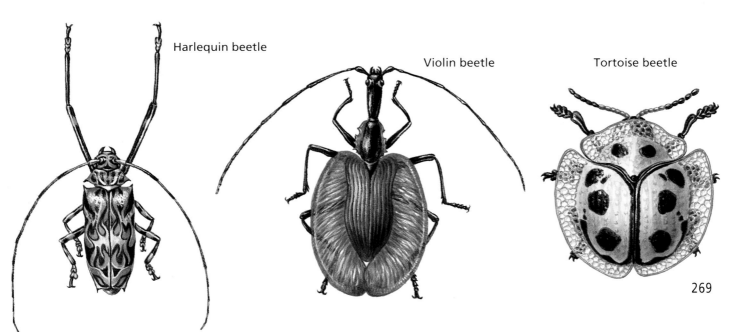

Harlequin beetle

Violin beetle

Tortoise beetle

269

CROP BUSTER

The Colorado beetle of North America originally ate wild plants. When potatoes were introduced, the beetle began to feed on this new food, devastating crops.

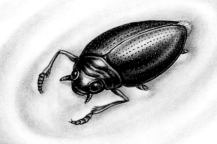

WHIRL POOL

Whirligig beetles dart across the surface of ponds and streams. They locate food and avoid obstacles by creating ripples and sensing how they bounce back.

Beetles find their food in a number of ways, including hunting by ambush or deception. For example, the larvae of some blister beetles climb onto flowers and grab hold of visiting bees. The bees then carry them back to their nest, where the larvae eat the bee's eggs. Other species let food come to them: Inhabitants of the harshest deserts, tenebrionid beetles eat scraps of organic debris blown by the wind.

All beetles need water, and some desert-dwellers have developed ingenious ways to collect it. One flying-saucer-shaped beetle in the Namib Desert, on the southwestern coast of Africa, comes to the surface when the sand starts to grow damp with fog. Using its body as a bulldozer, it plows a trench perpendicular to the fog wind. As the fog moves across the dunes, it condenses on the small ridges of the trench. The beetle then licks the fog droplets from the sand.

Code of Conduct

Beetles spend much of their adult life trying to attract the attention of members of the opposite sex. Like many other insects, male beetles often must compete with other males for females. For example, male carrion beetles on a dead animal will set up and defend territories against rival males in the hope of attracting mates.

Once mated, a female will lay her eggs on the carrion, then bury it. The carrion will provide a rich supply of food for her larvae.

The females of many species release pheromones to attract males. Other beetles, such as some longhorns, make squeaking noises. One little longhorn from Brazil has tufts of hair on its antennae and legs. These tufts look like pom-poms, and are perhaps waved to catch the eye of others.

Deathwatch beetles send messages to potential mates by tapping against wood with their head. This sound was once believed to predict death, but since the beetles tunnel through housing timber, their tapping is more likely to signal that the house is about

JOUSTING JAWS

Male hercules beetles use their greatly enlarged jaws to grapple with rivals for the right to mate with the females. These fights look ferocious, but they rarely produce lasting injuries.

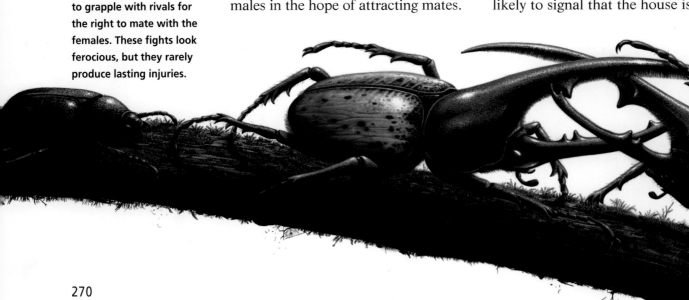

to collapse! Whirligigs also generate a code by tapping the water surface with their legs. Ten taps per minute means "I am female;" 90 taps per minute means "I am male." The beetles use their antennae to detect and interpret the code, then head toward its source.

Cryptic Critters

As prey of birds, lizards, and small mammals, beetles also spend much time trying to avoiding detection. Some species have evolved elaborate

WATER SLAUGHTER
The diving beetle lives in fresh water. A fierce predator, it is strong enough to kill vertebrates such as salamanders. If prey is scarce, it will fly to another pond.

camouflage. The click beetles of Africa have white patches on their elytra to make them blend into their tree bark habitat. The longhorn beetles of Madagascar resemble lichen, while longhorns in Africa and Asia mimic wasps to avoid being eaten by birds.

Some leaf beetles and weevils look like beads of gold, silver, or brass. The elytra of shining leaf chafers change color, from jewel-like greens and blues to stripes and highlights of purple

to orange. These sheens may help to conceal the beetles as they feed on shiny foliage. Like those of butterflies, they are produced by tiny hairs with structures that reflect light. Other beetles have elytra made of layers separated with spaces filled with air. The colors change according to the beetle's position in relation to the light, confusing a predator.

Loose Cannon

When some beetles are attacked they sit tight, either pretending to be dead, or cementing their feet to the leaf on which they are resting. Other species fight back. The larva of the tortoise beetle accumulates a huge shield or mace of droppings over its back, which it wields against predatory ants. Blister beetles and oil beetles secrete chemicals capable of blistering human skin.

The bombardier beetle has even more sophisticated weaponry. When attacked by a predator such as a toad or shrew, it breaks down chemicals called hydroquinone and hydrogen peroxide in special chambers in its abdomen. The resulting chemical reaction causes boiling, noxious gas to explode out of the beetle's anus with an audible bang. While the predator recovers from its shock, the beetle scuttles off to live another day

Ten-spotted ladybug

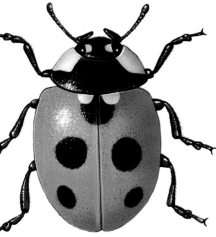

Five-spotted ladybug

SPOT THE DIFFERENCE
The bright colors of ladybug beetles warn predators that they have a bitter taste. The spots of each species are arranged in a different way.

Grasshoppers, Crickets, and Locusts

MEMBERS OF THE ORDER ORTHOPTERA, which includes katydids, all have leaf-chewing mouthparts and prominent, often powerful hind jumping legs. Their distinctive songs accompany warm evenings across the globe, but some are notorious for their tendency to swarm and mow through the environment.

Fans and Feelers

There are more than 23,000 species of Orthopteran, which means "straight wing." This refers to the insects' long, leathery, and narrow front wings. The broad hind wings, which are used for flying, can fold up like fans under the front wings when not in use.

Orthopterans also feature a pair of hair-covered sensory organs, called cerci, at the tip of their abdomen. The cerci supplement the other sense organs, including ears on the front legs or abdomen, large compound eyes, and antennae. Grasshoppers and locusts have relatively short antennae, but those of katydids and crickets can be as long as their body.

Home Cooking

Many grasshoppers are found near the ground, or on low shrubs or pasture. Other species prefer dry grasslands, and the dragon lubber grasshopper of southern California and Mexico is often found hopping on roads to eat insects killed by passing cars—including other dragon lubbers!

Most crickets spend their days in burrows, under shady, damp vegetation, or in cracks in the ground. Mole crickets use their strong, spadelike front legs to tunnel underground, while some desert crickets have feet like propellers to bury themselves in the sand.

Crickets come out at night to feed. The king crickets of Australia hunt for worms and insects, the adult snowy tree cricket of North America feeds on caterpillars and aphids, and the horned katydid of the Amazon eats snails. The secret cave cricket of Texas has been known to eat its own young, but most species and their nymphs use their strong, blunt jaws to saw and crush up leaves, fruits, fungi, and roots.

SHORT AND SWEET
Male speckled bush crickets use ultrasound to find a mate, making calls lasting one thousandth of a second. Such short calls may prevent bats from eavesdropping and eating the singers.

POCKET ROCKET
A grasshopper jumps to launch itself into flight. A springlike mechanism in its knees increases the force of the jump, and muscles in its hind legs flick backward to push it into the air.

Talk is Cheep

Katydids are at home in dense foliage. Their veined, leaflike front wings, which cover most of their green body, provide good camouflage. The mottled coloration of grasshoppers also helps them to hide from hungry predators, while the ragged wings of some South American bush crickets look like dead leaves. But the bright red and blue coloring of Leichhardt's grasshopper of northern Australia warns attackers that it contains toxins from its diet of poisonous plants. When disturbed, others flash their yellow, red, purple, or pink hind wings to startle enemies.

Sound communication has the advantage of allowing an insect to remain hidden from predators while it broadcasts its call. Orthopterans use sound to establish territories, send warnings, or attract mates. Grasshoppers "sing" during the day, but crickets trill at night by scraping their front wings together. Katydids communicate with sharp clicks and buzzes; only both sexes of the "true" katydid of North America sing "*katy*-DID" and, less often, "*katy*-DIDN'T."

Swarm Warning

Crickets can cause damage to plants when the females use their needlelike ovipositors to drill eggs into stems. But little compares to the devastation caused by locusts. They respond to changes in population by changing their behavior. They live alone when conditions are uncrowded, but under crowded conditions they form groups and migrate with the winds to places where food is plentiful. Swarms can fly 3,000 miles (5,000 km) in five days or less, eating everything in their path. Eventually, unsuitable breeding conditions, drought and a lack of food, or disease kills the swarm, and survivors go back to their solitary life.

MEGAPHONE HOME
The Y-shaped burrow of the male mole cricket amplifies his call, made by scraping his left front wing against his right—much like a fingernail against a comb.

LOCUST FOCUS
Locusts normally live alone, but swarms can number 300 million insects per square mile (2.6 km²)! They eat the equivalent of their own body weight every day, ruining crops and grasslands.

CHIRPY CHAPS

Insects were singing long before Buddy Holly and the Crickets hit the charts! A male grasshopper calls to attract mates by scraping pegs on his hind legs against the hard edges of his front wings. Called stridulation, this makes the wings vibrate and make a sound. Stridulation also gives females information about the identity and physical quality of the male, and where he is located.

Bees, Wasps, and Ants

THE 200,000 OR SO SPECIES of bees, wasps, ants, and their kin belong to the order Hymenoptera. These active insects have developed a variety of lifestyles and behavior, but most share similar body characteristics. These include a "waist" between the thorax and abdomen, and two pairs of wings joined by tiny hooks.

Nip and Tuck

Hymenopterans live on all continents except Antarctica. With their large body covered in a layer of insulating hairs, bumblebees can even survive as far north as the Arctic tundra.

All adults have chewing mouthparts, which for some species act as hands and tools for digging, building nests, and cutting up food. For example, female leafcutter bees clip out pieces of leaf with their jaws, and take the pieces back to their nests. They use them to make tube-shaped cells for larvae. In other species, such as the green metallic bees of North America, the tongue is long and pointed, and is used to suck nectar from flowers.

Not all hymenopterans have wings. In fact, most female ants and some female wasps are wingless, but their narrow waist, called a pedicel, gives their abdomen flexibility when laying eggs or using their stinger. Wasps sting to paralyze prey or to defend themselves—the sting of the American cow killer wasp is said to be painful enough "to kill a cow." But chalcid wasps curl up and play dead when threatened. Bees, which are vegetarians, sting only in self-defense.

Wax Works

Some of the best-known wasps and bees, such as hornets, bumblebees, and honeybees, are social insects.

CACHE AND CARRY
Worker honeybees collect pollen in basket-like notches on their back legs. They then take the pollen and nectar back to their nest.

HIVE OF ACTIVITY
Back in the hive, the bee regurgitates the nectar. It is then swallowed by another worker, who evaporates some of its water and adds proteins. The fluid is put into a wax cell to become honey.

worker bee

queen bee

nectar stores

honey stores

pollen stores

drone

capped pupae cells

queen cell

open larva cell

CARDBOARD CRADLE

A common wasp queen constructs a hanging cup from chewed wood fibers. She lays her eggs in cells inside the cup, and keeps them warm by wrapping layers of this paper-like material around them.

Queen starts building nest

First layer of cells is added

Workers hatch, then expand nest

antennae

compound eye

venom gland

venom sac

stinger

FEMME FATALE

Only female wasps and bees have stingers, evolved from the egg-laying tube, or ovipositor. When this wasp stings, venom flows from the venom sac, down the stinger, and into the victim.

The only species to produce honey, social bees live in colonies consisting of a queen, female workers, and male drones. They nest in hollow trees or human-made hives, constructing a water-resistant, waxen comb made up of a matrix of hexagonal cells. These building blocks provide homes for the larvae or storage bins for the honey that feeds the colony when flowers and nectar are scarce.

As with other social bees and wasps, the life of the colony focuses on the fertile queen, who produces all the larvae—sometimes more than 50,000—in her five or so years of life. She releases chemicals called pheromones which control the workers and prevent them from maturing and becoming able to breed. The purpose of the short-lived drones, which develop from unfertilized eggs, is to mate with the queen.

Social bee larvae are fed by the workers with a mixture of honey and pollen called bee bread. In spring or summer, the queen bee flies out of the hive, accompanied by a swarm of workers, to found a new colony. A daughter reared on "royal jelly," the nutritious food produced in glands on worker bees' heads, succeeds her mother as queen of the old hive.

Lone Rangers

Among the fiercest of the predatory wasps, the bald-faced hornet of North America patrols sunny walls in order to launch aerial assaults on flies. Like yellow jacket hornets, these social wasps build nests using layers of chewed wood "paper." The entrance hole is kept small to keep other insects out and to regulate the temperature of the nest. If their nest is disturbed, the enraged occupants pour out of the hole and sting the intruder repeatedly.

But most other wasps and bees are solitary insects. Instead of building large nests, they often dig burrows underground, like the cicada killer wasp and digger bee, or tunnel into rotting wood like the Asian carpenter bee. The gall wasp lays her eggs on

REPEAT OFFENDER

This wasp's stinger is like a syringe, so it can sting repeatedly. But once a honeybee stings, it dies. A bee's stinger has a barbed tip and cannot be extracted, so some of its organs are torn out when it flies away.

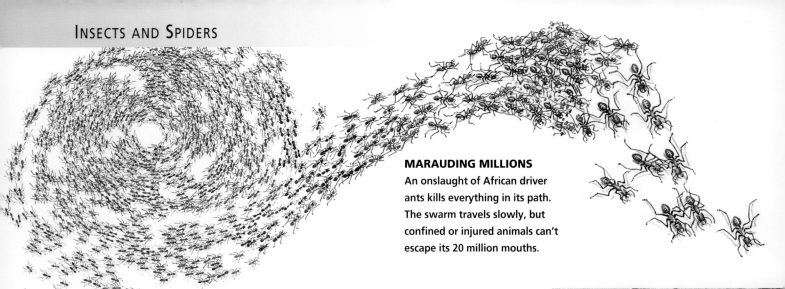

MARAUDING MILLIONS
An onslaught of African driver ants kills everything in its path. The swarm travels slowly, but confined or injured animals can't escape its 20 million mouths.

rosebuds. The mason bee lays hers in cells of clay attached to twigs or rocks or inside empty snail shells. Some even line their cells with flower petals!

Some wasps cruise the countryside to bring in fresh-killed caterpillars and other insects for their larvae. Polistine wasps even venture onto spider's webs to steal prey already entangled in the silk. Others, such as the brachonid wasps, lay their eggs on an insect host. So, too, does the tarantula hawk of tropical America. It stings a spider, drags it to a burrow, lays an egg on it, and then closes the burrow. When the larva hatches, the nutrients from the fresh spider meat enable it to grow and gnaw its way out of the burrow.

Parasitic bees, such as the cuckoo bee, lay eggs in the cells of other bees. Their larvae then either eat the host's larvae, or the food intended for them. Young cuckoo bees eat the honey and pollen stored for the larvae of the mining bee.

Sweet Smell of Success

Wasps and bees are termed "beneficial insects." When bees feed on flower nectar, they become dusted with pollen, which they carry to other flowers. By pollinating the flowers, they ensure that seeds are produced.

Ants are also beneficial. Some species help to break down plant material and refine the soil, while others spread seeds. For nearly 2,000 years, Chinese farmers have used green weaver ants to kill the insects that eat their crops.

There are 9,000 species of ant, most of which are social insects. Like social bees and wasps, they live in colonies divided into castes and controlled by a queen. A young queen, which has wings, leaves her old nest and mates once with a winged male. After biting off her wings, she starts a nest that is enlarged as her offspring, all female workers, hatch and become adults.

Like social bees, ants use scents containing pheromones to identify themselves and to communicate with each other. Pheromones are used by

POT BELLIES
Some honeypot worker ants are living reservoirs. Their abdomen swells like a balloon as it fills with nectar, used to feed the colony in times of drought.

LADY-IN-WAITING
In an ant colony, only one ant—the queen—lays eggs. The eggs are carried away by worker ants, who care for the larvae. Most termites also reproduce this way.

ANT WITH ATTITUDE
A bulldog ant guarding a nest recruits others to attack an enemy by sending out chemical signals, called pheromones, produced in the Dufor's gland. As few as 30 stings from these aggressive ants can kill a human.

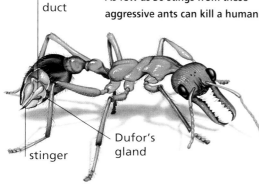

venom duct

stinger

Dufor's gland

the queen to sterilize the workers, and workers leave pheromone trails to guide other ants to food or the nest. Workers also create a chemical bond by regurgitating food to each other.

There's Power in a Union

Ants work hard to create their nests in leaves, soil, or wood. When the nest is attacked, some workers carry the larvae to safety deeper underground, while other workers rush to defend it. They attack in great numbers, biting the enemy with their sharp, powerful jaws or stinging it repeatedly. Some species that lack venom, such as sugar ants and honeypots, squirt formic acid from their abdomen, making the wound even more painful.

Although the South American *Dinoponera* ants hunt alone, other social ants work together to capture insects and carry them home. Even the tiniest ant is capable of amazing feats of strength: In relation to its size, an ant can carry an object equivalent to a human lifting an elephant!

But not all ants are carnivores. Adult bulldog ants also eat tree sap and honeydew, and leaf-cutter ants of South America grow fungus gardens.

These ants snip fragments from leaves and flowers and carry them back to their nest. There, the fragments are chewed into smaller pieces, mixed with saliva, fertilized with droppings, then inserted into spongelike mounds of fungus. As the fungus feeds on the leaves, it breaks down leaf fiber into food for the ants.

Ants in semidesert areas have found clever ways to avoid food and water shortages. Honeypot ants feed nectar to specialized workers, which store enough in their body to provide the whole colony with food and water during the dry season, when no flowers bloom. An Indian species decorates the entrance of its underground nest with birds' feathers, upon which dew forms at night. The dew is then collected by the workers, ensuring no ant dies of thirst.

FREELOADER
One species of beetle lives as a parasite inside ants' nests. It gains entrance by secreting substances that ants like to eat (above). It is then carried into the nest, where it breeds, fed by the ants.

LION'S SHARE

Antlions are not ants—they are in fact the larvae of lacewings. Some larvae, called doodlebugs, live at the bottom of steep pits dug in fine sand. When a doodlebug detects its ant prey, it moves sand at the bottom of the pit. This causes an avalanche, which sweeps the ant into the doodlebug's jaws. If the ant tries to clamber to the top, the doodlebug will throw sand at it to knock it back to the bottom again!

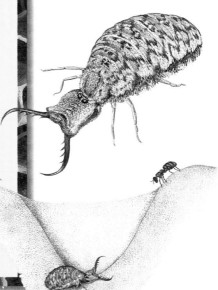

Termites

LIKE MANY SPECIES OF BEE AND WASP, AND MOST ANTS, termites are social insects. Worker termites build the nest, gather food, and feed and care for the young and the other castes. Soldier termites defend the colony. For termites, the survival of the colony is more important than that of any single insect, apart from the queen.

Castles in the Air

At 1,483 feet (452 m) high, the Petronas Towers in Malaysia are now the world's tallest buildings. They are the height of about 255 adults standing on each other's head. But at 20 feet (6 m) high, the highest termite nests are taller than 1,000 termite workers laid end to end. In fact, in proportion to their size, termites build the highest structures of all creatures.

Termite nests are often begun after a mating flight. Winged reproductive termites spend their life in the cool of the nest, eating the food collected by worker termites. But in the spring, or at the beginning of the rains in the tropics, thousands of reproductives leave their nests and swarm into the air in search of a partner. After landing, a "king" and "queen" break off their wings and mate. Depending on the species, they excavate a tiny cell below the surface of the soil, in which the first worker nymphs are hatched. The workers undergo an incomplete metamorphosis, then begin to extend the nest, constructing many tunnels and chambers. Unlike worker bees and ants, which are all female, worker termites are both male and female.

Bedrooms and Hallways

Some termite species build nests in the trunks or branches of trees. Blind and wingless, the workers toil in the dark, using their droppings and the fibrous wood chewed with their small jaws to create covered highways. Other species build fortress-like nests of soil mixed with saliva. When dry, this "cement" is often so strong that only dynamite can destroy it!

The royal cell is the foundation of the nest. The only fertile male in the colony, the king lives beside the queen, who can lay an

SOIL SOLDIER
Termites are often called white ants because of their pale appearance. They are not true ants, but like ants they are divided into castes. This soldier spinifex termite helps to defend the nest.

mud mix dries in the sun to create hard, porous walls

COMPASS POINT
Magnetic termites of northern Australia build nests aligned from north to south. They use temperature differences on the eastern and western sides of the nest to keep the temperature inside the nest constant.

egg every few seconds. The swollen abdomen of the queen makes her look like a small sausage. She is constantly fed and groomed by workers. If she grows too big, they increase the size of the cell, or carry her to a larger one.

Radiating out from the royal cell are the larval chambers, where the eggs are taken and cared for by the workers. Tunnels lead to food storage chambers, where species such as

harvester termites keep dry grass stems and leaves to eat during times of drought. Other species cultivate food in special fungi chambers. Unlike ants, termites are strictly vegetarian.

The nest is ventilated by a system of vents and ducts. Workers also control the temperature and humidity inside the nest by moistening the walls with saliva or damp soil. It is vital that the temperature is kept stable, because termites cannot tolerate extreme heat.

A Bug's Life

The king and queen may live for more than ten years and produce millions of eggs. Some nests can house as many five million termites at one time. Such large numbers are necessary, because a termite's life is fraught with danger. Most reproductives are eaten by birds, frogs, rodents, lizards, snakes, or ants almost as soon as they leave the nest. Geckos can stuff themselves with enough reproductives in one night to survive for months without a meal.

Even inside their nest, the termites are not always safe. The soldiers do their best to defend the colony, but they are often no match for hungry aardvarks, sloth bears, and pangolins, which rake nests open with their claws and suck up thousands of angry occupants.

GIMME SHELTER
This "umbrella" nest in West Africa starts underground and measures 18 inches (45 cm) high. Made of earth pellets and saliva, it has sloping roofs to shed rain.

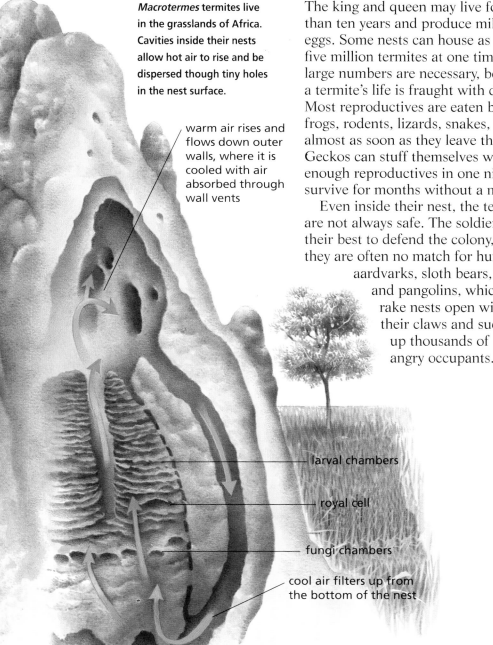

AIR CONDITIONING
Macrotermes termites live in the grasslands of Africa. Cavities inside their nests allow hot air to rise and be dispersed though tiny holes in the nest surface.

warm air rises and flows down outer walls, where it is cooled with air absorbed through wall vents

larval chambers

royal cell

fungi chambers

cool air filters up from the bottom of the nest

HOME INVASION
Some amphisbaenians, birds, and lizards, such as these goannas, use the regulated heat of termite nests to incubate their eggs. But when the young escape they often damage the nests.

279

Flies and Dragonflies

FLIES AND DRAGONFLIES ARE NOT RELATED, but both orders contain some well-known insects. Some flies are valuable because they pollinate flowers, scavenge carrion, and control other insect pests, but other species can carry deadly diseases. Dragonflies are looked upon more favorably. Although harmless to humans, they eat flies!

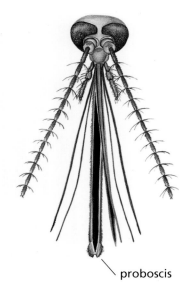

JAVELIN JAW
Before laying eggs, a female mosquito uses her stylets to stab skin, then sucks blood through her proboscis. The blood provides nutrients for her eggs. Males do not bite, and sip only plant juices.

proboscis

Acrobats and Leather Jackets

The order Diptera—the flies—consists of at least 120,000 known species. They live just about everywhere and are easy to distinguish because, unlike most other insects, they have only one pair of wings. The back wings have modified into two knobbed organs called halteres. These are thought to keep the insect balanced during flight.

Most flies have excellent eyesight, thanks to their large compound eyes. Because each foot has two claws and bristly pads, they are also capable of amazing stunts. For example, when a house fly is about to land on a ceiling, it flies the right way up, but lifts its front legs above its body. Its foot pads secrete an adhesive, and its claws catch hold of the ceiling. The fly's body then flips upside down. Its other legs make contact with the surface, and the fly is fastened securely. This tricky maneuver takes just a fraction of a second.

Most flies go through complete metamorphosis, transforming from blind, legless maggots to winged adults. Like many fly larvae, fruit flies mature inside rotting fruit. Others live in soil—crane fly maggots, called leatherjackets, have a bad reputation for ruining lawns. Some live as parasites on other insects: Pyrgotid fly eggs are inserted into the abdomen of May beetles and the

larvae eat their host from the inside out, eventually killing it. Screw-worm flies lay their eggs on live vertebrates, while other species prefer to use their dung. Flesh flies can turn carrion into a squirming mass of maggots.

Sucker Punch

All flies eat liquid food. Robber flies snatch insects in midair and suck their juices. Snipe flies, mydas flies, and

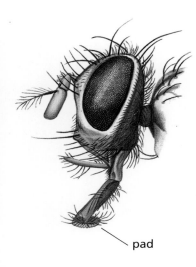

SLOP AND MOP
Unlike many other insects, which have jaws, house flies use a spongy pad to pour saliva over food. This pad is the equivalent of a lower lip. After the food is dissolved, it is sucked up.

pad

WASP WANNABES
Hover flies are often seen hovering over flowers. Their colors and fast forward, backward, and sideways actions mimic those of wasps.

DELICATE DRAGON
Members of Odonata cannot fold their wings up against their body. Dragonflies hold their wings out to the side, while damselflies hold theirs vertically behind them.

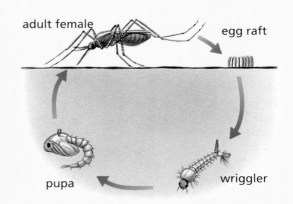

EYE-ZING UP
Male stalk-eyed flies from Southeast Asia use their weird eyestalks to threaten rivals and measure their size. Males with the longest stalks win the right to mate with the females.

hover flies are welcomed by gardeners because their larvae eat aphids and scale insects. Other species mop fluids from flowers or fruit. But the horsefly uses its heat-sensitive antennae to find its meal: the blood of mammals. Its saliva contains an anticoagulant that stops the blood from clotting.

Because many flies feed on rotting flesh, wounds, or dung, they can transmit a variety of bacteria and parasites. Even the common house fly can carry typhoid, dysentery, cholera, and worms. The blood-sucking tsetse fly of Africa spreads sleeping sickness, and mosquitoes can transmit viruses that cause yellow fever, dengue fever, and malaria. But some flies have also helped us to better understand the human body. Vinegar flies, from the family Drosophilidae, have for years been used in the study of genetics.

Damsels of Distress

The 5,000 or so species of dragonfly and damselfly are admired not only for their often jewel-like beauty but also for their predatory prowess. Dragonflies' four wings beat independently—up to 50 times per second—giving them great maneuverability as they whiz above ponds. Spectacular hunters, they destroy legions of mosquitoes, seizing prey with their long legs and slicing them with their sharp mouthparts.

Dragonflies first flew 350 million years ago. Even today adults spend most of their life in the sky—they can't walk well, so they even mate in midair, then lay eggs on water plants or drop them as they fly. Some males improve their mating chances by defending egg-laying sites, waiting for females who must come there to lay their eggs.

WRITHES OF PASSAGE

Most flies lay their eggs on rotting remains. But mosquitoes lay theirs, either singly or in floating rafts, on the surface of quiet waters such as puddles or stagnant ponds. Their twisting, writhing larvae, called wrigglers, breathe from a siphon on their abdomen. Tiny brushes on their head sweep food particles into their mouth.

adult female

egg raft

pupa

wriggler

True Bugs

PEOPLE OFTEN USE THE TERM "BUG" to refer to any insect, but true bugs are really only those species belonging to the order Hemiptera. There are about 82,000 species of true bug, such as plant bugs, seed bugs, lace bugs, and pond-skaters. They are all characterized by their mouthparts, used to pierce and suck food.

Spear Throwers

True bugs can be a small as a speck or as big as your thumb. The name Hemiptera, which means "half-wings," refers to their front wings, which are often leathery at the base but clear at the tips. They overlap when the insect is resting. The hind wings are shorter than the front wings, and are completely transparent.

True bugs' mouthparts are long and form a beaklike organ called a rostrum. The rostrum is on the front of the head, and in many species it curves beneath the body when not in use. It consists of a central tube and four sharp-tipped stylets. Inside the tube are two channels that carry liquid up or down.

To feed, the bug pierces the food source with its stylets and then pushes the tube into the wound. Down one of the channels it pumps toxic saliva, which partly digests the food. It sucks up the food with the other channel. Assassin bugs also rasp their rostrum against a filelike structure on their underside to produce a hissing noise.

Blood-Sucking Cone-Noses

Farmers and gardeners hate true bugs because of the damage they cause to crop and ornamental plants. The green stink bug attacks orange, apple, peach, and cherry trees and soybean, cotton, bean, pea, tomato, eggplant, and corn crops. Squash bug nymphs cause the leaves of melon, cucumber, and gourds to wilt and dry. Boxelder bugs blemish fruit, and stilt bugs puncture young fruit and make them drop before they are ripe.

Not all true bugs cause harm, however. Damsel bugs feed on pests such as aphids and caterpillars, while some predatory stink bugs eat grubs and mites. But one of the most notorious insects, the bedbug, feeds at night on the blood of birds and mammals—including humans. It hides in

TELL-TALE TRIANGLE
As in most true bugs, the thorax area between the wings of these milkweed bugs is enlarged. It forms a distinctive triangular shield called the scutellum.

WATER TORTURE
A frog is a hearty meal for a giant waterbug, which also grabs underwater prey such as snails and fish. Commonly found lurking in tropical waters, some stab at human feet. Nymphs eat each other.

282

crevices during the day and can live without food for up to 15 months!

The bite of assassin bugs can cause allergic reactions in humans, and some South American varieties can spread disease. The nymphs of some eat termites, but termite nests are guarded by soldiers which attack anyone who fails to carry the colony's smell. So the nymphs become "wolves in sheep's clothing:" They coat themselves in scent from nest sand to catch prey.

By contrast, ambush bugs lie in wait for their prey. Their notched shape and greenish-yellow or brown color provides good camouflage on flowers, where they often pounce on bees and wasps and suck them dry.

The Weighting Game

Most true bugs live on vegetation, and many spend winter hibernating in leaf litter or clumps of grass. Some other species, such as water boatmen, are aquatic, and use their legs like oars to move across water. The long, thin legs of water treaders, pond-skaters, and ripple bugs enable them to spread their weight and scoot across the surface of ponds without falling through. These predators use the ripples of a crashed or fallen insect to lead them to their food. Most water bugs lay their eggs on or in aquatic vegetation. Many terrestrial true bugs also insert their

eggs into soft plant tissue, while the jagged ambush bug and stink bugs glue their eggs firmly onto leaves.

After hatching, nymphs may molt up to six times before they are mature. During this process, they often change color. For example, harlequin bugs of Australia are red, orange, and blue as nymphs, but bright orange as adults.

KICKING UP A STINK
When disturbed, most true bugs squirt foul-smelling liquid from glands near their back legs. Many, such as this shield bug from Borneo, are also brightly colored to warn off birds.

SCUBA SWIMMER
The backswimmer swims upside down underwater. It stores bubbles of air under its wings, absorbing oxygen through its spiracles.

A Class Apart?

Leafhoppers, treehoppers, froghoppers, psyllids, aphids, mealybugs, scale insects, and cicadas (right) are usually considered true bugs. But their rostrum is located underneath their head, and their wings are completely transparent. This is why they are sometimes classed in the suborder Homoptera. All homopterans eat plants, but they reproduce in a variety of ways. Aphids do not even have to mate— one female aphid can breed billions of babies by herself!

stylets

rostrum

Focus on Spiders

FOR MOST PEOPLE, SPIDERS AROUSE MIXED EMOTIONS. While few fail to admire the sight of a web glistening with morning dew, a close encounter with the web's creator is for some a terrifying ordeal. But for the most part this fear is unjustified. Tough and resourceful, spiders help the planet by keeping insects in check.

World Wide Web

Everybody is familiar with spiders. It's difficult to avoid them! At least 40,000 species have been identified, and they live on all continents except Antarctica: in forests, grasslands, deserts, cliffs, caves, fresh water, and our homes. Spiders have even been found on Mount Everest, the highest mountain in the world.

Spiders developed from marine animals that took to the land about 400 million years ago. From these beginnings they continued to evolve through a process called adaptive radiation. For example, species such as funnel-web spiders have changed little over the course of time, but thousands of other species developed to take advantage of every available niche and habitat.

As a result, modern-day spiders can be as small as a pinprick or twice the size of your hand. They have a huge range of body and behavioral adaptations to suit their equally huge range of homes and lifestyles. Many of these adaptations came about in response to the need to catch food.

TAILOR-MADE TRAPS
Spiders build an enormous variety of webs, including the cocoon-like lair of the purse-web spider that extends from its burrow. The spider stabs its prey through the silk, then drags it through to be eaten.

Pinch or Punch?

All spiders have fangs at the end of their jaws, called chelicerae, and almost all use venom to subdue prey. While spiders' fangs have the same purpose—to bite, hold, and crush prey—their design differs according to each species' preferred food. Generally, smaller spiders eat smaller insects, while larger spiders tackle larger prey. For this reason, smaller spiders, most of which belong to

SIDE BITERS
Most spiders, such as this common garden spider, are "true spiders." Their jaws, or chelicerae, are attached below their head. The fangs move in a pinching action.

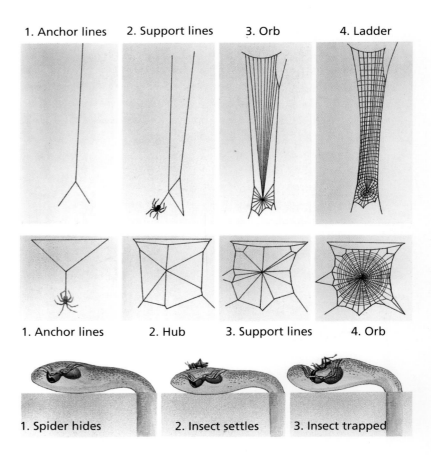

1. Anchor lines 2. Support lines 3. Orb 4. Ladder

1. Anchor lines 2. Hub 3. Support lines 4. Orb

1. Spider hides 2. Insect settles 3. Insect trapped

CLING WRAP

This argiope spider is lying in wait for prey. To make sure a meal cannot escape, it will vibrate its web to further ensnare its prey, then wrap it up in sticky silk.

Webs enable a spider to catch flying insect prey. Therefore spiders weave webs in places where these insects are most likely to go, such as across open spaces. The design of the web varies, from trip wires and untidy cobwebs to complex orbs. Likewise, the webs are constructed in a number of ways.

For example, an orb-weaving spider waits for a breeze to blow a silken thread from one plant stem to another. The spider adds more silk to make it strong and tight, then spins a loosely attached line. The spider sits in the centre of this line and pulls it into a V shape, then spins another line straight down to form a Y shape.

Working from the base of the V, or hub, the spider attaches radiating spokes of dry, non-sticky silk until the web looks like a sliced pie. The spider then walks around laying a spiral of

Hunting spider

Web-building spider

THE RIGHT FOOT

Hunting spiders usually have two claws on each foot, enabling them to cling to rough surfaces. Spiders that trap their prey in webs have three. The middle claw contracts to grip silk threads.

the suborder Labidognatha ("true spiders"), have sideways-biting jaws that pierce prey. The large spiders of the suborder Orthognatha (the mygalomorph spiders) wield their fangs with force, like a pair of pickaxes, to strike their large, often heavy prey.

When muscles in the spiders' venom glands contract, paralyzing venom is injected through the chelicerae and out tiny holes in the fangs. But how does a spider actually catch its prey? The answer lies within.

Come Into My Parlor

All spiders produce silk in glands in their abdomen, then squirt it through modified excretory glands called spinnerets. Silk may have first been used to create egg cases and to line nesting burrows. Now, half of the world's spiders use silk to make webs, not only as homes, but as traps for prey.

DEADLY DAGGERS

Australia's funnel-web spider is a mygalomorph. This kind of spider has jaws on the front of its head. Mygalomorphs raise their head to attack, and stab their prey with a downward motion, pinning it to the ground.

CRAFTY CATCH
A net-casting spider waits in ambush. If an insect walks beneath, it is scooped up in a sudden, spreading cast of the spider's sticky snare.

dry thread. Finally it returns to the hub and, following the outline, replaces the dry spiral with a spiral of sticky, insect-catching silk. (The dry spiral silk is eaten.) In some species of orb-weaver, the old web is replaced each night with a new one, spun in the dark by touch alone.

Stairway to Heaven

Some spiders incorporate crosses or zigzags of thick white silk into their webs, perhaps to make them more visible to birds and prevent them from accidentally blundering into the web. Spiders that specialize in larger aerial prey, such as moths, have also devised different web designs. This is because moths are not only big, fat, and fast, but because they are covered with tiny scales. These body scales readily peel off, allowing the insect to escape. So some moth-eating spiders build ladder webs: a group of long, sticky capture threads attached to a smaller orb. If a moth hits this web, it will struggle to escape, rolling down the ladder's length and shedding its scales. By the time it hits the orb it is plucked and ready for execution.

A VIEW FROM THE BRIDGE
The black widow spider's web consists of sticky lines stretching to the ground. When an insect is caught in a line, the line breaks from the ground and dangles. The spider then hauls its prey up to its platform in the middle.

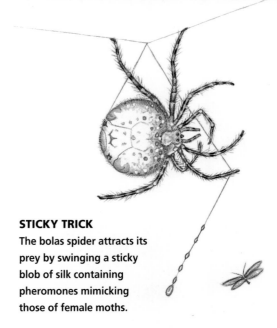

STICKY TRICK
The bolas spider attracts its prey by swinging a sticky blob of silk containing pheromones mimicking those of female moths.

Gate Crashers

Once the web is complete, spiders usually hang, head first, waiting for prey. Many sit on their web with their legs resting on the threads that lead to the web hub. Tuned to the web like antennae, their legs detect vibrations. If the source of the vibrations is edible, the spider grapples with it, trusses it in silk, and delivers the fatal bite. It may suck its prey dry straight away, or save it as a snack for later.

But even then a meal isn't always guaranteed. The webs of the *Nephila* spiders of the New Guinea rain forest are also home to other, smaller spiders

BEHIND YOU!
Many large spiders are called "tarantulas," but true tarantulas are found only in Central and South America and Australia. Nocturnal, they spend their day in crevices and burrows. They hunt mice, frogs, lizards, and small birds by touch.

which dart in and snatch small insects. Giant damselflies, polistine wasps, scorpion flies, and even hummingbirds may also pluck prey from webs—a male scorpion fly will then present its loot to a female fly as a courtship gift. One species of bug lives permanently on spider webs, eating insects already overpowered by the spider, and some colonial spiders share their webs with caterpillars, which munch the skeletal remains of the spiders' prey.

Lassoes and Lunges

Although a web is a sure sign that a spider is nearby, a high percentage of spiders don't weave webs. Webs are effective traps—when they work. But rain or wind makes a web less sticky, and a broken or tangled web takes time and energy to repair. Also, a spider on a broken web is an easy target for predators such as birds.

So instead of waiting for food to fly their way, many spiders have devised alternative hunting techniques. Some species, such as grass spiders, rely on their exceptional speed to chase and catch food. The common house spider can run proportionately six times faster than a sprinter at the Olympics! The thin-legged wolf spider of North America patrols a territory out in the open, basking in the sun and keeping warm and ready to chase down prey.

WHAT NEXT?
From vibrations spiders can identify kinds of prey and decide what action to take. A stinging wasp or kicking grasshopper must be tightly wrapped to avoid damage to the spider or its web.

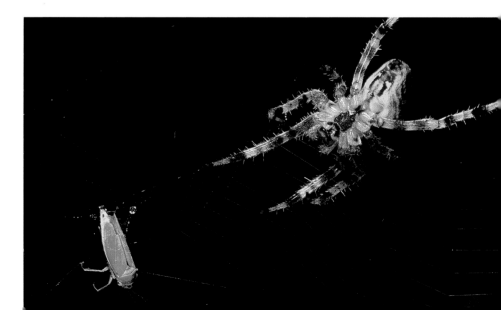

Other species use projectiles to snare a meal. Bolas spiders catch male armyworm moths by twirling a globule of liquid silk that imitates the scent of a female moth. As the males search for their "mate" they collide with the spider's snare—and meet a sticky end.

Spitting spiders squirt prey with a sticky, venomous secretion produced in their cephalothorax. Small—about ⅜ inch (9 mm)—and with just six eyes, they nevertheless have good aim. Some can spit "glue" up to 1 inch (2.5 cm), sticking prey in its tracks.

The aim of the jumping spider is even better. Its largest pair of eyes face forward, giving it binocular vision to judge depth and distance. Although some of the largest jumping spiders are only ⅝ inch (1.5 cm) long, they can locate and leap on prey 8 inches (20 cm) away. Before they jump they secure themselves with a dragline. If they don't like what they find, or if the prey escapes, they winch themselves back to where they started.

Boo! Boohoo!

Other species prefer to ambush their victims. For example, the raft spider perches on floating leaves, dangling its front legs in the water. It detects the presence of prey by sensing the

ripples they create. After stabbing an insect, fish, or tadpole with its fangs, the spider hauls its catch ashore.

Trapdoor spiders have the perfect hide-and-surprise strategy. These clever spiders fashion soil, silk, and debris into a hinged "door" for their silk-lined underground burrow. The spiders hold their door shut with their fangs, then fling it open and lunge at unsuspecting insects.

But perhaps the most enterprising species are the Australian bird-poo spiders. Their shiny brown and white appearance—complete with a white silk "splatter zone"—provides good camouflage. Most predators are not interested in eating bird droppings. But this method of defense doubles as a method of attack. Salt is vital

GRAY AREA
If disturbed, some fishing spiders dive underwater and stay there for up to 30 minutes. When on land, they try to blend with their surroundings, such as this lichen-covered rock.

CRAB GRAB
Camouflaged crab spiders lurk among flowers with their front legs wide open. If suitable prey lands within range, they strike instantly.

WHEEL OF FORTUNE
Wheel spiders live in the Namib Desert in Africa. Wasps try to dig them from their burrows to provide food for their larvae. But the spiders escape by curling in their legs and rolling away like wheels.

BAD HAIR DAY
This goliath bird spider has hairs with microscopic barbed spines that can make skin itch and burn. When in danger, it scrapes hairs off its abdomen and showers them on its enemy.

for effective body processes, but in tropical Australia salt is also hard to find. Because fresh bird droppings are salty, many insects sip from them. But sometimes the "bird poo" winds up sipping from the insect instead!

DOWN THE PLUGHOLE
If its burrow is discovered by a hunting wasp, this trapdoor spider plugs the tunnel with its leathery abdomen. This protects the spider from being stung and makes it difficult for the wasp to pull the spider out.

Fangs For the Memories

Spiders are effective hunters, but sometimes they become the hunted. Birds, mammals, lizards, amphibians, and centipedes all eat spiders, and some wasps paralyze them and use them as food for their larvae. To outwit their enemies, spiders use a range of defenses. Many are disguised to blend in with their environment, while others have conspicuous coloration. For example, the scarlet stripe of the black widow and the redback spider, and the red or orange knees of the Mexican red-kneed tarantula, warn others to stay away.

Some spiders also mimic other species. The black body and pale yellow spots and stripes of spotted racing spiders make them look like wasps. Other tropical species pretend to be ants by waving one pair of legs in front of their head like antennae, and moving with jerky, scurrying movements. Wary of ants' stings, bites, or sprays of formic acid, most predators leave these "ants" alone.

But when all else fails, spiders bite. Virtually all spiders are poisonous, but only about 500 species have fangs long enough to drive venom into human skin. Of this number, fewer than 30 species have venom that is dangerous to humans. Most spiders would rather run away than bite—with the exception of the Sydney funnel-web spider. It is quite willing to attack when disturbed, and before the development of an effective antivenin, bites generally proved fatal. But while its venom is deadly to humans and other primates, other domesticated and wild animals are immune to it!

Predators are not the only dangers spiders face, however. Being smaller, they heat up faster, and web-building spiders that need to stay on their webs during the day risk overheating. So the leaf-rolling spider hauls a leaf, empty snail shell, or paper scrap up to its web to create a shelter. *Nephila* spiders, whose huge webs are common in the tropics, reduce their exposure to the heat by aligning their body with the shadow cast by the changing angle of the Sun—rather like the hour hand of a clock.

MOMMIE DEAREST
A female black widow rarely bites, unless she is guarding her eggs. After mating, she may eat the male, earning her the name "widow."

HARD TO CRACK
The hard, shiny abdomen and spurs of this arrow-shaped *Micrathena* is a defense against bird bills. These features developed in response to the spider's exposed habitat.

Strained Relations

For male spiders, mating can also be a dangerous time. This is because in many species, the female is very much larger than the male. For example, a female black-and-yellow argiope can be up to five times the size of a male. Being small increases the male's chances of living unnoticed in some far corner of the female's web until she is ready to mate. However, his

SPIDER RIDERS
A wolf spider drags her egg sac, attached to her spinnerets, wherever she goes. When her spiderlings hatch, they ride on her abdomen until they can fend for themselves.

size also means that he runs the risk of being mistaken by her as a prey item when he finally approaches her.

To avoid being eaten, some male spiders signal to the female that they are a fellow spider, and not a fly, by vibrating her web in a special way. A nursery web male presents the female with an insect so that he can mate with her in safety while her jaws are busy eating his gift. The male sucks a drop of sperm up into his pedipalps, then transfers the sperm to the female. Some crab spiders even tie up the female to prevent her attacking them.

Web-building males detect the pheromones of mature females with the hairs on their legs. Hunting spiders that do not build webs are thought to follow a female's scented dragline. Wolf spiders wave their legs and pedipalps in courtship dances, or tickle their partner's legs. Jumping spiders take advantage of their species' keen eyesight to prance about flashing their abdomen, which in some species can be iridescent red, green, and blue.

All spiders wrap their eggs in a silk egg sac. A garden spider can lay up to 500 eggs; larger hairy mygalomorphs lay about 150 per brood. Females carry their sac with them, or hide it somewhere safe, such as under a rock or leaf. Most guard their sac, and some species, such as tarantulas, also keep a close watch on their young. But the females of other species die before their eggs hatch, leaving the young to fend for themselves. But they don't abandon their spiderlings completely: For some spiders, their mother's body is their first meal.

FLYING SPIDERS!

To travel to a new home, some spiderlings use a technique that is virtually unique in the animal kingdom—ballooning. The spiderling stands on tiptoes in an exposed position, such as the end of a branch. It then faces the wind and squeezes out a droplet of silk. Pulled by the wind, the droplet expands into threads, and the spiderling floats away.

SILKEN SAILS

Instead of ballooning, some spiderlings leave their nest by climbing to a high perch and dropping a dragline. The wind lifts the spiderling until the dragline breaks. The little spider then drifts gently to the ground.

Scorpions, Ticks, and Mites

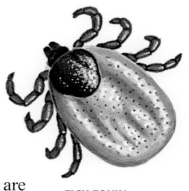

LIKE THEIR RELATIVES THE SPIDERS, scorpions, ticks, and mites are arachnids. There are 1,500 species of scorpion and 1,000 species of tick, but there could be millions of mite species that have never been studied, let alone named. Their tiny size means that many go unnoticed—except for those species that endanger human health.

Land Lobsters

About 435 million years ago scorpions were marine animals that grew up to 6½ feet (2 m) long. Today scorpions live in grasslands, mountains, rain forests, sea shores, and underground caves, but most species are found in hot, arid habitats. The largest, the imperial scorpion of west Africa, has a body length of 7 inches (18 cm).

Like spiders, scorpions have eight legs attached to their cephalothorax. Despite having as many as 12 eyes, they don't see well—a few species are even blind. Instead, they rely on hairs on each leg to sense vibrations. They also have a pair of sense organs, called pectines, on the tip of their abdomen.

Scorpions' most distinctive features are their modified pedipalps, which resemble large, lobster-like pincers.

Scorpions also differ from spiders in having an abdomen divided into 12 segments. The last five segments make up the upturned tail, which is equipped with a poisonous stinger.

Mincer Pincers

Scorpions don't have silk glands, so instead of building webs they live in dark crevices under bark, stones, or leaf litter. Desert species avoid the heat of the day by living in burrows underground. They emerge at dusk to hunt, lying in wait at their burrow entrance or actively searching for prey such as insects, spiders, and even small vertebrates.

When its pectines detect vibrations, the scorpion seizes and crushes the prey with its pincers. If the prey is large or struggling, the scorpion may paralyze or kill it with its sting. It then tears its prey to pieces and sucks up the juices.

Scorpions also use their stinger to defend themselves from enemies such as bats, owls, snakes, and mongooses.

TICK TOXIN

After feeding, the body of a female Australian paralysis tick can swell to 200 times its weight. Its saliva contains a toxin that can paralyze and even kill some animals unless the tick is removed.

A STING IN THE TALE

Muscles in a scorpion's tail squeeze poison down a tube and into its prey. But these male and female scorpions are not fighting—they are performing a mating dance.

SMALL STOWAWAYS

Mites don't have wings, so they travel by hitchhiking on a host. Nymphs of some species secrete a stalk that dries and hardens onto the host, while other species attach themselves with suckers.

LYME ALARM

In North America and Europe, deer ticks carry bacteria that cause Lyme disease. The symptoms include rashes, aches, and fever. If untreated, the infection can lead to arthritis, damage to the heart and nervous system—or death. To remove a tick, grasp the head with fine tweezers and pull it from the wound. Don't twist, or its mouthparts will stay stuck in the skin.

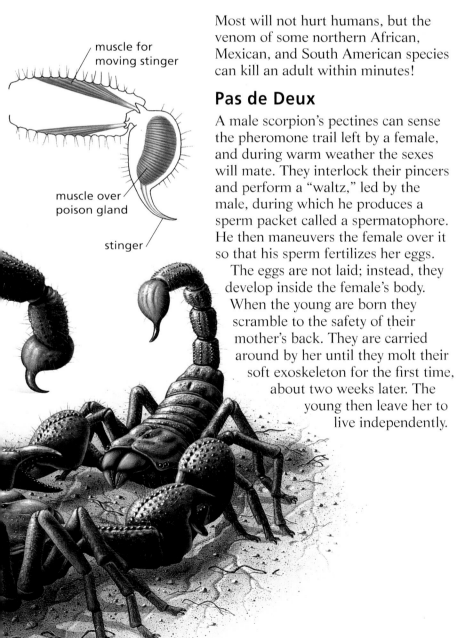

muscle for moving stinger

muscle over poison gland

stinger

Most will not hurt humans, but the venom of some northern African, Mexican, and South American species can kill an adult within minutes!

Pas de Deux

A male scorpion's pectines can sense the pheromone trail left by a female, and during warm weather the sexes will mate. They interlock their pincers and perform a "waltz," led by the male, during which he produces a sperm packet called a spermatophore. He then maneuvers the female over it so that his sperm fertilizes her eggs.

The eggs are not laid; instead, they develop inside the female's body. When the young are born they scramble to the safety of their mother's back. They are carried around by her until they molt their soft exoskeleton for the first time, about two weeks later. The young then leave her to live independently.

Skin Crawlers

Mites are found on land and in water throughout the world. Some mites eat aphid eggs and hunt roundworms; others improve soil by breaking down leaf litter. Still more are parasites of plants and animals, living in monkey lungs, bee tracheae, or bird nostrils. Some mites ride on ants. There are dust mites living on you right now!

Ticks are generally larger than mites, but like mites their body is not divided into segments. Most have three pairs of legs as larvae and four pairs as nymphs and adults. Mites take in liquid food with their piercing mouthparts, but ticks have a hook that anchors them to their host. They suck the blood of animals, and many carry diseases from one meal to another.

DUST DEVIL

Dust mites feed on the millions of dead skin and hair cells humans shed every day. Some people are allergic to their droppings, and can suffer from asthma if they inhale them.

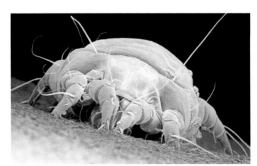

Arranging the Animals

E VERY ANIMAL must be named, described, and placed in an arrangement that shows its relationship to others. The science of classifying animals is called taxonomy. The most basic category in classification is the species. Species with features in common are placed into a genus. Related genera are classed as a family; related families comprise an order; and related orders make a class.

MAMMALS

The following list of orders and families is based on *A World List of Mammalian Species* by G.B. Corbet and J.E. Hill, 3rd edition, 1991, Facts on File Publications, New York/British Museum (Natural History), London.

CLASS MAMMALIA

SUBCLASS PROTOTHERIA

ORDER
MONOTREMATA   **MONOTREMES**
Tachyglossidae   Spiny anteaters
Ornithorhynchidae   Duck-billed
   platypus

SUBCLASS THERIA

INFRACLASS METATHERIA

ORDER
MARSUPIALIA   **MARSUPIALS**
Didelphidae   American
   opossums
Microbiotheriidae   Colocolos
Caenolestidae   Shrew-opossums
Dasyuridae   Marsupial mice,
   etc.
Myrmecobiidae   Numbat
Thylacinidae   Thylacine
Notoryctidae   Marsupial mole
Peramelidae   Bandicoots
Peroryctidae   Spiny bandicoots
Vombatidae   Wombats
Phascolarctidae   Koala
Phalangeridae   Phalangers
Petauridae   Gliding
   phalangers
Pseudocheiridae   Ringtail possums
Burramyidae   Pygmy possums
Acrobatidae   Feathertails
Tarsipedidae   Honey possum
Macropodidae   Kangaroos,
   wallabies
Potoroidae   Bettongs

INFRACLASS EUTHERIA

ORDER
XENARTHRA   **ANTEATERS,**
   SLOTHS, &
   ARMADILLOS
Myrmecophagidae   American
   anteaters
Bradypodidae   Three-toed sloths
Megalonychidae   Two-toed sloths
Dasypodidae   Armadillos

ORDER
INSECTIVORA   **INSECTIVORES**
Solenodontidae   Solenodons
Tenrecidae   Tenrecs,
   otter shrews
Chrysochloridae   Golden moles
Erinaceidae   Hedgehogs,
   moonrats
Soricidae   Shrews
Talpidae   Moles, desmans

ORDER
SCANDENTIA   **TREE SHREWS**
Tupaiidae   Tree shrews

ORDER
DERMOPTERA   **FLYING LEMURS,**
   COLUGOS
Cynocephalidae   Flying lemurs,
   colugos

ORDER
CHIROPTERA   **BATS**
Pteropodidae   Old World
   fruit bats
Rhinopomatidae   Mouse-tailed bats
Emballonuridae   Sheath-tailed bats
Craseonycteridae   Hog-nosed bat,
   bumblebee bat
Nycteridae   Slit-faced bats
Megadermatidae   False vampire bats
Rhinolophidae   Horseshoe bats
Hipposideridae   Old World
   leaf-nosed bats
Noctilionidae   Bulldog bats
Mormoopidae   Naked-backed
   bats
Phyllostomidae   New World
   leaf-nosed bats
Natalidae   Funnel-eared bats
Furipteridae   Smoky bats
Thyropteridae   Disk-winged bats
Myzopodidae   Old World
   sucker-footed bat
Vespertilionidae   Vespertilionid
   bats
Mystacinidae   New Zealand
   short-tailed bats
Molossidae   Free-tailed bats

ORDER
PRIMATES   **PRIMATES**
Cheirogaleidae   Dwarf lemurs
Lemuridae   Large lemurs
Megaladapidae   Sportive lemurs
Indridae   Leaping lemurs
Daubentoniidae   Aye-aye
Loridae   Lorises, galagos
Tarsiidae   Tarsiers
Callitrichidae   Marmosets,
   tamarins
Cebidae   New World
   monkeys
Cercopithecidae   Old World
   monkeys
Hylobatidae   Gibbons
Hominidae   Apes, humans

ORDER
CARNIVORA   **CARNIVORES**
Canidae   Dogs, foxes
Ursidae   Bears, pandas
Procyonidae   Raccoons, etc.
Mustelidae   Weasels, etc.
Viverridae   Civets, etc.
Herpestidae   Mongooses
Hyaenidae   Hyenas
Felidae   Cats
Otariidae   Sealions
Odobenidae   Walrus
Phocidae   Seals

ORDER
CETACEA   **WHALES,**
   DOLPHINS
Platanistidae   River dolphins
Delphinidae   Dolphins
Phocoenidae   Porpoises
Monodontidae   Narwhal,
   beluga
Physeteridae   Sperm whales
Ziphiidae   Beaked whales
Eschrichtiidae   Gray whale
Balaenopteridae   Rorquals
Balaenidae   Right whales

ORDER
SIRENIA   **SEA COWS**
Dugongidae   Dugong
Trichechidae   Manatees

ORDER PROBOSCIDEA	**ELEPHANTS**	Cervidae	Deer	Hystricidae	Old World porcupines
Elephantidae	Elephants	Giraffidae	Giraffe, okapi		New World porcupines
		Antilocapridae	Pronghorn	Erethizontidae	
ORDER PERISSODACTYLA	**ODD-TOED UNGULATES**	Bovidae	Cattle, antelopes, etc.	Caviidae	Guinea pigs, etc.
Equidae	Horses	**ORDER PHOLIDOTA**	**PANGOLINS, SCALY ANTEATERS**	Hydrochaeridae	Capybara
Tapiridae	Tapirs			Dinomyidae	Pacarana
Rhinocerotidae	Rhinoceroses	Manidae	Pangolins, scaly anteaters	Dasyproctidae	Agoutis, pacas
				Chinchillidae	Chinchillas, etc.
ORDER HYRACOIDEA	**HYRAXES**	**ORDER RODENTIA**	**RODENTS**	Capromyidae	Hutias, etc.
Procaviidae	Hyraxes	Aplodontidae	Mountain beaver	Myocastoridae	Coypu
		Sciuridae	Squirrels, marmots, etc.	Octodontidae	Degus, etc.
ORDER TUBULIDENTATA	**AARDVARK**	Geomyidae	Pocket gophers	Ctenomyidae	Tuco-tucos
Orycteropodidae	Aardvark	Heteromyidae	Pocket mice	Abrocomidae	Chinchilla-rats
		Castoridae	Beavers	Echymidae	Spiny rats
ORDER ARTIODACTYLA	**EVEN-TOED UNGULATES**	Anomaluridae	Scaly-tailed squirrels	Thryonomyidae	Cane rats
Suidae	Pigs	Pedetidae	Spring hare	Petromyidae	African rock-rat
Tayassuidae	Peccaries	Muridae	Rats, mice, gerbils, etc.	Bathyergidae	African mole-rats
Hippopotamidae	Hippopotamuses	Gliridae	Dormice	Ctenodactylidae	Gundis
Camelidae	Camels, llamas	Seleviniidae	Desert dormouse	**ORDER LAGOMORPHA**	**LAGOMORPHS**
Tragulidae	Mouse deer	Zapodidae	Jumping mice	Ochotonidae	Pikas
Moschidae	Musk deer	Dipodidae	Jerboas	Leporidae	Rabbits, hares
				ORDER MACROSCELIDEA	**ELEPHANT SHREWS**
				Macroscelididae	Elephant shrews

FISHES

The following list of orders and families is based on *Fishes of the World* (3rd edition) by Joseph S. Nelson, 1994, a Wiley-Interscience publication.

SUPERCLASS AGNATHA	***JAWLESS FISHES***	**ORDER SQUALIFORMES**	**DOGFISH SHARKS & ALLIES**	Mitsukurinidae	Goblin shark
				Pseudocarchariidae	Crocodile shark
CLASS MYXINI	**HAGFISHES**	Echinorhinidae	Bramble sharks	Megachasmidae	Megamouth shark
		Squalidae	Dogfish sharks		
ORDER MYXINIFORMES	**HAGFISHES**	Oxynotidae	Roughsharks	Alopiidae	Thresher sharks
Myxinidae	Hagfishes			Cetorhinidae	Basking shark
		ORDER PRISTIOPHORIFORMES	**SAW SHARKS**	Lamnidae	Mackerel sharks (makos)
CLASS CEPHALASPIDOMORPHI	**LAMPREYS & ALLIES**	Pristiophoridae	Saw sharks		
				ORDER CARCHARHINIFORMES	**GROUND SHARKS**
ORDER PETROMYZONTIFORMES	**LAMPREYS**	**ORDER HETERODONTIFORMES**	**HORN (BULL-HEAD) SHARKS**	Scyliorhinidae	Catsharks
Petromyzontidae	Northern lampreys	Heterodontidae	Horn (bullhead) sharks	Proscylliidae	Finback catsharks
Geotriidae	Pouched lampreys			Pseudotriakidae	False catshark
Mordaciidae	Shorthead lampreys	**ORDER ORECTOLOBIFORMES**	**CARPET SHARKS & ALLIES**	Leptochariidae	Barbled houndshark
		Parascylliidae	Collared carpet sharks	Triakidae	Houndsharks
SUPERCLASS GNATHOSTOMATA	***JAWED FISHES***	Brachaeluridae	Blind sharks	Hemigaleidae	Weasel sharks
		Orectolobidae	Wobbegongs	Carcharhinidae	Requiem (whaler) sharks
CLASS CHONDRICHTHYES	**CARTILAGINOUS FISHES**	Hemiscylliidae	Longtail carpet sharks	Sphyrnidae	Hammerhead sharks
		Stegostomatidae	Zebra shark		
Subclass Elasmobranchii	**SHARKS & RAYS**	Ginglymostomatidae	Nurse sharks	**ORDER SQUATINIFORMES**	**ANGEL SHARKS**
		Rhincodontidae	Whale shark	Squatinidae	Angel sharks
ORDER HEXANCHIFORMES	**SIX- & SEVEN-GILL SHARKS**	**ORDER LAMNIFORMES**	**MACKEREL SHARKS & ALLIES**	**ORDER RHINOBATIFORMES**	**SHOVELNOSE RAYS**
Chlamydoselachidae	Frill shark	Odontaspididae	Sand tigers (grey nurse sharks)	Platyrhinidae	Platyrhinids
Hexanchidae	Sixgill, sevengill (cow) sharks			Rhinobatidae	Guitarfishes
				Rhynchobatidae	Sharkfin guitarfishes

ORDER RAJIFORMES — SKATES
Rajidae — Skates

ORDER PRISTIFORMES — SAWFISHES
Pristidae — Sawfishes

ORDER TORPEDINIFORMES — ELECTRIC RAYS
Torpedinidae — Electric rays
Hypnidae — Coffinrays
Narcinidae — Narcinids
Narkidae — Narkids

ORDER MYLIOBATIFORMES — STINGRAYS & ALLIES
Potamotrygonidae — River rays
Dasyatididae — Stingrays
Urolophidae — Round stingrays
Gymnuridae — Butterfly rays
Hexatrygonidae — Sixgill rays
Myliobatididae — Eagle rays
Rhinopteridae — Cownose rays
Mobulidae — Mantas, devil rays

SUBCLASS HOLOCEPHALI — CHIMAERAS

ORDER CHIMAERIFORMES — CHIMAERAS
Callorhynchidae — Plownose chimaeras (elephant fishes)
Chimaeridae — Shortnose chimaeras (ghost sharks, ratfishes)
Rhinochimaeridae — Longnose chimaeras (spookfishes)

CLASS OSTEICHTHYES — BONY FISHES

SUBCLASS SARCOPTERYGII — LUNGFISHES & COELACANTH (FLESHY-FINNED FISHES)

ORDER CERATODONTIFORMES — LUNGFISHES
Ceratodontidae — Australian lungfish

ORDER LEPIDOSIRENIFORMES — LUNGFISHES
Lepidosirenidae — South American lungfish
Protopteridae — African lungfishes

ORDER COELACANTHIFORMES — COELACANTH
Latimeriidae — Coelacanth (gombessa)

SUBCLASS ACTINOPTERYGII — RAY-FINNED FISHES

ORDER POLYPTERIFORMES — BICHIRS
Polypteridae — Bichirs

ORDER ACIPENSERIFORMES — STURGEONS & ALLIES
Acipenseridae — Sturgeons
Polyodontidae — Paddlefishes

ORDER LEPISOSTEIFORMES — GARS
Lepisosteidae — Gars

ORDER AMIIFORMES — BOWFIN
Amiidae — Bowfin

GROUP TELEOSTEI — TELEOSTS

ORDER HIODONTIFORMES — MOONEYES
Hiodontidae — Mooneyes

ORDER OSTEOGLOSSIFORMES — BONYTONGUES, ELEPHANT-FISHES, & ALLIES
Osteoglossidae — Bonytongues
Pantodontidae — Freshwater butterflyfish
Notopteridae — Featherbacks
Mormyridae — Elephantfishes
Gymnarchidae — Aba

ORDER ELOPIFORMES — TARPONS & ALLIES
Elopidae — Tenpounders (ladyfishes)
Megalopidae — Tarpons

ORDER ALBULIFORMES — BONEFISHES & ALLIES
Albulidae — Bonefishes

ORDER NOTACANTHIFORMES — SPINY EELS & ALLIES
Halosauridae — Halosaurs
Notacanthidae — Spiny eels

ORDER ANGUILLIFORMES — EELS
Anguillidae — Freshwater eels
Heterenchelyidae — Shortfaced eels
Moringuidae — Spaghetti eels
Chlopsidae — False moray eels
Myrocongridae — Myrocongrid
Muraenidae — Moray eels
Nemichthyidae — Snipe eels
Muraenesocidae — Pike eels
Synaphobranchidae — Cutthroat eels
Ophichthidae — Snake eels, worm eels
Nettastomatidae — Duckbill eels
Colocongridae — Colocongrids
Congridae — Conger eels, garden eels
Derichthyidae — Narrowneck eels, spoonbill eels
Serrivomeridae — Sawtooth eels
Cyematidae — Bobtail snipe eels
Saccopharyngidae — Swallowers
Eurypharyngidae — Gulper eels
Monognathidae — Singlejaw eels

ORDER CLUPEIFORMES — SARDINES, HERRINGS, ANCHOVIES, & ALLIES
Denticipitidae — Denticle herring
Clupeidae — Sardines, herrings, pilchards
Engraulididae — Anchovies
Chirocentridae — Wolf herrings

ORDER GONORYNCHIFORMES — MILKFISH, BEAKED SALMONS, & ALLIES
Chanidae — Milkfish
Gonorynchidae — Beaked salmons
Kneriidae — Shellears
Phractolaemidae — Hingemouth

ORDER CYPRINIFORMES — CARPS, MINNOWS, & ALLIES
Cyprinidae — Carps, minnows
Psilorhynchidae — Psilorhynchids
Balitoridae — Hillstream loaches
Cobitidae — Loaches
Gyrinocheilidae — Algae eaters
Catostomidae — Suckers

ORDER CHARACIFORMES — CHARACINS & ALLIES
Citharinidae — Citharinids
Distichodontidae — Distichodontins, African fin eaters
Hepsetidae — African pike characin
Erythrinidae — Trahiras & allies
Ctenoluciidae — American pike characins
Lebiasinidae — Voladoras, pencil fishes
Characidae — African tetras (characins), characins, tetras, brycons, piranhas, & allies
Curimatidae — Toothless characins
Prochilodontidae — Flannelmouth characins
Anostomidae — Anostomins, leporinins
Hemiodontidae — Hemiodontids
Chilodontidae — Headstanders
Gasteropelecidae — Freshwater hatchetfishes

ORDER SILURIFORMES — CATFISHES & KNIFEFISHES

SUBORDER SILUROIDEI
Diplomystidae — Velvet catfishes
Nematogenyidae — Mountain catfish
Trichomycteridae — Spinyhead catfishes, candirus
Callichthyidae — Plated catfishes
Scoloplacidae — Spinynose catfishes
Astroblepidae — Andes catfishes

Loricariidae	Armored suckermouth catfishes
Ictaluridae	Bullhead catfishes, madtoms
Bagridae	Bagrid catfishes
Cranoglanididae	Armorhead catfishes
Siluridae	Sheatfishes, wels, glass catfishes
Schilbidae	Schilbid catfishes
Pangasiidae	Pangasiid catfishes
Amblycipitidae	Torrent catfishes
Amphiliidae	Loach catfishes
Akysidae	Asian banjo catfishes
Sisoridae	Hillstream catfishes
Clariidae	Labyrinth (air-breathing) catfishes
Heteropneustidae	Airsac catfishes
Chacidae	Square head (angler) catfishes
Olyridae	Olyrid catfishes
Malapteruridae	Electric catfishes
Ariidae	Sea catfishes
Plotosidae	Eeltail catfishes
Mochokidae	Upsidedown catfishes (squeakers)
Doradidae	Thorny catfishes
Auchenipteridae	Wood catfishes
Pimelodidae	Longwhisker, shovelnose catfishes
Ageneiosidae	Bottlenose (barbelless) catfishes
Helogenidae	Helogene catfishes
Cetopsidae	Carneros, shark (whale) catfishes
Hypophthalmidae	Loweye catfishes
Aspredinidae	Banjo catfishes

SUBORDER GYMNOTOIDEI

Sternopygidae	Longtail knifefishes
Rhamphichthyidae	Longsnout knifefishes
Hypopomidae	Bluntnose knifefishes
Apternotidae	Black knifefishes
Gymnotidae	Banded knifefishes
Electrophoridae	Electric eel (electric knifefish)

ORDER ARGENTINIFORMES

HERRING SMELTS, BARRELEYES, & ALLIES

Argentinidae	Herring smelts
Microstomatidae	Deepsea smelts
Opisthoproctidae	Barreleyes (spookfishes)
Alepocephalidae	Slickheads
Bathylaconidae	Bathylaconids
Platytroctidae	Tubeshoulders

ORDER SALMONIFORMES

Osmeridae	
Salangidae	
Retropinnidae	
Galaxiidae	
Lepidogalaxiidae	
Salmonidae	

ORDER ESOCIFORMES

Esocidae	
Umbridae	

ORDER ATELEOPODIFORMES

Ateleopodidae	

ORDER STOMIIFORMES

Gonostomatidae	
Sternoptychidae	
Phosichthyidae	
Stomiidae	

ORDER AULOPIFORMES

Aulopidae	
Bathysauridae	
Chlorophthalmidae	
Ipnopidae	
Synodontidae	
Scopelarchidae	
Notosudidae	
Giganturidae	
Paralepididae	
Anotopteridae	
Evermannellidae	
Omosudidae	
Alepisauridae	
Pseudotrichonotidae	

ORDER MYCTOPHIFORMES

Neoscopelidae	
Myctophidae	

ORDER LAMPRIDIFORMES

Lampridae	
Veliferidae	
Lophotidae	
Radiicephalidae	
Trachipteridae	
Regalecidae	
Stylephoridae	

SALMONS, SMELTS, & ALLIES

- Northern smelts, ayu
- Icefishes (noodlefishes)
- Southern smelts
- Galaxiids
- Salamanderfish
- Trouts, salmons, chars, whitefishes

PIKES, PICKERELS, & ALLIES

- Pikes
- Mudminnows

JELLYNOSE FISHES

- Jellynose fishes

DRAGONFISHES, LIGHTFISHES, & ALLIES

- Lightfishes, bristlemouths
- Hatchetfishes & allies
- Lightfishes
- Viperfishes, dragonfishes, snaggletooths, loosejaws

LIZARDFISHES & ALLIES

- Aulopids
- Bathysaurids
- Greeneyes
- Ipnopids, tripodfishes
- Lizardfishes, Bombay duck
- Pearleyes
- Waryfishes
- Telescope fishes
- Barracudinas
- Daggertooth
- Sabertooth fishes
- Omosudid
- Lancetfishes
- Pseudotrichonotids

LANTERNFISHES & ALLIES

- Neoscopelids
- Lanternfishes

OARFISHES & ALLIES

- Opahs
- Velifers
- Crestfishes
- Inkfishes
- Ribbonfishes
- Oarfishes
- Tube eye

ORDER POLYMIXIIFORMES

Polymixiidae	

ORDER PERCOPSIFORMES

Percopsidae	
Aphredoderidae	
Amblyopsidae	

ORDER GADIFORMES

Muraenolepididae	
Moridae	
Melanonidae	
Euclichthyidae	
Bregmacerotidae	
Gadidae	
Merlucciidae	
Steindachneriidae	
Macrouridae	

ORDER OPHIDIIFORMES

Ophidiidae	
Carapidae	
Bythitidae	
Aphyonidae	

ORDER BATRACHOIDIFORMES

Batrachoididae	

ORDER LOPHIIFORMES

Lophiidae	
Antennariidae	
Tetrabrachiidae	
Lophichthyidae	
Brachionichthyidae	
Chaunacidae	
Ogcocephalidae	
Caulophrynidae	
Ceratiidae	
Gigantactinidae	
Neoceratiidae	
Linophrynidae	
Oneirodidae	
Thaumatichthyidae	
Centrophrynidae	
Diceratiidae	
Himantolophidae	
Melanocetidae	

BEARDFISHES

- Beardfishes

TROUTPERCHES & ALLIES

- Troutperches
- Pirate perch
- Cavefishes

CODS, HAKES, & ALLIES

- Muraenolepidids
- Morid cods (moras)
- Melanonids
- Euclichthyid
- Codlets
- Codfishes, haddocks, & allies
- Hakes
- Steindachneriid
- Rattails (grenadiers)

CUSKEELS, PEARLFISHES, & ALLIES

- Cuskeels, brotulas, & allies
- Pearlfishes
- Livebearing brotulas
- Aphyonids

TOADFISHES & MIDSHIPMEN

- Toadfishes & midshipmen

ANGLERFISHES, GOOSEFISHES, & FROGFISHES

- Goosefishes (monkfishes)
- Frogfishes (shallow anglerfishes)
- Humpback angler
- Lophichthyid
- Warty anglers (handfishes)
- Seatoads (gapers, coffinfishes)
- Batfishes
- Fanfin anglers
- Seadevils
- Whipnose anglers
- Needlebeard angler
- Netdevils
- Dreamers
- Wolftrap angler
- Hollowchin anglers
- Double anglers
- Footballfishes
- Blackdevils

ORDER GOBIESOCIFORMES	CLINGFISHES & ALLIES
Gobiesocidae	Clingfishes
Callionymidae	Dragonets
Draconettidae	Draconettids

ORDER CYPRINODONTIFORMES	KILLIFISHES & ALLIES
Rivulidae	South American annuals
Aplocheilidae	African annuals
Profundulidae	Profundulids
Fundulidae	Killifishes
Valenciidae	Valenciids
Anablepidae	Four-eyed fishes (cuatro ojos)
Poeciliidae	Livebearers (guppies, etc)
Goodeidae	Goodeids
Cyprinodontidae	Pupfishes

ORDER BELONIFORMES	RICEFISHES, FLYINGFISHES, & ALLIES
Adrianichthyidae	Ricefishes
Exocoetidae	Flyingfishes
Hemiramphidae	Halfbeaks
Belonidae	Needlefishes
Scomberesocidae	Sauries

ORDER ATHERINIFORMES	SILVERSIDES, RAINBOW-FISHES, & ALLIES
Atherinidae	Silversides, topsmelts, grunions
Dentatherinidae	Dentatherinid
Notocheiridae	Surf silversides
Melanotaeniidae	Rainbowfishes
Pseudomugilidae	Blue eyes
Telmatherinidae	Sailfin silversides
Phallostethidae	Priapium fishes

ORDER STEPHANOBERYCIFORMES	PRICKLEFISHES, WHALEFISHES, & ALLIES
Stephanoberycidae	Pricklefishes
Melamphaidae	Bigscale fishes (ridgeheads)
Gibberichthyidae	Gibberfishes
Hispidoberycidae	Bristlyskin
Rondeletiidae	Orangemouth whalefishes
Barbourisiidae	Redvelvet whalefish
Cetomimidae	Flabby whalefishes
Mirapinnidae	Hairyfish, tapetails
Megalomycteridae	Mosaicscale (bignose) fishes

ORDER BERYCIFORMES	SQUIRRELFISHES & ALLIES
Holocentridae	Squirrelfishes (soldierfishes)
Berycidae	Alfoncinos
Anoplogasteridae	Fangtooth fishes

Monocentrididae

Anomalopidae

Trachichthyidae

Diretmidae

ORDER ZEIFORMES	DORIES & ALLIES
Parazenidae	Parazen
Macrurocyttidae	Macrurocyttids
Zeidae	Dories
Oreosomatidae	Oreos
Grammicolepididae	Tinselfishes
Caproidae	Boarfishes

ORDER GASTEROSTEIFORMES	STICKLEBACKS, PIPEFISHES, & ALLIES
Hypoptychidae	Sand eel
Aulorhynchidae	Tubesnouts
Gasterosteidae	Sticklebacks
Indostomidae	Paradox fish
Pegasidae	Seamoths
Aulostomidae	Trumpetfishes
Fistulariidae	Cornetfishes
Macroramphosidae	Snipefishes
Centriscidae	Shrimpfishes (razorfishes)
Solenostomidae	Ghost pipefishes
Syngnathidae	Pipefishes, seahorses

ORDER SYNBRANCHIFORMES	SWAMPEELS & ALLIES
Synbranchidae	Swampeels
Mastacembelidae	Spiny eels
Chaudhuriidae	Chaudhuriids

ORDER SCORPAENIFORMES	SCORPION-FISHES & ALLIES
Scorpaenidae	Scorpionfishes (rockfishes), stonefishes
Caracanthidae	Coral crouchers
Aploactinidae	Velvetfishes
Pataecidae	Prowfishes
Gnathanacanthidae	Red velvetfish
Congiopodidae	Pigfishes (horsefishes)
Triglidae	Sea robins (gurnards)
Dactylopteridae	Helmet (flying) gurnards
Platycephalidae	Flatheads
Bembridae	Deepwater flatheads
Hoplichthyidae	Spiny (ghost) flatheads
Anoplopomatidae	Sablefish, skilfish
Hexagrammidae	Greenlings
Zaniolepididae	Combfishes
Normanichthyidae	Southern sculpin
Rhamphocottidae	Grunt sculpin
Ereuniidae	Deepwater sculpins
Cottidae	Sculpins
Comephoridae	Baikal oilfishes
Abyssocottidae	Abyssocottids
Hemitripteridae	Hemitripterids

Pineapple (pinecone) fishes

Flashlight (lanterneye) fishes

Roughies (slimeheads)

Spinyfins

Psychrolutidae

Bathylutichthyidae

Agonidae

Cyclopteridae

Liparidae

ORDER PERCIFORMES	PERCHES & ALLIES
SUBORDER PERCOIDEI	
Ambassidae	Glassfishes
Acropomatidae	Acropomatids
Epigonidae	Epigonids
Scombropidae	Gnomefishes
Symphysanodontidae	Symphysanodontids
Caesioscorpididae	Caesioscorpidids
Polyprionidae	Wreckfishes
Dinopercidae	Cavebasses
Centropomidae	Snooks
Latidae	Giant perches
Percichthyidae	South temperate basses
Moronidae	North temperate basses
Serranidae	Sea basses, groupers
Callanthiidae	Rosey perches
Pseudochromidae	Dottybacks
Grammatidae	Basslets
Opistognathidae	Jawfishes
Plesiopidae	Roundheads
Notograptidae	Bearded snakeblennies
Pholidichthyidae	Convict blennies
Cepolidae	Bandfishes
Glaucosomatidae	Pearl perches
Terapontidae	Grunters
Banjosidae	Banjosids
Kuhliidae	Aholeholes
Centrarchidae	Sunfishes
Percidae	Perches, darters
Priacanthidae	Bigeyes (catalufas)
Apogonidae	Cardinalfishes
Dinolestidae	Dinolestid
Sillaginidae	Smelt whitings (whitings)
Malacanthidae	Tilefishes
Labracoglossidae	Labracoglossids
Lactariidae	False trevallies
Pomatomidae	Bluefish (tailor)
Menidae	Moonfish
Leiognathidae	Ponyfishes (slipmouths)
Bramidae	Pomfrets
Caristiidae	Manefishes
Arripidae	Australian salmons
Emmelichthyidae	Rovers
Lutjanidae	Snappers (emperors)
Lobotidae	Tripletails
Gerreidae	Mojarras (silver biddies)
Haemulidae	Grunts
Inermiidae	Bonnetmouths
Sparidae	Porgies (breams)
Centracanthidae	Centracanthids
Lethrinidae	Scavengers (emperors)
Nemipteridae	Threadfin, monocle breams
Sciaenidae	Drums, croakers
Mullidae	Goatfishes

Fatheads (blobfishes)

Bathylutichthyids

Poachers

Lumpfishes

Snailfishes, lumpsuckers

Monodactylidae	Moonfishes (fingerfishes)	Stichaeidae	Pricklebacks	Trichiuridae	Cutlassfishes
Pempherididae	Sweepers	Cryptacanthodidae	Wrymouths	Scombridae	Mackerels,
Leptobramidae	Beachsalmon	Pholididae	Gunnels		tunas, bonitos
Bathyclupeidae	Bathyclupeids	Anarhichadidae	Wolffishes	Xiphiidae	Swordfish
Toxotidae	Archerfishes	Ptilichthyidae	Quillfishes	Istiophoridae	Billfishes
Coracinidae	Galjoenfishes	Zaproridae	Prowfish		
Kyphosidae	Seachubs	Scytalinidae	Graveldiver	**SUBORDER STROMATEOIDEI**	
Girellidae	Nibblers			Amarsipidae	Amarsipids
	(blackfishes)	**SUBORDER NOTOTHENIOIDEI**		Centrolophidae	Medusafishes
Scorpididae	Halfmoons, mado	Bovichtidae	Thornfishes	Nomeidae	Driftfishes
	(sweeps)	Nototheniidae	Nototheniids	Ariommatidae	Ariommatids
Microcanthidae	Stripey	Harpagiferidae	Plunderfishes	Tetragonuridae	Squaretails
Ephippidae	Spadefishes	Bathydraconidae	Antarctic	Stromateidae	Butterfishes
Scatophagidae	Scats		dragonfishes		
Chaetodontidae	Butterflyfishes	Channichthyidae	Icefishes	**SUBORDER ANABANTOIDEI**	
Pomacanthidae	Angelfishes			Badidae	Chameleonfish
Enoplosidae	Oldwife	**SUBORDER TRACHINOIDEI**		Nandidae	Leaffishes
Pentacerotidae	Armorheads	Chiasmodontidae	Swallowers	Pristolepidae	False leaffishes
Oplegnathidae	Knifejaws	Champsodontidae	Champsodontids	Channidae	Snakeheads
Icosteidae	Ragfish	Trichodontidae	Sandfishes	Anabantidae	Climbing
Kurtidae	Nurseryfishes	Trachinidae	Weeverfishes		gouramies
Scombrolabracidae	Scombrolabracid	Uranoscopidae	Stargazers	Belontiidae	Gouramies
		Trichonotidae	Sanddivers	Helostomatidae	Kissing gourami
SUBORDER CARANGOIDEI		Creediidae	Sandburrowers	Osphronemidae	Giant gourami
Nematistiidae	Roosterfish	Leptoscopidae	Leptoscopids	Luciocephalidae	Pikehead
Carangidae	Jacks (trevallies)	Percophidae	Duckbills		
Echeneidae	Remoras	Pinguipedidae	Sandperches	**ORDER**	
Rachycentridae	Cobia (black	Cheimarrhichthyidae	Torrentfish	**PLEURONECTIFORMES**	**FLATFISHES**
	kingfish)	Ammodytidae	Sandlances	Psettodidae	Spiny flatfishes
Coryphaenidae	Dolphinfishes			Citharidae	Citharids
		SUBORDER BLENNIOIDEI		Bothidae	Lefteye flounders
SUBORDER CIRRHITOIDEI		Tripterygiidae	Triplefins	Pleuronectidae	Righteye
Cirrhitidae	Hawkfishes	Dactyloscopidae	Sand stargazers		flounders
Chironemidae	Kelpfishes	Labrisomidae	Labrisomids	Cynoglossidae	Tonguefishes
Aplodactylidae	Aplodactylids	Clinidae	Kelp blennies		(tongue soles)
Cheilodactylidae	Morwongs		(kelpfishes)	Soleidae	Soles
Latrididae	Trumpeters	Chaenopsidae	Tube blennies	Achiridae	American soles
		Blenniidae	Combtooth		
SUBORDER MUGILOIDEI			blennies	**ORDER**	
Mugilidae	Mullets			**TETRAODONTIFORMES**	**TRIGGERFISHES**
		SUBORDER GOBIODEI			**& ALLIES**
SUBORDER POLYNEMOIDEI		Rhyacichthyidae	Loach goby	Triacanthodidae	Spikefishes
Polynemidae	Threadfins	Odontobutidae	Freshwater Asian	Triacanthidae	Triplespines
			gobies	Balistidae	Triggerfishes
SUBORDER LABROIDEI		Gobiidae	Gobies, sleepers	Monacanthidae	Filefishes
Cichlidae	Cichlids		(gudgeons)		(leatherjackets)
Embiotocidae	Surfperches			Aracanidae	Robust boxfishes
Pomacentridae	Damselfishes,	**SUBORDER ACANTHUROIDEI**		Ostraciidae	Boxfishes,
	anemonefishes	Siganidae	Rabbitfishes		cowfishes,
Labridae	Wrasses	Luvaridae	Louvar		trunkfishes
		Zanclidae	Moorish idol	Triodontidae	Pursefish (three-
Odacidae	Rock whitings	Acanthuridae	Surgeonfishes		toothed puffer)
Scaridae	Parrotfishes		(tangs)	Tetraodontidae	Pufferfishes
					(toados)
SUBORDER ZOARCOIDEI		**SUBORDER SCOMBROIDEI**		Diodontidae	Porcupinefishes
Bathymasteridae	Ronquils	Sphyraenidae	Barracudas	Molidae	Ocean sunfishes
Zoarcidae	Eelpouts	Gempylidae	Snake mackerels,		(molas)
			gemfishes		

BIRDS

The following list of orders and families is based on *Check-list of Birds of the World* by J.L. Peters, E. Mayr, J.C. Greenway Jr., *et. al.*, 1931–1987, 16 volumes, Cambridge, Massachusetts, Museum of Comparative Zoology.

CLASS AVES		Casuariidae	Cassowaries	Procellariidae	Shearwaters
		Dromaiidae	Emu	Hydrobatidae	Storm petrels
ORDER		Apterygidae	Kiwis	Pelecanoididae	Diving petrels
STRUTHIONIFORMES	**RATITES &**				
	TINAMOUS	**ORDER**		**ORDER**	
		PROCELLARIIFORMES		**SPHENISCIFORMES**	**PENGUINS**
Struthionidae	Ostrich		**ALBATROSSES**	Spheniscidae	Penguins
Tinamidae	Tinamous		**& PETRELS**		
Rheidae	Rheas	Diomedeidae	Albatrosses		

299

ORDER GAVIIFORMES
Gaviidae

DIVERS
Divers (loons)

ORDER PODICIPEDIFORMES
Podicipedidae

GREBES
Grebes

ORDER PELECANIFORMES
Phaethontidae
Pelecanidae
Phalacrocoracidae

Sulidae
Fregatidae

PELICANS & ALLIES
Tropicbirds
Pelicans
Cormorants, anhingas
Gannets, boobies
Frigatebirds

ORDER CICONIIFORMES
Ardeidae
Scopidae
Ciconiidae
Balaenicipitidae

Threskiornithidae
Cathartidae

HERONS & ALLIES
Herons, bitterns
Hammerhead
Storks
Whale-headed stork
Ibises, spoonbills
New World vultures

ORDER PHOENICOPTERIFORMES
Phoenicopteridae

FLAMINGOS
Flamingos

ORDER FALCONIFORMES
Accipitridae

Sagittariidae
Falconidae

RAPTORS
Osprey, kites, hawks, eagles, Old World vultures, harriers, buzzards, harpies, & buteonines
Secretarybird
Falcons, falconets, caracaras

ORDER ANSERIFORMES
Anatidae

Anhimidae

WATERFOWL & SCREAMERS
Geese, swans, ducks
Screamers

ORDER GALLIFORMES
Megapodiidae

Cracidae

Phasianidae

GAMEBIRDS
Megapodes (mound-builders)
Chachalacas, guans, curassows
Turkeys, grouse, etc.

ORDER OPISTHOCOMIFORMES
Opisthocomidae

HOATZIN
Hoatzin

ORDER GRUIFORMES
Mesitornithidae
Turnicidae

Pedionomidae

Gruidae

CRANES & ALLIES
Mesites
Hemipode-quails (button quails)
Collared hemipode (plains wanderer)
Cranes

Aramidae
Psophiidae
Rallidae
Heliornithidae
Rhynochetidae
Eurypygidae
Cariamidae
Otididae

Limpkins
Trumpeters
Rails
Finfoots
Kagus
Sunbittern
Seriemas
Bustards

ORDER CHARADRIIFORMES

Jacanidae
Rostratulidae
Dromadidae
Haematopodidae
Ibidorhynchidae
Recurvirostridae
Burhinidae

Glareolidae

Charadriidae
Scolopacidae

Thinocoridae
Chionididae
Laridae

Stercorariidae
Alcidae

WADERS & SHOREBIRDS
Jacanas
Painted snipe
Crab plover
Oystercatchers
Ibisbill
Stilts, avocets
Stone curlews (thick knees)
Coursers, pratincoles
Plovers, dotterels
Curlews, sandpipers, snipes
Seedsnipes
Sheathbills
Gulls, terns, skimmers
Skuas, jaegers
Auks

ORDER COLUMBIFORMES

Pteroclididae
Columbidae

PIGEONS & SANDGROUSE
Sandgrouse
Pigeons, doves

ORDER PSITTACIFORMES
Cacatuidae
Psittacidae

PARROTS
Cockatoos
Parrots

ORDER CUCULIFORMES

Musophagidae

Cuculidae

TURACOS & CUCKOOS
Turacos, louries (plaintain-eaters)
Cuckoos, etc.

ORDER STRIGIFORMES
Tytonidae

Strigidae

OWLS
Barn owls, bay owls
Hawk owls (true owls)

ORDER CAPRIMULGIFORMES

Steatornithidae
Podargidae
Nyctibiidae
Aegothelidae
Caprimulgidae

FROGMOUTHS & NIGHTJARS
Oilbird
Frogmouths
Potoos
Owlet nightjars
Nightjars

ORDER APODIFORMES

Apodidae
Hemiprocnidae
Trochilidae

SWIFTS & HUMMINGBIRDS
Swifts
Crested swifts
Hummingbirds

ORDER COLIIFORMES
Coliidae

MOUSEBIRDS
Mousebirds

ORDER TROGONIFORMES
Trogonidae

TROGONS
Trogons

ORDER CORACIIFORMES

Alcedinidae
Todidae
Momotidae
Meropidae
Coraciidae
Upupidae
Phoeniculidae
Bucerotidae

KINGFISHERS & ALLIES
Kingfishers
Todies
Motmots
Bee-eaters
Rollers
Hoopoe
Wood-hoopoes
Hornbills

ORDER PICIFORMES

Galbulidae
Bucconidae
Capitonidae
Ramphastidae
Indicatoridae
Picidae

WOODPECKERS & BARBETS
Jacamars
Puffbirds
Barbets
Toucans
Honeyguides
Woodpeckers

ORDER PASSERIFORMES

SUBORDER EURYLAIMI

Eurylaimidae
Philepittidae
Pittidae
Acanthisittidae

BROADBILLS & PITTAS
Broadbills
Sunbirds, asitys
Pittas
New Zealand wrens

SUBORDER FURNARII

Dendrocolaptidae
Furnariidae
Formicariidae
Rhinocryptidae

OVENBIRDS & ALLIES
Woodcreepers
Ovenbirds
Antbirds
Tapaculos

SUBORDER TYRANNI

Tyrannidae

Pipridae
Cotingidae
Oxyruncidae
Phytotomidae

TYRANT FLYCATCHERS & ALLIES
Tyrant flycatchers
Manakins
Cotingas
Sharpbills
Plantcutters

SUBORDER OSCINES
Menuridae
Atrichornithidae
Alaudidae
Motacillidae
Hirundinidae

Campephagidae

Pycnonotidae
Irenidae

Laniidae
Vangidae
Bombycillidae
Hypocoliidae
Ptilogonatidae
Dulidae
Prunellidae

Mimidae

SONGBIRDS
Lyrebirds
Scrub-birds
Larks
Wagtails, pipits
Swallows, martins
Cuckoo-shrikes, etc.
Bulbuls
Leafbirds, ioras, bluebirds
Shrikes
Vangas
Waxwings
Hypocolius
Silky flycatchers
Palmchat
Accentors, hedge-sparrows
Mockingbirds, etc.

Cinclidae	Dippers	Sittidae	Nuthatches, sitellas, wallcreepers
Turdidae	Thrushes		
Timaliidae	Babblers, etc.	Certhiidae	Holarctic treecreepers
Troglodytidae	Wrens		
Sylviidae	Old World warblers	Rhabdornithidae	Philippine treecreepers
Muscicapidae	Old World flycatchers	Climacteridae	Australasian treecreepers
Maluridae	Fairy-wrens, etc.	Dicaeidae	Flowerpeckers, pardalotes
Acanthizidae	Australian warblers, etc.	Nectariniidae	Sunbirds
Ephthianuridae	Australian chats	Zosteropidae	White-eyes
Orthonychidae	Logrunners, etc.	Meliphagidae	Honeyeaters
Rhipiduridae	Fantails	Vireonidae	Vireos
Monarchidae	Monarch flycatchers	Emberizidae	Buntings, tanagers
Petroicidae	Australasian robins	Parulidae	New World wood warblers
Pachycephalidae	Whistlers, etc.	Icteridae	Icterids (American blackbirds)
Aegithalidae	Long-tailed tits		
Remizidae	Penduline tits	Fringillidae	Finches
Paridae	True tits, chickadees, titmice		

Drepanididae	Hawaiian honeycreepers
Estrildidae	Estrildid finches
Ploceidae	Weavers
Passeridae	Old World sparrows
Sturnidae	Starlings, mynahs
Oriolidae	Orioles, figbirds
Dicruridae	Drongos
Callaeidae	New Zealand wattlebirds
Grallinidae	Magpie-larks
Artamidae	Wood swallows
Cracticidae	Bell magpies
Ptilonorhynchidae	Bowerbirds
Paradisaeidae	Birds of paradise
Corvidae	Crows, jays

REPTILES AND AMPHIBIANS

The classification of reptiles and frogs changes as new knowledge is acquired. The following list of orders and families is based on the most recent information.

CLASS AMPHIBIA

SUBCLASS LISSAMPHIBIA

ORDER
CAUDATA — SALAMANDERS & NEWTS

SUBORDER SIRENOIDEA
Sirenidae	Sirens

SUBORDER CRYPTOBRANCHOIDEA
Cryptobranchidae	Hellbenders & giant salamanders
Hynobiidae	Hynobiids

SUBORDER SALAMANDROIDEA
Amphiumidae	Amphiumas (Congo eels)
Plethodontidae	Lungless salamanders
Rhyacotritonidae	Torrent salamanders
Proteidae	Mudpuppies, waterdogs, & the olm
Salamandridae	Salamandrids
Ambystomatidae	Mole salamanders
Dicamptodontidae	Dicamptodontids

ORDER
GYMNOPHIONA — CAECILIANS
Rhinatrematidae	South American tailed caecilians
Ichthyophiidae	Ichthyophiids
Uraeotyphlidae	Uraeotyphlids
Scolecomorphidae	Scolecomorphids
Caeciliidae	Caeciliids & aquatic caecilians

ORDER
ANURA — FROGS & TOADS
Ascaphidae	"Tailed" frogs
Leiopelmatidae	New Zealand frogs
Bombinatoridae	Fire-bellied toads & allies
Discoglossidae	Discoglossid frogs
Pipidae	Pipas & "clawed" frogs
Rhinophrynidae	Cone-nosed frog
Megophryidae	Megophryids
Pelodytidae	Parsley frogs
Pelobatidae	Spadefoots

SUPERFAMILY BUFONOIDEA
Allophrynidae	Allophrynid frog
Brachycephalidae	Saddleback frogs
Bufonidae	Toads
Helophrynidae	Ghost frogs
Leptodactylidae	Neotropical frogs
Myobatrachidae	Australasian frogs
Sooglossiidae	Seychelles frogs
Rhinodermatidae	Darwin's frogs
Hylidae	Hylid treefrogs
Pelodryadidae	Australasian treefrogs
Centrolenidae	Glass frogs
Pseudidae	Natator frogs
Dendrobatidae	Dart-poison frogs

SUPERFAMILY RANOIDEA
Microhylidae	Microhylids
Hemisotidae	Shovel-nosed frogs
Arthroleptidae	Squeakers
Ranidae	Ranid frogs
Hyperoliidae	Reed & lily frogs
Rhacophoridae	Rhacaphorid treefrogs

CLASS REPTILIA

SUBCLASS EUREPTILIA

SUPERORDER LEPIDOSAURIA

ORDER
RHYNCHOCEPHALIA — TUATARAS
Sphenodontidae	Tuataras

ORDER
SQUAMATA — SQUAMATES

SUBORDER IGUANIA — IGUANID LIZARDS
Corytophanidae	Helmeted lizards
Crotaphytidae	Collared & leopard lizards
Hoplocercidae	Hoplocercids
Iguanidae	Iguanas
Opluridae	Madagascar iguanians
Phrynosomatidae	Scaly, sand, & horned lizards
Polychrotidae	Anoloid lizards
Tropiduridae	Tropidurids
Agamidae	Agamid lizards
Chameleonidae	Chameleons

SUBORDER SCLEROGLOSSA

SUPERFAMILY GEKKONOIDEA
Eublepharidae	Eye-lash geckos
Gekkonidae	Geckos
Pygopodidae	Australasian flapfoots

SUPERFAMILY SCINCOIDEA
Xantusiidae	Night lizards
Lacertidae	Lacertids

Scincidae	Skinks		
Dibamidae	Dibamids		
Cordylidae	Girdle-tailed lizards		
Gerrhosauridae	Plated lizards		
Teiidae	Macroteiids		
Gymnophthalmidae	Microteiids		

SUPERFAMILY ANGUOIDEA

Xenosauridae	Knob-scaled lizards
Anguidae	Anguids; glass & alligator lizards
Helodermatidae	Beaded lizards
Varanidae	Monitor lizards
Lanthanotidae	Earless monitor lizard

SUBORDER AMPHISBAENIA   AMPHISBAENIANS

Bipedidae	Ajolotes
Amphisbaenidae	Worm lizards
Trogonophidae	Desert ringed lizards
Rhineuridae	Florida worm lizard

SUBORDER SERPENTES   SNAKES

INFRAORDER SCOLECOPHIDIA

Anomalepididae	Blind wormsnakes
Typhlopidae	Blind snakes
Leptotyphlopidae	Thread snakes

INFRAORDER ALETHINOPHIDIA

Anomochelidae	Stump heads
Aniliidae	Coral pipesnakes
Cylindrophidae	Asian pipesnakes
Uropeltidae	Shield tails
Xenopeltidae	Sunbeam snake
Loxocemidae	Dwarf boa
Boidae	Pythons & boas
Ungaliophiidae	Ungaliophiids
Bolyeriidae	Round Island snakes
Tropidophiidae	Woodsnakes
Acrochordidae	File snakes
Atractaspididae	Mole vipers
Colubridae	Harmless & rear-fanged snakes
Elapidae	Cobras, kraits, coral snakes, & sea snakes
Viperidae	Adders & vipers

SUPERORDER TESTUDINES

ORDER TESTUDINATA   TURTLES, TERRAPINS, & TORTOISES

SUBORDER PLEURODIRA   SIDE-NECK TURTLES

Chelidae	Snake-neck turtles
Pelomedusidae	Helmeted side-neck turtles

SUBORDER CRYPTODIRA   HIDDEN-NECKED TURTLES

SUPERFAMILY TRIONYCHOIDEA

Kinosternidae	Mud & musk turtles
Dermatemydidae	Mesoamerican river turtle
Carretochelyidae	Australian softshell turtle
Trionychidae	Holarctic & paleotropical softshell turtles

SUPERFAMILY CHELONIOEDEA

Dermochelyidae	Leatherback sea turtles
Cheloniidae	Sea turtles

SUPERFAMILY TESTUDINOIDEA

Chelydridae	Snapping turtles
Emydidae	New World pond turtles & terrapins
Testudinidae	Tortoises
Bataguridae	Old World pond turtles

SUPERORDER ARCHOSAURIA

ORDER CROCODILIA   CROCODILIANS

Alligatoridae	Alligators & caimans
Crocodylidae	Crocodiles
Gavialidae	Gavials

INSECTS AND SPIDERS

The classification of insects and arachnids changes as new knowledge is acquired. Only major orders and families are listed below. Gaps in the list indicate that the family has no common name.

CLASS INSECTA

ORDER PROTURA   PROTURANS

ORDER COLLEMBOLA   SPRINGTAILS

Entomobryidae	Entomobryid (elongated-bodied) springtails
Hypogastruridae	
Isotomidae	
Onychiuridae	
Poduridae	Podurid (elongated-bodied) springtails
Sminthuridae	Globular springtails

ORDER DIPLURA   DIPLURANS

Japygidae	Forcipate diplurans

ORDER MICROCORYPHIA   JUMPING BRISTLETAILS

Machilidae	Jumping bristletails

ORDER ARCHAEOGNATHA   COMMON BRISTLETAILS

ORDER THYSANURA   SILVERFISH

Lepismatidae	Silverfish (firebrats)

ORDER EPHEMEROPTERA   MAYFLIES

Baetidae	Small mayflies
Ephemerellidae	Midboreal mayflies
Ephemeridae	Burrowing mayflies
Heptageniidae	Stream mayflies
Leptophlebiidae	Spinners

ORDER ODONATA   DRAGONFLIES & DAMSELFLIES

Aeschnidae	Darners
Calopterygidae	Broad-winged damselflies
Coenagrionidae	Narrow-winged damselflies
Cordulegastridae	Biddies & flying adders
Corduliidae	Green-eyed skimmers
Gomphidae	Gomphid dragonflies (clubtails)
Lestidae	Spread-winged damselflies
Libellulidae	Common skimmers
Macromiidae	Belted & river skimmers
Petaluridae	Graybacks

ORDER BLATTODEA   COCKROACHES

Blaberidae	Blaberid cockroaches
Blattellidae	Blattellid cockroaches
Blattidae	Blattid cockroaches

ORDER MANTODEA   MANTIDS

Mantidae	Mantids

ORDER
ISOPTERA — **TERMITES**
Hodotermitidae — Rotten-wood termites
Kalotermitidae — Dry-wood, damp-wood, & powder-post termites
Mastotermitidae
Rhinotermitidae — Subterranean & damp-wood termites
Termitidae — Soldierless, desert, & nasutiform termites
Termopsidae

ORDER
ZORAPTERA — **ZORAPTERANS**
Zorotypidae — Zorapterans

ORDER
GRYLLOBLATTODEA — **ICE INSECTS**

ORDER
DERMAPTERA — **EARWIGS**
Chelisochidae — Black earwigs
Forficulidae — Common earwigs
Labiduridae — Long-horned earwigs
Labiidae — Little earwigs

ORDER
PLECOPTERA — **STONEFLIES**
Capniidae — Small winter stoneflies
Chloroperlidae — Green stoneflies
Isoperlidae — Green-winged stoneflies
Leuctridae — Rolled-winged stoneflies
Nemouridae — Spring stoneflies
Peltoperlidae — Roachlike stoneflies
Perlidae — Common stoneflies
Perlodidae — Perlodid stoneflies
Pteronarcidae — Giant stoneflies
Taeniopterygidae — Winter stoneflies

ORDER
ORTHOPTERA — **GRASSHOPPERS & CRICKETS**
Acrididae — Short-horned grasshoppers
Cooloolidae — Cooloola monster
Cylindrachetidae — Sand gropers
Eneopterinae; Trigonidiinae — Bush crickets
Eumastacidae; Tanaoceridae — Monkey grasshoppers
Gryllacrididae; Rhaphidophoridae — Camel crickets & kin, cave crickets
Gryllidae — True crickets
Gryllotalpidae — Mole crickets
Myrmecophilidae — Ant crickets
Oecanthinae — Tree crickets
Pyrgomorphidae
Stenopelmatidae — King crickets; Jerusalem or sand crickets
Tetrigidae — Pygmy grasshoppers

Tettigoniidae — Long-horned grasshoppers & katydids
Tridactylidae — Pygmy mole crickets

ORDER
PHASMATODEA — **WALKING-STICKS & TIMEMAS**
Phasmatidae — Stick insects
Phasmidae — Walkingsticks
Timemidae — Timemas

ORDER
EMBIOPTERA — **WEBSPINNERS**

ORDER
PSOCOPTERA — **BOOK LICE & BARK LICE**
Lepidopsocidae — Scaly barklice
Liposcelididae — Liposcelid booklice
Pseudocaeciliidae — Pseudocaeciliid barklice
Psocidae — Common barklice
Psyllipsocidae — Psyllipsocids
Trogiidae — Trogiid booklice

ORDER
PHTHIRAPTERA — **CHEWING LICE & SUCKING LICE**
Boopidae — Spiny sucking lice
Echinophthiriidae — Guinea pig lice
Gyropidae — Mammal-sucking lice
Haematopinidae
Hoplopleuridae — Bird lice
Laemobothriidae — Smooth sucking lice
Linognathidae — Poultry-chewing lice
Menoponidae — Human lice
Pediculidae — Bird lice, feather-chewing lice
Philopteridae — Bird lice
Ricinidae — Mammal-chewing lice
Trichodectidae

ORDER
HEMIPTERA — **TRUE BUGS**
Achilidae — Achilid planthoppers
Adelgidae — Pine aphids
Aleyrodidae — Whiteflies
Alydidae — Broad-headed bugs
Anthocoridae — Flower bugs, minute pirate bugs
Aphididae — Aphids
Aphrophoridae
Aradidae — Flat bugs, bark bugs, fungus bugs
Asterolecaniidae — Pit scales
Belostomatidae — Giant water bugs
Berytidae — Stilt bugs
Carsidaridae
Cercopidae — Spittlebugs & froghoppers
Chermidae — Pine & spruce aphids
Cicadellidae — Leafhoppers
Cicadidae — Cicadas

Cimicidae — Bed bugs
Cixiidae — Cixiid planthoppers
Coccidae — Soft scales, wax, & tortoise scales
Colobathristidae
Coreidae — Leaf-footed bugs, crusader bugs
Corixidae — Water boatmen
Cydnidae — Negro bugs
Dactylopiidae — Cochineal bugs
Delphacidae — Delphacid planthoppers
Derbidae — Derbid planthoppers
Diaspididae — Armored scale insects
Dictyopharidae — Dictyopharid planthoppers
Dinidoridae
Dipsocoridae; Schizopteridae — Jumping ground bugs
Eriosomatidae — Woolly & gall-making aphids
Eurymelidae; Membracidae — Treehoppers
Flatidae — Flatid planthoppers
Fulgoridae — Fulgorid planthoppers
Gelastocoridae — Toad bugs
Gerridae — Water striders
Hebridae — Velvet water bugs
Homotomidae
Hydrometridae — Marsh treaders, water measurers
Isometopidae — Jumping tree bugs
Issidae — Issid planthoppers
Kermidae — Gall-like coccids
Kerriidae; Lacciferidae — Lac insects
Leptopodidae — Spiny shore bugs
Lygaeidae — Seed bugs
Margarodidae — Giant scale insects, ground pearls
Mesoveliidae — Water treaders
Miridae — Leaf or plant bugs
Nabidae — Damsel bugs
Naucoridae — Creeping water bugs
Nepidae — Waterscorpions
Notonectidae — Backswimmers
Ochteridae — Velvety shore bugs
Ortheziidae — Ensign scales
Peloridiidae — Moss bugs
Pentatomidae — Stink bugs, shield bugs
Phylloxeridae — Gall aphids
Phymatidae — Ambush bugs
Polyctenidae — Bat bugs
Pseudococcidae; Eriococcidae — Mealybugs
Psyllidae — Psyllids, lerps
Pyrrhocoridae — Red bugs, stainers
Reduviidae — Assassin bugs
Rhopalidae — Scentless plant bugs
Ricaniidae — Ricaniid planthoppers
Saldidae — Shore bugs
Scutelleridae — Jewel bugs, shield-backed bugs

essaratomidae
Tettigarctidae — Hairy cicadas
Tingidae — Lace bugs
Triozidae
Veliidae — Ripple bugs

ORDER
THYSANOPTERA — **THRIPS**
Aeolothripidae — Banded thrips
Phloeothripidae — Tube-tailed thrips
Thripidae — Common thrips

ORDER
MEGALOPTERA — **ALDERFLIES,**
DOBSONFLIES,
& FISHFLIES
Corydalidae — Dobsonflies
& fishflies
Sialidae — Alderflies

ORDER
RAPHIDIOPTERA — **SNAKEFLIES**
Raphidiidae; Inocelliidae — Ocellated
snakeflies

ORDER
NEUROPTERA — **NET-VEINED**
INSECTS
Ascalaphidae — Owlflies
Chrysopidae — Green lacewings
Coniopterygidae — Dusty-wings
Hemerobiidae — Brown lacewings
Ithonidae — Moth lacewings
Mantispidae — Mantidflies
Myrmeleontidae — Antlions
Nemopteridae
Polystoechotidae — Giant lacewings
Psychopsidae — Silky lacewings
Sisyridae — Spongeflies

ORDER
COLEOPTERA — **BEETLES**
Anobiidae — Furniture beetles
Anthribidae — Fungus weevils
Bostrichidae — Branch & twig
borers, auger
beetles
Brentidae — Primitive weevils
Bruchidae — Seed beetles
Buprestidae — Metallic wood-
boring beetles,
jewel beetles
Cantharidae — Soldier beetles
Carabidae — Ground beetles
Cerambycidae — Longhorn
beetles,
longicorn beetles
Chrysomelidae — Leaf beetles
Cicindelidae — Tiger beetles
Cleridae — Clerid beetles,
checkered beetles
Coccinellidae — Ladybug beetles
Cucujidae — Flat bark beetles
Curculionidae — Snout beetles
& weevils
Dermestidae — Dermestid beetles
Dytiscidae — Predacious
diving beetles
Elateridae — Click beetles
Erotylidae — Pleasing fungus
beetles
Gyrinidae — Whirligig beetles
Haliplidae — Crawling water
beetles
Histeridae — Hister beetles

Hydrophilidae — Water scavenger
beetles
Laemophloeidae
Lampyridae — Fireflies,
lightning bugs
Lathridiidae — Minute brown
scavenger beetles
Lucanidae — Stag beetles
Lycidae — Net-winged
beetles
Lymexylidae — Ship-timber
beetles
Meloidae — Blister beetles
Melyridae — Softwinged
flower beetles
Mycetophagidae — Hairy fungus
beetles
Nitidulidae — Nitidulid beetles
Passalidae — Passalid beetles
or bessbugs
Psephenidae — Water pennies
Ptiliidae — Feather-winged
beetles
Ptinidae — Spider beetles
Pyrochroidae — Fire-colored
beetles
Rhipiphoridae — Rhipiphoridan
beetles
Scarabaeidae — Scarab beetles
Scolytidae — Bark &
ambrosia beetles
Silphidae — Carrion beetles
Silvanidae — Flat grain beetles
Staphylinidae — Rove beetles
Tenebrionidae — Darkling beetles
Trogidae — Carcass beetles
Trogositidae — Bark-gnawing
beetles
Zopheridae

ORDER
STREPSIPTERA — **TWISTED-**
WINGED
PARASITES
Mengeidae — Mengeids
Stylopidae — Stylopids

ORDER
MECOPTERA — **SCORPION-**
FLIES & KIN
Bittacidae — Hangingflies
Boreidae — Snow scorpionflies
Panorpidae — Common
scorpionflies

ORDER
SIPHONAPTERA — **FLEAS**
Dolichopsyllidae;
Ceratophyllidae — Rodent fleas
Leptopsyllidae — Mouse fleas
Pulicidae — Common fleas
Tungidae — Sticktight &
chigoe fleas

ORDER
DIPTERA — **FLIES**
Acroceridae — Bladder flies
Agromyzidae — Leafminer flies
Anthomyiidae — Anthomyiid flies
Apioceridae — Flower-loving flies
Asilidae — Robber flies
Bibionidae — March flies
Blephariceridae — Net-winged
midges
Bombyliidae — Bee flies
Braulidae — Beelice

Calliphoridae — Blowflies
Canacidae — Beach flies
Cecidomyiidae — Gall midges
Ceratopogonidae — Punkies, biting
midges
Chaoboridae — Phantom midges
Chironomidae — Midges
Chloropidae — Grass flies
Coelopidae — Seaweed flies
Conopidae — Thick-headed flies
Culicidae — Mosquitoes
Dolichopodidae — Long-legged flies
Drosophilidae — Pomace flies,
ferment flies, or
vinegar flies
Empididae — Dance flies,
water cruisers
Ephydridae — Shore flies
Fanniidae
Fergusoninidae — Eucalyptus flies
Heleomyzidae — Sun flies
Hippoboscidae — Louse flies
& sheep keds
Lonchaeidae — Lance flies
Micropezidae — Stiltlegged flies
Muscidae — Muscid flies or
house flies
& bushflies
Mycetophilidae — Fungus gnats
Mydidae — Mydas flies
Nemestrinidae — Tanglevein flies
Nerriidae — Cactus flies
Neurochaetidae — Upside-down flies
Nycteribiidae; Streblidae — Bat flies
Oestridae; Gasterophilidae — Botflies
Phoridae — Scuttle flies
Piophilidae — Skipper flies
Platypezidae — Flat-footed flies
Platystomatidae — Platystomatid flies
Psychodidae — Moth flies
Ptychopteridae — Phantom
crane flies
Pyrgotidae — Pyrgotid flies
Rhagionidae — Snipe flies
Sarcophagidae — Flesh flies
Scenopinidae — Window flies
Sciaridae — Black fungus
gnats
Sciomyzidae — March flies
Sepsidae — Ant flies
Simuliidae — Black or
sand flies
Sphaeroceridae — Short heel flies,
small dung flies
Stratiomyidae — Soldier flies
Syrphidae — Hover flies
Tabanidae — Horse &
deer flies
Tachinidae — Tachinid flies
Tephritidae — Fruit flies
Teratomyzidae — Fern flies
Therevidae — Stiletto flies
Tipulidae — Crane flies
Trichoceridae — Winter crane flies

ORDER
TRICHOPTERA — **CADDISFLIES**
Hydropsychidae — Net-spinning
caddisflies
Leptoceridae — Long-horned
caddisflies
Limnephilidae — Northern
caddisflies
Phryganeidae — Large caddisflies

Psychomyiidae	Trumpet-net & tube-making caddisflies

ORDER LEPIDOPTERA — **BUTTERFLIES & MOTHS**

Alucitidae	Many-plume moths
Anthelidae	
Apaturidae	Hackberry & goatweed butterflies
Arctiidae	Tiger moths
Bombycidae	Silkworm moths
Bucculatricidae	
Carposinidae	Carposinid moths
Carthaeidae	
Castniidae	
Citheroniidae	Royal moths
Coleophoridae	Casebearer moths
Copromorphidae	
Cosmopterygidae	Cosmopterygid moths
Cossidae	Wood moths
Ctenuchidae	Ctenuchid moths
Danaidae	Milkweed butterflies
Drepanidae	Hook-tip moths
Eupterotidae; Zanolidae	Zanolid moths
Gelechiidae	Gelechiid moths
Geometridae	Measuringworm moths, loopers
Gracilariidae	Leaf blotch miners
Hepialidae	Ghost moths, swifts
Hesperiidae	Skippers
Incurvariidae	Yucca moths & kin
Lasiocampidae	Tent caterpillar & lappet moths
Libytheidae	Snout butterflies
Limacodidae	Slug caterpillar moths, cup moths
Lycaenidae	Gossamer-winged butterflies
Lymantriidae	Tussock moths & kin
Lyonetiidae	Lyonetiid moths
Noctuidae	Owlet moths, semi-loopers
Notodontidae	Prominents
Nymphalidae	Brush-footed butterflies
Oecophoridae	Oecophorid moths
Papilionidae	Swallowtails & kin
Pieridae	Whites, sulphurs, & orange tips
Plutellidae	Diamondback moths
Pterophoridae	Plume moths
Psychidae	Bagworm moths
Pyralidae	Pyralid moths
Riodinidae	Metalmarks
Saturniidae	Giant silkworm moths
Satyridae	Satyrs, nymphs, & arctics
Sesiidae	Clear-winged moths
Sphingidae	Sphinx or hawk moths
Thaumetopoeidae	
Tineidae	
Tortricidae	Tortricid moths
Uraniidae	
Yponomeutidae	Ermine moths
Zygaenidae	Smoky moths

ORDER HYMENOPTERA — **BEES, ANTS, WASPS, SAW-FLIES, & KIN**

	Clothes moths & kin
Agaonidae	Fig wasps
Andrenidae	Andrenid bees
Apidae	Digger bees, carpenter bees, cuckoo bees, bumblebees, honeybees, & kin
Argidae	Argid sawflies
Braconidae	Braconids
Cephidae	Stem sawflies
Chalcididae	Chalcids
Chrysididae	Cuckoo wasps
Cimbicidae	Cimbicid sawflies
Colletidae	Yellow-faced & plasterer bees
Cynipidae	Gall wasps
Encyrtidae	Encyrtid wasps
Eulophidae; Aphelininae	Eulophid wasps
Eurytomidae	Seed chalcids
Evaniidae	Hatchet wasps
Formicidae	Ants
Halictidae	Halictid bees
Ibaliidae	Ibaliid wasps
Ichneumonidae	Ichneumonids
Megachilidae	Leaf-cutting bees
Melittidae	Melittid bees
Mutillidae	Velvet-ants
Mymaridae	Fairy wasps, fairy flies
Pelecinidae	Pelecinids
Pergidae	Pergid sawflies
Pompilidae	Spider wasps
Pteromalidae	Pteromalid wasps
Scelionidae	Scelionid wasps
Scoliidae	Scoliid wasps
Siricidae	Horntails
Sphecidae	Sphecid wasps, cicada-killers
Stephanidae	Stephanid wasps
Symphyta	Sawflies
Tenthredinidae	Common sawflies
Tiphiidae	Tiphid wasps
Torymidae	Torymid wasps
Vespidae	Vespid wasps

CLASS ARACHNIDA

ORDER ARANEAE — **SPIDERS**

Agelenidae	Funnel-web weavers
Antrodiaetidae	Folding trapdoor spiders
Araneidae	Orb weavers
Clubionidae	Sac spiders
Ctenidae	Wandering spiders
Ctenizidae	Trapdoor spiders
Dictynidae	Dictynid spiders
Linyphiidae	Sheet-web spiders
Loxoscelidae	Violin spiders
Lycosidae	Wolf spiders
Oxyopidae	Lynx spiders
Philodromidae	Philodromids
Pisauridae	Nursery web spiders
Salticidae	Jumping spiders
Scytodidae	Spitting spiders
Selenopidae	Selenopid crab spiders
Sparassidae	Giant crab spiders
Tetragnathidae	Large-jawed orb weavers
Theraphosidae	Tarantulas
Theridiidae	Comb-footed spiders
Thomisidae	Crab spiders

ORDER SCORPIONIDA — **SCORPIONS**

Buthidae	Buthid scorpions
Iuridae	Iurid scorpions

ORDER PSEUDOSCORPIONIDA — **PSEUDO-SCORPIONS**

Chernetidae	Chernetids

ORDER OPILIONES — **DADDY-LONG-LEGS**

Phalangiidae	Daddy-long-legs

ORDER ACARINA — **MITES & TICKS**

Argasidae	Soft ticks
Hydrachnellae	Water mites
Ixodidae	Hard ticks
Tetranychidae	Spider mites
Trombidiidae	Velvet mites

ORDER UROPYGI — **WHIPSCORPIONS**

Thelyphonidae	Vinegarones

ORDER AMBLYPYGI — **TAILLESS WHIPSCORPIONS**

Tarantulidae	Tailless whipscorpions

ORDER SOLPUGIDA — **WIND-SCORPIONS**

Eremobatidae	Eremobatid windscorpions

Glossary

abdomen   The part of an animal's body that contains the digestive system and the organs of reproduction. In insects and spiders, the abdomen makes up the rear of the body.

acid rain   Rain that has combined with pollution in the atmosphere to form an acid, killing plants.

adaptation   A change that occurs in an animal's behavior or body form to allow it to survive and breed in new conditions.

algae   The simplest forms of plant life.

altitude   The height of a place or object above sea level.

altricial   The condition of being helpless at birth, used to describe newly hatched chicks of some birds.

ambush   To attack prey by surprise.

amphibian   A vertebrate that can live on land and in water. Amphibians (frogs, toads, salamanders, caecilians, and newts) are similar to reptiles, but they have moist skin and they lay their eggs in water.

anal fin   An unpaired fin located on the lower surface of a fish's abdomen. It plays an important role in swimming.

ancestor   A plant or animal from which a later form of plant or animal evolved.

Antarctica   The extremely cold continent on which the South Pole is situated.

antenna   A slender organ on an animal's head that it uses to sense smells and vibrations in its surroundings. Insects have two antennae.

antivenin   A medicine to counteract the effects of venom from the bites or stings of venomous animals.

antlers   Bony growths from the head of deer that grow and shed during the year. They are used as weapons and for display.

aquatic   Living all or most of the time in water.

arachnid   An arthropod with four pairs of walking legs. Arachnids include spiders, scorpions, ticks, and mites.

Arctic   The very cold region at the North Pole. In contrast to the South Pole, which is on land, the North Pole is situated on frozen ocean.

arid   Having low rainfall and very little vegetation. A very arid area is a desert.

arthropod   An animal with jointed legs and a hard exoskeleton. Arthropods make up the largest group of animals on Earth and include insects, spiders, crustaceans, centipedes, and millipedes.

avian   Of or about birds. Birds form the class Aves in the animal kingdom.

baleen   The comblike, fibrous plates found in some whales. They hang from the upper jaw and are used to sieve food from sea water. Baleen is often referred to as "whalebone."

barb   A part of a bird's feather. Barbs emerge from the central shaft of a feather in a parallel arrangement, like the teeth on a comb.

barbel   A slender, fleshy outgrowth on the lower jaw of a fish. It is equipped with sensory and chemical receptors ("taste buds") and is used by the fish to find food.

barbules   Small structures arranged along the length of a barb of a feather. They have tiny hooks, which lock onto the barbules of a neighboring barb, giving the feather its strength.

birds of prey   Flesh-eating land birds that hunt and kill their prey. Hawks and eagles are known as diurnal birds of prey; owls are nocturnal birds of prey.

bony fish   A fish with a bony skeleton. Other characteristics include a covering over the gills, and a swim bladder. Most bony fishes also have scales on their skin.

book lungs   Lungs found in primitive insects, consisting of "pages" of tissue through which blood and oxygen circulate.

browser   A mammal that uses its hands or lips to pick leaves from trees, or from low-growing woody plants.

camouflage   The colors and patterns of an animal that enable it to blend in with the background. Camouflage conceals the animal from predators and helps it to ambush prey.

canine teeth   The teeth between the incisors and molars of mammals.

carnassial teeth   Special cheek teeth with sharp, scissor-like edges used by carnivores to tear up food.

carnivore   An animal that eats mainly meat. Most carnivorous mammals are predators, while some are both predators and scavengers. Most carnivores eat some plant material as well as meat.

carrion   The rotting flesh and other remains of dead animals.

cartilaginous fish   A fish with a skeleton made of cartilage, such as a shark, ray, or chimaera.

caterpillar   The larva of a butterfly or moth.

caudal fin   An unpaired fin located toward the tail end of a fish.

cephalothorax   In arachnids and crustaceans, a region of the body that combines the head and thorax. It is covered by a hard body case.

chelicerae   Pincerlike, biting mouthparts, such as the fangs, found in spiders, ticks, scorpions, and mites.

chitin   A hard, plastic-like substance that gives an exoskeleton its strength.

chrysalis   The form taken by a butterfly in the pupal stage of its metamorphosis, or the case in which it undergoes this stage.

claspers   The modified inner edges of the pelvic fins of male sharks, rays, and chimaeras, used for the transferring of sperm to the female.

climate The pattern of weather that occurs in a place over an extended period of time. The Earth can be divided into a number of climatic zones.

cloaca The internal chamber in fishes, amphibians, reptiles, birds, and some mammals (monotremes), into which the contents of the reproductive ducts and the waste ducts empty before being passed from the body.

clutch The full and completed set of eggs laid by a female bird or reptile in a single nesting attempt.

cocoon In insects and spiders, a case made of silk used to protect themselves or their eggs. In amphibians, a protective case made of mud, mucus, or a similar material, in which the animal rests during estivation.

cold-blooded Not able to keep the body at a stable, warm temperature by internal means. All arthropods, including insects and spiders, are cold-blooded. Reptiles are also cold-blooded, but they control their body temperature by their behavior.

colony A group of animals that live, hunt, and defend themselves together. Many insect colonies consist of a family of animals produced by a single queen.

competitors Two or more animals that may fight for the same food, territory, or mating partner.

complete metamorphosis A way of developing in which a young insect changes shape from an egg to a larva, to a pupa, to an adult. Insects such as beetles and butterflies develop by complete metamorphosis.

compound eye An eye that is made up from many smaller eyes, each with its own lens. Compound eyes are found in most insects, but not in spiders.

conservation Looking after the Earth's resources for future generations of plants and animals, including humans.

continent One of Earth's seven major land masses: Europe, Asia, Africa, North America, South America, Australia, and Antarctica.

convergent evolution The situation in which different, unrelated animal species in different parts of the world evolve to look similar because they live in similar ways.

coral reef A structure made from the skeletons of coral animals, or polyps, found in warm waters.

crest In a lizard, a line of large, scaly spines on the neck and back. In birds, a line of feathers on the top of the head. Lizards and many birds, such as cockatoos, can raise or lower their crest to communicate with other animals.

crop A thin-walled, saclike pocket of the gullet, used to store food before digestion or to feed chicks by regurgitation.

crocodilians Crocodiles, caimans, alligators, gavials, or the tomistoma. Members of the order Crocodilia.

crustacean A mostly aquatic animal, such as a lobster, crab, or prawn, that has a hard skeleton on the outside of its body.

deforestation The cutting down of forest trees for timber, or to clear land for farming or building.

desert A dry area with low rainfall and sparse vegetation that is adapted to withstand drought.

dewlap In a lizard, a flap of skin, sometimes brightly colored, on the throat. A dewlap usually lies close to the neck and can be extended to communicate with other lizards.

dinosaurs A group of reptiles that dominated Earth from the Triassic to the Cretaceous Period (245–65 million years ago). The largest land animals that ever lived, dinosaurs are more closely related to today's birds and crocodilians than they are to other living reptiles.

display Behavior used by an animal to communicate with its own species, or with other animals. Displays, which can include postures, actions, or showing brightly colored parts of the body, may signal threat, defence, or readiness to mate.

diurnal Active during the day. Most reptiles are diurnal because they rely on the Sun's heat to provide energy for hunting and other activities.

DNA A molecule, found in chromosomes of a cell nucleus, that contains genes. "DNA" stands for deoxyribonucleic acid.

domestication The process of taming and breeding an animal for human use. Domesticated animals include pets and animals used for sport or work, such as horses and dairy cattle.

dorsal fin The large fin on the back of some fishes and aquatic mammals. It helps the animal to keep its balance as it moves through the water. Some fishes have two or three dorsal fins.

drag The resistance caused by the shape of an animal to its movement through the air, soil, or water.

dragline A strand of silk that spiders leave behind them as they move about.

drone A male honeybee. Drones mate with young queens, but unlike worker bees, they do not help in collecting food or maintaining the hive.

echolocation A system of navigation that relies on sound rather than sight or touch. Dolphins, porpoises, many bats, and some birds use echolocation to tell them where they are, where their prey is, and if anything is in their way.

ecosystem A community of plants and animals and the environment to which they are adapted.

ecotourism Tourism, such as trips to see animals in their natural habitat, that promotes ecological awareness. By promoting respect for the environment and educating tourists in appropriate behavior, ecotourism also limits damage to the animals' often sensitive habitat.

egg sac A silk bag that some spiders spin around their eggs. Some egg sacs are portable, so the eggs can be carried from place to place. Others are more like a blanket, and are attached to leaves or suspended from twigs.

egg tooth A special scale on the tip of the upper lip of a hatchling lizard or snake. It is used to break a hole in the egg so that the newborn animal can escape. The egg tooth falls off within a few days of hatching.

electroreceptors   Specialized organs found in some fishes (such as sharks) and mammals (such as platypuses) that detect electrical activity from the body of other animals. Electroreceptors also help the animal to navigate by detecting distortions in the electrical field of its surroundings—for example, those caused by a reef.

elytra   The thickened front wings of beetles that cover and protect the back wings.

embryo   An unborn animal in the earliest stages of development. An embryo may grow inside its mother's body, or in an egg outside her body.

endangered   In danger of becoming extinct. A plant or animal can become endangered because of environmental changes or human activities.

environment   The natural surroundings of a community of plants and animals, particularly the shape of the land, the climate, and the soil.

estivate   To spend a period of time in a state of inactivity to avoid unfavorable conditions. During times of drought, many frogs greatly reduce their overall metabolic rate and estivate underground until rain falls.

estuary   The mouth of a river, where its currents meet the ocean's tides.

evolution   The gradual change, over many generations, in plants and animals.

exoskeleton   A hard external skeleton or body case. All arthropods are protected by an exoskeleton.

exotic   A foreign or non-native species of animal or plant, often introduced into a habitat by humans.

extinct   Describes a species of animal or plant that no longer survives because all the individual animals or plants of that kind have died.

feral   A wild animal or plant, or a species that was once domesticated but has returned to its wild state.

fledgling   A young bird that has recently grown its first true feathers and has just left its nest.

flippers   The broad front (and often, back) legs of some aquatic animals. Flippers are composed mainly of the bones of the fingers and hand, and act like paddles to "row" the animal through the water.

fossil   The remains or traces of a plant or animal, usually found between layers of rock.

frill   In a lizard, a collar around the neck. Like a crest or dewlap, a frill can be raised to signal to other lizards or to surprise a predator.

froglets   Frogs that are small, yet fully formed, when they hatch.

fry   Young or small fishes.

gastroliths   Stomach stones swallowed by animals such as crocodilians. They stay in the stomach to help crush food.

gestation period   The period of time during which a female animal is pregnant with her young.

gills   Organs that collect oxygen from water and are used for breathing. Gills are found in many aquatic animals, including fishes, some insects, and the larvae of amphibians.

gizzard   Found only in birds, a gizzard is the equivalent of the stomach in mammals. Grit and stones inside the gizzard help to grind up food. Food passes from the gizzard to the intestines.

global warming   The increase in the temperature of the Earth and its lower atmosphere, caused by the absorption of heat by water vapor and "greenhouse" gases, including carbon dioxide and methane. The trapped heat, which would otherwise be radiated out to space, will cause the polar icecaps to melt and ocean levels to rise. Global warming is also known as "the greenhouse effect."

grazer   An animal that feeds on grasses and plants that grow on the ground.

greenhouse effect   *See* **global warming**

grub   An insect larva, usually that of a beetle.

gullet   Found in birds, the gullet is the equivalent of the esophagus in mammals. This tube passes food from the bill to the gizzard.

habitat   The place where an animal naturally lives. Many different kinds of animals live in the same environment (for example, a rain forest), but each kind lives in a different habitat within that environment. For example, some animals in a rain forest live in the trees, while others live on the ground.

haltere   One of a pair of modified back wings of a fly. They help the fly to balance during flight.

harem   A group of female animals that mate and live with one male.

hatchling   A young animal, such as a bird or reptile, that has recently hatched from its egg.

heat-sensitive pit   Sense organs in some snakes that detect tiny changes in temperature.

herbivore   An animal that eats only plant material, such as leaves, bark, roots, and seeds.

hibernate   To remain completely inactive during the cold winter months. Some animals eat as much as they can before the winter, then curl up in a sheltered spot and fall into a very deep sleep. They live off the fat they have stored, and they slow their breathing and heartbeat to help conserve their energy until spring. Insects hibernate as either eggs, larvae, pupae, or adults.

hoof   The toe of a horse, deer, antelope, and related animal that is covered in thick, hard skin with sharp edges.

iceberg   A large, floating chunk of ice, broken from a glacier or ice sheet and carried out to sea.

incisors   The front teeth of an animal, located between the canines, used for cutting food.

incomplete metamorphosis   A way of developing in which a young insect gradually changes shape from an egg, to a nymph, to an adult.

incubate   To keep eggs in an environment, outside the female's body, in which they can develop and hatch. Most birds incubate their eggs by warming them with their body heat. The eggs of other birds and reptiles may incubate in soil, leaf litter, or a similar covering, with no further input from the parents.

insectivore   An animal that eats only or mainly insects or invertebrates. Some insectivores also eat vertebrates, such as frogs, lizards, and mice.

introduced   An animal or plant species imported from another place by humans and deliberately released into a habitat.

invertebrate   An animal that does not have a backbone. Many invertebrates are soft-bodied animals, such as worms, leeches, or octopuses, but most have a hard external skeleton, such as insects.

ivory   The hard, creamy white, bonelike substance that makes up the main part of the tusks of an elephant or walrus.

Jacobson's organ   Two small sensory pits on the top part of the mouth of snakes and lizards. They use this organ to analyse small molecules picked up from the air or ground with their tongue.

keratin   A protein found in horns, hair, scales, feathers, and fingernails.

krill   A small, shrimplike crustacean that lives in large numbers in Arctic and Antarctic waters.

lateral line   A sensory canal system along the sides of a fish. It detects moving objects by registering disturbances (or pressure changes) in the water.

larva   A young animal that looks completely different from its parents. An insect larva, sometimes called a grub, maggot, or caterpillar, changes into an adult by either complete or incomplete metamorphosis. In amphibians, the larval stage is the stage before metamorphosis that breathes with gills rather than lungs.

lift   The upward force that helps flying animals to stay in the air. Lift is produced when air flows over the wings.

live-bearing   Giving birth to young that are fully formed.

luminous   Describes something that either reflects or radiates light. Some deepsea fishes can produce their own light source by using luminous bacteria.

maggot   The larva of a fly.

mammal   A warm-blooded vertebrate that suckles its young with milk and has a single bone in its lower jaw. Although most mammals have hair and give birth to live young, some, such as whales and dolphins, have very little or no hair, and others, the monotremes, lay eggs.

mandibles   The biting jaws of an insect.

marine park   An area of the ocean set aside as a reserve to protect endangered species and to preserve the marine environment.

marsupial   A mammal that gives birth to young that are not fully developed. These young are usually protected in a pouch (where they feed on milk) before they can move around independently.

metamorphosis   A way of developing in which an animal's body changes shape. Many invertebrates, including insects and amphibians such as salamanders, undergo metamorphosis as they mature.

migration   A seasonal journey from one habitat to another. Many animals migrate hundreds or even thousands of miles to another location to find food, and often to mate and lay eggs or give birth.

molars   A mammal's side cheek teeth.

mollusk   An animal, such as a snail or squid, with no backbone and a soft body that is partly or fully enclosed by a shell.

molt   To shed an outer layer of the body, such as hair, skin, scales, feathers, or the exoskeleton.

monotreme   A primitive mammal with many features in common with reptiles. Monotremes lay eggs and have a cloaca. They are the only mammals that lack teats, although they feed their young milk released through ducts on their belly.

niche   The ecological role played by a species within an animal community.

nocturnal   Active at night. Nocturnal animals have special adaptations, such as large, sensitive eyes or ears, to help them find their way in the dark. All nocturnal animals rest during the day.

nomadic   An animal that has no fixed territory, instead wandering from place to place in search of food and water.

nymph   The young stage of an insect that develops by incomplete metamorphosis. Nymphs are often similar to adults, but do not have fully developed wings.

ocean   A very large stretch of sea.

ocellus   A kind of simple eye with a single lens. Insects usually have three ocelli on the top of their head.

omnivore   An animal that eats both plant and animal food. They have teeth and a digestive system designed to process almost any kind of food.

opposable   Used to describe a thumb that can reach around and touch all of the other fingers on the same hand, or a toe that can similarly touch the other toes on the same foot.

order   A major group that taxonomists use when classifying living things.

osteoderm   In reptiles, a lump of bone in the skin that provides protection against predators. Most crocodilians and some lizards are protected by osteoderms, as well as by thick, strong skin.

oviparous   Describes a fish that lays eggs. Little or no development occurs within the mother's body; instead, the embryos develop inside the eggs. Each egg eventually hatches into a young fish.

ovipositor   A tubelike organ through which female insects lay their eggs. The stinger of bees and wasps is an modified ovipositor.

ovoviviparous   Describes a fish that gives birth to live young which have developed and hatched from eggs within the mother's body.

pair bond   A partnership maintained between a male and a female animal, particularly birds, through one or several breeding attempts. Some species maintain a pair bond for life.

parasite   An animal or plant that lives and feeds on another living animal or plant, sometimes with harmful effects. "Parasitic" describes the activities or features of a parasite.

passerine   Any species of bird belonging to the order Passeriformes. A passerine is often described as a "songbird" or a "perching-bird."

pectines   On scorpions, sensory organs found on the underside of the abdomen. They are used for detecting scents, vibrations, and textures.

pectoral fins   In fishes and aquatic mammals, the paired fins attached to each side of the animal and used for lift and control of movement. In fishes, they are usually located just behind the gills.

pedicel   The narrow "waist" that connects an insect's head to its thorax, or a spider's cephalothorax to its abdomen.

pedipalp   One of a pair of small, leglike organs on the head of insects and the cephalothorax of spiders and scorpions, used for feeling or handling food. In spiders, they are also used for mating.

pelvic fins   Paired fins, located on the lower part of a fish's body.

pheromone   A chemical released by an animal that sends a signal and affects the behavior of others of the same species. Many animals use pheromones to attract mates, or to signal danger.

phytoplankton   Tiny, single-celled algae that float on or near the surface of the sea.

placental mammal   A mammal that does not lay eggs (as monotremes do), or give birth to underdeveloped young (as marsupials do). Instead, it nourishes its developing young inside its body with a blood-rich organ called a placenta.

plankton   The plant (phytoplankton) or animal (zooplankton) organisms that float or drift in the open sea. Plankton forms an important link in the food chain.

plumage   All the feathers on a bird.

poach   To hunt animals illegally. A person who does this is called a poacher.

pollen   A dustlike substance produced by male flowers, or by the male organs in a flower, and used in reproduction.

pollination   The process by which the pollen produced by the male organs of a flower come into contact with the female parts of the flower, thus fertilizing the flower and enabling seeds to form.

pores   Tiny openings in the skin.

precocial   The condition of being active and self-reliant at birth, used to describe newly hatched chicks of some birds.

predator   An animal that lives mainly by killing and eating other animals.

preen   Of a bird, to clean, repair, and arrange plumage.

prehensile   Grasping or gripping. Some tree-dwelling mammals and reptiles have prehensile feet or a tail that can be used as an extra limb to help them stay safely in a tree. Elephants have a prehensile "finger" on the end of their trunk so they can pick up small pieces of food. Browsers, such as giraffes, have prehensile lips to help them grip leaves. The prehensile tongue of parrots enables them to extract kernels from shells.

prey   An animal that is hunted, killed, and eaten by predators.

proboscis   In insects, a long, tubular mouthpart used for feeding. In some mammals, a proboscis is an elongated nose, snout, or trunk. The proboscis of an elephant has many functions, including smelling, touching, and lifting.

pupa   The stage during which an insect transforms from a larva to an adult.

pupil   The round or slit-shaped opening in the centre of the eye. Light passes through this to the back of the eye.

queen   A female insect that begins a social insect colony. The queen is normally the only member of the colony that lays eggs.

quills   Long, sharp hairs of porcupines, echidnas, and a few other mammals.

rain forest   A tropical forest that receives at least 100 inches (250 cm)

of rain each year. Rain forests are home to a vast number of plant and animal species.

raptor   A diurnal bird of prey, such as a hawk or falcon. The term is not used to describe owls.

regurgitate   To bring food back up from the stomach to the mouth. Many hoofed mammals use this process to break down their food into a more liquid form. This is called "chewing the cud." Birds also regurgitate partially digested food to feed to their chicks.

roost   A place or site used by some animals, such as birds and bats, for sleeping. Also, the act of traveling to or gathering at such a place.

retractile claws   The claws of cats and similar animals that are usually protected in sheaths. Such claws spring out when the animal needs them to capture prey or to fight.

rival   An animal competing for food, territory, and mates.

rostrum   A tubular, beaklike feeding organ located on the head of some insects.

rudimentary   Describes a simple, undeveloped, or underdeveloped part of an animal's body, such as an organ or wing. The rudimentary parts of some modern-day animals are the traces of the functional parts of an early ancestor, but now serve no purpose.

savanna   Open grassland with scattered trees. Most savannas are found in subtropical areas that have a distinct summer wet season.

scales   Distinct thickened areas of skin that vary in size, from very small to large.

scavenger   An animal that eats carrion—often the remains of animals killed by predators.

scrub   An area of land covered with shrubs and low trees.

scutes   In a turtle or tortoise, the horny plates that cover the bony shell.

sea   A body of water that is partly or completely enclosed by land.

semiaquatic   Living some of the time in water, and some of the time on land.

silk   A strong but elastic substance made by many insects and spiders. Silk is liquid until it leaves the animal's body.

social   Living in groups. Social animals can live in breeding pairs, sometimes together with their young, or in a colony or herd of thousands of animals.

solitary   Living alone. Solitary animals usually meet others of the same species during the breeding season. At other times they avoid each other's company.

spawn   To release eggs and sperm together directly into the water.

species   A group of animals with very similar features that are able to breed together and produce fertile young.

spermatophore   A container or package of sperm that is passed from male to female during mating.

spinnerets   The fingerlike appendages of spiders that are connected to silk glands, found near the tip of the abdomen.

spiracle   A small opening that leads into the trachea, or breathing tube, of an insect or spider. In cartilaginous fishes, spiracles are located behind the eyes. They take in water for breathing when the fish is at rest on the bottom, or when the mouth is being used for feeding.

squalene   A substance found in the liver oil of deepsea sharks. It is refined and used as a high-grade machine oil in high-technology industries; as a human health and dietary supplement; and in cosmetics.

stinger   A hollow structure on the tail of insects and scorpions that pierces flesh and injects venom.

streamlining   This gives an animal a smooth body shape to reduce drag.

stridulate   To make a sound by scraping things together. Many insects communicate in this way, some by scraping their legs against their body.

stylet   A sharp mouthpart used for piercing plants or animals.

subantarctic   Describes the oceans and islands just north of Antarctica.

swamp   An area of wet land containing plants adapted to growing in water. Also called a marsh or wetland.

swim bladder   A gas-filled, baglike organ in the abdomen of bony fishes. It enables the fishes to remain at a particular depth in the water.

tadpole   The larva of a frog, just after hatching. Tadpoles are aquatic and take in oxygen from the water through gills.

temperate   Describes an environment or region that has a warm (but not very hot) summer and a cool (but not very cold) winter. Most of the world's temperate regions are located between the tropics and the polar regions.

tentacles   On marine invertebrates, long, thin structures used to feel and grasp, or to inject venom. On caecilians, sensory organs located on the sides of the head, possibly used for tasting and smelling.

territory   An area of land inhabited by an animal and defended against intruders. The area often contains all the living resources required by the animal, such as food and a nesting or roosting site.

thermal   A column of rising air, used by birds to gain height.

thorax   The middle part of an animal's body. In insects, the thorax is divided from the head with a narrow "waist," or pedicel. In spiders, the thorax and head make up a single unit.

tide   The repeating rise and fall of the Earth's seas, caused by the pull of the Moon and Sun on the water.

trachea   A breathing tube in an animal's body. In vertebrates, there is one trachea (or windpipe), through which air passes to the lungs. Insects and some spiders have many small tracheae that spread throughout their body.

tropical   Describes an environment or region near the Equator that is warm to hot all year round.

tropical forests   Forests growing in tropical regions, such as central Africa, northern South America, and southeast

Asia, that experience little difference in temperature throughout the year. *See* **rain forest**

tundra   A cold, barren area where much of the soil is frozen and the vegetation consists mainly of mosses, lichens, and other small plants adapted to withstand intense cold. Tundra is found near the Arctic Circle and on mountain tops.

tusks   The very long teeth of mammals, such as elephants, pigs, hippos, musk deer, walruses, and narwhals. They are used in fights and for self-defense.

ungulate   A plant-eating mammal with hoofs.

venom   Poison injected by animals into a predator or prey through fangs, stingers, spines, or similar structures.

venomous   Describes an animal that is poisonous. Venomous animals usually attack by biting or stinging.

vertebrate   An animal with a backbone. All vertebrates have an internal skeleton of cartilage or bone. Fishes, reptiles, birds, amphibians, and mammals are vertebrates.

viviparous   Describes fishes that give birth to live young, such as some sharks. Like mammals, the shark embryos develop inside their mother and are nourished by a placenta. After nine months to a year, live young are born.

warm-blooded   Able to keep the internal body temperature more or less the same, regardless of the outside temperature, by internal means. Birds and mammals are warm-blooded.

woodland   An area of land covered with widely spaced trees and shrubs.

worker   A social insect that collects food and tends a colony's young, but which usually cannot reproduce.

zooplankton   The tiny animals that, together with phytoplankton, form the plankton that drifts on or near the sea's surface. Zooplankton is eaten by some whales, fishes, and seabirds.

zygodactylous   Describes the feet of some birds, on which two of the four toes point forward, and the other two toes point backward.

Index

Page references in *italics* indicate photographs or illustrations.

aardvarks 58, *58*, 279
adders
　death adder 206
　European adder 237
African hunting dogs 45, 77
Age of the Reptiles 200–1
agnathans 108, 110–11,
　122–3, 134, 135
albatross 27, 157, 159, 165,
　184, *185*, 185, 186
　wandering *162*, 162
algae 28, 31, 33, 113, 116,
　147, 306
　brown 32
　and coral polyps 119
alligators 33, 205, 206, *209*,
　209, *242*, 242, *243*, 307
　American 244, *247*, 247
　Chinese *246–7*, 246–7
Allosaurus 201
alpaca 25
alpine regions *24–5*, 24–5
alveoli 251
amber, trap for insects 254,
　255, 255
Amolops 221
amphibians 14, 51, *54*, 54, 88,
　196–7, *196–203*, 306, 307,
　309
　adaptations 202–03, 212–13,
　220, 221
　behavior 204–9, 307, 308
　classification 198–9
　eggs *198*, 198
　endangered species 210–11
　evolution 200–01, 216
　skin color 199, 207, 214,
　215, 221
　tadpoles 204, 209, 217–18,
　219, 220, 221, 311
　taxonomy 301–302
　temperature regulation 204–5
　see also caecilians; frogs;
　salamanders; toads
amphisbaenians 226, *238–9*,
　238–9, 279
ampullae of Lorenzini 127
anaconda *211*, 211, 232
anapsids 222
anemonefishes *116*, 116, *146*,
　146
angelfishes 145
anglerfishes 116, 138
Antarctica 26–7, 29, 146, 183,
　195, 306, 309
antbirds 166, 174
anteaters 10, 56
　collared *56*, 56

giant 48, 56, *57*, 57
　scaly *see* pangolins
　spiny *see* echidnas
antelopes 14, *16*, 16, *40*, *44*,
　44, 45, 95, 98, 101
　horns *101*, 101
antlers 42, 100, 306
　growth cycle *101*, 101
antlions 277
ants *251*, 251, 256, 260, 274–7
　army ant 256
　bulldog ant *277*, 277
　desert ant 258
　Dinoponera 277
　driver ant *276*, 276
　fire ant 22
　green ant 256
　green weaver ant 276
　honeypots *276*, 276, 277
　imitation by spiders 289
　leaf-cutter ant 257, 277
　nesting 256
　pheromones 260
　reproduction *276*, 276
　sugar ant 277
　weaver ant 256
　white ant *see* termites
　wood ant 259
　workers 251, 256, 311
apes 39, 68, *70*, 70
aphids 260, 263, 283
arachnids 252, 289, 292–3, 306
　see also mites; ticks;
　scorpions; spiders
arawana *135*, 135
Archaeopteryx 154, *155*, 155,
　173
Archelon 201, 201
archerfishes *114*, 114
Archosauria 242
Arctic 26–7, 70, 72, 86, 102,
　306, 309
armadillos 56, 57
Arsinoitherium 39, 39
arthropods 250, 252, 254, 264,
　306, 307
　see also insects; spiders
artiodactyls 98
asses 94
　domestic *see* burro
Atlantic guitarfish 132
auks *165*, 165, 178, 184
Australopithecus afarensis 39,
　39
Autarchoglossa 231
avocets *32*, 32, *157*, 157, 183
axolotl 215
aye-aye *41*, 41, 67

babirusa *98*, 98
baboons *42*, 42, 43–4, 69
backswimmer *282*, 283
badgers *81*, 81
bagworms 257
　caterpillars *256*, 256
baleen 84–5, 306
bandicoots 44, 54
barracuda 112, 116, 146
basilisks *207*, 207, 230
bass 146
bats 10, 62–5, 310
　disk-winged bat 10
　fishing bat 63
　free-tailed bat *63*, 63
　hammer-headed bat *65*, 65
　horseshoe bat *63*, 63
　lesser long-nosed bat *19*, 19
　long-eared bat *62*, 62
　moth hunting 267
　spotted evening bat *63*, 63
　tent-building bat 10, *62*, 62
　vampire bat 45, 63–4
bears 36, 38, 42, 46, 72–5
　black bear 22, *73*, 73, *74*, 74
　body parts for medicine
　46, 48
　brown bear 22, *73*, 73
　grizzly *see* bears, brown
　Kodiak *see* bears, brown
　polar bear *26*, 26, 27, *47*, 47,
　72, 73, 74, *75*, 75
　sloth bear 72, 73, 279
　spectacled bear 72
　sun bear 72, 73
　teeth 78
　winter sleep 74
beavers 22, *102*, 102
bedbugs 282–3
beehive 256, *274*, 274
bees 251, 264, 274–7
　bumblebee 27, 274
　carpenter bee 257, 275
　communication *259*, 259
　cuckoo bee 276
　digger bee 275
　drones 275, 307
　green metallic bee 274
　honeybee *250*, 250, *259*, 259,
　264, 264, *274*, 274, 275
　killer bee 259–60
　leafcutter bee 274
　mason bee 276
　mining bee 276
　orchid bee 260
　parasitic 276
　pheromones 260
　queens *260*, 260, 310

sting 275
　workers 256, *260*, 260, *274*,
　274, 311
　see also hornets; wasps
beetles 27, 264, 268–71
　antennae *268*, 268, *269*, 269,
　306
　auger beetle 268
　blister beetle 270, 271
　bombardier beetle 271
　camouflage 271
　carpet beetle 269
　carrion beetle 258, 270
　case-bearing leaf beetle 257
　chafer beetle 268
　clerid beetle 268
　click-beetle *259*, 259, 271
　Colorado beetle *270*, 270
　darkling beetle *268*, 268
　deathwatch beetle 270–1
　devil's coach-horse beetle 269
　diving beetle *271*, 271
　dung beetle 258, 261, 264,
　271, 271
　feather-winged beetle 268
　firefly 260
　goliath beetle 268
　ground beetle 269
　harlequin beetle 268, *269*
　hercules beetle 268, *270*, 270
　jewel beetle 269
　larvae 270
　leaf-mining beetle 257
　lily beetle 259
　longhorn beetle 268, 270,
　271
　May beetle 280
　metamorphosis *269*, 269,
　307, 308
　movement *263*, 263
　oil beetle 271
　parasitic *277*, 277
　pheromones 270
　rove beetle 268
　scarabs 268, *271*, 271
　spider beetle 269
　stag beetle 269
　tenebrionid 270
　tiger beetle 258, *264*, 264,
　269
　tortoise beetle *269*, 269, 271
　violin beetle *269*, 269
　whirligigs 269, *270*, 270, 271
belugas *85*, 85
bilby 54
billfishes 145
biodiversity 264, 265
birds 32, 150–1, 307, 308

adaptations 153, 155, 156–7, 161, 171, 173, 175, 178, 180, 183, 185, 187–8
behavior 158–63
bills *157*, 157, 177, 178–9, 180, *182*, 182, 183
body temperature control 156, 161
classification 152–3
courtship rituals *158*, 158–9, *170*, 170, 175, 180, 181, 183, 185, 188
effect of DDT on 165
egg-laying 180, 189, 194, 307, 309
endangered species 164–7
evolution 154–6
feathers 26, 150, 152–3, 182, 194, 306, 308
see also plumage
flight 24, 152–3, 156–7, *162*, 162, *186*, 186, 311
flightless 155, 178, 180, 192–5
food gathering 22, 156, 157, 161, 308
furcula 152, 154
gamebirds 168
land birds 168 77
migration 22, 27, 33, 162–3, 172, 178, 181, 182, 186–7, 309
molting 179–80, 309
nest building 159–60, 171, 173, *174*, 174, 174–5, 180, 182, 184, 188, 195
pecten 153
plumage *158*, 158, 181, 192, 310
raptors 186–91, 306
skeleton 152–3
syrinx 177
taxonomy 299–301
vision 153, *156*, 156
wading birds 33, 180–2
waterbirds 178–85
birds of paradise 167
raggiana *159*, 159
birds of prey *see* buzzards; caracaras; eagles; falcons; goshawks; griffons; gymnogene; harriers; hawks; kestrels; kites; owls; raptors; secretarybird; vultures
bison 21, 47, *48*
bittern 160–1
blackbuck 44, *101*, 101
Blanus cinereus 239, 239
blennies 117, *149*, 149
blowhole 84
blubber 26, 84
blue tit *175*, 175
bluefish *33*, 33

boas 233
constrictor 234, 235
sand boa 232–3
body temperature
amphibians 204–5
birds 156, 161
cold-blooded 307
mammals 40
regulation 60, 204
reptiles 204–5
warm-blooded 311
bongo 101
bony fishes *108*, 108, 109, 110, 134–49, 306, 311
bonytongues 135–6
boobies *183*, 183, 184
bovids 101
bowerbirds *158*, 158
boxfishes 149
Brachiosaurus 201
bristlemouths 138
bristletails *254–5*, 255
bristleworms 28
broadbills 166–7, *173*, 173
brush turkeys 160
buffalo 21, 101
Bufo (true toads) 216, 220–1
bugs
ambush bug 283
assassin bug 258, 282, 283
bedbug 282–3
boxelder bug 282
damsel bug 282
giant waterbug 261, *282*, 282
harlequin bug 283
jagged ambush bug 283
ladybug *256*, 256, *261*, 261, *262*, 262
milkweed bug *282*, 282
ripple bug 283
shield bug *283*, 283
squash bug 282
stilt bug 282
stink bug 282, 283
true bugs 282–3
water bug 283
bullfrogs *211*, 211, 219
bunting, painted *176*, 176
burro *95*, 95
bush babies 66
butcherbirds 176
butterflies 27, 264, 265, 266–7, 306, 307
antennae *267*, 267, 306
harvester butterfly 267
migration 263
monarch butterfly 260–1, *263*, 263, 264
painted lady 263
Queen Alexandra's birdwing 266
swallowtail *266*, 266
zebra butterfly *12*, 12
butterfly ranching 265

butterflyfishes 113, 135–6, 144–5
freshwater *134*, 134
long-nosed 145
Meyer's *145*, 145
ornate 145
buzzards 187, 188, 189

caddis flies 257, *261*, 261
caecilians 203, 212–13, 311
caimans *242*, 242, 247, 307
black 247
common 247
Cuvier's dwarf *242*, *245*, 245, *246*, 246
Schneider's dwarf 243
camels 17, *98*, 98
camouflage 23, 31, 206, 221, 230, 273, *288*, 288, 306
capybara 102, *103*, 103
caracal *78*, 78
caracaras 190
Carboniferous Period 254, 255
Carcharodon 111
cardinalfishes 117, 145
caribou 26, *27*, 27, *100*, 100
carnivores 39, 72, 73, 76, 78, 80–3, 252, 306
carp *137*, 137
cartilage 124
cartilaginous fishes *108*, 108, 118, 124–33, 306, 311
chimaeras 124
rays 108
sharks 108, 109
see also rays; sharks
cassowary 192, *193*, 193
caterpillars 257, 262, 264, *266*, 266, 287, 306, 309
bagworm *256*, 256
color *258*, 258
movement *262*, 262
puss moth *260*, 260
catfishes 14, 112, 139–40
electric catfish *139*, 139
European wels 139
royal catfish 139
walking catfish 140
cats 78–9, 310
fishing cat *33*, 33, 79
see also caracals; cheetahs; cougars; jaguar; leopards; lions; lynx; margay; pumas; servals; tigers
cattle 21, 98, 101, 307
cerci 272
cetaceans 84–7
see also dolphins; porpoises; whales
chameleons 202, 206, *207*, 207, 208, *227*, 227, 228, 230
Knysna dwarf *230*, 230
skin color 230
cheetahs 14, *40*, 47, 79

chelonians 222–5
see also tortoises; turtles
chimaeras 124, 306
chimpanzees *70*, 70, 71
Chiromantis 221
chitin 250, 251, 252, 306
Chondrichthyians 111
chrysalis 262, 266, 306
chuckwallas 228
cicadas 260, 262, *283*, 283
cichlids 115, 116, 121
ciguatera 137, 149
civets 12, 82, *83*, 83
banded linsang *82*, 82
Cladoselache 124
clams 29 30
claws *41*, 41, *51*, 51, 56, 66, *78*, 78, 79, 310
cleaner birds 162
cleaner fishes 116–17
Climatius 111, 111
cloaca 50, 241, 307
clownfish *see* anemonefishes
coatis *75*, 75
cobras 234, *235*, 235, 236
cock-of-the-rock *175*, 175
cockatoos 171, 307
cockroaches 251, *254*, 254, 260
codfishes 112, 146
coelacanths 111, *120*, 120, 134
coelurosaur *154*, 154
Coelurosauravus 201, 201
colocolo 55
condors *24*, 24, 186, 190, *191*, 191
conifers *8*, *22–3*, 22, 23
convergent evolution 41, 307
coots 182
coral bleaching 119–20
coral crouchers 143
coral reefs *30–1*, 30, 31, 33, 113, *118*, 118, 119–20, 307
cormorants 27, 184, *185*, 185
flightless *195*, 195
cornetfishes 142
cougar 22
cowfishes 149
coyotes 22, 76
cranes 159, 163, 164, 181–2
crowned crane *181*, 181
sarus crane *164*, 164
Siberian crane *166*, 166
whooping crane 167
Cretaceous Period 39, 154, 155
crickets 260, 272–3
bush cricket 259, 260, *272*, 272, 273
desert cricket 272
giant weta *258*, 258, 259
king cricket 272
mole cricket 272, *273*, 273
secret cave cricket 272
snowy tree cricket 272

crocodile icefish 146
crocodiles 14, 33, *204*, 204, 208, 209, *242*, 242, 307
  American 246
  dwarf 246
  Johnston's *244*, 244
  nest temperature 244
  Nile 206, 244, *245*, 245
  parenting 244
  saltwater (Indopacific) 206, 242, 245–6
  slender-snouted 246
crocodilians 242–7, 307, 308
crows 176
cuckoos 160, 170
curlews 182, 184
cuscus 54
cynodonts 38
Cynognathus 38

damselfishes 116, 146–7
damselflies 255, 262, 281, 287
deer 23, *27*, 27, 98, *100*, 100–1
  antlers 100, *101*, 101
  barking deer *see* muntjac
  foot *98*, 98
  water deer (Asian) 100
deforestation 12, 47, 97, 307
Deinonychus 200, 200
Deinosuchus 201, 201
Dermophis mexicanus 212, 212
deserts *8*, *16–17*, *18–19*, 16–19, 307
desman, Pyrenean *60*, 60
dholes 76
diapsids 222
Dicranurus 254, 254
Dimetrodon 201, 201
dingoes 50, 76
Dinoponera ants 277
Dinornis maximus 192, 192
dinosaurs 39, 154–5, 192, 200–2, 307
Diplodocus 201
dippers 174
diprotodonts 53
dodo *164*, 164
dogs 22, *45*, 45, 76–7, 90
  behavior 43, 76–7
  see also African hunting dogs; coyotes; dholes; dingoes; foxes; jackals; maned wolf; wolves
dolphinfishes *144*, 144
dolphins 31, 38, 40, 84, 86
  bottlenose dolphin *86*, 86
  common dolphin 87
  Fraser's dolphin 49
  Hector's dolphin *85*, 85
  orca (killer whale) 84, *85*, 85, 87
  pantropical spotted dolphin 49
  spinner dolphin *49*, 49, 87

dominance 43–4, 66, 76, 101
donkey *see* burro
dottybacks 145
doves *18*, 18, *169*, 169
dragonfishes *138*, 138
dragonflies 27, *33*, 33, 251, 258, *261*, 261, 263, *281*, 281
  Meganeura monyi 255
  wings *263*, 263
drones 275, 307
drongos *177*, 177
ducks 27, 156, 178–9, 180
  black-headed duck 180
  king eider duck *179*, 179
  sea duck 178, 179
  wood duck *166*, 166
dugongs 32, *89*, 89
duikers 101
Dunkleosteus 111, 111

eagles 10, 22, 32, 153, 156, 187
  bald eagle *187*, 187, 188
  giant eagle 47
  Great Philippine eagle *167*, 167
  harpy eagle *166*, 166, *187*, 187, 188
  sea eagle 191
ears 77, 91, 92–3, *104*, 104
earwigs 261
echidnas 45, 50–1, *51*, 310
echolocation *62*, 62, 63, 64, 86–7, 173, 267, 307
ecosystem 12, 307
ecotourism 119, 307
edentates *see* xenarthrans
eels 109, 116, *136*, 136
  Congo eel 136
  electric eel 136
  freshwater eel 137
  gulper eel *113*, 113
  moray eels 134, 136–7
    dragon moray 136
    leaf-nosed moray 136
    ribbon moray *31*, 31
egg-laying 50, *158*, 158, 160, 174, 261
  amphibians 198, 217
  birds 80, 189, 194, 307, 309
  fishes 115–16
  insects 256, 260–261, 275–6, 281, 283, 291
  reptiles 198, 223–4, 225, 227–8, 236, 309
egrets 181
  cattle egret *21*, 21, 181
  great egret *32*, 32
Elasmosaurus 201, 201
electric fish 114
electroreception 51, 114, 116, 126–7, 308
elephant shrew 58, *59*, 59
elephantnose fish *134*, 134

elephants 10, 21, 14, *37*, 37, 43, 49, 90–3
  African 90, *91*, 91, *93*, 93
  ancestors *59*, 59, *90*, 90
  Asian *12*, 12, 90, 91, *93*, 93
  ears 91, 92–3
  front feet *90*, 90
  temperature control 90–1
  trunk 90, *91*, 91–2, *92*, 93, 310
elks 23, 25
  American elk *see* wapiti
  antlers *101*, 101
emu 192, *193*, 193–4
endangered species 12, 21–2, 46–9, 54, 57, 59, 60, 72, 75, 77, 79–80, 94, 95, 96, 97, 118–21, 164–7, 169, 210–11, 218, 240, 241, 246, 264–5, 308
Eocene Period 155, 186
Epicrionops petersi 213, 213
estivation 14, 18, 205, 217, 224, 225, 308
estuaries *32–3*, 32–3, 308
euphonia 177
Euthenopteron 200, 200
exoskeleton 250, 252, 254
extinctions 39, 46, 164–7, 210
  see also endangered species

fairy-wrens *172*, 172
falconets 186
falconry 189
falcons 187, 188, *189*
  brown falcon 188
  Eleonora's falcon 186–7
  peregrine falcon *165*, 165, 187, 189–90
  pygmy falcon *188*, 188–9
felines (cats) 78–9, 83
ferrets, black-footed 21, 81–2
figbirds 176
filefishes *117*, 117, *148*, 148, 149
finches 157, 176, 177
  cardinal finch *157*, 157
  Gouldian finch *176*, 176
  woodpecker finch 162
fins
  anal 108, 306
  caudal (tail) 108, 306
  dorsal 108, 307
  pectoral 84, 108, 310
  pelvic 108, 306, 310
firefish *see* turkeyfish
fireflies *259*, 259, 260
fishes 14, 31, 32, 106–7, 307
  barbels 112, 128, 136, *138*, 138, 306
  behavior 114–17
  beneficial relationships 116–17
  camouflage 113, 116

classification 108–9
electroreception 114, 126–7, 308
endangered species 118–21
evolution 110–11
fins 84, 108, 306, 310
fossil record *110*, 110–11, *111*, 122, 129, 134
Garra species 112
gills 108, 109, 308
jawed fishes 108, 111
  bony fishes *108*, 108, 109, 110, 134–49, 306, 311
  cartilaginous fishes *108*, 108, 111, 118, 124–33, 306, 311
jawless fishes 108, 110–11, 122–3
jaws; teeth 134–5
lateral line 109, 114, 126, 309
light organs 113, 138, 143, 309
migration 22, 31, 32, 116–17, 123, 137
operculum (gill cover) 125
scales 108, *109*, 109, 125
sex change 114–15, 146, 148
swim bladder 125, 134, 137, 311
taxonomy 295–9
flamingos *180*, 180
flannel-mouthed characins 137
flashlight fishes *143*, 143
flatfishes *112*, 112–13
flathead, spiny 143
fleas *250*, 250
flies 27, 264, 280–1
  crane fly 280
  dance-fly 260
  disease carriers 281
  flesh fly 280
  fruit fly 280
  horsefly 250, *250–1*, 281
  house fly *280*, 280, 281
  hover fly *280*, 280–1
  liquid food 280–1
  metamorphosis 280
  mydas fly 280–1
  pyrgotid fly 280
  robber fly 280
  scorpion fly 287
  screw-worm fly 280
  snakefly fossil *255*, 255
  snipe fly 280–1
  stalk-eyed fly *281*, 281
  tsetse fly 281
  vinegar fly 281
flippers *36*, 36, 308
flounders 116
flycatcher, tyrant 175
flying fox, gray-headed *64*, 64
flyingfishes *141*, 141
fossa *82*, 82

fossilisation *110*, 110–11, *111*, 308
foxes 27, 76–7
  Arctic fox *41*, 41, 77
  bat-eared fox 77
  desert fox 76
  fennec fox 18, 76–7
  gray fox 22, 76
  red fox *76*, 76, 77
frigatebirds *159*, 159, 161–2, 184
froghoppers 283
frogmouths 173–4
frogs 10, 18, 22, 33, 203, 204, 205, 207, 216–21, 308, 311
  bell frog *217*, 217
  burrowing frog 220
  calls 208, 209, 216, 218–19
  clawed frog *219*, 219, 220
  corroboree frog *218*, 218
  Darwin's frog 217
  gastric brooding frog 218
  glass frog 217, *219*, 219
  horned frog 205
  leopard frog *218*, 218
  marsupial frog 209
  moor frog 216
  poison frog 205, 220, *221*, 221
  pygmy marsupial frog 203
  red-banded crevice creeper *219*, 219
  red-eyed leaf-frog *198*, 198
  reed frog 220
    painted *216*, 216
  shovel-nosed frog 220
  tailed frog 220
  tree frogs 203, 220, 221
    Mexican *209*, 209
    Pine Barren *216*, 216
    Wallace's *218*, 218
  túngara frog 216
  tusked frog 209
  water-holding frog 203
  wood frog 216
fruit bats 64–5
  dog-faced fruit bat 64
  Gambian epauletted fruit bat *65*, 65
  gray-headed flying fox *64*, 64
  lesser bare-backed fruit bat *65*, 65
  Old World fruit bat 62, 64
fulmars 160, 185
fur 36–7, 48, 74, 81

gallinules *180*, 180, 182
gamebirds 168
gannets 184, 185
garibaldi 147
gavials *210*, 210, *242*, 242, 244, 246 –7, 307
gazelles 14, 101
  Thompson's gazelle *40*

geckos 21, 202, 207, 208, 226, 227, 230–1, 279
  blue-tailed day gecko *231*, 231
  chameleon gecko 207
  eggs 227–8
  gliding gecko *203*, 203
  house gecko 228
  leaf-tailed gecko *227*, 227
  leopard gecko 226
  Virgin Islands gecko 226
geese 27, 162, 163, 178–9, 180
  bar-headed goose 178
  Hawaiian nene goose 178
  magpie goose 178
  Siberian red-breasted goose *179*, 179
  snow goose *178*, 178
geladas 68
gemsbok *see* oryx
genets 82
gerbils 18, *103*, 103
gerenuks *44*, 44
gibbons 70
giraffes 21, 98, 310
gliders *55*, 55
global warming 12, 29, 33, 39, 118, 119, 308
glycopeptide 146
gnat, fungus 258
gnu *see* wildebeest
goannas 204, 279
  see also monitor lizards
goats 98, 101
  alpine 25
  feral 210–11
gobies 145, *148*, 148
gopher, pocket 102
gorillas 12, 49, 70, 71
  hands and feet *67*, 67
  mountain gorilla 49
  silverback male *70*
goshawks 187, 191
gouramies *145*, 145
grasshoppers *251*, 251, *272*, 272–3, *273*, 273
  dragon lubber grasshopper 272
  Leichhardt's grasshopper 273
  long-headed grasshopper 259
grasslands 9, *20-1*, 20–3
grebes *160*, 160, 182
  little grebe 165
  western grebe's courtship rituals 159
greenhouse effect *see* global warming
griffons *191*, 191
group living 37, 42–4, 69, 87, 92
  hierarchy 43
  wolf packs *23*, 23, *76-7*, 76–7
groupers *115*, 115, *147*, 147–8

grubs 262, 309
guineafowl, vulturine *168*, 168
gulls 184
guppies 141
gymnogene *187*, 187

habitat destruction 47, 48, 49, 54, 59, 65, 97, 307
habitats 8–9, 308
  alpine regions *24–5*, 24–5
  deserts 8, *16–17*, *18–19*, 16–19, 307
  esturine *32-3*, 32–3, 308
  forests 9, *22-3*, 20–3
  grasslands 9, *20-1*, 20–3
  polar regions 9, *26–7*, 26–7, 29, 70, 72, 86, 102, 146, 195, 306, 309
  rain forest 8, 10–13, *11*, *12-13*, 118, 310, 311
  savanna grasslands 8, 14–15, *15*, 310
  temperate zones 20–3, 311
  tundra 27, 102, 311
  water 9, 28–33, *30-1*,112, 146, 310, 311
  woodlands *20-1*, 20–3
hagfishes 108, 110–11, *122*, 122, *123*, 123
halfbeaks 113
hare lip 104
hares *104*, 104, 105
  Arctic hare 27, 105
  form (bed) 105
  piping hare *see* pikas
  snowshoe hare *23*, 23
  whistling hare *see* pikas
harriers *14*, 14, 188, 191
hatchetfishes 138
hawkfish, long-nose *113*, 113
hawks
  bat hawk 191
  Galápagos hawk 188
  Harris's hawk 161, 188
  red-shouldered hawk *188*, 188
  Swainson's hawk *157*, 157
headstander, striped *137*, 137
hedgehogs *60*, 60
hellbenders 214, 215
Hemicyclaspis 110, 110
herbivores 39, 52, 96, 98
herons 178, 180, *181*, 181
  see also egrets
herpetology 198
herrings 117
Hesperornis 154, 154, 155
hibernation 22, 35, 60, 74, 205, 229, 205, 246, 263, 308
hippopotamuses 98, *99*, 99, 100
  dwarf hippopotamus 100
  pygmy hippopotamus 100
hoatzin 173

hog, red river *99*, 99
honeybees *see* bees
honeydew 257
honeyeaters 176
honeyguide 162
hoofs 94, 98, 308
  see also ungulates
hornbills *172*, 172
hornets 274, 275
horns 42, 47, 48–9, 96, 101
horses 40, 94
  domestication 94–5, 307
  Przewalski's 94
host (of parasite) 144, 258, 276
human threats 46–7, 48, 81, 118–19, 164, 192, 195
hummingbirds 10, 12, 153, *157*, 157, 172, 287
  bee hummingbird *150*, 150
  ruby-throated hummingbird *163*, 163
hyenas 14, *83*, 83, 96, *96–97*
Hylonomus 201, 201
hyraxes 39, 58, 104, *105*, 105

ibises 180, 181
Ichthyophis glutinosus 213, 213
Ichthyophis kohtaoensis 213, 213
Ichthyornis 155
Ichthyosaurus 201, 201, 202
Ichthyostega 200
idiotfishes 143–4
iguanas *209*, 209, *211*, 211, 227, 230
  crested iguana *228–9*, 229
  green iguana 230
  land iguanas *211*, 211
  marine iguanas 205, *209*, 209, 226, 228, 230
  rhinoceros iguana *204*, 204
impala 45
Indricotherium 95
indris 66–7, *67*
inkfishes 140
insecticides 264, 265
insectivores 60–1, 65, 309
insects 12, 21, 32, 248, 254–5, 307, 310
  antennae 251, 306
  behavior 256–7, 256–63, 311
  camouflage 258–9, 306
  classification 250–1
  endangered species 264–5
  evolution 254–5
  flight 255
  larvae 12, 262–3, 266, 308, 309
  legs *262*, 262
  mating 260
  migration 263, 273
  molting 250, 309
  ocelli 250, 255, 309
  parasitic 258

social 256, 274–5, 276, 278, 307, 311
sting 251
taxonomy 302–305
tracheae 251
wings 263, 263, 308
ivory 49, 92, 309

jacanas 183, 183
jackals 76
jackrabbit, black-tailed 18, 104, 104
Jacobson's organ 199, 229, 229, 231, 232, 309
jaguar 56, 79, 79
jawless fishes 108, 110–11, 122, 123, 122–3
jays 176, 176
jerboas 102
joey 53, 53
juncos 177
Jurassic Period 39

kakapo 170, 170
kangaroos 22, 52
red kangaroo 52, 53, 53
reproduction 52 3, 52–3
tree kangaroos 52, 53, 53
kangaroo rat 18
katydids 272, 273
keratin 109, 152, 222, 309
kestrels 188, 188, 189
killdeer 161, 161
killer whale see dolphins
killifishes 140–1
annual killifish 141
clown killifish 141, 141
four-eyed killifish 141, 141
steel-blue killifish 10, 10
kingfishers 32, 171
belted kingfisher 171, 171
kookaburra 171–2
shovel-billed kingfisher 171
kinkajou 75, 75
kites 189
black kite 191
black-shouldered kite 189, 189
snail kite 186
kiwi 192, 192, 193, 194
koala 22, 41, 41, 42, 52, 52, 53
kookaburra see kingfishers
kraits 235, 235

lacewings 251, 251, 277
ladybugs 256, 256, 263, 264
five-spotted 271, 271
ten-spotted 271, 271
lampreys 108, 110–11, 122, 122
horny teeth 123, 123
pouched lamprey 123
sea lamprey 123
langurs 14, 14
lanternfishes 117

larks 177
larvae 12, 262–3, 266, 308, 309
doodlebugs 277, 277
mosquitoes 281, 281
salamanders 214, 214
leaf chafers 271
leafhoppers 283
leafy seadragon 31, 31
lemming, collared 27, 41
lemurs 10, 66
aye-aye 41, 41, 67
indris 66–7, 67
mouse lemurs 66
pygmy 66
red-ruffed lemur 66, 66
ring-tailed lemur 66, 66
leopards 14, 78, 78
snow leopard 25, 25, 42, 48
limpkin 182
linsang, banded see civets
lionfish see turkeyfish
lions 14, 37, 37, 40, 78, 79, 79
prides 37, 79
lizardfish 139, 139
lizards 21, 207, 206–7, 208, 226–31, 230, 307
adaptations 17, 202
agamids 227, 230
alligator lizard 228, 231
Angolosaurus skoogi 17, 17
anoles 208, 230
Cuban brown 231, 231
Cuban knight 227, 227
armadillo girdle-tailed lizard 207–8
beaded lizard 227, 231
collared lizard 209, 228, 228, 230, 230
dragon lizard 209, 228
flap-footed lizard 227
frilled lizard 206, 206, 230
galliwasp 231
Gila monster 210, 210, 227, 231
glass lizard 231
horned lizard 208, 230
Komodo dragon 211, 226, 228, 228
leopard lizard 209
Mohave fringe-toed lizard 202
Namib dune lizard 229
night lizard 228, 231
regal horned lizard 207
sand lizard 230
temperature regulation 204, 205, 241
tree dragon 229, 229
wall lizard 228
whiptails 227, 228, 231
see also geckos; iguanas; monitor lizards; skinks
llama 25

loaches
saddled hillstream loach 112, 112
slimy freshwater loach 136, 136
locusts 251, 251, 259, 263, 264, 272–3
loons 22, 182
loosejaws (fishes) 138
lorises 66
lotus birds 183, 183
lungfishes 14, 14, 111, 115, 134
lynx 78, 78
lyrebirds 22, 158, 158, 175

macaques 69
macaws 10, 167, 167, 171, 171
mackerel 109, 146
maggots 262, 280, 309
magpies 176
mammals 34–41, 58–9, 307, 309
adaptations 40–41
behavior 42–3, 42–5
classifying 36–7
endangered species 46–9, 54, 57, 59, 60, 72, 75, 77, 79–80, 94, 95, 96, 97
evolution 38–40, 41, 56, 59, 62, 72, 88, 90, 94, 95
jaw, hinged 36
migration 14, 25, 31, 44–5, 85
skin 37
taxonomy 294–5
see also marsupials; monotremes; placental mammals
mammary glands 36
mammoths 59
family tree 59, 59
woolly mammoth 46
manakins 159
manatee 89
mandarin fish 139, 139
mandibles 252
mandrills 68, 68
maned wolf 41, 41
body parts as medicine 48
mangroves 32, 32
mantids
flower mantis 258
praying mantis 257, 257, 258
wings 263, 263
mara, Patagonian 102, 102
margay 36
marlin 109, 116, 146
marmoset, pygmy 69
marsupials 21, 22, 36, 44, 52–5, 55, 309
martens 22, 81
martins 175

mating, for life 44, 59, 61, 70, 102, 180, 181, 185, 188, 309
mayflies 262
mealybugs 283
medicinal use of animals 46, 48–9, 59, 96, 120, 121, 311
meerkats 20, 43, 43, 83
melanin 152
mergansers 178–9
Mesonyx 38
metamorphosis 262, 269, 269, 280, 307, 309
mice 102
midshipmen 114
migration 22, 309
birds 22, 27, 33, 162–3, 172, 178, 181, 182, 186–7, 309
fishes 22, 31, 32, 116–17, 123, 137
insects 263, 273
mammals 14, 25, 31, 44–5, 85
reptiles 31, 223
milk, for survival 42, 50, 84, 86, 89
mink 81
mistletoebird 176
mites 252, 292, 292, 293, 293, 306
moas 47, 192
mockingbirds 174
mola mola 148, 148
mole-rats 102
moles 36
European mole 60, 60
tunnels 61, 61
mollies 141
mongooses 82 3, 83, 83
monito del monte see colocolo
monitor lizards 14, 209, 227, 228, 228, 231
monkeys 10
baboons 42, 42, 43–4, 69
colobine monkey 68–9
gelada 68
howler monkey 69, 69
langurs 14, 14
macaques 69
mandrill 68, 68
marmosets, pygmy 69
New World monkeys 68, 68, 69
night monkey 69, 69
Old World monkeys 68, 68
proboscis monkey 69
snow monkey see macaques
squirrel monkey 69–70
tamarins 48, 48, 68, 68
titis 69
woolly spider monkey 69, 69
monotremes 36, 50–1, 307, 308, 309

moonrats *61*, 61
moorhens 182
moose 100, *101*, 101
Morganucodontids 38, 38
mosquitoes 27, 264, *280*, 280,
   egg-laying *281*, 281
moths 263, 266–7
   antennae *267*, 267, 306
   armyworm moth 288
   atlas moth *266–7*, 266
   hawk moth *257*, 257
   jumping bean moth 266
   life cycle *266–7*, 266
   locust-bean moth 266
   looper moth 267
   meal moth 267
   polyphemus moth *258*, 258,
      267
   puss moth *260*, 260
   pygmy moth 266
   silk moth larva *266*, 266
      in spiders' webs 286
   tear moth 267
   tiger moth 260
   yellow emperor moth *267*,
      267
mousebirds 170
mudpuppy *214–15*, 214
mullet 146
multituberculates 39
munia, white-rumped 176
muntjac 100–1
musk oxen 26, *101*, 101
musk turtle (stinkpot) 207
mustelids 80–2
muttonbird *184*, 184
mygalomorphs *285*, 285, 291
mynah, Indian 177
narwhal 86
newts 214–15
   alpine newt *215*, 215
   marbled newt *215*, 215
nightjars 173
Nile perch 121
ningauis *17*, 17, 52
non-passerines (birds) 168
noseleaf *62*, 62, *63*, 63
nostrils 58, *68*, 68
numbat 22, *55*, 55
nymphs 262, 283, 309

oarfishes 140
ocean sunfish 31, 115, *148*,
   148, 149
oceans 28–33
oil glands 37, 82, 169
oilbirds 173, 174
okapi *100*, 100
oldsquaw 179
olm 215
omasum 98
omnivores 54, 72, 98
oncilla 78
opahs *140*, 140

opossums 52, 54–5
   Virginia opossum 54
   woolly opossum *54*, 54
opposable thumb *67*, 67, 70,
   309
orangutans 10, *47*, 47, 70–1, *71*
oryx *16*, 16, 101
osprey *187*, 187, 191
ostrich 150, *151*, *192*, 192,
   193, 194
otters 80
   river otter 22, *80*, 80
   sea otter 32, *80*, 80, *81*, 81
ovenbirds 174–5
overfishing 120, 147–8
owls 22, 173, 174, 187
   barn owl 153, *156*, 156, 173
   burrowing owl 20
   eagle owl *156*, 156
   fishing owl 174
   great horned owl 160
   snowy owl 27, 174
oxpeckers *96*, 96, 162
oystercatchers 183

Pachyrachis 201
paddlefishes 134, *135*, 135
pandas
   giant panda 48, *72*, 72, 74–5
   red panda *72*, 72, *74*, 74
pangolins *58–9*, 58–9, 279
pantherines (cats) 78
parasites 280, 281, 310
parrotfishes 108, *112*, 112,
   114–15, 114–15, 117, 135,
   147
parrots 21, 22, 166, 167, 170,
   171, 310
   hanging parrot 171
   hawk-headed parrot *171*, 171
   monk parrot 171
   see also cockatoos; macaws
passerines (songbirds) 168,
   174, 176, 177, 310
peafowl 169
   tail display 158
peccaries 98–9
pectines *292*, 293, 310
pelicans *183*, 183, 184
penguins 26, *27*, 27, 31, 155,
   160, 184, 192, *194*, 194 5
   Adélie penguin *194*, 194, 195
   chinstrap penguin *194*
   emperor penguin 27, *160*,
     160, *194*, *195*, 195
   fairy penguin *194*
   fjordland penguin *194*
   Galápagos penguin 195
   gentoo penguin 195
   king penguin 195
   Magellanic penguin *194*
   rockhopper penguin *195*, 195
   yellow-eyed penguin *194*
perches 121, 145, 146

perissodactyls 94
petrels *27*, 27
   giant petrel 185
phainopepla *160*, 160
pheasants 169
pheromones 209, 260, 267,
   270, 276–7, 286, 290, 293,
   310
pigeons 169–70
   crowned pigeon *168*, 168
   passenger pigeon *165*, 165
pigfishes 143
pigs 98, 99
pikas *105*, 105
pike 116
pineapplefish *143*, 143
pinnipeds 88–9
pipefishes 108, 142
   banded pipefish *142*, 142
piranhas *10*, 10, 135, *136*, 136
pitohui *161*, 161
pittas *173*, 173
placenta 36, 310
placental mammals 36, *61*,
   56–105, 310
placoderms 111
plankton 30, 31, 113, 310
Planocephalosaurus 201, 201
platyfishes 141
platypus 50–1, *51*
   electromagentic pulses 51,
     308
Pleistocene Era 56, 155
plesiosaurs 201, 202
plover, Egyptian 184
poisonous animals 215, 311
   antivenin 290, 306
   color signals *206*, 206, 207,
     213, 215
   frogs *221*, 221
   moray eels 136–7
   pitohui *161*, 161
   platypus 50
   pufferfishes 116, 149
   salamanders 215
   scorpions 293
   solenodon 60
   spiders 252, 264, 289–90
   stonefishes 142, 144
polar regions 9, *26–7*, 26–7, 29,
   70, 72, 86, 102, 146, 195,
   306, 309
pollination 276, 310
pollination corridors 265
pollution 48, 118
   acid rain 22, 306
   air pollution 22
   avoiding pollution 121
   marine pollution 33, 118,
     119
pond-skaters 283
porcupinefishes 149
porcupines 22, *40*, 40, 103,
   310

porpoises 84, *87*, 87
   see also dolphins; whales
possums 10, 22, 53–4
   brushtail possum 53
   ringtail possum 53–4
   striped possum *41*, 41
prairie dogs 82
   black-tailed *103*, 103
praying mantids *257*, 257, 258
prehensile tails 68, 69, *75*, 75,
   202, *227*, 227, 233, 310
pride, of lions 37, 79
primates 36, 66–71
   apes 10, *39*, *47*, 47, 49, 68,
     70, 70–1, *71*
   bush babies 66
   monkeys 10, *42*, 42, 43–4, *48*,
     48, *68*, 68, 69, 68–70
   lemurs 10, *41*, 41, *66*, *67*,
     66–7
   lorises 66
   tarsiers *66*, 66
prions 185
Priscacara 110, 110
proboscis 90, *257*, 257, 267,
   280, 280
procyonids 75
Proganochelys 201, 201
psyllids 283
ptarmigans *26*, 26
Pteranodon 154, 154, *201*, 202
pterosaurs 154, 201–2
pudu *100*, 100
puffer, black-saddled *117*, 117
pufferfishes 112, *116*, 116, 149
puffins 178, *182*, 182, 184
puggle 50
pumas 25
pupae 262, 310
purplequeen *146*, 146
pygmy-possum 54
pythons *208*, 208, *233*, 233,
   234, 235, 236
   tree pythons 209
     green 233, *236*, 236
   woma python 206

quail 22, 157
   California quail *169*, 169
quetzal 10, *170*, 170

rabbits *104–5*, 104, 105
   warren *104–5*, 105
raccoon 22, *74*, 74, 75
rails 178, 180, 182
rain forests *8*, 10, *11*, 11, 310
   canopy 10
   destruction 12, 118
   forest floor 10–11
   medicinal plants 13
rainbow bee-eater *170*, 170
rainbow cale *146*, 146
raptors 186–91, 310
   talons *187*, 187, 188

wing span *186*, 186
see also birds of prey
ratites 192–4
rats 102–3
    fish-eating rat 103
    speckled harsh-furred rat 103
rattlesnakes *18*, 18, *204–5*,
    204–5, 234
rays 108, *109*, 109, 111, 124,
    127, *130*, 130, 132–3, 306
    blue-spotted ribbontail ray
      132, 132
    buoyancy 125
    cownose ray 133
    eagle ray 133
    electric rays 133
      short-nose 132
      short-tailed 132
    major orders *133*, 133
    manta ray *30*, 30, 31, 132,
      133, 133
    ocellated freshwater stingray
      132, 132
    sixgill stingray *133*, 133
    spotted eagle ray *120*, 120
    torpedo ray 133
reefs, artificial 121
reefs, coral *see* coral reefs
reindeer *see* caribou
remora *144*, 144
reproduction 52–3, 65, 69, 80,
    92, 103
reptiles 38, 196–203, 307
    behavior 204–9, 307
    classification 198–9
    eggs *198*, 198, 307
    endangered species 210–11
    evolution 200–02, 222, 226,
      232,
    migration 31, 223
    outer skin *199*, 199
    skin color 199
    temperature regulation
      204–5
    taxonomy 301–302
    see also crocodilians;
      lizards, snakes; tortoises;
      turtles
rhea 192, 193
rhinoceros 21, *43*, 43, *47*, 47,
    94, 95–6
    black rhino 48–9, *96*, 96
    horns 47, 48–9
    Indian rhino *96*, 96
    Javan rhino *96*, 96–7
    Sumatran rhino *96*, 96
    white rhino *96*, 96, *97*, 97
ribbonfishes *140*, 140
roadrunners 18, 170
rodents 21, 42, 76, 102–3
    see also beavers; gerbils;
      mice; porcupines; rats;
      squirrels
rollers 172

rufous hornero 174–5
rumen 98

sailfishes 146
salamanders 22, 207, 209,
    214–15
    fire salamander 214
    giant salamander *24*, 24, 214,
      215
    lungless salamander 214, 215
    mole salamander 214, 215
    red salamander *214*, 214
    spotted salamander *199*, 199,
      215
    tiger salamander 204
salmon *22*, 22, 27, 32, 116
    sockeye salmon 116, *138*,
      138
sandgrouse 169, 170
savanna grasslands *8*, 14–15,
    15, 310
sawfishes *118*, 118
scale insects 264, 283
scavengers 45, *54*, 54, *83*, 83,
    185, *190*, 190, 310
scent glands 66
scent marking 61, 66
scorpionfishes 113, 143
scorpions 10, 22, 252, *292–3*,
    292–3, 306, 310, 311
    fossils 254
    imperial scorpion 292
    pectines 292, 293
    water scorpion *251*, 251
scoters 178
screamers *178*, 178
scrub-birds 174
sea cows *89*, 89
sea kraits 30, *235*, 235
sea lions *88*, 88
sea spiders 28
sea urchins 149
seadragons
    leafy seadragon *31*, 31
    weedy seadragon 115–16
seahorse farming 121
seahorses 31, 32, *121*, 121,
    134, 142
    reproduction *115*, 115
seals 26, 27, 31, 88, 89
    crabeater seal 89
    elephant seal 89, 129
    fur seal *27*, *88*, 88, 130
    harp seal *89*, 89
    leopard seal 88
    monk seal 48
    Weddell seal *27*, 27, 89
seamoths 142
secretarybird 154, *189*, 189,
    190
servals 14
sharks 31, 108, 109, 111, 112,
    124, 306
    adaptations 127–8

angelshark 128, *131*, 131
barbels 128, 306
basking shark 113, 128
binge feeding 130
blacktip reef shark *128*, 128
blind shark 128
blue shark *124*, 128, 129,
    130
bronze whaler shark *124*
bull shark 128
bullhead shark 128, *129*,
    129, 131, 132
buoyancy 125
camouflage 128, 306
catshark 132
cookiecutter shark *126*, 126,
    129, 129
denticles 125
diet 128–30
dogfish shark 131
dominance hierarchy 130–1
egg case *109*, 109
electroreception 109,114,
    308
epaulette shark 129
evolution 124
exploitation *120*, 120
frilled shark *130*, 130
goblin shark 125
gray reef shark 131
great white shark 111, *121*,
    121, *125*, 125, 128–9, 131
    jaws *124*, 124
hammerhead shark *126*,
    126, 129, 130
jaw 124, 125 6, *131*, 131
lemon shark 126
mako shark 125, 128, 129
necklace carpet shark *128*,
    128
nurse shark *126*, 126, *127*,
    127, 128
oily liver 125, 311
oviparous 109, 132, 309
ovoviviparous 132, 309
placoid scales 109
porbeagle shark *127*, 127
reproduction 130, 131,
    131–2
sand tiger shark 132
sawshark *131*, 131
schooling 130
sevengill shark 130
silvertip shark 131
spiny shark *111*, 111
swellshark 131
tail shapes 126 7
teeth 111, 126, 128, *129*,
    129
thresher shark *127*, 127
tiger shark *124*, *127*, 127, 129
viviparous 109, 131–2, 311
whale shark 30, *119*, 119,
    128, 132

whitetip shark *127*, 127, 129,
    131
wobbegongs *113*, 113, 128
shearwaters 184
    short-tailed shearwater *163*,
      163, *184*, 184
sheathbills 183
sheep 21, 98
    Barbary sheep 101
    mountain sheep *42*, 42
shingleback *227*, 227
shrew-opossums 55
shrews 10, 27, 60–1
shrikes 175–6
shrimp, ghost *33*, 33
siamang 70
sifaka 67
silverfish 255
sirens 214
siskin, red 166
skates 111
skimmers *182*, 182, 184
skinks 207, 227, 229, 231
    blue-tongue skink *226*, 226
    five-lined skink *231*, 231
    green-blooded skink 231
    red-tailed skink *231*, 231
    tails *227*, 227
skuas 161–2, 184, 195
skunks *44*, 44, 82
sloths 10, *41*, 41, 56, 56–7, *57*
    giant sloth 46, *56*, 56
slow worms 231
snaggletooths 138
snakes 10, 12, 20, 202, 205,
    206, 207, 226, 233–7, 307
    agile racer 236
    blind snake 237
    boomslang 235
    burrowing snake *233*, 233
    coral snake 235
    false coral snake *206*, 206
    fangs *234*, 234–5
    garter snake 22, 236
    hognose snake 208, 234
    internal organs *232–3*, 233
    king snake 234
    mambas 235
    Mandarin rat snake *234*, 234
    mangrove snake 233
    mating 236
    Mayan coral snake *206*, 206
    scales *232*, 232, 310
    sea snakes 232, 233, 235
      sea kraits 30, *235*, 235
      yellow-bellied *28*, 28, 235
    skin shedding *236*, 236
    small-scaled snake 234
    Sonoran whipsnake *19*, 19
    taipan 235
    thread snake 232
    tree snake *233*, 233
    twig snake 206
    venomous snakes 234–5

vine snake *203*, 203
water snakes 235–6
see also adders; anaconda;
 boas; cobras; rattlesnakes
snapper 146
soldierfishes, blackbar *117*, 117
sparrow, crowned 177
sparrowhawks *187*, 187, *188*,
 188
spermatophore 260, 293, 311
spiders 10, 32, 248, 254–5,
 264, 306, 307, 311
 argiope spider *285*, 285, 290
 ballooning *291*, 291
 behavior 284–91
 bird-poo spider 288–9
 black widow spider 286, 289,
 290
 body parts *253*, 253, 311
 bolas spider *286*, 286, 288
 carnivores 252
 chelicerae 252, 306
 classification 252–3
 colonial spider 287
 crab spider *288*, 288, 290
 egg sacs *290*, 290, 291, 307
 endangered species 264–5
 evolution 254, 255, 284
 fishing spider *288*, 288
 funnel-web spider 284, *285*,
 285, 290
 garden spider *284*, 284, 291
 goliath bird spider *289*, 289
 grass spider 287
 happy-faced spider 265
 house spider 287
 hunting spiders *285*, 285,
 287–9, 290
 jumping spider *252*, 252,
 288, 291
 leaf-rolling spider 290
 mating 290–1, 310
 Micrathena spider *290*, 290
 Nephila spider 253, 286–7,
 290
 net-casting spider *286*, 286
 nursery web spider 290
 orb-weaving spider 285–6
 purse-web spider 284
 raft spider 288
 redback spider 289
 silk 253, 285
 spitting spider 288
 spotted racing spider 289
 spruce-fir moss spider 265
 tarantula, red-kneed *265*,
 265, 289
 taxonomy 305
 tooth cave spider 265
 trapdoor spider 288, *289*,
 289
 venom 284 5, 289–90
 web-building 253, *284*, 284,
 285, 285 6, *286*, 290

wheel spider *288*, 288
wolf spider 287, *290*, 290–1
spines *51*, 51, *60*, 60
spinnerets *253*, 253, 285
spinynose sculpin 113
spoonbills 178, 180, *181*, 181
springbok *40*
spurs *50*, 50, 66
squeakers (frogs) 220
squirrels 20, 22, *45*, 45, 102
 antelope ground squirrel *19*,
 19
 black giant squirrel *102*, 102
 flying squirrel 10, 103
 red squirrel 103
starlings *177*, 177
Stegosaurus 201, 201
sticklebacks 115, 142–3
stifftails 178
stingrays 132
 ocellated freshwater
 stingray *132*, 132
 sixgill stingray *133*, 133
stomach
 complex 98
 simple *95*, 95
stonefishes 113, 144
 purple stonefish *142*, 142
storks 180, 190
 New World vultures 190–1
 painted stork *180*, 180
 white stork 181
 yellow-billed stork 181
streamcreepers 175
stridulation 273
sturgeons 109
sunbirds
 crimson sunbird 177
 regal sunbird *174*, 174
surgeonfishes 147
suricates *see* meerkats
swallows 163, 175
 cliff swallow *174*, 174
swans 27, 153, 160, 178, *179*,
 179, 180
 trumpeter swan 180
sweat glands 37
swiftlets, cave-dwelling 172
swifts 172
swordfish 146
swordtails 141
synapsids 38, 222

tadpoles 204, 209, 217–18,
 219, 220, 221, 311
tailor *see* bluefish
Takifugu 149
talons *187*, 187, 188
tamandua *see* anteaters,
 collared
tamarins
 cotton-top tamarin *68*, 68
 golden lion tamarin *48*, 48
tanagers 176

tapirs 94, *97*, 97
tarantula hawk wasp 276
tarantulas 22, 287, 291
 red-kneed tarantula *265*, 265,
 289
tarsiers *66*, 66
Tasmanian devil *54*, 54
Tasmanian tiger *see* thylacine
tayra 81
teeth 36, 53, 104, 306, 308,
 309
 canine 38, 306
 carnassial 72, *73*, 73, 76
 sharks 111, 126, 128, *129*,
 129
Temminck's tragopan *169*, 169
temperature regulation 40, 83,
 104, 104, 156, 161, 204–5
tenrec, streaked *60*, 60
Teratornis merriami 155, 155
teratorns *155*, 155
termites 18, 256, 257, 264,
 276, 278–9, 283
 harvester termite 279
 magnetic termite 278
 nests *278 9*, 278–9, 283
 soldiers 259, *278*, 278
 spinifex termite *278*, 278
terns 159, 184, *185*, 185
 Arctic tern *162*, 162
terrapin, painted 225
territory marking 44, 61, 66
therapsids 38
thermals *186*, 186
theropods 154
thorny devil *202–3*, 203, 208,
 230
thrips *263*, 263
thrushes 162, 177
thylacine *55*, 55
ticks 252, 264, 292, 293, 306
 deer tick *293*, 293
 paralysis tick *292*, 292
tigers 37, *46*, 46, 48, *79*
 Siberian tiger 78
titis 69
toadfishes *119*, 119, 137
toads 20, 33, 203, 208, 216–21
 burrowing toad *220*, 220
 crucifix toad *18*, 18
 eastern narrow-mouthed
 toad *221*, 221
 golden toad 25
 horned toad *221*, 221
 natterjack *208*, 208
 Nicoll's toadlet 208
 oriental fire-bellied toad *207*,
 207
 ornate horned toad *220*, 220
 spadefoot toad 220
 Surinam toad 220
tomistoma 242, 244, *245*, 245,
 307
tortoises 209, 222–5, 310

giant tortoise 225
gopher tortoise 225
hidden-necked tortoise 222
land tortoise *222*, 222, 225
pancake tortoise *224*, 224
saddleback shell tortoise
 224, 224
shell; carapace *222*, 222
spider tortoise 225
straight-necked tortoise 225
toucans 10, *173*, 173
tragus *62*, 62
tree kangaroo *53*, 53
tree shrew *61*, 61
treecreepers 174
treehoppers 283
tremblers 174
Triassic Period 38
triggerfishes 117, 148–9
 clown triggerfish *149*, 149
 queen triggerfish *119*, 119
trilobites *254*, 254
tripodfish 28
trogons 170
tropicbirds *184*, 184
true bugs 282–3
 rostrum 282, *283*, 283, 310
truffles 99
trumpetfishes 142, *143*, 143
trunk 90, *91*, 91–2, *92*, 93
tuataras 222, *240–1*, 240–1
tube-eyes 140
tubenoses 185
tubeworms 28, 30
tuna 116, 145, 146
tuna fishing *49*, 49
tundra 27, 102, 311
turacos *168*, 168, 170
turkeyfish 113, *142*, 142, 144
turkeys 22, 168
turnstone, ruddy 178
turtles 32, *205*, 205, 209, 222–5,
 310
 alligator snapping turtle *223*,
 223
 big-headed turtle 223
 box turtle *20*, 20
 helmeted turtle 224
 hidden-necked turtles 222
 musk turtle 224
 northern snake-necked turtle
 224
 painted terrapin 225
 pond turtles *222*, 222, 223,
 224
 red-eared turtle 208
 river turtles 224
 sea turtles *202*, 202, *222*,
 222, 223, 225
 green *31*, 31, 223, *225*,
 225
 leatherback 222, *224*, 224
 Pacific hawksbill *211*, 211
 Sepik turtle *222*, 222

side-necked turtles *222, 222*
softshell turtles 222, *223*, 223, 224
tusks 42, 49, 86, *89*, 89, *92*, 92, *98*, 98, 311
Typhlonectes natans 213, 213
Tyrannosaurus 201
  T. rex 154

ungulates 311
  even-toed 98–101
  odd-toed 94–7
unicornfishes *145*, 145
Ursavus 38

vertebrates 36, 198, 200, 232, 254, 309, 311
viperfishes 138
vipers 206, 233, 234, 236
  horned viper *233*
  rhinoceros viper *234*, 234
vision 153
  binocular 36, 66, 78, 156, 187–8, 288
  color 36, 73, 199, 243
  night 78, 173, 243
viverrids 82
voles 20, 27
vultures 14, 186, *187*, 187, 189, *190*, 190–1, *191*
  bearded vulture *191*, 191
  black vulture 189
  lappet-faced vulture *190*, 190

New World vultures 190–1
Old World vultures *190*, 190, 191
  palm nut vulture 191

wallabies 21, 52
walrus *26*, 26, 88, *89*, 89
wapiti 100
warblers 159, 174
warty prowfish 117
wasps 256, 257, 264, 274–7
  bald-faced hornet 275
  brachonid wasps 276
  chalcid wasp 274
  cicada killer 275
  cow killer wasp 274
  gall wasp 275–6
  ichneumon wasp *260*, 260
  polistine wasp 276, 287
  potter wasp *256*, 256
  spider hunters *288*, 288, 289
  sting *275*, 275
  wings *263*, 263
  wood wasp larva *260*, 260
water boatmen 283
water chevrotain *10*, 10
water opossum *see* yapok
water snakes 235–6
water treaders 283
waterbirds 178–85
wattlebirds 176
waxwings 174
weasels 27, *81*, 81, 88

weaver birds *159*, 159, 188–9
weedy seadragons 115–16
weevils 264, *268*, 268, 269, 271
  Eupholus bennetti 268, 268
  giraffe weevil *268*, 268
  hazelnut weevil 257
wetlands 33
whales 27, 31, 36, 38, 40, *43*, 43, 84
  baleen whales 31, 48, 84, 85, 89
  migration 85
  blue whale 84, 86
    size *85*, 85
  bowhead whale 85
  gray whale 85
  humpback whale *28-9*, 45, *84*, 84, 85–6, *86*
    bubblenetting 86
    protection *49*, 49
    size *85*, 85
  minke whale *84*, 84
  right whale *84*, 84
  sperm whale *86*, 86
    size *85*, 85
  stranding 87
  toothed whales 85, 86, 243
  see also dolphins; porpoises
white-eyes *174*, 174
whydah 177
wildebeest *40*, *44–5*, 44, 101
wolverine 81

wolves 25, 27, 37, 43, 45, 76
  communication *77*, 77
  pack animals *23*, 23, 76–7, 76–7
wombats 22, 53
woodpeckers 22, 172
  gila woodpecker *19*, 19
worm lizards *see* amphisbaenians
wrasses 108, *114–15*, 114, 115, 117
wrens
  cactus wren *19*, 19
  fairy-wrens *172*, 172
  Stephen Island wren 164
wrigglers 281
wrybill, New Zealand 183

xenarthrans 56–7

yak 25
yapok *54*, 54

zebra 14, *44–5*, 44, *94*, 94, 95
  Burchell's zebra 95
  Grèvy's zebra 95
  mountain zebra 95
  plains zebra 95
zooplankton 31, 84, 85, 89, 185, 311
zooxanthellae 119
zygodactylism 170, 193, 311

Credits

Weldon Owen would like to thank the following people: Sarah Anderson; Dan Bickel, Department of Entomology, Australian Museum, Sydney, Australia; Lisa Boehm; Trudie Craig; Peta Gorman; Michael Hann; Dr. Pat Hutchings, Department of Marine Invertebrates, Australian Museum, Sydney, Australia; Aliza Pinczewski; Jackie Richards; Jo Rudd (index)

(t=top, b=bottom, l=left, r=right, c=center)

Photographs Ad-Libitum/Stuart Bowey, 72. Auscape: 52, 292, 293; S. Yves Lanceau, 123; Osolinski, 68; Tui De Roy, 184; V. Steiger/Peter Arnold, 293. Bruce Coleman: B.J. Coates, 161; F. Labhardt, 252; W. Layer, 57; R. Maier, 104; B. Ward, 279; S. Widstrand, 89; R. Williams, 61. Corel Corporation, 41, 46, 47, 47, 47, 47, 47, 57, 65, 79, 91, 92, 94, 97, 99, 109, 112, 113, 116, 117, 118, 119, 120, 127, 128, 130, 132, 133, 136, 137, 143, 144, 145, 147, 148, 149, 156, 159, 159, 160, 162, 164, 166, 167, 168, 171, 174, 177, 180, 181, 188, 190, 193, 194, 195, 198, 199, 209, 210, 211, 211, 218, 222, 227, 235, 247, 258, 260, 265, 271, 278, 281, 282, 283, 285, 287, 288, 289, 290, 290. Stephen Dalton, 12. Frits Jan Maas, 185, 185. Oxford Scientific Films: R. Bush, 170, 240; M. Hamblin, 189. The Photo Library: 276; M. Kage/SPL, 7, 258.

Illustrations Susanna Addario, 259c, 262b, 263c, 274b, 275b. Mike Atkinson/Garden Studio, 6tl, 33tr, 150c, 192tr, 193. Graham Back, 121b. Alistair Barnard, 36bl, 38t, 50, 73tr. Andrew Beckett/Garden Studio, 20-21. Sally Beech, 280tl & cl, 283. Andre Boos, 74b, 80b, 81tr, 82l, 83t & b. Anne Bowman, 6cl, 110b, 196l, 244tl & b, 254c, 255l. Martin Camm, 7tr, 14c, 36tl, 41cr, 68t & cl, 78tl, 84, 86t& cl, 91, 93t & b, 124l, 129cl, 133r, 264t, 269t. Fiammetta Dogi, 31. Simone End, 1, 6br, 20br, 26, 27r, 37t, 53l, 58bl, 66, 75t, 88, 103r, 104t, 105l, 202tl, 203tr, 208c, 223bl, 224t, 227b, 228, 233cl, 236c, 237b, 246b, 250c, 268bl & r, 269b, 270t, 271r. Christer Eriksson, 7tl, 18t, 37c, 47, 53b, 79t, 87b, 95b, 97t, 125b, 135t, 155t, 206b, 209t, 223t, 237t, 245t, 247, 248, 256bl & r, 257b, 262t, 270b, 272b, 287, 293. Alan Ewart, 92, 285b. Guiliano Fornari, 285t, 286l. Chris Forsey, 119t. John Francis/Bernard Thornton Artists UK, 202-203, 204-205b, 224b, 234l. John Gittoes, 26-27, 56t, 71t, 81c, 89t, 105r, 194b, 195cr, 282b, 288b. John Gittoes, 11. Mike Gorman, 184b, 186b. Ray Grinaway, 12t, 30, 49t, 70tr, 99b, 113b, 126b, 127b, 128, 129t, 131t & c, 257t, 263b, 266c, 268t, 286t, 288t. Gino Hasler, 38b, 85b, 86br, 131l. Tim Hayward, 8-9, 80c, 81b. Tim Hayward/Bernard Thornton Artists UK, 23b, 44cl, 45tl, 260b, 276b, 284t, 290, 291b. Robert Hynes, 201, 207r, 209b, 230b, 258, 256t, 275t, 278. David Kirshner, 4br, 5tl, br & l, 6bl, 10, 14b, 16, 17, 18b, 18-19, 22, 23tl, 24tl, 28, 41cl, 53tr, 54bc, 55t & c, 57bl, 60br, 61c, 63tl & b, 64, 65t & br, 67r, 68br, 69t & b, 72, 73tl & br, 74l & tr, 75c & b, 76-77b, 77r, 78bl, 82tr, 83c, 94, 96t & b, 97b, 98t & cr, 99t, 100tr & tl, 101tl & bl, 102l & r, 106, 108, 109r, 110t, 111t & b, 112t & r, 113t, 114b, 115b, 117, 119b, 120c, 122, 123, 125t, 132, 134, 135b, 136, 137, 138, 139, 140, 141, 142t, 143, 144, 145, 146, 147, 148, 149, 150t, 151c, 152, 153bl & r, 154t & b, 155b, 156tl, 157c, 158c, 162b, 164, 165t, 166t, 168, 169t & c, 170, 171tr, 172, 173, 174r, 175t, 176t & c, 177, 178t, 179, 180, 181c, 182, 183c, 187bl & tl, 188l, 192tr, 194t, 196-197, 198, 199t, 199c, 200c & b, 204t & c, 206t, 207t & b, 210-211, 211, 212, 213, 214, 215, 216, 218c, 219, 221, 222, 223r, 224c, 226t, 228-229, 229, 230t, 231, 232, 232-233, 234t & b, 235, 238, 239, 242, 243, 244cr, 245br, 246t, 250b, 252, 254t, 281b, 292, 293cl, 294r, 295, 299l, 300, 301. Frank Knight, 12b, 25br, 33cr, 35, 36br, 39br, 40b, 44tr, 45cl, 46, 59bc, 61b, 62b, 76-77b, 78cr, 79b, 90, 93r, 95t, 114tl, 115t, 116, 153tl, 156bl & tr, 157tr, 158t, 161t, 166b, 184c, 199b, 208tl, 217, 225, 236t, 261t, 266-277, 284b. Stan Lamond, 163t. Jeff Lang, 71b, 158bl. Alex Lavroff, 124r. Jillian B. Luff, 24-25. John Mac/FOLIO, 57br, 60l, 62r, 63tr, 65bl, 100b, 101r, 259t. Robert Mancini, 157tr & br, 160l, 161c, 176b, 181b. Iain McKellar, 265. James McKinnon, 40t, 52, 54t, 58c, 68tr, 102b, 103t & b, 200t, 240, 241, 289. Robert Morton, 165c, 185, 192bl. Colin Newman, 32, 33cl. Colin Newman/Bernard Thornton Artists UK, 202b, 204b, 227t, 230r. Nicola Oran, 282t. Tony Pryzakowski, 5tr & cr, 6tr, 14t, 24bl, 49b, 85t, 87t, 109l, 120b, 121t, 126c, 127c, 151tl, 154l, 167, 186r, 187r, 188r, 189, 190, 191, 210, 246-247, 291t. Oliver Rennert, 89b. John Richards, 39bl, 259b, 273c & b. Edwina Riddell, 255r, 260t, 262cl. Barbara Rodanska, 42, 42-43, 76l, 151bl, 162t, 169b, 175b, 183b, 208bl, 264bl, 274t, 277t & br, 299r. Trevor Ruth, 7c, 16-17, 24-25, 41t, 45b, 163b, 203b, 205, 233tr, 266b, 280br, 281r, 297. Claudia Saraceni, 27cl, 58tr, 93cl, 264br, 270c, 273tr. Michael Saunders, 111l. Peter Schouten, 2, 4cl, 34c, 39t, 56b, 64-65, 70-71, 226b, 279. Peter David Scott, WILDlife ART Agency, 15. Rod Scott, 28-29. Kevin Stead, 51, 183t, 195, 216-217, 218 t, 250t, 251, 253b, 254b, 261b, 267, 271l, 272r, 275c, 276t, 277l, 286b, 302r. Roger Swainston, 118, 127bl, 129b, 133l. Bernard Tate, 142b. Thomas Trojer, 253t & r. Genevieve Wallace, 23tr, 95c, 104-105. Patrick Watson, 165b. Trevor Weekes, 21tr, 157cr, 160t, 171b, 174l, 178b. Rod Westblade, 294l. Anne Winterbotham, 98bl.